The Modern Turn

Studies in Philosophy and the History of Philosophy

General Editor: John C. McCarthy

Volume 60

The Modern Turn

Edited by Michael Rohlf

The Catholic University of America Press
Washington, D.C.

The paper used in this publication meets the minimum requirements of American National Standards for Information Science—Permanence of Paper for Printed Library Materials, ANSI Z39.48-1984.
∞

Library of Congress Cataloging-in-Publication Data
Names: Rohlf, Michael, editor.
Title: The modern turn / edited by Michael Rohlf.
Description: Washington, D.C. : The Catholic University of America Press, [2017] | Series: Studies in philosophy and the history of philosophy ; volume 60 | Includes bibliographical references and index.
Identifiers: LCCN 2017023753 | ISBN 9780813230054 (cloth : alk. paper)
Subjects: LCSH: Philosophy, Modern—History.
Classification: LCC B790 .M63 2017 | DDC 190—dc23
LC record available at https://lccn.loc.gov/2017023753

Contents

Acknowledgments

Richard F. Hassing, "Modern Turns in Mathematics and Physics" (chapter 7), incorporates material from the author's article "History of Physics and the Thought of Jacob Klein," *The New Yearbook for Phenomenology and Phenomenological Philosophy* 11 (2011), which is reprinted here with permission from Taylor and Francis.

Michael Rohlf, "Happiness in Rousseau and Kant" (chapter 9), originally appeared in *Estudos Kantianos* 1, no. 2 (2013), and is reprinted here with permission from *Estudos Kantianos.*

Paul Guyer, "Kant, Autonomy, and Modernity" (chapter 10), appears in the author's book *Virtues of Freedom: Selected Essays on Kant* (Oxford University Press, 2016) and is reprinted here with the permission of Oxford University Press.

Harvey C. Mansfield, "Tocqueville on Religion and Liberty" (chapter 11), originally appeared in *American Political Thought* 5, no. 2 (2016), and is reprinted here with permission from *American Political Thought.*

The Modern Turn

Michael Rohlf

Introduction

What is the modern turn in philosophy? In other words, what are the features that make modern philosophy distinctively "modern" in contrast with the premodern philosophy from which it emerged—for example, medieval scholasticism, Renaissance philosophy, and ancient Greek and Roman thought? How did the modern turn in philosophy transpire? That is, what did specific philosophers contribute that shaped the distinctive character of modern philosophy? The twelve essays in this volume seek to address these questions, and in doing so they exemplify and contribute to a rich debate about the nature and value of modern philosophy.

It may seem on the face of it that the first step toward identifying the distinctive features of modern philosophy would be to recognize a well-defined time period as "modernity," so that we can then go on to look for distinctive features of the philosophical texts written during this period. But on closer examination it becomes apparent that this approach would either beg the questions at issue or be arbitrary. It would be question-begging to define modern philosophy from the outset as, say, the philosophy that emerged in Europe between 1637 (the publication year of Descartes's *Discourse on Method*) and 1790 (the year in which Kant's *Critique of Judgment* was published) on the grounds that this is the period when ideas emerged that we already know to be distinctive of modern philosophy. Moreover, this question-begging approach would also assume that every philosophical text written during the modern period (thus defined) exhibits the relevant features, which will turn out to be false with any interesting list of such features. But it would be arbitrary to define limits for the time period of modern philosophy on the basis of anything other than the content of ideas expressed in philosophical texts. We cannot carve up the history of philosophy, for example, purely on the basis of historical or political events, since that would simply avoid or presuppose answers to important questions about the relationship between those events and philosophical ideas.

So how, then, is one to begin looking for the distinctive features of modern philosophy? The approach taken in this volume is to recognize some common associations with the phrase "modern philosophy" as fallible starting points for more rigorous reflection. For example, it is now common in the United States for academic curricula in philosophy to contain a course entitled either "modern philosophy" or "early modern philosophy." Most often the material covered in this course runs from Descartes through Kant, which conveys the impression that modern philosophy begins with Descartes and reaches its zenith in Kant. Along the way, major figures such as Spinoza, Locke, Leibniz, and Hume are typically read and discussed as well. Around half of the essays in this volume approach the question of what is distinctive about modern philosophy by asking what, if anything, these specific philosophers who are commonly recognized as modern contribute to the modern turn. In some cases these essays reach conclusions that are consistent with widely accepted views about modern philosophy, and in many cases they challenge common interpretations.

But our contemporary associations with the term "modern philosophy" go beyond the typical content of "early modern philosophy" courses in at least two main ways. First, those courses typically focus mainly or exclusively on metaphysics, epistemology, and the philosophy of science, while portraying the development of modern philosophy as tightly bound up with the early modern Scientific Revolution. Practically everyone recognizes, however, that other areas such as ethics and political philosophy are also central to philosophy in general and to modern philosophy in particular. Moreover, marking the beginning of modern philosophy with Descartes seems much more artificial when its scope is expanded to include these other topics. Machiavelli, for example, who was writing at the beginning of the sixteenth century, more than a century before Descartes, is widely regarded as a major influence especially on modern political thought. Consequently, the essays in this volume address what is distinctive about modern philosophy in each of these areas—metaphysics, epistemology, the philosophy of science, ethics, and political philosophy—and several of the essays illuminate connections between modern contributions in multiple areas. Furthermore, this volume approaches the modern turn in philosophy not as an event that occurred all at once, but rather as a series of shifts in different areas of philosophy at different times. So Machiavelli may have contributed significantly to the modern turn even though he wrote much earlier than other philosophers who also shaped modern thought on the same or different topics.

Second, if our contemporary associations with the term "modern philosophy" do not mark a clear beginning in time for the modern period, it is even less clear when or whether it has ended. The wide use of "early modern philosophy" in reference to a period ending with the eighteenth century suggests that after it came a period of "late modern philosophy" extending at least through much of the nineteenth century. In some respects we speak of modernity as continuing into (not just as influencing) the present, so that "modern" in this sense overlaps with "contemporary." But we also have the term "postmodern" and sometimes use it to suggest that the modern period has ended and we are now in a new age. This volume does not attempt to sort out these conflicting ideas, since its focus is the turn *to* the modern period in philosophy, not any putative turn away from it. In recognition of this ambiguity concerning how far forward in time modern philosophy extends, however, several of the essays in this volume extend their scope into the nineteenth and twentieth centuries. This is useful both for identifying the distinctive character of modern thought once it has largely taken shape, and for raising and addressing evaluative questions about how we should respond to the legacy of modern philosophy today.

The essays are arranged broadly in chronological order of the topics they treat, beginning with two chapters on Machiavelli. In chapter 1, Michael Gillespie addresses Machiavelli's relation to the Christian tradition. He argues that Machiavelli's modernity does not involve a rejection of Christian morality, as some hold, but rather lies in his way of synthesizing antiquity and Christianity in order to provide a new answer to the old question of how to produce and sustain good government. The novelty of Machiavelli's answer to this question, according to Gillespie, consists in his introduction of the general principle that morality enjoins princes to do what is necessary for the common good, and to do so in the least vicious way possible. Vicious actions undertaken by princes do not thereby cease to be vicious, but they nevertheless do not incur blame if, as is often the case, they are necessary for creating or sustaining a regime that is more friendly to virtue or that avoids worse evils. Thus Machiavelli does not generally seek to redefine traditional Christian views about the nature or importance of either the virtues or vices, and Gillespie defends the consistency of Machiavelli's principle with Renaissance Christianity by locating it in the intellectual context of his humanist predecessors' response to the fourteenth-century nominalist attack on scholastic realism. In this context, without a natural law to provide order in the world, chaos and war were seen as universal, both within each human being and in the natural world writ large. Consequently, a strong prince, willing to use violence and vice in the interest of both the common good and his own glory, is necessary for imposing order and establishing peace. Such a prince is loved by God and exercises a power that is analogous in a way to divine omnipotence that transcends a preexisting natural law.

In chapter 2, Nathan Tarcov approaches the question of Machiavelli's modernity from a different angle by focusing on his relation to antiquity. Tarcov argues that Machiavelli rejects the views of ancient writers in several crucial respects. For example, according to Tarcov but contrary to Gillespie's reading, Machiavelli robs virtue and vice of their moral meaning by characterizing them as whatever qualities lead to one's security or ruin, respectively, in given circumstances. In so doing he adopts an adverbial rather than a substantive account of virtue, according to which qualities traditionally considered virtues or vices may be used either well or badly. But Tarcov argues that Machiavelli obscures this and other disagreements with earlier writers by calling for imitation of ancient virtue, because the aim of writing for Machiavelli is not to communicate knowledge of the past for its own sake but rather to shape future action. So Machiavelli feels free to invent the past and does so without drawing attention to it because he considers himself to be in competition with earlier writers for influence or rule over the lives of active men. Indeed, this is the core of Machiavelli's modern turn and may have led to his other departures from antiquity, on Tarcov's view: namely, that he rejects the glorification of contemplative over active men, which had been common ground for both classical philosophy and Christianity.

Although there is disagreement about what Machiavelli's modernity consists in, he is often credited as the first modern and specifically political thinker. Descartes, however, is widely regarded as the father of modern philosophy *tout court*. One reason for this is Descartes's critique of scholastic teleology, which is often understood to imply a complete rejection of natural teleology in favor of mechanism. In chapter 3, Tad M. Schmaltz argues on the contrary that Descartes's attitude toward teleology is more flexible than this stark contrast between teleology and mechanism suggests. In fact, Schmaltz argues, Descartes does not reject just any sort of appeal to final causes but only the appeal to divine purposes in physics. Descartes allows for genuine final causation in the case of finite minds, the possibility that God's action is conditioned by (indifferently created) ends, and a kind of finality in human sensation that does not depend on divine teleology. In the latter case, Schmaltz claims both that Descartes is in some respects more like Aristotle than the medieval scholastics, and also that Descartes's acceptance of a kind of natural teleology that does not need to be understood in terms of final causation marks him out as modern in light of the later Darwinian revolution.

Chapter 4 returns to politics, this time to the modern ideal of a tolerant and secular society. Steven Nadler argues that Spinoza's commitment to toleration goes further than anyone else's in the seventeenth century (including Locke's), but that Spinoza does not hold views about freedom of religion (or the separation of church and state) that are often attributed to him. It is often assumed that Spinoza defends the separation of church and state, and in fact he does hold that people should be left alone to believe or not to believe whatever they want. However, according to Nadler, Spinoza distinguishes between inner belief and the outer forms of religion, the latter of which are to be determined and supervised by the civil government. Thus Spinoza's views on freedom of religion are in fact not that different from those of Hobbes, insofar as both hold that there is to be only one established religion and that it will be overseen by the sovereign. Spinoza goes further than Hobbes and everyone else in the seventeenth century, however, in defending toleration, not just in the sense of toleration of belief, but especially in the sense of the freedom of citizens to express their beliefs in speech or writing, according to Nadler. Yet Nadler argues that Spinoza does not go far enough by his own standards, because he does not support absolute freedom of speech and leaves room in his account for unreasonable censorship of the expression of ideas. He claims that Spinoza does not consistently follow the logic of his own reasoning, which in fact leads to an absolutist position that draws the boundary between protected and unprotected speech at the border of belief (and its expression) and true action.

In chapter 5, Michael Pakaluk analyzes different notions of "right" in Locke and argues that one of them is inconsistent with the classical natural law tradition and constitutes Locke's distinctive contribution to the modern turn in political philosophy. This notion of "right" is the authorization that Locke attributes to everyone in a state of nature to exact punishment for transgressions of the law of nature. According to Pakaluk, this right is inconsistent with natural law as understood by the classical tradition because Locke does not restrict it by considerations of either the common good or merit. It is a kind of power that previous philosophers attributed only to sovereign governments, not to individual persons, let alone to every individual person. The rest of Pakaluk's essay claims that Locke's detachment of this right from natural law, and his transference of the semi-divine power of sovereignty from states to individuals, is responsible for a variety of faults that he finds with liberalism today, among which he includes the endorsement of slavery and abortion. The apparent implication of Pakaluk's argument is that Locke's modern turn in political philosophy is a disaster insofar as it, and consequently all of modern liberalism through today, diverges from the classical natural law tradition.

Each of the previous chapters discusses the contribution that some philosopher makes to the modern turn, but chapter 6 is different. Nicholas Jolley distinguishes between seventeenth-century and more recent textbook senses of "modern" and argues that Leibniz is not a modern philosopher in either of these standard senses. According to Jolley, to be modern in the seventeenth-century sense is to be committed to the mechanical model of scientific explanation, and to be modern in the more recent textbook sense is to have a special interest in foundationalist epistemology and the mind-body problem. But arguably Leibniz is not a modern philosopher in either of these senses, although he may be counted as a modern philosopher in the less standard sense that he shares the seventeenth-century ambition of providing a metaphysical foundation for the new science. Leibniz's deepest philosophical allegiance, Jolley argues, is to the thought of the Renaissance, because of his commitment to views inspired by Neoplatonism, such as his thesis that this is the best of all possible worlds and his doctrine of monads, and because of the pervasive syncretism or eclecticism of his philosophy. So Leibniz is better understood as a premodern (rather than modern) philosopher, although this does not imply and Jolly does not claim that Leibniz made no important contributions to the modern turn.

In chapter 7, Richard F. Hassing provides a detailed account of what is distinctively modern in classical physics, especially but not exclusively in Newton, by contrasting it with both Aristotelian and quantum physics. Through this contrast Hassing identifies two fundamental features of classical physics. First, Newton's forces and particles model posits species-neutral laws of nature instead of the species-specific natural forms and ends of Aristotelian physics. This leads to Newton's radical thesis of universal transformism, according to which the parts of one species are indifferent to their membership in that whole and therefore can be removed from it and put into any other kind of whole, and which implies a vast expansion of human powers to predict, control, and transform nature. Hassing also associates the species-neutrality of classical Newtonian physics with reductionism and contrasts it with the form-limited holism of Aristotelian physics. Second, in contrast to both Aristotelian and quantum physics, classical physics assumes that any differences between mathematical and physical objects make no difference for the conduct of physics, which Hassing calls the physico-mathematical secularism of classical physics. Together, these two features of classical physics lead to the homogenization of heterogeneities in both mathematics and physics, which undoubtedly has certain advantages, such as removing the mistaken heterogeneity of the celestial and terrestrial in pre-Newtonian physics. But Hassing argues that removing all heterogeneity from nature—including that of the living and nonliving, human and nonhuman—leads both to the breakdown of classical physics and to confusion concerning the place of human beings in the whole. Although quantum physics does not retain the species-neutrality, reductionism, and physico-mathematical secularism of classical physics and in those respects bears affinities to Aristotelian physics, according to Hassing, the immoderate ambition to transform nature that is the moral legacy of classical physics continues today in some areas of contemporary science.

Thomas W. Merrill's essay in chapter 8 complements the previous chapter by finding in Hume a related (but less technical and more Socratic) critique of the ambitions of modern science. When Hume writes that "reason is and ought to be slave of the passions," on Merrill's reading, what he means is that science is and ought to be slave of philosophy. By "reason" in this context, Hume means the use of empirical observations, judgments of probability, and theory building to arrive at well-founded generalizations about the world, which Merrill associates especially with the Cartesian conception of science. Thus understood, science is an enterprise that aims to find means to any given ends but relies on some other source to set those ends, and this is precisely Hume's point. The passion to which science is and ought to be subjected for the setting of ends is curiosity or the love of truth, that is, philosophy. Thus Hume proposes a quasi-Socratic turn toward moral and political philosophy, according to Merrill, on the grounds that Cartesian science cannot account for its own presuppositions and leads to skepticism when enshrined as if it were first philosophy. Instead of using science as our starting point, Hume proposes that we puzzle through the perplexities inherent in pretheoretical and prescientific life as it is lived, according to Merrill. In political terms, he proposes a coalition of mutual benefit between philosophers and honest gentlemen, with the latter bringing common sense and the former standing guard against superstition. This coalition is the basis for a social contract between science and political society, in which unfettered inquiry is protected in exchange for serving human passions, especially the fear of death and disease.

In chapter 9, I argue that modern conceptions of happiness become increasingly subjectivist but nevertheless preserve much that is of value in ancient conceptions of happiness while eliminating their narrowness. In particular, I analyze Rousseau's and Kant's conceptions of happiness and compare both with Aristotle's conception. While Rousseau understands happiness fundamentally in terms of the feeling of pleasure and the avoidance of pain, and Kant understands it in terms of satisfying desires, each of them holds that some of the same objective goods that Aristotle thinks happiness consists in—including virtue, the development of rational powers, and love of others—are either necessary for or at least tend to promote one's own happiness. Moreover, while Aristotle's account is extremely narrow in characterizing only the life of the politically engaged philosopher as (at least ideally) happy, there is more flexibility in Rousseau's and especially Kant's accounts of what kinds of lives can be happy. Like Machiavelli and Hume, according to earlier essays in this volume, Kant also prioritizes the cultivation and exercise of practical reason over theoretical reason. But Kant still holds that the development of theoretical reason is an objective good, because we have a duty to promote that end; and his account of happiness is flexible enough to allow that the happiness of some people who choose to place a high value on theoretical reasoning may thereby come to depend on and be enhanced by their satisfying desires to cultivate and exercise that capacity.

In chapter 10, Paul Guyer argues that both Kant's positive conception of autonomy and the non-foundationalist method by which he eventually argues for it are distinctively modern. Not all aspects of Kant's idea of autonomy should be regarded as distinctively modern, according to Guyer, because some of them are anticipated by the ancients. For example, Plato pioneers the anti-voluntarist idea that moral claims must be tested against the lights of our own reason; and both Plato and the Stoics develop a negative conception of autonomy, according to which the rule of reason over desires can rescue us from being controlled by desires and from the dissatisfaction of having too many (or too strong) unfulfilled desires. But none of the ancients anticipated Kant's idea that autonomy in the sense of setting our own ends is unconditionally valuable and a positive source of satisfaction that outweighs the frustration of having unfulfilled desires. So this positive conception of autonomy is distinctively modern—and, Guyer claims, so is Kant's non-foundationalist method of arguing for it. After a false start in *Groundwork* III that is inconsistent with his own epistemological strictures, on Guyer's interpretation, Kant adopts a method of argument in the *Critique of Practical Reason* that recognizes the impossibility of proving fundamental principles without prior assumptions and instead confines itself to reconciling conflicts among fundamental commitments. Guyer suggests that this defensive and non-foundationalist method of argument in moral philosophy, which he associates with John Rawls's method of reflective equilibrium, is as distinctively modern and innovative as Kant's positive conception of autonomy.

The themes of foundationalism and of prioritizing practice over theory are developed further in chapter 11, in which Harvey C. Mansfield analyzes Tocqueville's account of the alliance between religion and liberty in America. On Mansfield's interpretation, Tocqueville opposes foundations from philosophy but holds that America needs foundations from religion in order to preserve its democratic liberty. Some sort of foundation of fixed ideas is required to guide practical life, but (Cartesian) philosophy cannot provide this foundation because it leads only to doubt, especially doubt about the authority of everyone except oneself. So Tocqueville associates (Cartesian) philosophy with an extreme notion of democratic equality, and this in turn he associates with materialism, on the grounds that only material comforts are available as ends for democratic citizens to pursue once they cease believing in superiors with natural authority to identify more distant goals for their lives. But materialism and democratic equality are enemies of liberty, because in fact mild despotism is most effective at absorbing us in the pursuit of material pleasures. Liberty, on the contrary, requires tension rather than too much comfort, and it requires belief in distant ideals toward which one strives. In democratic America, on Mansfield's reading of Tocqueville, these ideals are provided by religion, especially by the teaching that each of us has an immortal soul, which does not elevate any of us above anyone else but provides each of us with a goal worth devoting one's life to that is elevated above material comforts. Religion is thus practically useful for preserving liberty in a democratic society, as in America, and it does not impede liberty too much because there are no aristocrats to look down on the delusions of the multitude. Consequently, society itself exerts enormous pressure on individuals to identify the useful with the true, since religion will be useful in this way only if it is believed to be true. So Mansfield ascribes to Tocqueville a non-foundationalist, indeed almost pragmatist, form of justification for religious faith in America. In a collective exercise of liberty, we adopt religious faith in order to preserve our liberty, and this faith then sets limits (but not excessively narrow limits) on the freedom of individuals as a consequence.

In the final essay of this volume, Rémi Brague argues that the modern project fails in principle to answer the question: why should there be human beings? It fails to answer this question precisely because it understands itself as a project. A project, for Brague, is to be distinguished from a task, which one is assigned by another, to which one may not be equal, but which one is solely responsible for completing. By contrast, a project in the modern sense, as Brague characterizes it, is assigned by oneself, can be completed by definition, and guarantees progress when passed on to others in the future. So against the premodern view that life is a task set for us by some higher power (God, nature, being, etc.), the modern turn is toward viewing life instead as a project that is its own content, which may also be expressed by saying that radical self-determination or autonomy define the modern outlook. Brague also associates this view with the different notion that humankind is the passive object of an experiment conducted by an indifferent nature, and he raises the possibility that this experiment might fail. But even if the human experiment does not fail outright due to nuclear war or catastrophic climate change, Brague argues that the modern project cannot explain why it is better for human beings to exist than not to exist. In other words, it cannot explain why it would be a bad thing if dwindling birthrates eventually led to the extinction of our species. Some kind of higher metaphysics than the modern project can allow, Brague claims, is needed to explain why it would be bad for the human species to go extinct or why it is good for human beings to exist and to enjoy goods such as living decently under the rule of law or having access to education and museums.

Among the themes that recur most often in these essays are, first, that modern philosophy is characteristically preoccupied with questions about foundations and, second, that it ultimately prioritizes practice over theory. As Merrill points out in his chapter on Hume, the latter theme is not uniquely modern but revives a kind of Socratism. Perhaps the modern version of Socratism is distinctive, however, insofar as it intersects with the other theme about foundations. The relevant context suggested by several of the essays in this volume is that, by rejecting natural law and other aspects of scholastic metaphysics, late medieval nominalists open the door to a variety of questions about new, alternative foundations that would take center stage in modern philosophy—new foundations in the sciences but also for practical life. Eventually the latter type of question about new foundations for the good life and for the organization of political society becomes more pressing, either because the new science provides a model that some philosophers want to imitate in and extend to the ethical and political sphere, or because some philosophers react against the expansion of the sciences beyond their proper sphere and into areas of human life where the scientific model is inappropriate. These explanations are not incompatible with one another, and both are represented in this volume. Several essays also imply that the trajectory of modern philosophy moves from an endorsement of foundationalism (in Descartes) to a subtler concern with (both epistemological and practical) foundations that seeks to ground them in some non-foundationalist way. There is disagreement, however, both among contributors to this volume and among the modern philosophers they are discussing, about what sort of non-foundationalist method of justification can ground our commitment to, for example, the modern liberal values of tolerance, free expression, and autonomy—whether it should be the common sense method that Merrill attributes to Hume, the quasi-coherentist method that Guyer attributes to Kant and Rawls, or the quasi-pragmatist method that Mansfield attributes to Tocqueville. The challenge articulated by Brague in reference to the entire modern project, and also by Pakaluk in reference to Locke specifically, concerns whether any of these methods of grounding fundamental values and orienting practical life can succeed. That we still face this challenge today is a key part of the legacy of the modern turn.

Michael Gillespie

1 Machiavelli's Modernity and the Christian Tradition

In 1340 Ambrogio Lorenzetti completed the frescoes called the *Allegory of Good and Bad Government* in the town hall of the Sienese Republic. They lay out in elaborate detail the reciprocal character of virtue and good government as well as the connection between vice and bad government. Good government is personified as the saint-like, quasi-avuncular figure of the Common Good, and the consequences of good government are portrayed as peace, prosperity, and happiness. The consequences of bad government, represented by the devil-horned figure of Tyranny, are also starkly presented as fear, desolation, and misery. As simplistic as this binary depiction may at first appear, it would be a mistake to conclude that the artist was unaware of the harsh realities of political life. In fact, he clearly recognized that even in the best regimes some men must be harshly punished to protect law-abiding citizens. Good government, if we take Lorenzetti's frescoes at face value, thus inevitably requires the use of force. The men bound and awaiting punishment, beneath the feet of Temperance and Justice as well as the criminal hanging from a gallows in the hands of an angel are an indication that he recognized this harsh political reality. The artist was also clearly aware of the danger posed by faction and subtly indicates how essential cooperation is by painting a cord descending from Justice to Concord and passing through the hands of all the citizens before ending tied to the wrist of the Common Good.[1]

1. Randolph Starn, "The Republic Regime of the 'Room of Peace' in Siena, 1338–40," *Representations* 18 (Spring 1987): 12.

This concern with faction was not accidental. Civil strife was endemic in Siena and the city reformed its political institutions ten times between 1325 and 1352 in an effort to eliminate it.[2] Lorenzetti himself spoke on at least one occasion "with words of wisdom" concerning constitutional reform.[3] His frescoes are thus not the imaginary representations of an apolitical artist, but the work of an engaged and thoughtful citizen.

The purpose of such a presentation is not hard to imagine. The frescoes decorate the Sala dei Nove, the Room of the Nine, that was the meeting place of the group of nine men who served as the chief authorities of the republic. The paintings were almost certainly intended to represent the activities of a well-ordered regime to remind the republic's rulers—who held their offices for only two months—of their responsibilities and to make clear to them what would happen should they stray from the path of virtue. Given the continuing conflict within the city, the paintings were clearly a needed, although not entirely successful, reminder.[4]

While these frescoes are perhaps the most elaborate depiction of political life in the history of Western art, the lessons they teach were not new in 1340.[5] In fact the frescoes reflect a traditional understanding of political life that goes back to Plato and Aristotle and that was integral to Roman and medieval political theory. This tradition firmly believed that moral virtue was the irreducible foundation for good government. In explicating this relationship, these thinkers sought to explain *what* good government was, the shape it took, and the ends it served. This is what is painted on the walls of the Sala dei Nove. The question that Lorenzetti and the others in this tradition did not answer was how such a government could come into being and how it could be sustained.

The absence of concern with the origins of such a regime was not accidental, but rooted in a fundamental pessimism about its possibility. This pessimism is hardly surprising—political philosophy, after all, came into being in response to the execution of Socrates, that is, the execution of the most virtuous citizen by the best, or at least one of the best regimes. From the very beginning, then, classical political philosophy was struck by a contradiction—it recognized that virtue was essential to

2. Ibid., 1.

3. Ibid., 5.

4. Starn characterizes the painting as a republican fiction, wistfully suggesting that good and evil could be kept separate. Ibid., 26–27.

5. Ibid., 2.

good government but that real regimes were almost always hostile to virtue. The conclusion that many classical thinkers reached was that virtue and politics could not coexist and that the idea of such a combination was at best an ideal. Thus a truly good regime might be founded "in one's soul" or among a community of friends but never in an actual city.

Such pessimism, however, was not rooted in a single event—even one as emblematic as the death of Socrates. It had deeper foundations in the sense of fatality that characterized ancient thought, the melancholic recognition that overwhelmed them even in victory, tying their moment of triumph to a future defeat that would inevitably swallow them up as well. Christianity radically changed this view of things but, in a sense, only for the worse, since it preached not the inevitability of a future fall but the stark reality of a primordial fall that had long ago tainted human nature and that could only be overcome by an apocalyptic transformation and the reestablishment of the rule of God. Seen from this point of view, Lorenzetti's frescoes do not aim at bringing a good regime into being but at encouraging rulers to live virtuously in anticipation of the reinstitution of divine rule.

These frescoes are in many respects a terrestrial analogue of the poetic portrait of the afterlife Dante had painted thirty years before in his *Divine Comedy.* There he laid out in great detail what awaits human beings in the world to come, and in this way set moral standards for actions in this world. Like Lorenzetti, he delineates a doctrine of virtue and vice that is meant to underpin a decent political order. In contrast to Lorenzetti, however, he does not depict merely good and bad but also the realm of more ambiguous actions in between, represented in the afterlife by purgatory.

Like Lorenzetti, Dante was well aware that good government was not a given. He suffered greatly as a consequence of the factional struggles in Florence and spent the last nineteen years of his life in bitter exile. He consequently knew at first hand that good government could not be sustained by mere virtue. Thus, in *De monarchia* he laid out a vision for a virtuous overlord who would bring an end to the conflicts among and within cities and kingdoms. He assumed that this overlord would defend the common good, but never asked how he could come to rule or maintain the peace without using means that were less than virtuous.[6]

6. He particularly did not ask if such a ruler could come to be without sinning or acting viciously. He asserts of the Roman case, "that in subduing the world the Roman people had in

The character of the origins of states is a crucial question because in a world of faction and strife, there is no royal road to the establishment of good government, no divine hand that sets the virtuous man upon the throne. Thus, while everyone within the tradition that culminates in Dante and Lorenzetti recognized that the common good was the appropriate end of politics and that it depended upon the rule of a virtuous leader or leaders, no one understood (barring divine intervention) how such leaders could come to rule or maintain their rule without acting viciously and committing mortal sins. In what follows I argue that Machiavelli offers an answer to this question that recognizes the importance of individual virtue but also teaches potential founders and princes the importance of knowing how *not* to be good in order to bring the good regime into existence and sustain it. I argue further that Machiavelli formulates this answer by drawing on the prevailing notion of morality and reshaping it crucial ways.[7] Finally, I suggest that in this effort to reshape the moral code Machiavelli does not reject Christianity in favor of antiquity but combines elements of both into a new modern notion of morality.

During the late Middle Ages and Renaissance factional strife was more the rule than the exception in Italian city states and left almost all of the Italian republics (with the exception of Venice) weak and divided. Many cities struggled for a long time within republican forms before giving themselves over to strong men or tyrants, such as the Visconti, to live in peace. In most cases their new rulers eliminated not merely strife but public life itself. Dante and Machiavelli both blamed this strife and the lack of unity in Italy on the church's pursuit of temporal dominion. Not only did this lead to the corruption of spiritual power within the church, but it also was the source of the extensive foreign intervention in Italian

view the aforesaid good, their deeds declare. We behold them as a nation holy, pious, and full of glory, putting aside all avarice, which is ever adverse to the general welfare, cherishing universal peace and liberty, and disregarding private profit to guard the public weal of humanity. Rightly was it written, then, that 'The Roman Empire takes its rise in the fountain of pity.'" *De monarchia* 2.5.2. Machiavelli had a much more realistic notion of Roman motives. Peterman suggests that for Dante world monarchy is directed not at temporal goodness but toward the end of time. Larry Peterman, "Dante and the Setting for Machiavellianism," *American Political Science Review* 76, no. 3 (September 1982): 634.

7. I thus agree with Cary Nederman that Giuseppe Prezzolini is wrong in his claim that Machiavelli is thoroughly anti-medieval and anti-Christian. Cary J. Nederman, "Amazing Grace: Fortune, God, and Free Will in Machiavelli's Thought," *Journal of the History of Ideas* 60, no. 4 (1999): 619. Giuseppe Prezzolini, *Machiavelli Anticristo* (Rome: Gherardo Casini, 1954), 86–87.

politics by European powers called in by the church to help defend its temporal authority.[8]

The Florentine world into which Machiavelli was born had a long history of strife. However, this strife diminished in the latter half of the fifteenth century with the rise of the Medici banking family, who ruled through republican structures but exercised nearly princely power. Machiavelli was the oldest son of a respectable Florentine family and was educated for a career in the civil service. His opportunity for advancement came with overthrow of the Medici and the reestablishment of the republic under Piero Soderini in 1494. Soderini, however, rose to power with the support of the charismatic religious leader Savonarola, whom Machiavelli opposed; and it was thus only after Savonarola's execution in 1498 that Machiavelli rose to prominence, becoming the second secretary of the Florentine Republic, responsible for foreign affairs, a position he held until the Medici returned to power in 1512. Shortly thereafter, Machiavelli was accused of taking part in a conspiracy against the Medici, questioned under torture, imprisoned, and finally exiled to his modest estate outside Florence as part of a general amnesty when Giovanni de Medici became Pope Leo X in 1513. He repeatedly tried to regain the confidence of the Medici but was never again given a position of real responsibility. During this period he turned to literary activities, writing poetry, plays, his two great political works, the *Discourses* and *The Prince*, as well as the *History of Florence*, the *Art of War*, and a number of other shorter works.

Machiavelli tried to answer the question that had bedeviled political theorists from the time of Plato and Aristotle—*how* to produce and sustain good government. This question also had immediate bearing on Florence and the other Italian city-states of Machiavelli's time. Machiavelli's answer to this question has been widely understood as the hallmark of his modernity, but what that answer is has been just as widely debated. He has been characterized as one of the first to reject the moral teachings and constraints of Christianity and to adopt a secular view that denies the existence of a highest human good. From this perspective, he

8. Both Dante and Marsilius of Padua had blamed the church for the troubles of Italy long before Machiavelli did. Sebastian de Grazia, *Machiavelli in Hell* (Princeton, N.J.: Princeton University Press, 1989), 90, 173. Machiavelli traces the church's pernicious influence back to the rise of the Langobards. *Florentine Histories*, trans. Harvey Mansfield and Laura Banfield (Princeton, N.J.: Princeton University Press, 1988), 19, 34.

appears to defend the practice of politics as a form of technique separable from the question of values. He is thus seen as an early proponent of the fact-value distinction that Max Weber defended. Others have argued that Machiavelli was a civic republican or Renaissance humanist who not only rejected Christianity but sought to revive the thought of antiquity in order to revivify republicanism.[9] His modernity in this context is tied to his attempt to make antiquity meaningful for modern political life. Still others see him abandoning both medieval political theology and ancient political philosophy in favor of something like moral nihilism, denying that there is a meaningful distinction between good and evil and hence valorizing sheer force and violence in pursuit of political power. From this perspective, he is often described as a teacher of evil or a teacher of tyrants. All of these readings of Machiavelli are unsatisfying. Machiavelli's modernity is the result not of the rejection of either antiquity or Christianity but a combination of both in a new synthesis that he imagines will help answer the question of how one can constitute a good regime using means that while not good are also not evil.

Machiavelli was at heart a republican.[10] For him, "a man is under no greater obligation than to his country; he owes his very existence, and later, all the benefits that nature, and fortune offer him to her."[11] Not everyone, however, takes statements like this at face value. Some have argued that Machiavelli's patriotic rhetoric was merely camouflage for his true aim, which was to encourage and teach new founders the methods needed to establish dictatorial rule. Such a reading of Machiavelli, however, requires one to believe that most of what he wrote, as well as his repeated assertions to his closest friends and family over many years were disingenuous. While this is not impossible, it seems to be highly

9. This view is often identified with J. G. A. Pocock, but has its origins in the work of Hans Baron.

10. An unjust state in his view is ruled for private gain, a just state for the common good. On this point see de Grazia, *Machiavelli in Hell*, 175, 192; and Isaiah Berlin, "A Special Supplement: The Question of Machiavelli," *The New York Review of Books* 17, no. 7 (November 4, 1971): 9, 13, 14.

11. "A Dialogue on Language," in *The Literary Works of Machiavelli*, ed. J. R. Hale (London: Oxford University Press, 1961), 175. See also Peterman, "Machiavelli's Dante," 248. De Grazia argues that Machiavelli's love of country led to a new moral reasoning and re-dimensioning of the world visible and invisible, balancing heaven and hell and making room for a different earth (*Machiavelli in Hell*, 21). He also points to Machiavelli's late claim that "I love my country more than my soul" (342).

unlikely. That Machiavelli hoped to do something extraordinary, to play a glorious role as a founder or as a teacher of or adviser to founders of new regimes seems to me incontestable, but again and again he states his preference for republicanism. This does not mean that he did not consider other possibilities. He seems to have concluded at a later point in his life, for example, that under the circumstances in which Italy found itself a republican regime could not succeed and thus that a more centralized or dictatorial regime was necessary to preserve Italy from predation by foreign powers. There is little to suggest, however, that he saw such a regime as preferable to a republic. Moreover, even the more princely regimes he recommends seem to be tilted in a republican direction with Machiavelli repeatedly trying to convince the potential prince that his true self-interest was coincident with the common good. His hopes in the end, however, were almost all for a revival of Florentine, or Tuscan, or Italian patriotism and republicanism.[12]

This dedication to this goal is obvious in the *Discourses*, where he argues that the true lawgiver's intention "is to govern not in his own interest but for the common good, and not in the interest of his successors but for the sake of the fatherland which is common to all."[13] This concern also guides the argument in *The Prince*, although less obviously. In part the obscurity of this point in *The Prince* is the result of the rhetorical task of the work, which is to convince a potential prince that his self-interest lies more in maintaining the common good than in gratifying his personal passions. As a result of this rhetorical approach, the work is often taken as a manual for dictatorial rule. Machiavelli tries to dispel such an opinion by distinguishing heroic founders who will do anything to secure what is best for the state from those who come to power through crime and seek to upset the state merely for the purpose of gaining rule, but those who want to see Machiavelli as an immoralist treat this distinction as mere camouflage for his sinister adherence to pure power politics.[14]

12. As Berlin remarks, Machiavelli is not especially concerned with the opportunism of the ambitious individual because the ideal before his eyes is a shining vision of Florence or of Italy. For Berlin he was a typically impassioned humanist but interested in politics and not in art ("The Question of Machiavelli," 9). This cannot be entirely correct since he clearly considered himself a poet.

13. *Discourses*, 132.

14. Interestingly, as de Grazia points out, Aristotle shows none of the niceties that Machia-

Their argument has great traction in the post-Kantian world because we are prone to see morality as concerned above all with means and not with ends. From this point of view the distinction that is so central to Machiavelli between those who act treacherously in the public interest and those who act treacherously in their own interest may not seem compelling. This distinction, however, was well established in Machiavelli's own time as we can see by a comparison of the thought of Machiavelli and Dante.

Dante was a Christian thinker who held views similar to those of Aquinas. Despite this, Dante's account of virtue and vice seems to have been surprisingly important for Machiavelli. Machiavelli knew Dante's works well and had an extraordinary respect for his thought. He asserts that Dante "shows himself at every point to have excelled in genius, learning, and judgment," except in his anger at Florence over his exile.[15] Indeed, as we will see, Machiavelli generally agreed with Dante about the nature and order of the moral virtues and vices but disagreed with him about the way in which they applied to founders and princes.

In the *Divine Comedy*, Dante describes good and evil in terms of the rewards and punishments accorded human beings in the afterlife. He first discusses those damned to hell for committing mortal sins; then those in purgatory who must expiate their sins before they can enter paradise; and finally those whose places in heaven reflect their virtuous lives.

Guided by Virgil, Dante enters the afterlife through limbo, the first circle of hell, which is populated by the good pagans.[16] These men and women were not evil but can never attain salvation because they did not know Christ.[17] The succeeding circles of hell contain those who are guilty of the increasingly serious sins of lust, gluttony, greed, wrath, heresy, violence, fraud, and treachery. The sins of those in purgatory in or-

---

velli does in distinguishing those who come to power through crime and those who come to power through virtue (*Machiavelli in Hell*, 86).

15. "A Dialogue on Language," 178. He describes regularly reading Dante (de Grazia, *Machiavelli in Hell*, 250).

16. These include Cicero, Virgil, Averroes, Avicinna, Electra, Aeneus, Julius Caesar, Saladin, Homer, Horace, many of the Presocratic philosophers, Ovid, Lucan, Socrates, Plato, Aristotle, Pentheselia, Euripides, Agathon, Antiphon, Simonides, and Antigone, to name the most prominent.

17. I.4.42; II.3.40–44.

der of decreasing severity are pride, envy, wrath, sloth, greed, gluttony, and lust. The orders of paradise mirror the order of the heavens and include in ascending order those who lacked the courage to sustain their vows, those who were ambitious but deficient in justice, immoderate lovers, the wise, courageous warriors for the faith, just rulers, contemplatives who were models of moderation, the saints who practiced the virtues of faith, hope, and charity, and the angels.

The only sinners Dante unequivocally condemns to hell are those guilty of heresy, violence, fraud, or treachery. The worst of these are those who betray their kindred, their state, their guests, and their lords and benefactors. Machiavelli agrees wholeheartedly with Dante that treachery is inexcusable. In the *Discourses* he goes so far as to assert that our basic notions of good and evil arise from the sight of someone injuring his benefactor.[18] Even in *The Prince,* where he seems more tolerant of political violence, he argues that those who use such criminal methods to gain power can never win glory because they sacrifice the common good to satisfy their lust to rule.[19]

Like Dante, Machiavelli also sees heresy as wicked. He remarks in the *Discourses* that the most detestable men are those who extirpate religion.[20] In *The Prince,* he recommends that the ruler avoid the appearance of impiety, and that he refrain from anything that could be construed as heresy. He claims in the *Discourses* that Roman religious institutions were essential to their success, and that Italy had been ruined by a lack of religion brought about by the corruption of the Roman church. He even argues that if Christian states had maintained their beliefs they would have been more united and happy.[21] The wickedness of mercenary troops in his view is due to their lack of religion.[22] Thus, while Machiavelli may not have been personally particularly religious, it would be a mistake to believe that he was irreligious or thought that men could do without religion.

18. *Discourses,* 107.

19. De Grazia, *Machiavelli in Hell,* 100.

20. *Discourses,* 135. Leo Strauss, among others, has argued that Machiavelli's ultimate goal was to extirpate religion and that a careful reading of his text reveals his heretical position. But Machiavelli was never accused of blasphemy, although it was often said that that he did not have much faith to spare. On this point see de Grazia, *Machiavelli in Hell,* 4.

21. *Discourses,* 144–45. Christianity, he argues, was corrupted by men who interpreted it according to indolence and not according to virtue (de Grazia, *Machiavelli in Hell,* 104).

22. "Exhortation to Penitence," 170.

Like Dante, Machiavelli also generally condemns the use of violence, but he recognizes that no prince can rule without it and is convinced that a prince who tries to do so will need to use much greater violence in the long run. The prince, in his view, must combine the virtues of the lion and the fox, ruling principally by law but using violence when necessary. Too great a reluctance to use violence will lead to disorder but too great a willingness to use it will generate hatred, which Machiavelli believes must be avoided at all costs since it gives rise to wrath and an unquenchable desire for revenge.

Machiavelli similarly agrees with Dante that fraud is generally unacceptable. Indeed, he argues that it is one of the duties of the prince to provide justice to those who have been defrauded. These rules, however, do not apply to the prince himself who as Machiavelli repeatedly asserts must know how *not* to be good. In this case, that means knowing how to use fraud on occasions when one would otherwise have to use violence or treachery. Taking a citadel by deceit is thus preferable to a hard-fought battle with many casualties. Indeed, under those circumstances fraud is not a sin but a virtue. The use of deceit in his view is also initially crucial in securing one's rule. Machiavelli claims that any prince who will do great things and establish new modes and orders must begin by practicing deceit until he is strong enough to sustain his rule without it. Even the Romans had to follow this path.[23] While fraud is generally reprehensible, it is thus also always justifiable in times of necessity. Indeed, for Machiavelli, it is always good to defend your country in whatever way possible.

This points to the general principle that seems to underlie Machiavelli's moral and political theory: those who act in their own self-interest are subject to the general rules of morality, but those who act in pursuit of the common good can and must act in ways that are often *not* good and can do so without incurring blame because their actions help to create or sustain a regime that is more friendly to virtue or that avoids worse evils. In extreme cases the pursuit of the common good by a prince or founder may even justify killing one's own friends or relatives, as in the case of Romulus or the first Brutus. It always justifies the use of violence or fraud that makes treachery or greater violence unnecessary. Machiavelli's general principle thus seems to require the prince to do what is necessary for

23. *Discourses*, 311–12.

the common good and to do it in the least vicious way possible. He thus holds up as models Moses, Theseus, Cyrus, and Romulus, all of whom used violence and deceit against others.[24] They were not always good but they were never wicked. Machiavelli contrasts these founders with those who used treachery to attain power for themselves in opposition to the common good, such as Agathocles and Oliverotto. Even though Agathocles was successful, Machiavelli regards him as a criminal and not a hero or great man.[25] Oliverotto who was not successful is characterized as both a criminal and a fool.[26]

While Machiavelli seeks to convince men to act in ways that are not good in order to establish the new modes and orders he believes are necessary, not all those who use the means he recommends aim at the common good and not all those who use such means and aim at the common good are entirely successful or exemplary. It is especially difficult to evaluate those who fail. Castruccio Castracani and Cesare Borgia are cases in point. From Machiavelli's account it is difficult to determine what they ultimately hoped to accomplish and thus whether they sought only their own personal gain or the common good of their people. Both surely used means that were not good. Those who think that Machiavelli in fact is a teacher of tyrants see them as models he holds up for emulation, but his actual treatment of them is mixed. That they were willing to do what was necessary to succeed is clear but it is also clear that both failed in many respects. In contrast to Agathocles, Machiavelli does not describe Borgia as cruel, but only deceitful. However, in the first *Decannale* he describes Borgia's fate as fitting for "rebels against Christ."[27] And in *The Prince*, he remarks that Borgia's actions were not ordained by God.

There are two other examples brought up in *The Prince* that fall somewhere between Machiavelli's heroic founders and his rapacious tyrants. The first is the Roman emperor Severus who comes to power with the support of his army and sustains his rule by satisfying them and stu-

24. Nederman argues that Moses is the true model for Machiavelli ("Amazing Grace," 620, 629–32).

25. Machiavelli points to his bestial cruelty (de Grazia, *Machiavelli in Hell*, 305).

26. The distinction that Machiavelli is trying to make here is akin to the distinction between those leaders who are described as great (such as Peter the Great) from those who are described as terrible (such as Ivan the Terrible).

27. John McCormick, "Prophetic Statebuilding: Machiavelli, Weber, and the Passion of the Duke," unpublished conference presentation at UCLA (April 25, 2008).

pefying the people. However, lest one think Machiavelli is recommending him as an example for his own time, he goes on to point out that in modern times it is crucial to satisfy the people rather than the army, exactly the reverse of Severus's situation. Thus a prince today, according to Machiavelli must combine the harshness of Severus with the gentleness of Marcus Aurelius.

The other example he points to is Ferdinand of Aragon who began as a weak king but made himself lord of Spain and much of Italy. According to Machiavelli, he was extraordinarily astute, an excellent combination of the lion and the fox. However, Machiavelli also remarks in one of his letters that he was niggardly and avaricious, and that this vice lay behind his pious (but wicked) cruelty with respect to the Marranos, whom he banished from Spain purportedly on religious grounds but actually in order to seize their property.[28] Machiavelli holds these men up as examples not because they are perfect and not because a founder or ruler should emulate them in every detail, but because they show what is possible using the methods that he recommends.

When it comes to the lesser vices (lust, gluttony, greed, wrath, sloth, envy, and pride) Machiavelli generally agrees with Dante about their order of importance. For Dante, these sins (except for pride and envy) in their most severe form merit eternal damnation but in their lesser forms can be expiated by penance. Machiavelli suggests they are all serious impediments to successful rule but some cause greater problems than others. He argues that lust is exceedingly dangerous to the prince's rule when it leads him to take women who belong to his subjects against the will of their husbands or fathers, but it is much less dangerous (and more excusable) when the prince simply takes a willing woman as his mistress. Machiavelli has little to say explicitly about gluttony, although he clearly urges the prince to avoid self-indulgence and to prepare himself for war with daily exercise and riding. With respect to these and similar self-regarding sins or vices, however, Machiavelli's general advice to the prince seems to be to avoid them if possible but not to worry too much about them if he cannot.

Greed and wrath are much more important in Machiavelli's view because they pose a greater danger to the state. For this reason Machiavelli

28. On the cruelty of Ferdinand of Aragon, see de Grazia, *Machiavelli in Hell,* 85.

is adamant that the prince must keep his hands off the property of his subjects, suggesting infamously that, if one has to choose, it is better to kill a man's father than steal his patrimony, presumably because in the former case the son then inherits the father's property and thus has his hatred diminished by his gratitude. Machiavelli even cautions the prince against generosity (and thus against both the ancient virtue of liberality and the Christian virtue of charity) because it inevitably requires taking property from others. It is important to note here that Machiavelli does not argue that charity itself is not good but only that a prince who practices it may produce a worse evil, hatred, which is likely to undermine his authority.

Machiavelli, like Dante, believes that there is a close connection between greed and pride. In his "Tercets on Ambition" Machiavelli asserts that a hidden power, which is inimical to humans and sets them at war with one another, sent two furies—ambition and greed along with their companions envy, sloth, and hatred—to disrupt human life.[29] The desire to lord it over others in Machiavelli's view is the most politically disruptive passion and any ruler who aims at the common good must constrain it. However, Machiavelli vacillates when it come to the question of how widespread such a desire is, arguing at times that all men are dominated by it and at other times that it is more characteristic of the nobles while the plebs typically want merely to be left alone. However, in constituting a commonwealth he believes the founder must assume that all men are wicked and will take advantage of any opportunity to despoil or repress others when it arises.[30] Envy in his view is similarly widespread and all founders and princes must recognize that men are always more ready to belittle others than praise them, and to climb by crushing them.[31] This means that the prince must be relentless in his efforts to suppress such behavior and to restrain his own acquisitive passions and beware of flatterers who play on his envy and appeal to his pride.

It is also crucial that the prince be respected by his people or he will be unable to maintain order. Such respect in Machiavelli's opinion is

29. "Tercets on Ambition," in Machiavelli, *The Chief Works and Others*, trans. Allan Gilbert (Durham, N.C.: Duke University Press, 1965), 2:735–36. He makes a similar argument in "On Ingratitude." On this point see de Grazia, *Machiavelli in Hell*, 74.

30. *Discourses*, 111–12. He does believe however that the nobility want to dominate while the plebs for the most part want not to be dominated (116).

31. *Discourses*, 97. See also "Tercets," 737.

a combination of love and fear. While there is perhaps a greater desire among most men to be loved, Machiavelli argues that it is much more important for rulers to be feared. Therefore, they must beware of being excessively merciful, and insist that good modes and orders are in place and observed. Machiavelli recognizes, though, that this will be difficult because, as he notes in the *Discourses*, it is difficult to find a good man who will use bad means to make a people good.[32]

While Machiavelli generally agrees with Dante about the nature and the order of the vices, he clearly recognizes that successful rulers must not only know how not to be good but also know what the good is and be willing to act in ways that would be considered vicious if they were not necessary. We get a fuller idea of what Machiavelli believes is necessary in a ruler when we examine the ways in which he differs from Dante about the nature of the virtues.

In his description of those in heaven Dante organizes his discussion around the four cardinal virtues, courage, justice, moderation, and wisdom, and the three Christian virtues, faith, hope, and charity. From the lowest to the highest, the spheres of heaven include those who were deficient in courage and violated their vows, those who were ambitious but deficient in justice, immoderate lovers, the wise, courageous warriors for the faith, just rulers, contemplatives who lived moderately, saints who practiced faith, hope, and charity, and angels.

Machiavelli does not disagree with Dante about the importance of the cardinal virtues but he is more tolerant of founders and princes who practice them "deficiently." Machiavelli knows that they are often in a position where they have to do what is *not* good in the public interest. Thus while it is a defect for most people to violate their promises or vows, the prince must do so whenever it is necessary to secure the common good. Machiavelli, however, does not denigrate the courageous warriors for the faith that Dante praises. In fact he is convinced that armed prophets are essential to the founding of the state, and that an armed militia is essential to its preservation. Machiavelli like Dante also praises the ambitious, although he has better things to say about the earlier republican Romans than their imperial counterparts.[33] This said, he does admire Justinian, whom Dante too holds up as a model, both as a lawgiver and

32. *Discourses*, 163.
33. Peterman, "Machiavelli's Dante," 251.

as a strong leader. In contrast to Dante, however, he does not see Rome's dominance of the world as divinely ordained but much more rooted in republican courage and a dedication to the common good.[34]

While Machiavelli admires the ambitious, he believes ambition is only laudable when properly directed. He recognizes the disasters that ambition can bring when combined with cowardice and bad government, but he is convinced that ambition cannot be eliminated and therefore must be educated, by amalgamating it with good judgment and sound intellect as well as method and vigor.[35] Machiavelli is also anxious for potential princes and founders to understand that they can be saved if they do what is necessary for the common good. Machiavelli seeks to justify this assertion by redefining two of the most important virtues that Dante points to, love and wisdom.

Love, for Dante, is the essential capacity that elevates human vision toward God. Love, however, also takes the form of lust, which has the capacity to lure men into immorality and damnation. Machiavelli sees love not in this binary fashion but through the lens of humanists such as Petrarch and Ficino who, drawing on Plato, saw love as a ladder leading from the carnal lust to the love of God. The chief task of the founder or ruler in Machiavelli's view is to coordinate all of the various kinds of love to secure the common good. A comic example of such coordination is described in Machiavelli's *Mandragola,* where Ligurio, the masterful manipulator, makes possible the satisfaction of the harmonious loves of a husband who wants an heir, a priest who wants money, a lover who wants a woman, as well as a wife who wants a wealthy husband, an heir, and, as she eventually realizes, a lover. The goal of the founder or ruler in Machiavelli's mind is to bring about such a harmonious solution to the factional fighting in the state and this requires above all else the inculcation of love of the fatherland and a dedication to the pursuit of the common good. Living in a world in which most men strive to attain their own interest

34. Like Dante, Machiavelli also recognizes that the pursuit of fame and glory involve risk taking. Dante's Virgil points out that "he who rests on down or under covers cannot come to fame; and he who spends his life without renown leaves such a vestige of himself on earth as smoke bequeaths to air or foam to water." This is certainly a sentiment that Machiavelli shares. He disagrees, however, with what Oderisi the painter claims, that "worldly renown is nothing other than a breath of wind that blows now here, now there; and changes name when it has changed its course."

35. "Tercets on Ambition," 737–39.

and that of their families and friends, the prince must know how to turn their self-interested desires toward a higher goal and a higher love, which is the love of their fatherland. This was what distinguished the Romans and what Machiavelli finds sorely lacking in his fellow citizens.

While founders and princes may not be motivated by the love of God, it is crucial to their success that they convince their people that God wants them to love their state and be willing to die for it, for without this belief the founders will never be able to inspire their people to live according to the laws and institutions that are essential to the common good. This was the genius of Numa's establishment of religious institutions. Indeed, this act completed and perfected the Roman founding that Romulus had begun and that could never have been sustained by force alone. He reduces a ferocious people to obedience through religion.[36] Machiavelli thus asserts that Numa was more important than Romulus.[37] It is also important that founders and princes believe that God loves those who do what is necessary for the common good, even if it is contrary to conventional morality.[38] If not, the rulers' fear of damnation may prevent them from doing what they must.

While the prince must be strong and resolute, Machiavelli is convinced that he must also know how to get things done. Like Dante he thus sees wisdom as one of the highest virtues but in contrast to Dante he regards it as preeminently practical and not theoretical. Thus while Dante praises the scholastics, Machiavelli praises and draws upon Roman and Greek historians and biographers who reveal the deeds of great men and the rules that govern the rise and fall of states and princes. This does not mean, however, that he elevates ancient thought over Christian thought. He is equally dismissive of ancient metaphysicians and idealists. It does mean that he tries to draw what practical wisdom he can from ancient and modern thinkers and examples to develop a practical science for the prince or founder that will make it possible for him to promote the common good.

Machiavelli thus does not seek to abandon or to overturn Christian-

36. Peterman, "Machiavelli's Dante," 261.

37. *Discourses*, 140.

38. De Grazia points out that the deeds of great men in Machiavelli's view are most gratifying to God (*Machiavelli in Hell*, 121).

ity but to transform it.[39] In keeping with this much more practically oriented vision of Christianity, Machiavelli does not have as high an opinion of contemplatives and ascetics as Dante does. While he asserts that St. Francis and St. Dominic led exemplary lives that deserve emulation, he does not believe that such lives are possible for most men and is also convinced that in his world most of those who pretend to lead such lives are in fact hypocrites.[40] Moreover, even if more men could live in this way, it would not be good for the state since the basic teaching that governs them is to be humble and endure suffering, virtues which are antithetical to good and effective government.

While Machiavelli thus disagrees in a number of ways with Dante's account of the cardinal virtues, the differences between them are much more apparent when we turn to the Christian virtues of faith, hope, and charity, which Machiavelli almost entirely neglects, and the saints and angels who play no role at all in his thought.[41] This does not mean though that Machiavelli is unconcerned with these matters but that he believes they must be deemphasized within the political realm.

In a strange sense though Machiavelli does remain concerned with the afterlife. In his famous letter to Vettori in which he recounts dressing in his finest clothes to spend his evenings with the greatest men of antiquity, he also prominently discusses Dante. Seen against this background, it might be fair to describe Machiavelli as sojourning during the evening in Dante's limbo, a region that Dante largely neglects in his journey toward paradise.[42] Machiavelli in this light can be understood to bring the wisdom he learns from these ancients back to the Christian world he inhabits, a wisdom that can help transform his world in ways that will

39. Marjorie O'Rourke Boyle, "Machiavelli and the Politics of Grace," *MLN* 119 Supplement (2004): 5237. This said, it is probably only fair to admit that Machiavelli claims that new religions wipe out old ones (*Discourses*, 288).

40. "An Exhortation to Penitence," in Machiavelli, *The Chief Works*, 1:178; *Discourses*, 389. Peterman suggests that the accomplishments of St. Francis and St. Dominic were sufficient to move men irrespective of fortune ("Machiavelli's Dante," 257).

41. The fallen angels as discussed in his short story, Belfagor, reveal creatures who are subject to the same desires and failings as men. Whether this has to do with their fallen state or with their basic natures (in the absence of divine guidance) is a question Machiavelli does not answer. "The Tale of Belfagor," *The Literary Works of Machiavelli*, 191–202.

42. Mark Hulliung points to Machiavelli's supposed deathbed remark that he would rather go to hell to converse with men Dante has condemned there than to heaven. *Citizen Machiavelli* (Princeton, N.J.: Princeton University Press, 1984), 210–11.

make it better able to sustain the republicanism he longs for. And the chief lesson he brings back and seeks to instill in the potential princes of his time is the importance of glory as the end of their striving.

Glory, however, seems problematic on Christian grounds. For Christians all sin springs originally from pride, beginning with Satan's rebellion and Adam's fall. Similarly, virtue arises out of a humble reliance on God. Machiavelli's notion of virtue and vice in this respect seems to be almost diametrically opposed to that of Christianity. He recognizes that vice is the result of putting self-interest above the common good, but in his efforts to encourage founders and princes to aim at the common good, Machiavelli argues that attaining glory is ultimately what they should most want, what is in their highest self-interest. But what does it mean to suggest that the highest goal of the human action is glory? Is this not the epitome of the lust to dominate? And in this respect is it not essentially a return to antiquity and paganism against Christianity? Such a conclusion is understandable but it rests on the false assumption that Christianity and pagan morals are essentially incompatible with one another. In his efforts to encourage new founders and effective rule, Machiavelli does not reject Christianity but draws on his humanist predecessors in combining Christianity and antiquity into a new synthesis that he hopes will make possible a refounding of Florentine and Italian republicanism.

While our notion of pre-Reformation Christianity is often shaped by an idealized vision of the church as a single whole, unified by doctrine and dedicated to spirituality, the reality was quite different. Christianity had multiple forms and practices. Moreover, as an economic and political institution, it was deeply immured in the secular world. While at some level Christianity opposed pride, the church itself was filled with proud and ambitious men and often encouraged the ambition of secular rulers at least when what they sought was also in the church's interest. Dante, as we have seen, is ambiguous on this point, finding places for the proud and ambitious in hell, purgatory, and paradise.[43]

The intellectual world in which Machiavelli grew up was radically different than that of Dante. This change began with the fourteenth-century nominalist attack upon scholastic realism. The realist universe was a

43. For example, all of the Roman Caesars whose acts were motivated by a desire for honor and fame but whose aim was righteous in his view are in paradise (III.6.112–14).

closed world, created as a rational whole of ordered universals accessible to human reason. Realists also insisted that God had built into human nature a desire for the good and directed human beings by a natural law that they only had to follow to attain peace and happiness. Beginning with William of Ockham, the nominalists rejected this vision which they believed undermined God's divinity by subordinating divine will and power to reason and nature. The nominalists imagined a God whose omnipotence transcended both. If God were truly God then he was no man's debtor and could do anything that was not contradictory. Today he could save the saints and damn the sinners and tomorrow do exactly the reverse. Such a God, they reasoned, could not have created universals without limiting his own power. As a result, the natural world was not an orderly whole but a chaos of bodies in motion, and there thus could be no natural law such as Aquinas and other scholastic realists had imagined. Francesco Petrarch, the contemporary of Ockham, spelled out the consequences of this insight in a way that became definitive for humanism: "*Mother nature has created nothing without strife and hatred*."[44] War in his view was universal: "From the foremost of the angels to the smallest of the worms—the battle is unceasing and relentless."[45] This war is not merely among things in the external world but within human beings as well. The particular set of passions that characterized each human being, in Petrarch's view, was unique and as a result there was no single highest good or form of perfection for humans as a species. Rather each man or woman had to find and develop his or her own virtue. Human beings were principally willing and not rational beings and their excellence was thus measured by the strength of their wills. Later humanists from Salutati to Ficino developed this theme more explicitly, emphasizing not man's fallenness but the fact that like God he was a willing being, treating him less as a creature than as the *imago dei*. From this point of view the dignity of man, as one of Machiavelli's favorite thinkers Pico della Mirandola argued, consisted in attaining godlike power and perfection.[46]

Such a Promethean view of man may seem antithetical to Christianity today, but it was considered orthodox during the Renaissance. This heroic vision drew not merely on Christian notions of man as the *imago*

44. *Remedies for Fortune Fair and Foul*, 3:4.
45. Ibid., 3:10.
46. De Grazia, *Machiavelli in Hell*, 64.

dei but also on ancient models of exemplary human beings that reappeared as human possibilities in the newly discovered works of the historians and biographers such as Plutarch, Livy, and Tacitus. Petrarch pointed the humanist project in this direction when he set its goal as combining Roman virtue and Christian piety under the rubric of Platonic philosophy. This process of amalgamating ancient and Christian thought was given great impetus by Ficino's discovery and publication of the *Corpus hermeticum*, in the mid-fifteenth century. This led to the development of a powerful syncretistic interpretation of Christianity that persisted well into the seventeenth century, rooted in the notion that Hermes Trimegistus, whose thought Ficino believed he had recovered, was the teacher of both Moses and Orpheus and thus the common wellspring of the Greco-Roman and Christian traditions. This development within Christianity played a powerful role until and even in some cases well into the Reformation and had a particularly powerful impact on the understanding of political life.

If war is the basic state of the world, then the idea of universal peace under the reign of a virtuous ruler that Dante had dreamed of is impossible. Therefore, anyone who hopes to succeed in politics must accept the fact that faction and war are endemic, and can be controlled only by modes and orders that channel the conflict in ways that are conducive to the general good. A good regime thus depends upon men who are willing and able to do what is necessary to see that the state succeeds under such brutal conditions. Such men rise above the human level in creating and managing the institutions that channel conflict and give men some measure of control over fortune. In this way they win not just power but glory, which in part comes from their contemporaries but also partly because they are loved by God. At the core of this new understanding was an elevation of pride from the source of all sin to a place of honor in the panoply of human values.

The Prince and the *Discourses* were both written in 1513. In the same year, Albrecht Dürer completed his most famous engraving, *Knight, Death and the Devil*. A comparison to Lorenzetti's frescoes is illuminating and helps us understand the impact of humanism on morality and politics. Lorenzetti portrayed a fixed and unchanging world of good and evil. Dürer's world is a world at war, and at the center of this world is a solitary knight. He is headed toward a city, but not really part of it.

Indeed, in the context of the painting the individual looms large while the city is clearly in the background. The knight is also a rider; he is underway, active, and not a fixed element of an established order. His face is resolute and tells us little about his passions. His eyes appear slightly sad but a small smile or perhaps a sneer seems just about to surface on his face. His character, however, is revealed indirectly in the faces of his companions, his horse and dog, both of whom display an innate ferocity and determination that is truly extraordinary. The knight is armed and ready for battle. Indeed, his armor seems almost to be a part of him, a second skin. He clearly has no fear of death, who rides beside him, nor of the devil who waits behind him to catch him when he falls. The natural world around him is not an orderly whole but a chaotic jumble of rocks, bare trees, and weeds. There is no agriculture, no fertile or fallow fields, but only a wild and untamed world confronting him. There are no overt references to heaven (except perhaps the church in the city whose cross is obscured by a tree limb), but there are numerous references to hell from the devil and the snake wound round the neck of death, to the lizard under the horse's hooves. The knight's path leads him to the city and thus to politics. If we were to describe him in the language of Machiavelli's *The Prince*, we might characterize him as a lion. But this would not be entirely correct unless we also noted the prominent fox tail on his spear. He is not only virile and virtuous, he is also clever and deceptive. Dürer gives us a hint about what he represents in the small "S" carved into the plaque that contains his initials. The S stands for "Sanguinity," which literally means bloodiness but is generally defined as boldness. However, it might perhaps be better understood as the self-certainty that one's own power is sufficient for anything and that it gives one a good chance of success. This knight is a man in pursuit of glory and willing to do what is necessary to attain it. He is not bargaining with either death or the devil and relies only upon himself and his animal passions. He is an autonomous, self-sufficient, commanding human being, a Christian soldier to use the term Erasmus made famous, who also captures many of the aspects of Machiavelli's founder and prince.[47]

47. This is not surprising. During this period of his life Dürer was deeply influenced by Ficino and Italian humanism as well as the great northern humanist Erasmus, and particularly by his *Enchiridion militis Christiani*, his *Handbook for a Militant Christian*. This knight, like Machiavelli's great men, is a combination of Christian and ancient notions of morality.

Machiavelli's theory of the virtues and the vices is not anti-Christian. He is concerned above all with the common good, and the question with which he constantly wrestles is how to bring it into being in the face of rabid self-interest and endemic factionalism. For Machiavelli the realization of the republican regime depends upon effective rule and that means on a ruler or rulers who are able and willing to do what is necessary to found and maintain a regime. To be effective they must know how *not* to be good without becoming evil; or to put it in other terms, they must be willing to act violently or deceitfully in the face of those who are violent and deceitful, and must be willing to use violence effectively in order to avoid greater violence, all in the service of the common good. The ruler must also have an understanding of what the common good is and be concerned with what is possible and not be distracted by theories or ideals. This requires him to understand how states actually come into being and pass away in order to prepare for as many contingencies as possible. To achieve this end he needs a well-armed and well-trained citizen army and the support of a martial religion.[48]

The principal model of a republic that Machiavelli drew upon was Rome. For Machiavelli Rome was founded by and on military force and a harsh religion, and sustained its independence with its own arms. Its civil liberty was maintained by the competition and conflict between the two principal classes of the republic. This conflict did not lead to the dominance of one over the other in part because of Rome's continual need to use force against its external enemies and in part because its pagan religious beliefs legitimated inequality. The internal conflict in this way preserved the virtue needed for conquest and the danger from without put limits on the intensity and extent of party strife.

The contrast to Machiavelli's native Florence could not have been more pronounced. The Florentine republic was rooted not in military strength but in commerce. It was maintained not by its own arms but by the arms of hired mercenaries and the auxiliaries of other princes. It was thus ultimately incapable of defending itself. It too suffered from internal

48. Machiavelli himself remarks that our ceremonies are delicate rather than imposing and not ferocious; we beatify the humble rather than the glorious and we seek the strength to suffer rather than to do bold things. In his view, this seems to have made the world weak and prey to the wicked, but he believes that this due to those who interpret our religion according to indolence instead of virtue, and thus points to his project for a transformation, rather than a rejection, of Christianity (*Discourses*, 278).

conflict, but this conflict did not produce virtue. Instead, it led to the sequential subjugation of one group by another and the repeated murder or banishment of one's opponents. Again in contrast to Rome, religion also did not strengthen the republican character of the regime but weakened it because its implicit egalitarianism stoked the envy, greed, and resentment of the subjects against whoever was in power.

While Machiavelli, like his predecessors, held up the Roman model for emulation, such a model was ill suited to his Italy and was actually only successful in martially oriented Switzerland. Moreover, Machiavelli's demand for martial virtue was deeply at odds with the bourgeois character of the regimes that were unsuited for the kind of republicanism he had in mind. It was thus only in the seventeenth century, at the end of the Reformation and the Wars of Religion, that Machiavelli's martial republicanism could be transformed into a commercial republicanism that devalued the warrior virtues and the glory associated with the Roman model in favor of peace and commodious living. Good government in this context took on a meaning different in practice but not necessarily in its goals from what was portrayed on the walls of the Sala dei Nove. While Machiavelli certainly played an important role in the transition to the modern age, the idea of such a commercial republic was far from his thinking.

Nathan Tarcov

2 Machiavelli's Modern Turn

In conformity with the theme of this volume, I focus on Machiavelli's presentation of his break with the thought of classical antiquity rather than on his break with Christianity or biblical religion, since the latter break could be compatible with a return to antiquity rather than a distinctively *modern* turn.[1] And Machiavelli's relation to the Christian tradition is a subject of the previous chapter in this volume.

In both his major political works, *The Prince* and the *Discourses on Livy*, Machiavelli presents himself as an ardent advocate of the imitation of ancient virtue and a severe critic of modern weakness and idleness, and he invokes the authority exclusively of ancient writers. His famous letter to Francesco Vettori of December 10, 1513, beautifully describes his communing with the ancients: "I enter the ancient courts of ancient men, where, received by them lovingly, I feed on the food that alone is mine and that I was born for. There I am not ashamed to speak with them and to ask them the reason for their actions; and they in their humanity reply to me."[2]

In his dedicatory letter to *The Prince* Machiavelli writes that he got his knowledge of the actions of great men from "long experience with

1. See my "Machiavelli's Critique of Religion," *Social Research* 81, no. 1 (Spring 2014): 193–216. This paper benefited from the comments of Adrienne Black, Michael Dink, Hillel Fradkin, Michael Gorman, Christopher Lynch, Hannes Kerber, Alan Levine, Charles McCarthy, Colin Pears, Philip Neri Reese, Michael Rubin, Robert Sokolowski, Susan Tarcov, and other participants in the discussion after my lecture at the Catholic University of America on September 17, 2010.

2. Quoted from Niccolò Machiavelli, *The Prince*, trans. Harvey C. Mansfield, 2nd ed. (Chicago: University of Chicago Press, 1998), 109–10.

modern things and a continuous reading of ancient ones."[3] And the book ends with a quotation from Petrarch's *Italia mia* proclaiming that "the ancient valor in Italian hearts is not yet dead." In between, Machiavelli frequently recommends imitation of ancient rulers and republics, whose wisdom and success sometimes are contrasted with the folly and failure of modern counterparts.

The first example of an ancient-modern contrast in *The Prince* and the focus of Chapter III is the contrast between the wisdom, virtue, and prudence of the ancient Romans in conquering Greece and the errors of the modern French king Louis XII in attempting to conquer Italy. In Chapter IV two ancients, Alexander the Great and the Romans, are the examples of successful conquerors; and in Chapter V the Romans are the examples of successful conquerors yet again. What Machiavelli calls in Chapter VI "the greatest examples," princes who founded new principalities through their own arms and virtue, are all ancient: the Hebrew Moses, the Persian Cyrus, the Roman Romulus, and the Greek Theseus, and the lesser example he adds is the Syracusan Hiero. In contrast, when he turns in Chapter VII to the inferior case of those who became princes not through their own arms and virtue but through the arms of others and fortune, he briefly mentions unnamed Greek and Roman examples but discusses at length the modern example of Cesare Borgia, who is said there to have acquired and lost his state through the fortune of his father, Pope Alexander VI, and whose ultimate ruin resulted from his own error. In Chapter VIII, on those who acquired principalities through crimes, Machiavelli explicitly gives "two examples, one ancient, the other modern," the ancient being Agathocles of Syracuse who lived "for a long time secure in his fatherland," and the modern being Liverotto da Fermo who, after holding his principality for a year, was murdered by Cesare Borgia.

When Machiavelli recommends in Chapter XIV that a prince should exercise his mind by reading histories and should imitate the actions of excellent men, especially their imitation of someone praised and glorified before them, the examples are all ancient: "as they say Alexander the Great imitated Achilles; Caesar, Alexander; Scipio, Cyrus." Machiavelli then identifies the ancient Socratic philosopher Xenophon as the writer

3. Quotations from *The Prince* unless otherwise noted are from the Mansfield translation. References are by the Roman chapter numbers.

Scipio followed in his imitation of Cyrus. Modern imitators would thus be at least three removes from ancient originals: imitating what ancient writers wrote about ancient predecessors who imitated more ancient predecessors as described by poetic, historical, or philosophic writers such as Homer, Xenophon, or Plutarch.

Machiavelli refers to only two ancient authors by name in *The Prince*: Xenophon, a Greek writing not about a Greek but about the Persian Cyrus (Chapter XIV), and Virgil, a Roman quoted not about a Roman but about the Carthaginian Dido (XVII). Machiavelli does not name the ancient writers who were his sources for his ancient Greek and Roman examples in *The Prince*, such as Livy, Plutarch, Suetonius, Cicero, Diodorus Siculus, Justin, Herodian, and Polybius. Whereas Machiavelli emphasizes his use of ancient examples, he slights his dependence on ancient writers for those examples. And his peak of apparent adherence to the ancients in the passage on imitation at the end of Chapter XIV is immediately followed by his famous proclamation in Chapter XV that he departs from the orders of others by going directly to the effectual truth rather than to the imagination of things. "Many have imagined republics and principalities that have never been seen or known to exist in truth." The ancient writers therefore should not be trusted, and the republics and principalities they wrote about should not be believed in or imitated.

How are we to understand Machiavelli's self-proclaimed modernity, his departure from the orders and imagined republics and principalities of his predecessors for his effectual truth? He explains (61):

> For it is so far from how one lives to how one should live that he who lets go of what is done for what should be done learns his ruin rather than his preservation. For a man who wants to make a profession of good in all regards must come to ruin among so many who are not good. Hence it is necessary to a prince, if he wants to maintain himself, to learn to be able not to be good, and to use this and not use it according to necessity.

The descriptive observation that the wicked often prosper and the good often suffer in this world is not new: it was well known to biblical and classical writers. It is rather Machiavelli's prescriptive inference from this observation that departs from his predecessors, that it is therefore necessary for a prince to learn to be able not to be good and to use that ability according to necessity, that is, according to whatever may be necessary to maintain himself in power.

This conclusion is sometimes seen as a regretful departure on Machiavelli's part from the counsel of the biblical and classical traditions that princes should adhere to virtue, a departure made by Machiavelli only as a reluctant concession to necessity. Thus Machiavelli remarks in Chapter XV that "I know everyone will confess that it would be a very laudable thing that a prince should be found with all the qualities written above that are held good," but he notes that human conditions do not permit a prince to have them all or entirely observe them.[4] Similarly, in Chapter XVIII he writes that a prince should "not depart from good, when possible, but know how to enter into evil, when necessitated."

Machiavelli's departure from his predecessors, however, is less regretful and more radical than that. Machiavelli's acknowledgment that a quality is "held good" or is even confessed by everyone to be "laudable" does not imply he himself regards it as truly good or deserving of praise. Indeed, in Chapter XV Machiavelli carefully refrains from calling the qualities held to be good *virtues,* calling them instead merely qualities that bring praise or that are held to be good or that appear to be virtues. His list of the pairs of qualities that bring praise or blame varies their order in such a way that one cannot always be sure which is supposed to be praised and which to be blamed.

Machiavelli divides vices into three categories based solely on their relation to a prince's ability to maintain his state: (1) those whose infamy would take away his state; (2) those that would not take away his state; and (3) those without which he can with difficulty save his state. While Machiavelli argues that a prince should be so prudent that he knows how to avoid the infamy of those that would take away his state, he concedes that a prince should guard himself against those vices that would not take away his state if he is able to, but if he is not able to then he can with less respect or hesitation indulge in them. This allowance is not a matter of political necessity but a concession to the prince's own ability or inability to refrain from indulging in such vices. But does Machiavelli advise refraining from such vices as would take away a prince's state or only avoiding *the infamy* of indulging in them if one can indulge in them without incurring infamy? Does he even truly regard them as vices?

4. Author's translation. I translate as "very laud*able*" rather than "very praise*worthy*" since Machiavelli uses *laudabilissima* rather than *laudevolissima,* indicating merely that it can or will be praised, not necessarily that it is worthy of being praised.

Most tellingly, he concludes Chapter XV with his advice about the third kind of vice, "one should not care about incurring the fame [or infamy] of those vices without which it is difficult to save one's state; for if one considers everything well, one will find something *appears to be* virtue, which if pursued would be one's ruin, and something else *appears to be* vice, which if pursued results in one's security and well-being" (emphasis added). Thus Machiavelli leaves the reader at the end of Chapter XV with the thought that the qualities that are praised and blamed only *appear to be* virtues and vices but are not so in truth, that a quality that leads to one's ruin cannot truly be a virtue and a quality that leads to one's security and well-being cannot truly be a vice, that virtue is instead whatever quality in a given circumstance leads to one's security and well-being and vice is whatever quality in a given circumstance leads to one's ruin. Virtue and vice thus are robbed of their moral meaning. Machiavelli takes his bearings by the goals men actually pursue—wealth and glory (XXV)—rather than by the ancient standard of the right order of their souls or the biblical standard of the salvation of their souls. Indeed he never mentions the soul in either *The Prince* or the *Discourses.*

Machiavelli's destructive analysis of the virtue of liberality in Chapter XVI indicates a more general rejection of ancient virtue as understood by the ancient writers (in this case most obviously Aristotle).[5] His critique is presented at first as if it were directed not against the virtue of liberality as such but merely against liberality "used so that you may be held liberal." He objects that if a prince "wants to maintain a name for liberality," he will "consume all his resources," be necessitated to burden the people excessively with taxes, and become both hated for his taxation and despised for his poverty. (Machiavelli famously or infamously counsels princes that it is safer to be feared than loved, but he warns sternly against being hated or despised.) Such a prince will have "offended the many and rewarded the few," whereas a prince who does not care about getting a name for meanness will instead with time be held more and more liberal since he turns out "to use liberality with all those from whom he does not take, who are *infinite*, and meanness with all those to whom he does not give, who are *few*" (emphasis added).

Machiavelli's rejection of the classical praise of liberality as a virtue is

5. Cf. Clifford Orwin, "Machiavelli's Unchristian Charity," *American Political Science Review* 72 (1978): 1217–28.

therefore at least threefold. First of all, he suggests that whereas the classical praise of virtue praises its practitioners for practicing it for its own sake, they actually do so only for the sake of getting a name for virtue. Thus although he teaches princes to manipulate appearances (XVIII), he teaches them, as did the ancient writers, to see through appearances and reject them for the truth. Second, he accuses the writers who praise the classical virtues and those who practice them of favoring the few at the expense of the many. In this respect his destructive analysis of the biblical virtue of mercy in Chapter XVII parallels his destructive analysis of the classical virtue of liberality in Chapter XVI: he counsels a prince not to care about incurring the infamy of cruelty because with *very few* examples of cruel punishments he will be more merciful than those who for the sake of "too much mercy" allow disorders to continue that hurt *a whole community.*

Third, Machiavelli accuses the classical virtues of consuming themselves: "there is nothing that consumes itself as much as liberality: while you use it, you lose the capacity to use it; and you become either poor and contemptible or, to escape poverty, rapacious and hateful." The classical praise of what are held to be virtues, according to Machiavelli, leads to self-contradiction because it pays insufficient attention either to the conditions or to the effects of their exercise. In contrast to the classical writers' neglect of the conditions or capacities for the exercise of their virtues, Machiavelli emphasizes *acquisition* ("and truly it is a very natural and ordinary thing to desire to acquire," III); in contrast to the classical writers' neglect of effects, Machiavelli emphasizes what he calls "the effectual truth," considering whether the effects of exercising those qualities add to or subtract from one's security and well-being. In calculating effects, Machiavelli counts negative effects as well as positive ones, those from whom one does *not* take and crimes that are *not* committed, whereas according to him those who praise liberality and mercy count only positive effects, those to whom one gives or those whom one pardons.

Instead of regarding such qualities as virtues in the sense of dispositions that contribute to the perfection of one's soul, Machiavelli treats them as qualities that may be used either "virtuously" or badly. Virtue thus becomes adverbial rather than substantive. What are ordinarily considered vices may also be used either well or badly: Machiavelli writes of cruelties "well used (if it is permissible to speak well of evil)," parenthetically admitting that he speaks adverbially well of what is held to be substantive evil. The only true virtue not subject to the adverbial modification of being used well or badly is prudence, which "picks the less bad as good" (XXI) and determines the prudent use of those other qualities praised and blamed by the writers as virtues and vices.

In Chapter XVII Machiavelli stresses that for a prince with his army it is above all necessary not to care about getting a name for cruelty, contrasting Hannibal's "inhuman cruelty," which Machiavelli treats as one of his virtues because it kept his army united, with Scipio's "excessive mercy" that led his soldiers to mutiny. Machiavelli accuses "the writers" of admiring Hannibal's action but inconsiderately damning its principal cause, his inhuman cruelty. This accusation is directed tacitly in the first place against Livy, the one who condemned Hannibal's "inhuman cruelty" as a vice along with his perfidy, lack of truthfulness, lack of fear of the gods, and disrespect for oaths and religion.[6] More generally, this accusation treats the ancients' insistence on condemning vices even when they lead to good effects as hypocrisy or, worse, as a failure to understand the causes of the actions and accomplishments of great men.

Machiavelli's condemnation of Scipio's "excessive mercy" seems to call into question what I earlier called the peak of Machiavelli's apparent adherence to the ancients in *The Prince,* his praise in Chapter XIV of Scipio as one of the excellent men in the past said to have imitated someone praised and glorified before him: "whoever reads the life of Cyrus written by Xenophon will then recognize in the life of Scipio how much glory that imitation brought him, how much in chastity, affability, humanity, and liberality Scipio conformed to what had been written of Cyrus by Xenophon." Putting these two passages together, the reader gets the impression that Scipio was misled by Xenophon into imitation of damaging qualities such as excessive mercy, that Xenophon was one of those writers about imaginary principalities who forgot how far it is from how one does live to how one should live, and that Machiavelli's apparent endorsement of imitation of the models offered by the ancient writers is in fact a warning against imitating them.

Machiavelli is referring, however, to two different Scipios. The Scipio said to have imitated Xenophon's Cyrus in Chapter XIV was Scipio Af-

6. Livy, XXI.4.

ricanus *Minor,* who destroyed Carthage in 146 B.C., whereas the Scipio criticized for excessive mercy in Chapter XVII is Scipio Africanus *Major,* who defeated Hannibal and spared Carthage in 202 B.C.[7] In excuse of Machiavelli's frequently not bothering to distinguish one member of a family from another, one could cite his explanation in *Discourses* III.46 that one family keeps the same customs for a time owing to the differences in education between one family and another. Nevertheless, Machiavelli gives the reader the impression that imitation of Xenophon's Cyrus led "Scipio" astray. We can therefore still say that Machiavelli recommends the imitation of ancient excellent men not as written about by ancient writers but as written about by Machiavelli himself.

In Chapter XVIII of *The Prince* Machiavelli explicitly invokes "the ancient writers." He reveals that they "taught covertly to princes" that it is necessary to have recourse to force, which is proper to beasts, as well as to law, which is proper to man, by writing that Achilles and many other ancient princes were given to be raised by Chiron the centaur, "a half-beast, half-man." Even in apparently invoking their authority, however, Machiavelli departs from the ancient writers. Even if we assume that his interpretation of the ancient writers is correct, we must conclude that by *openly* teaching what he claims they taught only covertly, Machiavelli rejects their scrupulous concern for the dangerous effects of broadcasting such a teaching, whether encouraging excessive reliance by princes on force rather than on law or opening the eyes of the people to the bestial side of their rulers. Machiavelli departs here from the ancient writers not only in mode but in substance: he moves swiftly from the teaching he attributes to the ancient writers that a prince needs to know how to

7. Cicero recounts in a letter to his brother Quintus (I.1.23) that "Xenophon wrote of Cyrus not faithfully to history but as an image of just rule, and his supreme gravity was joined with singular courtesy by that philosopher; not without cause was Africanus used not to putting those books from his hands; no duty of diligent and moderate rule is omitted from those books" (author's translation). Similarly, in his *Tusculan Disputations* (II.62) Cicero writes that "Africanus always had the Socratic Xenophon in his hands." This is clearly Scipio Africanus Minor, whom Cicero makes the chief speaker in his *Republic,* for as Cicero notes (*Tusculan Disputations* IV.5), there were no philosophers in Rome before the time of the later Scipio. Cicero's account confirms Machiavelli's charge that philosophers like Xenophon imagined principalities never known to exist in truth. I owe these references to Meng Li. Giorgio Inglese and William J. Connell, however, identify the Scipio of Chapter XIV as Africanus Major: Niccolò Machiavelli, *Il Principe,* ed. Giorgio Inglese (Turin: Einaudi, 1995), 101; *The Prince by Niccolò Machiavelli with Related Documents,* trans. and ed. William J. Connell (Boston: St. Martin's, 2005), 86.

use both the nature of the beast and the nature of man to his own teaching that a prince needs to be both a fox and a lion (XVIII, also Severus in XIX), omitting the nature of man altogether. Leo Strauss comments that "the imitation of the beast takes the place of the imitation of God" and that Machiavelli "replaces the imitation of the God-Man Christ by the imitation of the Beast-Man Chiron."[8] Since my subject is Machiavelli's turn away from the ancients rather than his turn away from Christianity, I will add that this turn also seems to include a turn away from Plato and Aristotle's orientation toward the divine and toward the divine in man: intellect and love of wisdom.[9]

The only ancient identified as a philosopher in *The Prince* is Marcus Aurelius, "Marcus the philosopher" in Chapter XIX (the only mention of philosophy in the book). Machiavelli seems to praise Marcus for being of modest life, a lover of justice, an enemy of cruelty, humane, benign, and accompanied by many virtues that made him venerable, so that he lived and died honorably. It is not clear, however, that Machiavelli regards Marcus's modesty, love of justice, hostility to cruelty, humanity, and benignity as the virtues that made him venerable and enabled him to live and die honorably. Instead, Machiavelli writes, Marcus's having succeeded to the empire by (adoptive) hereditary right without owing it to either the soldiers or the people and his keeping both those orders in line led to his success. Machiavelli implicitly illustrates the perils of hereditary succession and Marcus's own imprudence, however, by tracing the subsequent decline to Marcus's son and heir, Commodus, whose cruel and bestial spirit led him to indulge the soldiers and make them licentious so as to practice his own rapacity on the people. In addition, Commodus failed to maintain his dignity, descending into the arena to fight with gladiators, and was put to death. Once the soldiers had been corrupted by Commodus, they could no longer endure an honest life, and later emperors were "forced not to be good" and either satisfied the soldiers by letting them vent their avarice and cruelty on the people or were themselves put to death. Although Marcus was adopted himself, he disastrously

8. Leo Strauss, *Thoughts on Machiavelli* (Chicago: University of Chicago Press, 1995), 10, 59, 78.

9. Plato, *Republic* 497bc, 500cd, *Laws* 631b–d, 716c–e, 726a, 792d, 804b, 818c, 966cd; Aristotle, *Politics* 1287a29, 1323b21–29, 1325b26–32; Aristotle, *Nicomachean Ethics* 1177a12–18, 1177b27–34, 1178b8–24.

allowed the succession of his son rather than adopting an heir like himself. Machiavelli claims in the *Discourses* (I.10) that of the twenty-six emperors from Caesar to Maximinus, all but one of those who succeeded by inheritance were bad, whereas all those who succeeded by adoption were good, and as the empire fell to heirs it met its ruin. The failure of the philosopher-emperor to perpetuate his rule through a suitable successor recalls the failure of the philosopher-kings in Plato's *Republic* to overcome chance and perpetuate their rule through successors like themselves.[10] Machiavelli, in contrast, in *The Prince* holds out the possibility of overcoming Fortuna (XXV), and in the *Discourses* he holds out the promises of regulating fortune, founding a "perpetual republic" ruled by ambitious princes rather than philosophers, and achieving perpetual fame or eternal memory (I.27, II.30.2, 30.5, and III.22.3). In this respect he imitates the promises of religion rather than of classical philosophy.

In turning to the *Discourses* I must of necessity be extremely selective as it is a much longer book and is engaged with antiquity on almost every page. The duality of return to classical antiquity combined with claims to radical innovation marks the *Discourses* as well as *The Prince*. Machiavelli's preface to Book I claims both that he has found new modes and orders by taking a path yet untrodden by anyone and that he writes to turn men from the error of judging imitation of the ancients impossible. The work is therefore not simply a commentary on Livy but a set of reflections on modern times and original interpretations of antiquity. When he explains how it is still possible to imitate the ancients, he nonetheless leaves room for innovation. He writes:

> In all cities and in all peoples there are the same desires and the same humors, and there always have been. So it is an easy thing for whoever examines past things diligently to foresee future things in every republic and to take the remedies for them that were used by the ancients, or, if they do not find any that were used, to think up new ones through the similarity of accidents.[11]

Machiavelli praises pagan antiquity at the expense of Christian modernity, but he also criticizes classical writers and even Rome itself. In

10. *Republic* 546.

11. I.39.1. References to Machiavelli's *Discourses on Livy* are to *Discourses on Livy*, trans. Harvey C. Mansfield and Nathan Tarcov (Chicago: University of Chicago Press, 1996), by book, chapter, and paragraph numbers.

waging a two-front war he fights one enemy at a time (III.11), hoping to gain the initial sympathy of humanist admirers of classical antiquity before revealing his critique of their classical models.

Before turning to some of the most salient of Machiavelli's criticisms of the ancients in the *Discourses,* I should stress his most fundamental agreement with classical philosophy, which makes him a philosopher. He avows that "it is good to reason about everything" (I.18.1) and "I do not judge nor shall I ever judge it to be a defect to defend any opinion with reasons, without wishing to use either authority or force for it" (I.58.1). Thus in *The Prince,* although Machiavelli declares that "one should not reason about Moses, as he was a mere executor of things that had been ordered for him by God," he nonetheless proceeds to do so on the grounds that Moses's actions and orders were no different from those of such founders as Cyrus, Romulus, and Theseus (VI). Similarly, although he writes in *The Prince* of ecclesiastical principalities such as the papacy that "being sustained by superior causes, to which the human mind does not reach, I will leave out speaking of them: because being exalted and maintained by God, to discourse of them would be the office of a presumptuous and reckless man," he nonetheless proceeds to reason about them (XI). In the dedicatory letter to *The Prince* Machiavelli declares that the possession he cares for and esteems most is his *knowledge* of the actions of great men. His willingness to reason about everything without relying on authority and his esteem for knowledge mark him as a philosopher like his ancient predecessors.

The first point I will discuss at which Machiavelli does break with his ancient predecessors in the *Discourses* regards the status of founding. He seems at first to accept the ancient notion of the superiority of a single wise founder like Lycurgus when he acknowledges that "that republic can be called happy whose lot is to get one man so prudent that he gives it laws ordered so that it can live securely under them without needing to correct them," whereas "that city has some degree of unhappiness that, by not having fallen upon one prudent orderer, is forced of necessity to reorder itself" (I.2.1). But as so often when Machiavelli seems to accept an ancient notion, he swiftly reverses course and innovates. Rome, where "so many accidents arose ... through the disunion between the plebs and the Senate that what an orderer had not done, chance did," he calls "a perfect republic," praising it more highly than Sparta, which observed the laws given at a stroke by Lycurgus "for more than eight hundred years without corrupting them or without any dangerous tumult" (I.2.6).[12] According to Machiavelli, "in Rome, ordered by itself and so many prudent men, every day new causes emerged for which it had to make new orders in favor of a free way of life" (I.49.3), and more generally "a republic has need of new acts of foresight every day," because "in a great city accidents arise every day that have need of a physician" (III.49.1 and title). For Machiavelli, reason or prudence rules not through a single act of founding but through continuous response to chance and accidents.[13]

Machiavelli's praise of internal discord and enmity as the first cause of Roman freedom (in I.3–6) stands in sharp contrast to the frequent praise of internal concord and blame of internal discord in Livy and to Plato's and Aristotle's praises of civic harmony and friendship.[14] Machiavelli prefers the tumultuous Roman republic, where the plebs held the guardianship of liberty through the tribunate, over the stabler, more united Spartan and Venetian republics, dominated by their nobles. He favors the Roman model as more conducive to expansion and empire. Machiavelli makes a brief concession to the advocates of a state strong enough to deter attack but not so great as to provoke attack and prohibited from expansion by its constitution and laws: "Without doubt I believe that if the thing could be held balanced in this mode, it would be the true political way of life and the true quiet of a city" (I.6.4). He immediately rejects this possibility, however, on the ground that "since all things of men are in motion and cannot stay steady, they must either rise or fall; and to many things that reason does not bring you, necessity brings you." He concludes that internal enmities must be tolerated for the sake of conquering external enemies; he proceeds on the basis of the primacy of enmity. Machiavelli follows reason, but for him reason must recognize and follow what he considers necessity or risk becoming mere imagination. He regards the "reason" he rejects as the wishful thinking of those who take their bearings by "republics and principalities that have never been seen or known to exist in truth," in contrast to true reason that

12. Seven chapters later Machiavelli acknowledges that Sparta deviated from those laws and suffered dangerous tumult less than eight hundred years after Lycurgus (I.9.4).

13. Cf. Plato, *Laws* 709.

14. Livy, e.g., II.31–33, 44, 57, III.54, 57, 65, 67–69, IV.7, 10, 43; Plato, *Laws* 628, 693b–d, 701d; Plato, *Republic* 431e–432a; Aristotle, *Politics* 1295b22–24; Aristotle, *Nicomachean Ethics* 1155a23–25.

takes its bearings by necessity. The "true political way of life and the true quiet of a city" that Machiavelli rejects on the grounds of the primacy of enmity, war, and foreign policy and the necessity to conquer or be conquered is the best regime of Plato and Aristotle.[15]

The *Discourses* differs from the works of its classical predecessors in Machiavelli's willingness, not only to advise the governors of republics how to maintain their freedom, but to advise would-be tyrants how to deprive their states of freedom, a willingness mitigated or aggravated by his implicitly advising the leaders of republics to employ tyrannical modes to establish or preserve freedom (I.16–18, 25–26, 55). In doing so he at one point even pointedly calls tyranny merely what "is called tyranny by the authors," calling it instead "absolute power" or simply a "new prince" (I.25–26). This openness to tyranny seems to result from his intense focus on the extreme case of corruption, such as he discerns in Florence and the modern Christian world generally, which requires extraordinary remedies (I.17–18).

Machiavelli wishes to defend a thing, as he says, "accused by all the writers" when he rejects the affirmation of Livy that the multitude is inconstant and by nature "either serves humbly or dominates proudly" (I.58). It is in this context that he makes the statement that "I do not judge nor shall I ever judge it to be a defect to defend any opinion with reasons, without wishing to use either authority or force for it." His defense of the relative wisdom and constancy of the multitude is in line with his preference for the relatively democratic Roman republic over the relatively aristocratic republics of Sparta and Venice. In this respect Machiavelli's modern turn can be called democratic. His defense of the multitude, however, rapidly turns into an accusation against "the nature of every man": princes no less than peoples are inconstant and imprudent when not shackled by laws, and are no more constant and prudent when they are shackled by laws. Therefore "someone accusing peoples and princes together might be able to say the truth," as Machiavelli himself does. The variations arise "not from a diverse nature—because it is in one mode in all." This accusation of human nature is in line with Machiavelli's claim that "it is necessary to whoever arranges a republic and orders laws in it to presuppose that all men are bad" and that "laws make men good" (I.3).

15. Plato, *Republic* 422a–423c; Aristotle, *Politics* 1324b23–1325a5, 1325b23–29.

He presents that claim, however, not as a departure from all the writers but as something "all those demonstrate who reason on a civil way of life."[16] His departure from the writers is ultimately not in accusing but in *excusing* human nature: both good and bad manifest the same natural desires to oppress and not to be oppressed (*Prince* IX; *Discourses* I.5.4, 16.5, 37.1, 46).

Machiavelli explicitly departs from the ancient writers' understanding of the Roman model he offers and even from the Roman self-understanding, when he refuses to confess with Plutarch, Livy, and the Roman people itself that it owed its victories and empire more to fortune than to virtue (*Discourses* II.1). But more often he does so only tacitly. The model Machiavelli offers is not the Rome of the classical writers but Rome as he reinterprets and even improves upon it.[17] He explicitly criticizes Rome for not changing its political orders as it became more corrupt, for not instituting agrarian laws early on, for initially making the term of the censors too long at five years, and for being ordered so that a citizen could be punished for promulgating a law conforming to a free way of life ("it must be either that the historian is defective or that the orders of Rome in this aspect are not good") (I.18, 37, and quotation at 49). He blames Roman humility or patience for increasing the arrogance of the Latins and blames Roman acquisitions of provinces such as Capua that led to their own corruption (II.14, 19, 20, 32). He rewrites Roman history to make his own models, creating a Romulus who does not resort to the gods and a Coriolanus who does not resort to foreign forces (I.11.7, corrected at III.13).[18] Since Machiavelli's concern is with knowing the past not for its own sake but for the sake of future action (preface to I; I.39.1; preface to II), he is free to invent the past. His invocations of the examples of classical rulers and republics reveal a critique of classical writers and an aspiration to replace them as the interpreter or creator of those examples.

Since men of action imitate the examples created by writers according to Machiavelli, writing can be a form of indirect ruling that in turn may spawn other forms of spiritual rule based on writings such as

16. Plato, *Laws* 853bc.

17. See Vickie B. Sullivan, *Machiavelli's Three Romes* (DeKalb: Northern Illinois University Press, 1996).

18. Cf. Livy, I.10, 12.

ecclesiastical principalities (*Prince* III, XI), and Machiavelli can aspire through his writing to replace the classical and biblical writers in indirectly ruling over ordinary princes.[19] He does not consider himself to be replacing true history with his own fiction; on the contrary, he indicates that writers such as Livy, Sallust, and Xenophon "made" their characters do things and "put words in their mouths," whereas he reconstructs, on the basis of his knowledge of human nature and politics, what those characters must have truly done to accomplish what the writers say they did.[20] His rewriting of history is therefore ultimately a form of reason rather than imagination or authority. He replaces not only the classical writers' accounts of their models but also the biblical writers' accounts of Moses and David, especially apt examples for him as they were traditionally regarded as both rulers and writers who wrote about themselves (*Prince* VI and XIII; *Discourses* I.19.2, 26, II.8.2, III.30.1). Whereas for the classical philosophers (who generally avoided writing about themselves), indirectly ruling through writing was incidental to leading readers toward the truth, Machiavelli gives the impression that it is an independent end. He may, however, share the "logocentric" (rather than "graphocentric") orientation of the classical writers, who subordinated writing to thinking, speech, and dialogue. His famous letter to Vettori quoted above presents his reading of the ancients from which *The Prince* emerged as a conversation: he "spoke" to them and they "replied." *The Prince* merely expressed in writing that prior thinking and dialogue. *The Prince* itself contains accounts of his own conversations (III, VII) and dialogues with hypothetical objectors, doubters, and questioners (III, VIII, X, XI, XII, XVI, XIX).

Although I began by explaining that I would focus on Machiavelli's break with the thought of classical antiquity rather than on his critique of Christianity and biblical religion, I am nonetheless compelled to consider his most explicit critique of the Christian religion in the *Discourses* for what it may imply about his view of classical philosophy. He explains that peoples were more lovers of freedom and men were stronger in ancient times than in his time because of "the difference between our education and the ancient, founded on the difference between our

19. I owe this point to Monsignor Robert Sokolowski.

20. See, e.g., *Discourses* I.46, II.13, 23, III.31, 38. See also Cicero on Xenophon quoted in note 7 above.

religion and the ancient" (II.2.2). He explains further that whereas the Gentiles placed the highest good in worldly honor, greatness of spirit, and strength of body and "beatified" men full of worldly glory, "our religion has glorified humble and contemplative more than active men" and "placed the highest good in humility, abjectness, and contempt of things human." We should note, however, that since Machiavelli traces this weakness back to a prior cause, that the Roman Empire eliminated all republics and civil ways of life, return to the ancients cannot be the solution to the problem of modern weakness and loss of liberty.

Machiavelli's own ranking of contemplative and active men and view of the relation of theory and practice are obscure.[21] Although he indicates in the dedicatory letter to *The Prince* that he cares most for his knowledge, it is his knowledge of the *actions* of great men. In the dedicatory letter to the *Discourses*, he writes that he chose to address it to "those who know, not those who can govern a kingdom without knowing," but it seems to be to those who know how to govern. Knowledge of the world does not guarantee good fortune but it enables excellent men to keep their spirits firm in good fortune and bad (*Discourses* III.31). Although, as mentioned above, Machiavelli holds out to men of action the promises of overcoming fortune, founding a perpetual republic, and achieving eternal glory, he knows that the names of most excellent men who deserve more praise than Alexander the Great have been forgotten, that Cesare Borgia could not foresee the date of his own death or illness, that all worldly things have a limit to their life so it is impossible to order a perpetual republic, that St. Gregory burned the works of the poets and historians, that most of Livy's work did not survive, and that his own might not (*Discourses* I.1.4, II.5.1, III.1.1, 17.1; *Prince* VII).[22] Not republics or glory but only truth is eternal, even if it was only first discovered after many ages by him and might be forgotten again for many ages, even if his effectual truth was not destined to have the effects he believed it deserved to have.

Machiavelli's description in *The Prince* (XIV) of Philopoemen, who

21. See my "Machiavelli in *The Prince*; His Way of Life in Question," in *Political Philosophy Cross-Examined: Perennial Challenges to the Philosophic Life*, ed. Thomas L. Pangle and J. Harvey Lomax (New York: Palgrave Macmillan, 2013).

22. *The Prince* and the *Discourses* were not published in his lifetime and they were put on the Index not long after publication. See Strauss, *Thoughts on Machiavelli*, 281–89.

was praised by the ancient writers (Livy and Plutarch), sounds almost like a description of the life and friendship of an ancient philosopher: he "reasoned" with his friends, asked them questions, listened to their opinions, gave his opinion, and supported it with reasons.[23] The difference, of course, is that Machiavelli's Philopoemen reasoned with his friends only about war and how to counter the enemy. Machiavellian friendship and philosophy as exemplified by Philopoemen exist in a context in which war and enmity possess primacy over peace and friendship.[24] Machiavelli's polemical philosophizing in his political books is constrained by what he perceives as the necessity to conquer or be conquered by those writers ancient and modern whom he considers to be his enemies.

In the *Discourses,* Machiavelli at first offers the choice between tyranny and private life, excluding certain middle ways (I.26). Later on he offers the choice between keeping one's distance from the prince and making oneself his close friend, both with the intent of ruining him, again ruling out a middle way (III.2). He then rules out keeping one's distance:

> Nor is it enough to say: "I do not care for anything; I do not desire either honors or useful things; I wish to live quietly and without quarrel!" For these excuses are heard and not accepted; nor can men who have quality choose to abstain even when they choose it truly and without any ambition, because it is not believed of them; so if they wish to abstain, they are not allowed by others to abstain.

Private life, including the contemplative life, is thus not a practical option for men of any quality. Machiavelli does not deny that such men may truly be without ambition and not desire honors or useful things, but he warns that they will not be believed and will be forced into active life. The character of Socrates in the *Republic* presents this as their corruption, but he admits that good men may be compelled to rule to avoid being ruled by worse men and that philosophers may be justly compelled to rule. Plato himself went to Syracuse to advise the tyrants Dionysius the Elder and Younger but his advice was, to put it mildly, ineffectual (Dionysius the Elder responded to Plato's first lesson by ordering

23. Machiavelli uses the verb for reasoning (*ragionare*) in *The Prince* with reference only to Philipoemen and to his own activity; see Chapters II, VI, VIII, XI, XIX.

24. Cf. Carl Schmitt, *The Concept of the Political,* trans. George Schwab (Chicago: University of Chicago Press, 2007), 30–32.

him killed or sold into slavery), and Plato's star pupil Dion later overthrew Dionysius the Younger only to fall victim to a conspiracy himself (I.17.1, III.6.20).[25] Accordingly, Machiavelli's only mention of Plato illustrates this halfway effect: two of his disciples conspired against two tyrants but killed only one of them, leaving the other alive to avenge him (III.6.16). Machiavelli himself led a private life after 1512 only because the Medici had destroyed the republic he served and excluded him from public life. In *The Prince* (XXIII) Machiavelli offers the "general rule that never fails," that if a prince who is not wise himself submits himself to be counseled and governed by someone very prudent, "it would not last long because that governor would in a short time take away his state," as if no wise man would be content merely to advise an unwise prince rather than to become prince himself. (Thus the only general rule that never fails is that there is no substitute for prudence: there are no foolproof rules. Machiavelli equates wisdom with prudence here.) The glorification of contemplative over active men and contempt of things human were not original with Christianity but already marked classical philosophy.[26] It may be this common ground between classical philosophy and Christianity that led Machiavelli to reject them both and make his modern turn.

25. *Republic* 347b–d, 494a–495b, 519e–521b; Plutarch, *Life of Dion.*

26. Plato, *Republic* 486a, 500b, 517cd; Plato, *Laws* 803bc, 804b; Aristotle, *Politics* 1325b14–21; Aristotle, *Nicomachean Ethics* 1141a33–b1, 1177a12–1178a8.

Tad M. Schmaltz

3 Descartes's Critique of Scholastic Teleology

It is of course a familiar claim that Descartes is "the father of modern philosophy."[1] I propose to focus here on an aspect of his system that would seem to have played a particularly important role in the transition from traditional scholasticism to a more modern outlook. I have in mind his emphatic claim in the Fourth Meditation that "the common search for final causes [has] no use in physics" since "it is not without temerity that I take myself to be capable of investigating the ends of God."[2] In place of the teleological natural philosophy of the scholastics, Descartes proposes a mechanistic physics that explains natural change by appealing not to the pulls of ends and final causation, but rather to the pushes of contact action and efficient causation. We would seem to have at least in Descartes's account of the material world what Dennis Des Chene has called "an unbending opposition to finality."[3]

It turns out, however, that Descartes's attitude toward teleology is considerably more flexible than my sketch of a stark contrast with scholasticism suggests. I illustrate this flexibility by focusing on a critique of scholastic teleology that might seem at first to indicate resolute opposition. This critique involves Descartes's charge that teleological explanations in scholastic physics derive from the confused sense that there are

1. On the history of this appellation, see Hans-Peter Schutt, *Die Adoption des "Vaters der modernen Philosophie": Studien zu einem Gemeinplatz des Ideengeschichte* (Frankfurt am Main: Klostermann, 1998).

2. René Descartes, *Œuvres de Descartes*, ed. Charles Adam and Paul Tannery (Paris: J. Vrin, 1964–74), 7:55 [hereafter "AT"].

3. Dennis Des Chene, *Physiologia: Natural Philosophy in Late Aristotelian and Cartesian Thought* (Ithaca, N.Y.: Cornell University Press, 1996), 170.

mind-like entities that guide the action of inanimate bodies. The emphasis in the "little souls objection," as we might call it, is on explanations of the "heaviness" of bodies that appeal to the teleological action of a special kind of "real quality."[4] Descartes offers as an alternative to the postulation of queer little souls an explanation of bodies entirely in terms of mechanistic interactions of bits of extension.

The claim that the scholastics considered real qualities to be little souls of course involves a gross caricature of their views. However, the caricature is useful in drawing attention to some respects in which Descartes's own opposition to teleology is less than absolute. The first is broached by the fact that the caricature assumes that there is final causation only in the case of the intentional action of minds. Indeed, there is reason to take Descartes's own view of human action to be informed by the scholastic account of final causality.

In fact, according to a prominent position in later scholasticism, final causality is restricted to agents that can cognize their ends. According to this position, the response to Descartes's little souls objection would be not that heaviness can act in a teleological manner without a mind, but rather that the cognition of the end of the activity of this quality must occur in the divine mind. This of course brings us to the prohibition in the Fourth Meditation of the appeal to divine purposes in physics. However, a consideration of the context of this proclamation reveals that Descartes takes it to be consistent with an (albeit conjectural) appeal to divine ends. Despite initial appearances, moreover, such an appeal is consistent as well with his doctrine of the creation of eternal truths.

Finally, it is significant that Descartes's little souls objection is linked to our conception of the mind-body union. In his view, the union involves a kind of teleology in the case of the bodily causation of sensation. Descartes's discussion in the Sixth Meditation may seem to suggest—in line with the late scholastic position—that the ends in this case are God's ends. Though the Fourth Meditation proclamation may allow for some sort of appeal to divine ends, it does not allow for the attribution of the ends of sensation to God. Indeed, according to Descartes we are not in a position to assert that any mind is required to cognize these ends. What

4. Following Des Chene, *Physiologia*, 393. In Daniel Garber, *Descartes Embodied: Reading Cartesian Philosophy through Cartesian Science* (Cambridge: Cambridge University Press, 2001), there is a reference to Descartes's objection to the appeal to "tiny souls" (270).

he leaves us with in the case of sensation, then, is a kind of natural teleology that does not need to be explained in terms of genuine final causation.

THE LITTLE SOULS OBJECTION

In his earlier (i.e., pre-*Meditations*) writings, Descartes tends not to attack scholastic natural philosophy directly, but rather to emphasize the empirical adequacy of his own simpler explanations of the material world. This strategy is reflected in his claim in the *Meteors*—published with the 1637 *Discourse on the Method*—that

> so as not to rupture the peace with the philosophers, I have no wish to deny that what they imagine in bodies over and above what I have mentioned [viz., small parts of matter with different sizes, shapes and motions], such as their *substantial forms*, their *real qualities*, and similar things, but it seems to me that my arguments must be all the more approved as I can make them depend on fewer things.[5]

During the 1640s, however, Descartes offers rather a more direct attack on the scholastics that emphasizes the problematic nature of the entities they posit "over and above" the mechanistic features of matter. At several points he illustrates the problems by focusing on the scholastic conception of the bodily quality of "heaviness" (*gravitas*) or "weight" (*pesanteur*).

Descartes's most detailed consideration of this particular case occurs in the Sixth Replies appended to the *Meditations*. There he is concerned to respond to the charge of his critics that he has failed to show that the idea of the soul "contains nothing of a corporeal nature."[6] Rather than repeating his arguments for the real distinction of mind from body, Descartes provides a kind of intellectual autobiography that is supposed to draw attention to the psychological source of the failure to recognize this distinction. Descartes notes that in his youth, a preoccupation with the senses led him to take "extension and thought to be one and the same thing" and to "refer to the body all the notions that it had of intellectual things."[7] He offers as an example of this kind of confused thought his

5. AT 6:239.
6. AT 7:420.
7. AT 7:441.

conception of heaviness (*gravitas*) as a real quality that is a *quality* insofar as it referred to the body in which it inheres, but that is *real* insofar as it is a substance. The model here is provided by the human mind, which "even though it is in fact a substance, can nonetheless be said to be a quality of the body to which it is joined."[8]

Of course, no scholastic would grant that a real quality is a substance. However, Descartes indicates that heaviness is conceived to have three features that mark it out as a non-bodily entity. The first is the extension of heaviness, which is conceived to be distinct from the extension of a body insofar as the latter excludes any interpenetration of parts. Whereas the extension of a body is whole in the whole and part in each part, heaviness is wholly contained not only in the whole of the heavy body, but also in each part. In this respect, heaviness is coextensive with the heavy body in the same way a mind is coextensive with a body to which it is joined: "the whole mind in the whole body and the whole mind in any one of its parts."[9]

The second distinctive feature of heaviness is the fact that it can exercise all of its force in a particular part of a body, even though it is spread out throughout that body. Thus, a body hung from a rope exerts its force on the rope "just as if the heaviness existed in the part actually touching the rope instead of being scattered throughout the remaining parts."[10] Here again, the case of a mind that is joined to a body provides the model. For on Descartes's mature view, a mind that is united to the whole of the human body nonetheless acts on a particular part of that body—namely, and notoriously, the pineal gland.[11]

The argument to this point shows at most that heaviness must be

8. AT 7:442. We must understand the claim here that the human mind "is a quality of the body to which it is joined" in light of Descartes's comment in the Fourth Replies that a substance can be said to be incomplete "insofar as it is referred to some other substance in conjunction with which it forms something which it forms something that is a unity in its own right" (AT 7:222). Thus, to say that the human mind is a quality of the body is to say that it is related to the body in such a way that together they form a unified human being. In a similar manner, heaviness is conceived to join with a body to form a single heavy body. Thanks to Gideon Manning for indicating the need for this clarification.

9. AT 7:442.

10. AT 7:442.

11. See *Passions of the Soul* I.30–31 (AT 11:351–52). Whereas Descartes holds that the mind can act only on the pineal gland, he allows that heaviness is conceived as being able to act on any part of the body in which it is spread out.

conceived as an incorporeal substance. What appears to be missing, though, is any support for the claim that it must be conceived as a *thinking* substance. Even if heaviness has a special kind of extension and a special location of action that only something that is incorporeal can possess, it still may be the case that it is distinguished from a mind by the fact that it lacks any sort of thought.

Enter the third and final feature of heaviness that Descartes emphasizes in the Sixth Replies, a feature that he claims "makes it especially clear that my idea of heaviness was taken largely from the idea I had of the mind." He observes that in his youth he "thought that heaviness carried bodies toward the center of the earth just as if [*tanquam si*] it had some cognition of the center within itself. For this surely could not happen without cognition, and there can be no cognition except in a mind."[12] The fact that the heaviness is conceived as directing the motion toward a particular terminus is supposed to require the assumption that this quality has some sort of basic cognition of that terminus. And since cognition can take place only in a mind, heaviness must be conceived as a rudimentary sort of mind, a "little soul" that directs the motion of the heavy body to its end.

The discussion of heaviness in the Sixth Replies can be seen as relying on what from a scholastic perspective would be an illicit "cartesianization" of scholastic ontology.[13] That is, the argument seems to be that any bodily feature the scholastics posit that is "over and above" the features of the mere extension that Descartes identifies with material substance must be conceived in terms of the only other kind of created substance that he allows, namely, thinking substance. This line of argument would help to explain why Descartes thought that the fact that heaviness has a special sort of extension and a special location for action shows that it must be conceived as some kind of mind, rather than merely as an incorporeal thing.

Nonetheless, Descartes's point about the directedness of the action of heaviness raises issues concerning final causation that are internal to scholasticism. In Aristotle himself, there is no suggestion that final causality requires cognition. Indeed, he emphasizes in the *Physics* that even though plants and animals act for an end, they act neither by art nor after deliberation. Rather, they are directed toward their end in a

12. AT 7:442.
13. See Garber, *Descartes Embodied*, 267.

non-intentional manner by their form.[14] Even in the version of Aristotelianism in Thomas Aquinas, there is an endorsement of the position that every agent—including those that act "by nature" rather than "by intellect"—directs itself to an end.[15] As Des Chene has noted, however, in post-Thomistic scholastic accounts of final causality, there is "a significant step away from Aristotle and toward Plato."[16] Just as in the *Phaedo* the character of Socrates ties final causation to the deliberations of a mind, so in later scholasticism there is an emphasis on the fact that such causation must involve cognition of the ends that are pursued.[17]

We can see this sort of "Platonizing" of the account of final causation in the work of the influential early modern scholastic Francisco Suárez. For Suárez, as for earlier Aristotelians such as Avicenna and Soncinus, the end can act as a final cause only by virtue of existing in the intellect of the agent who acts for that end. In the case of created intellects, Suárez holds that the "causality of the final cause" consists in a "metaphorical motion" in virtue of which the will is moved by desire for a cognized end to pursue that end.[18] In order to understand this position, we must keep in mind the scholastic view that a *motus* consists in the actualization of a *potentia*. One can speak of a "motion" in the intentional action of the will since the will by nature has the potential to desire any end that the intellect presents to it as good. However, the motion is merely "metaphorical" insofar as the only actual motion in this case consists in the volitional act

14. See *Physics* II.8.198b10–199b30.

15. See, e.g., his claim that "the agent that acts with nature as its principle is just as much directed to a definite end, in its action, as is the agent that acts through intellect as its principle." *Summa contra gentiles* III.1, chap. 2, trans. and ed. V. J. Bourke (South Bend, Ind.: University of Notre Dame Press, 1975), 3:39. In contrast to Aristotle, Thomas allows that agents that act with nature as its principle must be directed to their end by God (see ibid., chap. 7, 3:71–74). In contrast to later scholastics such as Suárez (see below), however, he also allows that God can implant a source of final causality in the agents themselves. Thanks to Jeff McDonough for pointing out Thomas's intermediate position on this point.

16. Des Chene, *Physiologia*, 187.

17. In this dialogue, Socrates criticizes Anaxagoras for attempting to provide a causal explanation of human action that does not appeal to the thought that this action is best (98c–99d).

18. Francisco Suárez, *Disputationes Metaphysicae* (Hildesheim: G. Olms, 1965), XXIII.4.4 [hereafter "*DM*"]. In this section, Suárez notes that the notion of metaphorical motion derives ultimately from Aristotle; see *On Generation and Corruption* I.7.324b14–15, in *The Complete Works of Aristotle*, ed. J. Barnes (Princeton, N.J.: Princeton University Press, 1984), 530. In connection with this notion, Suárez also cites Avicenna and Soncinus, among others, at *DM* XXIII.4.8.

to pursue the end that the will produces as an efficient cause. The cognition of the end provides only a condition for that actual motion.[19]

One way to eliminate this sort of final causality would be to argue that the cognition of the end is an efficient cause of a volitional change in the will. There would be no reason at this point to appeal to any sort of metaphorical motion.[20] However, I do not think that this is the route taken by Descartes. For one thing, to my knowledge he never speaks of intellectual cognition as an efficient cause of our acts of will. Indeed, his emphasis is on the fact that our will is *self*-determining, as when he notes at one point that the will has "a positive faculty of determining [itself] to one or other of two contraries."[21] Moreover, Descartes tends to stress the passivity of the intellect, which merely offers up ideas for consideration, in contrast to the activity of the will, which acts on the basis of those ideas.[22] Finally, he explains the determination of our will in terms not of an efficient cause external to that faculty, but rather of the orientation of the will itself toward the true and the good. It is in virtue of this orientation that "the will of a thinking thing is carried [*fertur*] voluntarily and freely (for this is the essence of the will), but nevertheless inevitably, toward a clearly known good."[23] This "carrying" would seem to correspond not to efficient causality, but rather to the sort of "metaphorical motion" that Suárez identified with the causality of the final cause in the case of created intellects. Though Descartes does not use the notion of final causality in describing the relation of our intellect to our will, it seems that for him the relation between these faculties is better conceived in terms of an agent being drawn to a perceived end, as in Suárez, rather than in terms of an efficient cause producing an effect in a patient. If this is correct, then there is in fact a remnant in Descartes of the scholastic account of final causation.

19. The qualification that this account applies only to *created* intellects is necessary because though Suárez allows—and indeed, as we will see, insists—that God is a final cause, he denies that there can be even a metaphorical motion in God. In the case of God, the cognition of an end serves merely as a "reason" (*ratio*), and not any sort of cause, of his action (*DM* XXIII.9.6).

20. I draw this point from Des Chene, *Physiologia*, 191.

21. AT 4:173.

22. See Descartes's claim that will and intellect "differ only as the activity and passivity of the same substance. For strictly speaking, understanding is the passivity of the mind and willing is its activity" (*To Regius*, May 1641, AT 3:372).

23. AT 7:166.

However, the fact that this account is restricted to intelligent agents may seem only to reinforce Descartes's point that scholastics must conceive of heaviness as a "little soul." For insofar as the scholastics conceived of heaviness as a final cause of motion toward the center of the earth, they seem to be committed to the view that this quality has a cognition of the end that conditions its action. But then they appear to be conceiving of heaviness as having some kind of mind, just as Descartes charged.

One way for the scholastic to avoid conceiving of heaviness as a little soul would be to deny that this quality itself is a source of final causality. And this is the route that Suárez in fact took, with respect not only to heaviness but also to any natural agent—that is, any agent that does not produce its effects by willing them. This is clear from his claim that in the case of "those actions, that are from natural agents, there is properly no final causality, but only an inclination [*habitudino*] toward a certain terminus."[24] Even when created intellectual agents act by some means other than will, according to Suárez, they are merely natural agents, and so do not exhibit final causality.[25] Of course, Suárez continues to allow for the fact—which he takes to be evident from experience—that the actions of natural agents are directed toward ends. Moreover, he holds that where there is direction toward an end, there must be final causality, and so some cognition of that end. Nonetheless, he insists that this final causality is grounded not in the natural agents themselves, as Aristotle claimed (and Thomas later suggested), but only in God. Thus, after citing Aristotle's view that "nature wants this or that on account of an end," Suárez adds that this "cannot be understood of nature, unless on account of its author."[26] The actions of natural agents can involve final causality only insofar as "their first principle is the First Cause; and thus in the adequate principle of such actions is included an intelligent cause intending their ends."[27] So in the case of heaviness, the motion of a heavy body that is directed toward the center of the earth requires a cognition of the center, but this is found in God, not in the quality of heaviness. Similarly,

24. *DM* XXIII.10.6.

25. *DM* XXIII.3.18.

26. *DM* XXIII.10.5.

27. *DM* XXIII.10.6. Though, as indicated in note 19, God's intending of the end is not brought about by the sort of final causality that operates in the case of created intellects.

Suárez himself insists that the reason for the rushing of water into a void can be found "neither in the peculiar nature of the water nor in its own impetus, but in the end, which resides in the perfection of the entire universe, which requires being intended by another superior agent"—which, one can add, we call God.[28]

As we have seen, though, Descartes concludes in the Fourth Meditation that "it is not without temerity that I think myself capable of investigating the purposes of God."[29] Though he can be read as issuing an absolute prohibition of any sort of appeal to divine ends, closer consideration reveals that his position is significantly more qualified than this.

THE APPEAL TO DIVINE PURPOSES

In the Fourth Meditation, Descartes considers the appeal to divine purposes in the context of attempting to offer an explanation of error. The central problem here is how the fact that we fall into error is to be reconciled with the fact that we are the products of an omniperfect creator. This problem divides into two sub-problems. The first arises from the possibility that our error derives from what Descartes calls a "positive imperfection" in our cognitive faculties.[30] If error did have its source in a positive imperfection, then God, as the creator of these faculties, would be subject to what we could call a "manufacturer culpability."[31] Descartes's response depends on his theory of judgment, according to which error derives from our freely applying our will to what we do not clearly and distinctly perceive. Since we are able to prevent this misapplication of the will, God is not culpable for our error, but rather we are subject to what we could call "user culpability."[32] As Descartes puts the point elsewhere, "our errors, if considered in relation to God, are merely negations; if considered in relation to ourselves they are privations."[33]

28. *DM* XXIII.10.10.

29. AT 7:55.

30. See AT 7:376.

31. Following Lex Newman, "The Fourth Meditation," *Philosophy and Phenomenological Research* 59 (1999): 561–69.

32. Again, following Newman.

33. AT 8–1:17. Our errors are mere negations with respect to God since he is not obliged to create us with a more powerful intellect, but they are privations with respect to us since we are obliged to refrain from misusing our will.

But even if our errors are mere negations with respect to God, and thus God is free from manufacturer culpability in this case, there is still the question of why God permits our cognitive malfunction. This second problem—the problem of permission, as we could call it—derives from the assumption that God "always wills what is best," and that he "could have given me a nature such that I was never mistaken."[34] As Descartes explains later, God could "have endowed my intellect with a clear and distinct perception of everything about which I was likely to deliberate; or he could have simply impressed it unforgettably on my memory that I should never make a judgment about anything which I did not clearly and distinctly understand."[35] So why did God, in willing the best, not bring it about that I am more perfect than I am now?

Descartes's initial answer is that given our weakness and limitations, we should not be surprised that we do not understand the reasons behind all of God's actions. He takes this skeptical consideration to show the futility of the search for final causes in physics, claiming, in a passage cited earlier, that "it is not without temerity that I think myself capable of investigating the purposes of God."[36] It is initially noteworthy that Descartes does not reject any sort of appeal to final causes, but only the appeal to *divine* purposes *in physics*. He therefore allows, first, for the appeal to final causes other than God; this is consistent with the previously noted implication in his writings that there is something like final causation in the case of our own intentional action. Moreover, Descartes seems to allow for the appeal to divine purposes in contexts other than physics. Indeed, he explains in the Fifth Replies, in response to Gassendi's objections, that his injunction against the appeal to divine purposes does not apply to conjectures regarding such purposes "in ethics," since "it may admittedly be pious on occasion to guess what purpose God may have had in mind in his direction of the universe." It is only because explanations in physics must be "backed up by the strongest arguments" that appeals to divine purposes in physics "are futile."[37]

34. AT 7:55.

35. AT 7:61.

36. AT 7:55.

37. AT 7:375. Cf. the claim in the *Principles* that though it may be permissible in ethics to claim that God made everything for our benefit in order impel us to worship him, such a claim would be precluded in physics by the fact that there are many things in the visible universe that are beyond our knowledge and hence of no use to us (*Principles* III.3, AT 8.1:81).

In fact, Descartes appears to employ teleological conjectures in the Fourth Meditation itself. After all, in setting up his problem of permission, he relies on the assumption that God wills what is best. Given this assumption, it seems that we can say that God creates the world that he does *because* it is the best. Additionally, Descartes offers a teleologically-laden answer to the question of why God creates a world with creatures that are prone to error: "there may in some way be more perfection in the universe as a whole because some of its parts are not immune to error, while others are immune, than there would be if all the parts were exactly alike."[38] The conjecture that diversity adds to the perfection of the universe makes sense only if one assumes the possibility that God created this universe *because* it has this feature.

Descartes's appeals to divine purposes here are striking given Suárez's explanation of the rushing of the water into the void in terms of the fact that it contributes to the divine end of enhancing the perfection of the universe. One might well ask how Descartes can allow for his appeals while condemning teleological explanations of the sort Suárez offers in physics as involving "temerity."

The answer is that Descartes's invocations of divine purposes are qualified in ways that Suárez's are not. In particular, Descartes emphasizes the merely conjectural nature of his divine teleology. Thus, he remarks to a correspondent that "I do not know that it can be laid down that God always does what he knows to be the most perfect, and it does not seem to me that a finite mind can judge of that," and that "I tried to solve the difficulty in question, about the cause of error, on the assumption that God had made the world most perfect, since if one makes the opposite assumption, the difficulty disappears altogether."[39] Descartes is not claiming that God wills what is best; he is only determining whether there is a problem with God's permission of error if one allows that he does. Moreover, he is not asserting that God produces creatures that are prone to error because they contribute to the perfection of the universe by making it more diverse; rather, he is saying only that for all we know it is possible that God produces such creatures for this reason. In terms drawn from contemporary discussions in the philosophy of reli-

38. AT 7:61.
39. To [Mesland], May 2, 1644 (AT 4:113).

gion, Descartes is offering here a defense instead of a theodicy of error.[40]

Even so, Descartes's remarks in the Fourth Meditation indicate that he allows for at least the unrefuted possibility of some version of optimism.[41] To be sure, these remarks also indicate that this possibility is of no consequence to his physics. And indeed, in contrast to Suárez, Descartes's explanations in physics do not invoke God's role in enhancing the perfection of the universe as a final cause. Instead, such explanations emphasize laws of nature that derive from the immutability of God's action as the primary efficient cause of motion.[42] Nevertheless, these explanations seem to be consistent with the supposition that God chooses a world governed by these laws because it is the best world possible, which would explain why Descartes thinks he can employ the supposition in the Fourth Meditation.[43]

Des Chene disagrees, citing the denial in Descartes of any preexisting standards of goodness that inform God's act of creation. Thus, there is Descartes's remark in the Sixth Replies:

> If we attend to God's immensity, it is manifest that nothing whatsoever can exist that does not depend on him; not only no subsistent thing, but also no order, no law, nor any reason of truth or goodness; since otherwise ... he would not have been entirely indifferent in creating what he created. If a reason of goodness had preceded his pre-ordering [of the world], it would have determined

40. See the classical source for this distinction in Alvin Plantinga, *God, Freedom, and Evil* (Grand Rapids, Mich.: Eerdmans, 1977). Notice, however, that with respect to the first problem that error seems to derive from a positive imperfection in us, Descartes offers something closer to a theodicy in denying that we have any such imperfection.

41. "Some version": As I indicate below, Descartes's doctrine of the creation of eternal truths is incompatible with features of Leibniz's own optimism.

42. See *Principles* I.28 and II.36 (AT 8.1:15–16 and 61–62).

43. Newman has urged that there are textual and doctrinal reasons to conclude that Descartes in fact rejects the principle that God wills the best. The textual consideration is that the argument in the Fourth Meditation requires only that allowing for diversity makes the world *more* perfect than it would be without that diversity, whereas the doctrinal consideration is that Descartes's own argument in the Third Meditation that knowledge in a created intellect can always increase further (AT 7:47) reveals that the notion of a most perfect created world is incoherent (Newman, "Fourth Meditation," 571n29). However, I have cited Descartes's comment to a correspondent that if one does not assume that God always does what is most perfect, then the difficulty concerning error "disappears completely" (AT 4:113). The clear suggestion here is that the argument in the Fourth Meditation requires this assumption. Moreover, it is not clear that Descartes's argument in the Third Meditation shows that the notion of a most perfect world is incoherent. Even if no particular created intellect can have actually infinite knowledge, still it seems there could be a most perfect world that includes the best combination of created intellects. Such, in fact, would appear to be Leibniz's position.

him to do what is best; but the contrary is true, because he determined himself to make the things that now exist, they were for that reason, as it says in *Genesis*, *They are exceedingly good*—the reason for their goodness, that is, depended on his willing that they be made thus.[44]

This passage of course reflects Descartes's famous—or infamous—doctrine of the creation of eternal truths, according to which eternal truths are what they are because God indifferently willed that they be so. Given this doctrine, there are no "reasons of goodness" that lead God to create in a particular manner; all such reasons derive from God's will itself. For Des Chene, the implication here—contrary to the proposal in the Fourth Meditation—is that "it is vain for me to complain about my error-prone condition in this world, and to wish that I had a more perfect nature, not because my condition is necessary to the greater perfection of the whole, but because such comparisons have no basis."[45] The fact that standards for goodness are created along with the world itself is supposed to reveal that the standards cannot reveal why a particular world exists.

As Des Chene recognizes, his anti-teleological reading of Descartes has a decidedly Spinozistic cast. Indeed, at one point in his *Ethics*, Spinoza notes that the "opinion, which subjects all things to a certain indifferent will of God, and makes all things depend on his good pleasure, is nearer to the truth than that of those who maintain that God does all things for the sake of the good." For Spinoza, those who defend the latter, more Leibnizian, opinion "seem to place something outside God, which does not depend on God, to which God attends, as a model, in what he does, and at which he aims, as at a certain good."[46] This opinion seems to Spinoza to require the "absurdity" that God is determined to act by some end external to himself. To be sure, he also objects to the former, more Cartesian, opinion on the grounds that it allows for alternative ways God could have acted, and thus conflicts with the implication of his system that all things follow with necessity from the divine nature. However, Spinoza also holds that this opinion is closer to the truth insofar as it allows that there is no goal or end that determines God's action. Thus for Spinoza, as for Des Chene, Descartes is distinctive in introducing a "God or nature" devoid of any finality.

44. AT 7:435–36, cited in Des Chene, *Physiologia*, 396.
45. Des Chene, *Physiologia*, 397.
46. 1p33s2, in *Spinoza Opera*, ed. Carl Gebhardt (Heidelberg: Carl Winters, 1925), 2:76.

Nevertheless, it may be possible to reconcile Descartes's doctrine of the creation of the eternal truths with his suggestion in the Fourth Meditation that God might have hidden purposes by distinguishing between antecedent and consequent purposes. It is an implication of the doctrine that God can have no purposes antecedent to the act of creation that lead him to create in a certain way. For this reason, Descartes is committed to rejecting Leibniz's own form of optimism, according to which God's will is conditioned by uncreated eternal truths concerning creatures in his intellect. Even so, there seems to be the possibility for Descartes that the act of creation itself yields ends or purposes that condition the creation of the actual world. We can understand this possibility in terms of Descartes's claim in the Fifth Replies, with respect to his eternal truths doctrine, that

> just as the poets suppose that the Fates were originally established by Jupiter, but that after they were established he bound himself to abide by them, so I do not think that the essences of things, and the mathematical truths that we can know concerning them, are independent of God; nevertheless I do think they are eternal and immutable, since the will and decree of God willed and decreed that they should be so.[47]

Though God indifferently wills essences and the truths concerning them, these essences and truths explain why creatures must have certain properties. Likewise, though any divine end or purpose would have to derive from God's indifferent will, nonetheless the fact that he has willed such ends or purposes could explain why he creates a particular world. Among these ends could be one that requires a sort of diversity that derives from there being creatures prone to error. Antecedent to divine creation there can be no such end that determines the divine will, but once God has produced that end, it can inform his decision to create a particular world. With reference to Spinoza's remarks, it must be admitted that there is no end here external to God (though it can also be added that there is no such end in Leibniz either). But in contrast to Spinoza (and Leibniz), Descartes can allow that the divine will produces its own ends. If we take the discussion in the Fourth Meditation to be reflective of Descartes's considered position, then we have what from a Spinozistic perspective would be an entanglement in a premodern view that allows for genuine divine teleology.

47. AT 7:380.

THE TELEOLOGY OF SENSATION

Earlier I focused on the discussion of the case of heaviness in the Sixth Replies. However, there is another important consideration of this case in Descartes's 1643 correspondence with Princess Elisabeth of Bohemia. In this correspondence Descartes mentions the conception of "weight" (*pesanteur*) as a real quality that "has the power to move the body that possesses it toward the center of the earth."[48] But whereas Descartes held in the Sixth Replies that we draw our conception of heaviness from the idea of mind, in the discussion in his correspondence it is the "primitive notion" of the body-soul union that is more prominent with respect to our conception of weight. Descartes emphasizes to Elisabeth that this notion is distinct from the primitive notions of body and soul, the former of which is just the notion of extension, and the latter just the notion of thought. In contrast, the notion of the union involves the notion of "the soul's power to move the body, and the body's power to act on the soul, causing its sensations and passions."[49] In particular, it is the conception of the soul's power to move the body that provides the model for the conception of the power of the weight to act. Descartes concludes that a consideration of the scholastic understanding of this quality draws our attention to an understanding of the soul's action on body that derives from the primitive notion of the union.

This line of argument from the correspondence with Elisabeth is consistent with the suggestion in the Sixth Replies that any sort of teleological action, including the action of heaviness or weight, must be conceived in terms of the intentional action of a mind. What creates some difficulty for this suggestion, however, is the claim that the notion of the union also involves "the body's power to act on the soul, causing its sensations and passions." For whereas Descartes indicates that the bodily action on the soul is teleological, he clearly does not think that this action is intentional. The indication I have in mind is from the Sixth Meditation, where Descartes observes that "any given movement occurring in the part of the brain that immediately affects the mind produces just one corresponding sensation," and in particular the sensation which, "of all possible sensations, is the most especially and most frequently

48. May 21, 1643 (AT 3:667).
49. AT 3:665.

conducive to the conservation of the healthy man."[50] The discussion in the Sixth Replies might seem to require Descartes to say that the brain acts by means of a little soul that cognizes the end of producing the sensation most conducive to the conservation of the union. But Descartes says no such thing; rather, his position is that the brain is simply constituted "by nature" to produce such a sensation. But why could one not say in the same way that heaviness is constituted by its nature to move a body toward the center of the earth?

Admittedly, for Descartes the human body is special in a way in which the heavy body is not. The difference between a mere body and a body united to a human mind is clear from his discussion in the Sixth Meditation of two senses of "nature." Descartes notes that when it is considered in itself, a clock cannot be said to depart from its nature in functioning poorly, since it follows the laws of nature whether it tells the correct time or not. The nature attributed to the poorly functioning clock is something that has been foisted upon it by the wishes of the clockmaker. According to Descartes, nature in this sense is "nothing other than a denomination depending on my thought" and "extrinsic to the things of which it is said."[51] Likewise, when the human body is considered apart from the human mind, it is a mere machine that can be considered as functioning well or poorly only when attributed a nature that is extrinsic to that body. Thus, when my body suffers from dropsy and leads me to drink even though that action is harmful, there is nothing unnatural in the body itself: it is simply undergoing the changes that the laws of nature require.

It also is the case, however, that the human body is joined to a mind. And it is in virtue of being so joined that it has a nature in terms of which it can truly be said to function well or poorly. In the case of dropsy, then, there is what Descartes calls a "true error of nature," a deviation from the nature of the mind-body composite. The indication here is that there is an intrinsic nature in virtue of which the human body can truly be said to have the end of producing those sensations beneficial to the conservation of the human composite, an end that is frustrated in the case of dropsy. Even though there is no mind that directs the body toward this end, the body can be said to have this end insofar as it is united with the human mind.

50. AT 7:87.
51. AT 7:85.

The distinction between the two kinds of nature is relevant to Descartes's prohibition of the appeal to purposes in physics. For what is foundational for Descartes's physics is the nature of matter as mere continuous quantity or extension. Whereas this nature can ground mechanistic explanation, as in the case of the clock, it does not allow for ends to be anything other than extrinsic denominations imposed on bodies by the mind. This nature is thus distinct from the teleologically-oriented natures invoked in scholastic physics.

However, Descartes allows for one case in which there is something like a scholastic nature that involves a body. As he tells a correspondent, the human mind is the only true substantial form in the created world.[52] Just as scholastic substantial forms provide the basis for the proper functions of the bodies they constitute, so for Descartes the human soul provides the basis for the goal-directed activity of the human composite. The mind-body union thus constitutes the one exception to the principle in Descartes that bodies can be explained entirely in mechanistic terms, with no appeal to ends or purposes.

For Suárez, as we have seen, in the case of natural agents, teleology requires in addition to a particular kind of nature the directive action of God. It might be thought that for Descartes as well, God is required for an explanation of the teleology of sensation. After all, in the Sixth Meditation emphasis is placed on the fact that there is nothing in our sensation "that does not testify to the power and goodness of God."[53] The suggestion here appears to be that the divine mind directs bodily motion to its end of producing the sensation most frequently conducive to the union.

The suggestion may seem to be confirmed by the fact that the discussion of dropsy in the Sixth Meditation to some extent mirrors the discussion of the problem of permission in the Fourth Meditation. Recall that in the latter Meditation Descartes confronts the problem that God's permission of our cognitive deficiencies appears to be incompatible with his supreme perfection. He addresses this problem by conjecturing that God permits such deficiency for the purpose of enhancing the perfection of the universe as a whole. In the Sixth Meditation, he confronts the apparently related problem, deriving from the case of dropsy, that the fact that there are true errors of nature with respect to the mind-body

52. To Regius, January 1642 (AT 3:505).
53. AT 7:88.

composite appears to be incompatible with divine goodness. And his solution to that problem seems to reflect his solution to the problem of cognitive deficiency: God permits true sensory error for the purpose of producing a sensory system that most often serves the good of the composite. In both cases, the solution to the problem of the conflict of our imperfections with divine perfection involves an appeal to the divine end of increasing overall perfection, whether of the universe as a whole or the mind-body composite.

I have argued that the solution in the Fourth Meditation is compatible with the strictures there on the appeal to divine purposes insofar as the purposes invoked are merely conjectural and also not put to work in physics. However, such strictures would seem to preclude the purposes that Descartes purportedly invokes in the Sixth Meditation. For the ends of sensation considered there are not merely conjectural; rather, we are "taught by nature" to accept conclusions regarding those ends as true. If these ends were God's ends, then we would indeed be capable of knowing the purposes of God, contrary to the official position of the Fourth Meditation. To be sure, issues concerning the mind-body composite do not fall within the purview of Descartes's physics insofar as this is restricted to body-body interactions. However, these issues are relevant to sciences such as medicine and morals, which Descartes takes to be branches of the tree of knowledge that sprout from the trunk of physics.[54] Given that the rejection of the appeal to divine purposes in physics is supposed to apply to sciences that emerge from physics, it applies as well to the study of the mind-body composite.

I think it is beyond dispute that the purposes that Descartes invokes in the Fourth Meditation are supposed to be divine purposes. However, there is reason to doubt that the ends of sensation that he considers in the Sixth Meditation are supposed to be God's ends. Here it is helpful to keep in mind the distinction Alison Simmons has introduced between "the ends that move God to create" and "the ends of the things he creates."[55]

54. This description is from the preface to the French translation of the *Principles* (AT 9–2:14). Medicine and morals are two of the three "principal sciences" that emerge from physics; the third is mechanics, understood as the study of machines constructed for our purposes as embodied beings. In this way, the nature of the mind-body composite is relevant to all three of the principal sciences.

55. Alison Simmons, "Latent Teleology in Descartes' Account of Sensation," *Journal of the History of Philosophy* 39 (2001): 66.

Clearly, the ends of sensation are ends of the composite: sensations on the whole are beneficial for the conservation of the mind-body union. But do the ends of sensation provide the reason for God's decision to give me the particular nature I have as a composite? It is not clear that the discussion in the Sixth Meditation requires that they do. The goodness of God is brought into question by the fact that he permits true errors of nature. But that question can be resolved by showing simply that the sensory system that gives rise to these errors has other features that are consistent with divine goodness. The system could have these features even if God chose to create it for some other reason, or even for no reason at all. Here the contrast with the Fourth Meditation seems to be evident: in the latter text, Descartes needs to appeal to God's intentions in permitting cognitive deficiencies. In the Sixth Meditation, it is not God's intentions but rather the nature of what he produces that is at issue.

We can understand the position in the Sixth Meditation in terms of Jean Laporte's contrast between "immanent" or "internal" finality, on the one hand, and "transcendent" or "external" finality, on the other.[56] Nature itself teaches us that our sensory system exhibits a certain kind of internal finality that is reflected in the fact that it for the most part produces sensations beneficial to the mind-body composite. But what remains hidden from us is the external finality the system has in virtue of its relation to God's intentions. In the case of external finality, we would have true final causality involving an intentional direction to an end. External finality clearly is at issue in the Fourth Meditation, where we are concerned with God's plan for the universe as a whole. But as far as the discussion in the Sixth Meditation is concerned, the sensory system could have its particular internal finality even if this finality does not track God's reasons for creating it.

Insofar as he allows that our sensory system has an internal finality that does not require an appeal to external finality, Descartes is in one respect closer to Aristotle's own teleology than is a scholastic such as Suárez. As I have indicated, Aristotle claimed that something can exist for the sake of an end even though there is nothing that intentionally directs it to that end. For Suárez and other later scholastics, this claim is unintelligible since whenever a natural being is directed to an end, there

56. Jean Laporte, "La finalité chez Descartes," *Revue d'histoire de la philosophie* 2 (1928): 388.

must be some mind that directs it to that end, and in particular, the divine mind as first cause. The principle is this: any teleology must be understood to derive from genuine final causality, that is, causality that involves the intentional action of a mind. Though Descartes's remarks concerning heaviness in the Sixth Replies may seem to suggest that he accepted this scholastic principle, his account of sensation in the Sixth Meditation indicates otherwise. For according to that account, nature teaches us that the human body is directed to the end of producing sensations that on the whole are conducive to the conservation of its union with the human mind, even though this end cannot be attributed to God (on pain of violating the prohibition of any non-conjectural appeal to divine purposes in explanations of natural events), and even though no other mind intentionally directs the body to that end. The result here is that Descartes must allow for an Aristotelian sort of teleology that does not require explanation in terms of a mental consideration of ends.

Nonetheless, there is another respect in which Descartes is separated from Aristotle by the Suárezian position in later scholasticism. For though he allowed that there is teleology in the case of sensation, Descartes did not claim—as Aristotle would have—that there must therefore be genuine final causality in this case. The discussion of heaviness in the Sixth Replies reveals that Descartes followed the later scholastic position in holding that such causality must involve intentional action, and so cannot be present when there is no direction by a mind. I began with the observation that Descartes's rejection of scholastic teleology has been seen as an indication of his modernity. But in light of the later Darwinian revolution, his acceptance of a kind of natural teleology that does not need to be understood in terms of final causation might appear as well to mark him out as modern.[57]

57. I presented earlier versions of this essay to the Workshop in Early Modern Philosophy at Harvard University, to the Society of the History of Modern Philosophy at the Ohio State University, to the Toronto Modern Philosophy Research Group at the University of Toronto, to the Symposium on Causality in Early Modern Philosophy at Acadia University, to the Quebec Seminar in Early Modern Philosophy at l'Université de Sherbrooke, at the Ecole Normale Supérière de Lyon, and as part of the lecture series on "The Modern Turn" at the Catholic University of America; thanks to the audiences at these presentations for helpful discussion. Thanks also to Gideon Manning, Jeff McDonough, and Sydney Penner for instructive comments on earlier drafts of the essay.

Steven Nadler

4 Spinoza and Toleration

Baruch Spinoza, the seventeenth-century Dutch philosopher of Portuguese-Jewish background, is the most important and eloquent advocate for toleration in the early modern period, even perhaps in all of the history of philosophy. But toleration is a notoriously complicated topic; it all depends on what is supposed to be tolerated, by whom, for whose sake, and to what extent. Even in the case of Spinoza, who is nothing less than a hero in this regard, it is not entirely clear how far he believes the toleration of ideas should be carried.

In this essay, I approach the issue of toleration in Spinoza's philosophy from two perspectives. First, I shall examine a common conception about Spinoza's views on the relationship between religion and the state and show why it is, in fact, a *mis*conception—that Spinoza is not, in fact, who he is very often taken to be on the question of religious toleration. Second, I would like to argue that Spinoza, despite his well-deserved reputation for being a strong defender of toleration in general, in fact does not go far enough, and makes a potentially troubling concession to the legitimacy of state censorship. When I say that he does not go far enough, I mean not only with respect to our broad contemporary ideals of toleration (since I do not want to hold Spinoza to any anachronistic standards), but also and especially with respect to his own standards—standards that were indeed exceedingly liberal for his time, but that, I shall suggest, he did not stand by with sufficient consistency.

I

The first amendment of the U.S. Constitution says, among other things, that "Congress shall make no law respecting an establishment of religion, or prohibiting the free exercise thereof." This complex (and oft-debated) proposition, comprised of both an "establishment" clause and a "free exercise" clause, is usually taken to be a clear and paradigmatic statement of the doctrine of separation of church and state. The government may not contribute to the promotion of any religious worship, but neither may it prevent people from observing any religious rites or ceremonies they wish.

Two hundred years earlier, freedom of religion was enshrined among the founding tenets of the United Provinces of the Netherlands. The thirteenth article of the Union of Utrecht states that "every individual should remain free in his religion, and no man should be molested or questioned on the subject of divine worship." The leaders of the Dutch Republic in the seventeenth century may not always have been faithful to this principle, and they certainly did not believe in the separation of church and state in the Republic, where the Reformed church was, if not the *established* church, at least a formally privileged one. Still, there was for the period an unusually high freedom of religion in Holland and the other provinces.

As the author of a "theological-political" work, and having prepared the ground in its early chapters with his discussions of prophecy, faith, scripture, and political theory, Spinoza must finally address in the *Tractatus Theologico-Politicus* what he views as the proper relationship between the state and religion. And it is often assumed that he was a strong early proponent of the separation of church and state and that he, along with John Locke, laid the foundation for future religious toleration. One recent commentator, echoing what many others have claimed, even writes that "the spirit of Spinoza lives on in the opening words of the First Amendment of the U.S. Constitution, the phrase referred to as the establishment clause."[1]

In fact, nothing could be further from the truth. The separation of church and state can mean a number of things. Spinoza did believe that when it comes to religious *belief* people should be left alone to believe (or

1. Rebecca Goldstein, *Betraying Spinoza: The Renegade Jew Who Gave Us Modernity* (New York: Schocken, 2006), 11.

not believe) whatever they want. It is impossible to control people's beliefs anyway; there is no way to monitor what goes on in their minds. True piety, "the inward worship of God," is an entirely personal matter. It should, as a matter not only of necessity but of right, be left to the individual alone.

> Since [religion] consists in honesty and sincerity of heart rather than in outward actions, it does not pertain to the sphere of public law and authority. Honesty and sincerity of heart is not imposed on man by legal command or by the state's authority. It is an absolute fact that nobody can be constrained to a state of blessedness by force or law.... As the sovereign right to free opinion belongs to every man even in matters of religion, and it is inconceivable that any man can surrender this right, there also belongs to every man the sovereign right and supreme authority to judge freely with regard to religion, and consequently to explain it and interpret it for himself.[2]

As we shall see, Spinoza also argues that the free expression of one's religious beliefs, verbally or in writing, should be tolerated by the state. No one should be prosecuted for heresy or irreligion.

However, if the separation of church and state means what it is usually taken to mean in the free exercise and establishment clauses of the U.S. Constitution, that government may not regulate or formally endorse any particular set of religious practices or outward forms of worship, then here the founders of the American republic have parted company with Spinoza.

According to Spinoza, in the properly ordered state, the sovereign power is charged with all matters of public well-being. Any actions or practices that enter into the public sphere and therefore may possibly affect the welfare of the people and the state are the responsibility of the government. The state's laws and decrees must be directed toward peace, security, and the stability of the polity, and its legislators must take care to regulate institutions whose activities have some bearing on these. (By contrast, anything that is not related to the public good, such as private belief, is not within the sovereign's purview.)

It follows, then, that the sovereign's power extends not only to the promulgation of civil laws but to laying down religious laws as well, at least insofar as these are related to the exercise of piety in the form of

2. *Tractatus Theologico-Politicus* VII, in *Spinoza Opera*, ed. Carl Gebhardt (Heidelberg: Carl Winters, 1972 [1925]), 3:117 [hereafter "TTP"]; also found in *Theological-Political Treatise*, 2nd ed., trans. Samuel Shirley (Indianapolis, Ind.: Hackett, 2001), 103.

public activities. The inner worship of God and the feelings of love toward one's neighbors, which for Spinoza constitute "true religion," are to be left to the individual. But the outer form in which this worship and love are to be practiced—the rites and ceremonies observed and, especially, the expression of the obedience of God and the love of one's neighbor through justice and charity in action—all fall within the public domain and, thus, within the sovereign's sphere of authority.

The welfare of the people is the highest law, to which all other laws, both human and divine, must be made to conform. But since it is the duty of the sovereign alone to decide what is necessary for the welfare of the people and the security of the state, and to command what it judges to be thus necessary, it follows that it is also the duty of the sovereign alone to decide what form piety towards ones' neighbor should take, that is, in what way every man is required to obey God.[3]

This means that the sovereign is responsible for what Spinoza calls the "interpretation of religion." Individual citizens are, of course, free to read and interpret the Bible for themselves and to discover its exhortations to justice and charity. They are at liberty to do this however they can and with whatever metaphysical, theological, and historical beliefs may help them toward obedience.[4] But in a democracy, Spinoza's preferred form of government, the governing assembly is to decide how God's law is to be translated into practice, since that assembly has sole authority to decide what activities are consistent with the public welfare.

No one can exercise piety toward his neighbor in accordance with God's command unless his piety and religion conform to the public good. But no private citizen can know what is good for the state except from the decrees of the sovereign, to whom alone it belongs to transact public business. Therefore, no one can practice piety aright nor obey God unless he obeys the decrees of the sovereign in all things.[5]

Notice that Spinoza says that the organization and control of religion is the duty of the sovereign *alone*. Among those "private citizens" who

3. TTP XIX, 3:232 (215–16).

4. In fact, Spinoza insists that there are certain beliefs that are necessary and sufficient for obedience to "God's law," the practice of justice and charity—e.g., the belief that "God, that is, a Supreme Being, exists, supremely just and merciful" (TTP XIV, 3:177 [162]). These constitute what he calls the "dogmas of the universal faith." However, it remains the case that no one can or should be compelled to believe them.

5. TTP XIX, 3:232–33 (216).

are not qualified to make judgments about the public good and thus dictate outward forms of worship (including, presumably, ceremonial rites) are clergy. Spinoza has fully removed the supervision of religion from sectarian leaders and put it firmly in the hands of the civil authority. The sovereign is free to appoint ecclesiastics to act as its "ministers" in religious affairs, but these representatives serve at the pleasure of, and are fully subordinate to, the secular authority.

Civil control of religious affairs, while no doubt offensive to early modern ecclesiastics, was in fact a prominent theme in seventeenth-century Dutch republican thought, and Spinoza was not alone in his views on this matter. Hugo Grotius had proposed secular regulation of preaching and worship, while Pieter de la Court, foreshadowing Spinoza, insisted that the state, insofar as it is responsible for peace, security, and prosperity, should have power over all religious activities (while, at the same time, tolerating a diversity of religious *beliefs*).[6] Meanwhile, the Englishman Thomas Hobbes also, unsurprisingly, argued that the sovereign is to have absolute command over religion within its dominion: not just the organization and content of public preaching, but even in determining what is scripture and what is the word of God. For Hobbes, there may be many pastors in a state, but they must all be subordinate to a single chief pastor. And, he says, "who that chief pastor is, according to the law of nature, hath been already shown, namely, that it is the civil sovereign."[7] The alternative to "this consolidation of the right politic and ecclesiastic" is, Hobbes believes, "civil troubles, divisions, and calamities of the nation."

For Spinoza, then, in the ideal state there is to be one and only one form of public devotion, and it is to be determined and supervised by the civil government. Now those who would claim that Spinoza was indeed a defender of the separation of church and state might argue that, in fact, what Spinoza insists upon is something weaker than what I have suggested: not a single form of public worship, but only the idea that all forms of public worship—and there may be many—must nonetheless be consistent with the civil laws and public welfare, as these are determined by the sovereign. Thus, he says that "no one can obey God unless his practice of

6. See Noel Malcolm, *Aspects of Hobbes* (Oxford: Clarendon Press, 2002), 41.

7. *Leviathan* III.29.v, in Hobbes, *Leviathan*, ed. Edwin Curley (Indianapolis, Ind.: Hackett, 1994), 316.

piety … *conforms with* the public good."[8] Rather than being the establisher of religion, then, government would thereby be only its watchdog. But it seems to me that Spinoza does in fact intend the stronger claim, that there is to be only one form of public worship and it is to be determined by the sovereign; after all, immediately before this passage, he says that "it is the duty of the sovereign alone to decide what form piety towards one's neighbor should take."

Spinoza's intention is most definitely *not* to institute a state religion with compulsory church attendance and religious observance. And he especially does not want the sovereign to dictate religious dogma. No one is to be forced to believe or to worship anything, to join any gathering or to engage in any ceremonial practices. Such enforced (and therefore false) piety and mandated uniformity would not be consistent with the primary aim of the state (or of Spinoza's political project): increasing the rationality and freedom of its citizens and ensuring civic peace. Spinoza is not interested in seeing totalitarian control over people's lives. Rather, his position is based on the fear that, without such singular and secular control over religious matters, there is a real danger to the well-being of the commonwealth.

In Spinoza's view, the greatest threat to civil peace—both in theory and, as ancient (biblical) and contemporary (Dutch) events have shown, in fact—are the divisions introduced into society by sectarian religion. The multiplication of sects, even the existence of *one* sect distinct from the official public one, will ultimately bring down even a powerful and prosperous society. Sectarian religions set citizens against each other—Christians against Jews, Protestants against Catholics—and, more importantly, against the state itself. As soon as there are alternative sources of authority besides the sovereign, the loyalty of citizens is divided. There are now states within the state. It becomes a legitimate question as to whether the citizens are devoted to the polity at-large and the general welfare or to their more narrow sectarian causes. And a commonwealth within which there is such a division of loyalties, with piety opposed to patriotism, cannot last long. It will eventually disintegrate under the pressure of civil discord. As Hobbes succinctly puts it, "no man can serve two masters."[9]

8. TTP XIX, 3:232 (216); emphasis added.

9. *De Cive* VI.11, in Hobbes, *Man and Citizen*, ed. Bernard Gert (Indianapolis, Ind.: Hack-

The problem becomes particularly acute when the "religious functionaries" themselves seek influence over not just the hearts and minds of their congregants, but the social and moral lives of citizens. It is, in fact, inevitable that ecclesiastics, once allowed their independent sectarian domains, will encroach upon the civil power and strive for supremacy over it. The result of such a usurpation of political authority is a division of sovereignty in the commonwealth and, in the end, its downfall.

This is precisely the lesson that Spinoza finds in ancient Israelite history. As long as political and religious authority were combined in one man (such as Moses) or one body acting on behalf of God (the true sovereign), the Hebrew commonwealth thrived as a theocracy. There was no confusion regarding to whom obedience was owed. A priestly caste existed, but its members were completely subordinate to the sovereign; they were consultants on religious matters, not leaders. After the monarchy was instituted under Saul, however, things deteriorated as power in the kingdom devolved into political and religious spheres. The kings were forced to recognize "a dominion within their dominion" as the priests exercised greater influence within and, subsequently, beyond the confines of the sanctuary. This was the beginning of the end for the Israelite commonwealth.[10]

With the return from exile in Babylon and the restoration of independence in the Second Temple period, "the priests usurped the right of government, thereby holding absolute power." In a reading of biblical history that has clear resonance for the contemporary Dutch scene—where, in the late 1660s, the orthodox Calvinist elements in Dutch society exerted their considerable influence on behalf of the Orangist bloc and the return of the stadtholder, and thus opposed the domestic and foreign policies of Jan de Witt and the States-party—Spinoza notes that "the priests became inflamed with the desire to combine secular and religious rule," with ruinous consequences for the Israelite polity.[11] The Dutch Republic, heeding the lesson of the Kingdom of Judah, should not allow ecclesiastics to influence civic affairs.[12] When priests and preach-

ett, 1991), 179–80: "For no man can serve two masters; nor is he less, but rather more a master, whom we believe we are to obey for fear of damnation, than he whom we obey for fear of temporal death."

10. TTP XIX, 3:235 (218).

11. TTP XVII, 3:221 (203–4).

12. TTP XVIII, 3:225 (208).

ers acquire "the authority to issue decrees and to transact government business," their individual ambitions will know no bounds and they will each seek "self-glorification both in religious and secular matters." They will fall out among themselves, increasing sectarian divisions in society. Corruption will necessarily follow as the affairs of state will be run according to the self-interest of whichever sect happens to gain the reins of power. Meanwhile, the religion they enforce, now for the perpetuation of their rule, will degenerate into "pernicious superstition."[13]

Thus, for Spinoza, in the model state, there is to be only one established religion, and it will be overseen by the sovereign. His views on this matter, then, are not that different from those of Hobbes, as these appear in both *Leviathan* and *De Cive*. In the *Political Treatise*, Spinoza does allow that there can be independent congregations of worship—even, it seems, sects. However, there will be restrictions: "Large congregations should be forbidden, and so, while those who are attached to another religion [besides the state religion] are to be allowed to build as many churches as they wish, they are to be small, of some fixed dimensions, and some distance apart." The houses of worship of the "national religion," by contrast, "should be large and costly."[14]

II

I now turn to the more general question of toleration. Spinoza is, without question, one of history's greatest proponents of a secular democratic society, and the strongest advocate for freedom and toleration in the early modern period. After all, the ultimate goal of the *Theological-Political Treatise* is enshrined in both the book's subtitle and in the argument of its final chapter: to show that the "freedom of philosophizing" not only *can* be granted "without detriment to public peace, to piety, and to the right of the sovereign, but also that it must be granted if these are to be preserved."[15]

To begin with, there is the question of the toleration of *beliefs*. And what we have already seen Spinoza say about the freedom of religious

13. TTP XVIII, 3:222 (205–6).

14. *Political Treatise* VIII.46 (3:345) [hereafter "TP"]; in Spinoza, *Complete Works*, trans. Samuel Shirley, ed. Michael Morgan (Indianapolis, Ind.: Hackett, 2002), 740.

15. TTP XX, 3:247 (229).

belief holds for all opinions whatsoever: they are to be absolutely free and unimpeded, both by right and in fact. "It is impossible for the mind to be completely under another's control; for no one is able to transfer to another his natural right or faculty to reason freely and to form his own judgment on any matters whatsoever, nor can he be compelled to do so." Indeed, any effort on the sovereign's part to rule over the beliefs and opinions of citizens can only backfire, as it will ultimately serve to undermine the sovereign's own authority. In a passage that strikes the reader as both obviously right and extraordinarily bold for its time, Spinoza writes that

> a government that attempts to control men's minds is regarded as tyrannical, and a sovereign is thought to wrong his subjects and infringe their right when he seeks to prescribe for every man what he should accept as true and reject as false, and what are the beliefs that will inspire him with devotion to God. All these are matters belonging to individual right, which no man can surrender even if he should so wish.

A sovereign is certainly free to try and limit what people think, but the result of such a foolhardy policy would be only to create resentment and opposition to its rule. "It is true that sovereigns can by their right treat as enemies all who do not absolutely agree with them on all matters, but the point at issue is not what is their right, but what is to their interest."[16] The freedom of opinion is, for Spinoza, an "inalienable right."

Still, the toleration of belief is easy, because necessary. Even Hobbes saw that citizens cannot be forced to believe anything.[17] The more difficult case, the true test of a philosopher's commitment to toleration, concerns the liberty of citizens to *express* those beliefs, either in speech or in writing. And here Spinoza goes further than anyone else in the seventeenth century.[18] "Utter failure will attend any attempt in a common-

16. TTP XX, 3:240 (223).

17. Edwin Curley, "Bayle vs. Spinoza on Toleration," *Mededelingen vanwege het Spinozahuis* 95 (Voorschoten: Uitgeverij Spinozahuis, 2009), suggests that, in fact, beliefs are not so immune to external coercion, and that Spinoza himself recognized this.

18. Hobbes explicitly denies the right to freedom of speech, and insists that the sovereign should exercise careful control over what ideas are expressed in the commonwealth. "It is annexed to the sovereignty to be judge of what opinions and doctrines are averse, and what conducing, to peace; and consequently, on what occasions, how far, and what men are to be trusted withal, in speaking to multitudes of people, and who shall examine the doctrines of all books before they be published" (*Leviathan* II.xvii.9 [113]).

wealth to force men to speak only as prescribed by the sovereign despite their different and opposing opinions .... The most tyrannical government will be one where the individual is denied the freedom to express and to communicate to others what he thinks, and a moderate government is one where this freedom is granted to every man."[19]

Spinoza's argument for freedom of expression is based both on the right (or power) of citizens to speak as they desire, as well as on the fact that (as in the case of belief) it would be self-defeating for a sovereign to try to restrain that freedom. No matter what laws are enacted against speech and other means of expression, citizens will continue to say what they believe (because they can), only now they will do so in secret. "It is far beyond the bounds of possibility that all men can be made to speak to order. On the contrary, the greater the effort to deprive them of freedom of speech, the more obstinately do they resist."[20] The result of the suppression of freedom is, once again, resentment and a weakening of the bonds that unite subjects to sovereign. In Spinoza's view, intolerant laws lead ultimately to anger, revenge, and sedition. The attempt to enforce them is a "great danger to the state."

Spinoza also argues for freedom of expression on utilitarian grounds. It is necessary for progress in the discovery of truth and the spread of creativity. Without an open marketplace of ideas, science, philosophy, and other disciplines are stifled in their development, to the technological, economic, and even aesthetic detriment of society. In this respect, Spinoza's defense of liberty foreshadows the one that John Stuart Mill would offer two centuries later in his *On Liberty*. As Spinoza puts it, "this freedom [of expressing one's ideas] is of the first importance in fostering the sciences and the arts, for it is only those whose judgment is free and unbiased who can attain success in these fields."[21]

For Spinoza, then, there is to be no criminalization of ideas in the well-ordered state. *Libertas philosophandi*, the freedom of philosophizing, must be upheld for the sake of a healthy, secure, and peaceful commonwealth and for material and intellectual progress. "What greater misfortune can be imagined for a state than that honorable men should be exiled as miscreants because their opinions are at variance with au-

19. TTP XX, 3:240 (223).
20. TTP XX, 3:243 (226).
21. TTP XX, 3:243 (226).

thority and they cannot disguise the fact? What can be more calamitous than that men should be regarded as enemies and put to death, not for any crime or misdeed, but for being of independent mind?"[22] One cannot but think that Spinoza had his unfortunate friend Adriaan Koerbagh—who had recently died in prison, incarcerated for his philosophical writings—in mind when he wrote these words.

Spinoza's views on liberty go beyond what was envisioned by another philosopher renowned for his defense of toleration: John Locke. Locke was primarily interested in the toleration within a society of a variety of religious ideas, so that individuals may enjoy the uninhibited personal communion with God in which religion consists. In his "Letter on Toleration," written in 1685, Locke argued that no religious group, nor even the state, has the right to persecute those who belong to other sects. Membership in a community of believers is voluntary, and thus no church may use force (or engage the power of the state) to further its narrow sectarian aims. Different forms of worship and theological dissent are to be allowed, even encouraged, in the commonwealth.

Like Spinoza, Locke also makes his case for toleration with utilitarian considerations. Such freedom, insofar as it fosters the search after truth, brings great benefits for society, and not just intellectual ones. Locke was clearly impressed by the economic fruits of toleration that he saw in the Dutch Republic, where he was residing when he wrote the Letter. However, Locke makes one significant exception to the general policy of openness for religious and secular ideas: there is to be no toleration of atheism and other forms of irreligion. Since atheists do not believe in God, they have no foundation for morality, and thus they cannot be trusted not to act in ways that are harmful to their fellow citizens. "Those are not at all to be tolerated who deny the being of God ... promises, covenants, and oaths, which are bonds of human society, can have no hold upon an atheist."[23] Locke's refusal to grant the same freedom to atheists that he provides for believers is therefore made on political and ethical rather than religious grounds. And apparently it is not only freedom of expression that is being denied to them, but freedom of belief, since their

22. TTP XX, 3:245 (227).

23. From Locke's "A Third Letter for Toleration," quoted in Jonathan Israel, *Radical Enlightenment: Philosophy and the Making of Modernity 1650–1750* (Oxford: Oxford University Press, 2001), 266; for a comparative discussion of Locke and Spinoza on toleration, see 265–70.

mere presence in the state is supposed to be a threat to its welfare. I believe this represents an inconsistency in Locke's thought and a striking failure of toleration, one that is absent from Spinoza's account.

However—and this brings me to my main point—Spinoza does not support *absolute* freedom of speech. He explicitly states that the expression of "seditious" ideas is *not* to be tolerated by the sovereign. There is to be no protection for speech that advocates the overthrow of the government, disobedience to its laws or harm to fellow citizens. The people are free to argue for the repeal of laws that they find unreasonable and oppressive, but they must do so peacefully and through rational argument. If their argument fails to persuade the sovereign to change the law, then that must be the end of the matter. What they may not do is "stir up popular hatred against [the sovereign or his representatives]."[24]

Absolutists about the freedom of speech will be troubled by these caveats on Spinoza's part, and rightly so. After all, who is to decide what kind of speech count as seditious? May not the sovereign declare to be seditious simply those views with which it disagrees or that it finds contrary to its policies? Spinoza, presumably to allay such concerns, does offer a definition of "seditious political beliefs" as those that "*immediately* have the effect of annulling the covenant whereby everyone has surrendered his right to act just as he thinks fit."[25] The salient feature of such opinions is "the action that is implicit therein"—that is, they are more or less verbal incitements to act against the sovereign and thus they are directly contrary to the tacit social contract of citizenship. "Other beliefs," he says, "in which there is no implication of actions such as the breaking of the covenant, the exaction of revenge, the indulgence of anger and so forth, are not seditious."

But this still leaves a considerable gap for unreasonable censorship of the expression of ideas. Engaging in speech that "immediately" contributes toward weakening the political compact could be done directly, by incendiary words intended to stir up civil disobedience. But it could also be done in a more subtle and indirect way, by spreading subversive beliefs about the sovereign, such as a rumor that its policies are treasonous, or even that its rule is illegitimate—in the United States, this might be exemplified by the so-called birther movement, a right-wing fringe belief

24. TTP XX, 3:241 (224).
25. TTP XX, 3:242 (225); emphasis added.

that President Obama was not born in the United States and thus does not satisfy one of the necessary conditions for the presidency. Among the things that Spinoza says are not to be allowed is accusing a magistrate of injustice. If there is an "implication of action" or an "immediate" effect of "annulling the covenant" in such a case, it is at best obscure.

It is not clear, then, that Spinoza's position really amounts to the view, as Jonathan Israel (for example) reads it, that the expression of opinions "only becomes subversive and hence liable for punishment ... if it directly obstructs implementation of laws and decrees."[26] It seems a rather hazy boundary here between legitimate dissent and protest (which, for Spinoza, is protected) and being "an agitator and a rebel" (which is not). The U.S. Supreme Court, in a troubling 6–3 decision, recently upheld a federal law which makes it a crime to provide help to a foreign group designated as a "terrorist organization," even if the help one provides involves only speech intended to encourage that organization to adopt nonviolent means for resolving conflicts.[27] Would such a ban be permissible under Spinoza's principles?

Spinoza may feel that he has provided an unambiguous criterion and identified a small and well-circumscribed domain for what is to count as seditious speech, and thereby set a firewall against the arbitrary abuse of state power over the expression of ideas. But still, there appears to remain a loophole for a clever sovereign to engage in and justify a potentially extensive suppression of ideas, including prior restraint of the press, the censorship of books and even the prohibition of meetings.[28]

Perhaps Spinoza should have more consistently followed the logic of his own reasoning by drawing the line not within the realm of belief (including its expression) but at the border of belief (and its expression), on the one hand, and true action, on the other hand, as he sometimes seems to do. "It was only the right to act as he thought fit that each man

26. Jonathan Israel, *Enlightenment Contested: Philosophy, Modernity and the Emancipation of Man 1670–1752* (Oxford: Oxford University Press, 2006), 158. See also Etienne Balibar, *Spinoza and Politics* (London: Verso, 1998), 27.

27. Holder v. Humanitarian Law Project, No. 08–1498. See "Justices Uphold a Ban on Aiding Terror Groups," *New York Times*, June 22, 2010. The court's majority argued that such speech would help the group achieve its ends, as well as free up other resources at its disposal.

28. In this respect, it may be that while Spinoza's views on toleration seem much more liberal than those of Hobbes, when the sovereign's ability to censor ideas in the name of public peace and political stability are taken into account, the two thinkers in fact are not that far apart; see note 17 above.

surrendered, and not his right to reason and judge. So while to act against the sovereign's decree is definitely an infringement of his [the sovereign's] right, this is not the case with thinking, judging, and consequently with speaking, too."[29] Although, again, Spinoza adds the warning: "provided one does no more than express or communicate one's opinion, defending it through rational conviction alone, not through deceit, anger, hatred, or the will to effect such changes in the state as he himself decides."

Now it might be argued that Spinoza does, in fact, draw the line between what the sovereign can and cannot legitimately monitor right at the border between ideas and action, on the grounds that the *expression* of ideas properly falls under the latter category (since such expression—whether in speech or in a publication—is a public action). It would then be perfectly consistent with his principles of toleration for Spinoza to allow the sovereign to censor speech.[30] However, Spinoza does not actually argue in this way. He does not say that the expression of ideas is an action and therefore is in the domain of the sovereign's control. Rather, he argues that those verbal expressions that have an "action that is implicit therein"—that is, speech that is a call or incitement to action—are subject to government control. Thus he maintains the distinction between ideas (and their expression), on the one hand, and action, on the other, and allows censorship to extend into the former. It must be confessed, however, that the boundary between thought and action does seem a little blurred with the category of the expression of ideas that is not itself action but "implies" action.[31]

Spinoza is certainly conscious of, and willing to allow for, some potentially unpleasant consequences entailed by the broad respect for civil liberties. There will be public disputes, even factionalism, as citizens express their opposing views on political, social, moral, and religious questions. This is, however, what comes with a healthy democratic and tolerant society. As he concedes, "what cannot be prohibited must necessarily be allowed, even if harm often ensues."[32] The proper state will be very much like Amsterdam itself, which, while not truly democratic, Spinoza

29. TTP XX, 3:241 (224).

30. See Daniel Garber, "Should Spinoza Have Published His Philosophy?," in *Interpreting Spinoza*, ed. Charles Huenemann (New York: Cambridge University Press, 2008), 170.

31. As Israel notes in *Enlightenment Contested*, whether there really can be "so clear and evident a distinction between action, on one side, and thought and expression, on the other, as this theory presupposes, may well appear unlikely" (158).

32. TTP XX, 3:243 (225).

greatly admires for the freedom it allows its denizens and the flourishing such toleration has brought the city.

Take the city of Amsterdam, which enjoys the fruits of this freedom, to its own considerable prosperity and the admiration of the world. In this flourishing state, a city of the highest renown, men of every race and sect live in complete harmony; and before entrusting their property to some person they will want to know no more than this, whether he is rich or poor and whether he has been honest or dishonest in his dealings. As for religion or sect, that is of no account, because such considerations are regarded as irrelevant in a court of law; and no sect whatsoever is so hated that its adherents—provided that they injure no one, render to each what is his own, and live upright lives—are denied the protection of the civil authorities.[33]

It is surprising to see Spinoza writing this. As we have seen, one of his close friends has just died in prison, condemned by the city of Amsterdam—in a brutal act of intolerance at the instigation of the Calvinist consistory—for philosophical and religious ideas. So perhaps there is a good deal of bitter irony in Spinoza's words here. On the other hand, Amsterdam was the most liberal and tolerant city in a republic renowned in its own time for religious and political toleration, and Spinoza, while aware of the city's shortcomings, also knew well and appreciated its virtues.

One can hope that perhaps Spinoza himself was uncomfortable with the restriction he had placed on freedom of speech, and that deep down he really was an absolutist on this matter. In the penultimate paragraph of the *Theological-Political Treatise*, he does draw a clear line between ideas and their expression, on the one hand, and actions, on the other hand, and insists—this time without any qualification—that the sovereign's authority should (if only out of prudence) be restricted to the latter: "The state can pursue no safer course that to regard piety and religion as consisting solely in the exercise of charity and just dealing, and that the right of the sovereign, both in religious and secular spheres, should be restricted to men's actions, with everyone being allowed to think what he will and to say what he thinks."[34] This sentence, a wonderful statement of the principle of toleration, is perhaps the real lesson of the *Treatise*, and should be that for which Spinoza is remembered.

33. TTP XX, 3:245–46 (228).
34. TTP XX, 3:247 (229).

Michael Pakaluk

5 From Natural Law to Natural Rights in John Locke

The common liberal democratic understanding of political society and its citizens differs in basic ways from the classical accounts one sees for instance in Aristotle, Cicero, and St. Thomas. What are some of the main differences? How shall we properly understand the modern turn in political philosophy?

One difference is that in classical theory, the first object of study is society, and then the nature of government is thought to follow from the nature of society; in modern theory, the nature and limits of government and "sovereignty" are considered first, and then society is left to shift for itself, as whatever results from sovereignty so conceived. Second, in classical theory, political society and government arise organically and naturally; in modern theory, society and government are conceived of as artificial, the result of deliberate human intervention, compact, and choice. Third, in classical theory, the common good of political society is prominent; in modern theory, the good or rather the rights of individuals are prominent. Fourth, in classical theory the government and citizens share the same goal, which is happiness, understood in the same way by both, but in modern theory the government has a different and limited goal, involving typically the negative aim of defense against attacks (either from without or from within, to keep one citizen from attacking another). Fifth and finally, in classical theory the law is regarded as pertaining in principle to any matter of good or bad, right or wrong, but in modern theory the law is held to be competent to deal only with matters in which citizens in some uncontroversial way harm one another.

The modern turn has this basic contour, then, and my concern here is with John Locke's contribution to it. Commentators often take that contribution to be contained in Locke's celebrated doctrine of natural rights. It is thought that Locke, with his introduction of natural rights, produced a political theory that is either incoherent on classical grounds or incompatible with classical political thought. In that spirit MacIntyre in *After Virtue*, holding forth for the classical view, famously asserted that "there are no such rights, and belief in them is one with belief in witches and unicorns."[1] Leo Strauss for different reasons reached a similar view: "The premodern natural law doctrines taught the duties of man; if they paid any attention at all to rights, they conceived of them as essentially derivative from his duties."[2]

Locke himself seems to make a transition from natural law to natural rights, since as a young man he delivered a series of lectures in Oxford defending the natural law strenuously, especially against Hobbes, and then two decades later he wrote what is generally regarded as the primary foundational text in the modern philosophy of natural rights. So we may wonder, what is involved in Locke's apparent change from emphasizing natural law to emphasizing natural rights?

We shall see that Locke's contribution to the modern turn, however, has nothing to do with his emphasis on natural rights *per se*, as indeed his main notion of natural right depends upon natural law and is incoherent without it. Rather his contribution consists in his assigning originally to individuals the kind of power and authority that in classical accounts could meaningfully be attributed only to those responsible for the common good of political society. This power and authority Locke also calls a "right," and it is only a right in that sense which is incompatible with classical accounts and constitutes Locke's distinctive contribution to the modern turn.

1. Alasdair MacIntyre, *After Virtue: A Study in Moral Theory*, 2nd ed. (South Bend, Ind.: University of Notre Dame Press, 1984), 69.

2. Leo Strauss, *Natural Rights and History* (Chicago: University of Chicago Press, 1953), 182.

TWO NOTIONS OF NATURAL RIGHT COMPATIBLE WITH NATURAL LAW

Let us begin by distinguishing two senses of the word "right" when we speak of someone's having or possessing a "right." In both senses rights are compatible with laws; indeed, in the first sense the notion of right depends upon the notion of law.

First, we may understand by "a right" simply a power, that is, an authority to act, as conferred by the relevant law. Laws either forbid, command, or permit, and sometimes permission takes the form of authorization, where someone is permitted to act according to his discretion to achieve some purpose intended by the law. This authorization may be referred to as a "power" to act which that person holds "by right of" that law. We may therefore say that he has the "right" to act in a certain matter according to his discretion. In that case our use of the word "right" is simply an abbreviation for "power to act in that way *by right of* that law." The appeal to a "right" like that is obviously not at odds with an appeal to law, since a right is a power assigned by a law; to appeal to a right is to assert a title which is underwritten by a law.

This meaning of the word "right" is very old and goes back to the Roman law of inheritance and before that. Actually, it is a commonsense notion that persons are given authority to act by law, which may be called a "power," a "power by right," or simply a "right." For example, St. Paul writing in 55 A.D. claims a power and then justifies his title to that power by reference to a law: "Have we not power to eat and drink? [...] Have we not power to carry about a woman, a sister, as well as the rest of the apostles? [...] Speak I these things according to man? Or doth not the law also say these things? For it is written in the law of Moses: Thou shalt not muzzle the mouth of the ox that treadeth out the corn" (1 Cor 9:4–9). He might just as well have said, "Have we not a right to eat and drink?"

We sometimes speak of rights in this sense as being different in kind, if the laws by which they are underwritten differ in kind. For instance, we might say that someone empowered to act in a certain way by federal law had a "federal right" to act as he did, and someone empowered to act by international law had an "international right." Similarly, if we believed that there was a natural law and that it empowered persons to act in certain ways, then we could say that those persons had a "natural right" to act as they did. On this way of speaking, again, far from "natural right" being some kind of innovation incompatible with natural law, a natural right would actually be completely a creature of natural law, since someone's claim to possess an authority "by right of" the natural law would make no sense if there were no natural law.

Note that when an authorization is conferred by a law, it is conferred to certain persons for certain kinds of actions, and for certain ends, as directed to or at least not incompatible with a regard for the common good. Thus police officers (certain persons) are authorized to stop vehicles and issue tickets for violations of the traffic code (certain kinds of actions), but only in order to keep the public peace (certain ends)—since an officer would be acting improperly if it were found that he gave tickets only to get revenge on his personal enemies. Thus an authorization is a kind of trust to use the authority for the purposes of the law, with a view toward the common good.

The second sense of "right" I wish to consider has reference to what is due a thing. Suppose that certain kinds of treatment are due or not due to certain kinds of things. Then to treat them in the way that is due and to refrain from treating them in manners not due would be "right treatment" of them. We might accordingly say that they have a "right" to the first kind of treatment and a "right" not to be treated in the second way. For instance, someone preoccupied with business fails to greet an old friend who has just arrived. We might say in that case, criticizing the thoughtlessness, that the friend had "a right" to be shown special regard, and by that we would mean no more than that certain things were due to him in virtue of his being an old friend.

Rights in this sense of right treatment are as transient and shifting as what makes for right treatment. Nonetheless, when people occupy offices or roles with definite purposes, and thus there is stability in their relationships, it is often possible to make statements about what is *always* due certain classes of persons or *never* due. For example, sufficient understanding of proposed medical treatment is due to someone who occupies the role of patient from someone who occupies the professional role of physician, and so we may speak in that case of "patient's rights." In this more restricted use, a "right" refers to certain sorts of actions toward certain sorts of persons which are always due or never due to them.

Just as we saw that we could distinguish different kinds of right in the first sense with reference to the different kinds of law that might authorize someone, so we can distinguish different kinds of right in this second sense with reference to the different grounds on which certain kinds of treatment may be always or never due. If the ground is an acquired or conventional role, then that is the sort of right that it is, as for example patients' rights, in our example. We are only sometimes sick and sometimes seeking professional medical assistance—only then do we have patients' rights. Suppose however that it were thought that human beings by nature, that is, simply as being human beings, occupied some kind of role or status relative to one another—for example, all being equal as made in the image of God, or all being brothers and sisters as having a common heavenly Father—and that as a consequence of that status certain kinds of treatment were always due or never due, as regards one holder of this role by nature toward another. Those who thought in such a way could speak of "natural rights" and mean simply these kinds of treatment that were always or never due.

Since laws either command, forbid, or permit, it is clear that corresponding to any right in this second sense there would be a "law," either articulated or not, which commands that treatment is always due and forbids that treatment is never due. The "law" would simply be the practical precept that would be recognized by anyone with sufficient knowledge acting in those circumstances. It makes little difference whether we say that patients have a right to informed consent or that physicians by the law or code of their profession are obliged to insure the informed consent of their patients. Similarly, if there are natural rights in this second sense of "right," then it makes little difference whether we say, for example, that those made in the image of God have a right to be treated in certain ways by others like that, or that there is a "natural law" obliging everyone like that to treat everyone else in that way. The first way of speaking calls attention to the basis and the other to the upshot.

The first sense of right was obviously related to the common good, since law is for the common good, and the first sense of right is a creature of law. But rights in the second sense are also related to the common good, albeit less obviously. A common good enters in implicitly with the necessary talk of roles or offices that makes this notion of right intelligible (that is, as pertaining to treatment always or never due). We can see this by asking whether rights in this second sense are directed toward anything, such that they become interpreted or even circumscribed with respect to other considerations—and it is plain that they are. For example, a patient suffering a heart attack in the emergency room cannot give informed consent, so that that "right" gets interpreted relative to the goal of that patient's health, and consent to appropriate medical intervention is presumed. It turns out that treatment "always" due to patients is due relative to certain purposes shared by physicians as physicians and by patients.

Another important point is that although equality seems important for rights in this second sense, equality is a derivative notion, dependent upon what first constitutes something in a relevant class. For example, without doubt, all patients equally have a right to informed consent; but that they each have a right that is "equal" follows trivially from the fact that they are in the class of patients. Membership in the class is primary, and their "equality" as being alike members of that class is a trivial consequence. (This is exactly the same "equality" that Aristotle remarks on when he says in the *Categories* that nothing of a certain kind is more or less that kind of thing than anything else of that kind; all horses are equally horses, all human beings equally human beings.)

Because natural rights in both of these senses imply natural law and are subordinated to considerations of the common good, they are entirely consistent with the classical tradition in political philosophy. One could not assert that they were fictions without implying that the natural law and the dignity of the human person are also fictions.

NATURAL RIGHTS IN LOCKE'S *SECOND TREATISE*

Natural rights in the first sense play an important role in Locke's *Second Treatise*, but they are seen by Locke as completely consistent with and a consequence of his continuing commitment to natural law. Natural rights in the second sense actually play little role, although they are thought to play a great role by those who confuse Locke's political philosophy with that of the Declaration of Independence and the founding of America. Locke's real innovation consists in his introducing a third sense of right, which he presents as though it were a right in the first sense, but which is entirely different and becomes a fundamental notion for modern political liberalism.

Let us review briefly the structure of Locke's argument in the two *Treatises*. Locke wishes to refute Robert Filmer's *Patriarcha*. Filmer claims that kings have the power of absolute rule. But what is their claim to this power? By what right do they rule? They have this power, Filmer thinks, by right of divine law, which is precisely what is meant by the phrase "divine right of kings." Hence, to refute Filmer, Locke thinks he must show that kings have no such power by right of divine law, but to seal the case he also argues that kings have no such power by right of natural law. As there are two types of law, divine and natural, so there are two treatises: the *First Treatise* argues that kings have no title to such power through divine law, and the *Second Treatise* argues that kings have no title to such power through natural law.

Locke's presuppositions about natural law in the *Second Treatise* are exactly those which he defends in his earlier *Essays on the Law of Nature*. In both works, Locke follows Calvin in holding that all power descends from God and is on loan from God. Calvin wrote in his *Institutes*: "How can the idea of God enter your mind without instantly giving rise to the thought, that since you are his workmanship, you are bound, by the very right of creation [*creationis iure*], to submit to his authority?"[3] Locke in his *Essays on the Law of Nature* similarly states that the obligation of law can be imposed only by someone who has "right and power" over us (*qui in nos jus et potestatem habet*), that is, by someone who possesses power "by that right which a creator has over his own creation [*a jure illo quod creator habet in creaturam suam*]."[4] "God has created us out of nothing," Locke states, "and, if He pleases, will reduce us again to nothing; we are, therefore, subject to Him by the highest right and highest necessity [*summo iure et summa necessitate*]."[5] Since only God has power, every other alleged authority can have power rightly only by donation. "The reason why we ought to be subject to magistrates is, because they are constituted by God's ordination," Calvin wrote in his commentary on Romans 13:1. "God is the highest power, yea the power of powers, from him is derived all power," wrote John Ponet, bishop of Rochester, in his *Short Treatise*

3. Jean Calvin, *Institutes of the Christian Religion*, trans. Henry Beveridge (Grand Rapids, Mich.: Eerdmans, 1959), 41.

4. John Locke, *Essays on the Law of Nature*, ed. W. von Leyden (Oxford: Clarendon Press, 1954), 157.

5. Ibid., 48.

on Political Power, an early prototype of Locke's *Second Treatise.*[6] Locke similarly states in his *Essays* that "every obligation is traceable ultimately back to God" (*in Deum enim ultimo resolvitur omnis obligatio*).[7]

Locke typically refers to God's sharing or donation of power with the verb *mutuor,* meaning "to borrow, to take out a loan": a subordinate power does not so much participate in God's authority as have that authority on loan. God manifests his will to loan power through either divine law or natural law. Hence, any claim to power must be traced back to God, either through the intermediary authority of the law of nature, or directly through some revelation of God's will: "Of itself and by its intrinsic force [*per se et vi sua*] and only so is the divine will binding," Locke teaches, "and either it can be known by the light of nature, in which case it is that law of nature which we are discussing; or it is revealed by God-inspired men or in some other manner, in which case it is the positive divine law."[8] Thus Locke's challenge to Filmer twenty years later in the *First Treatise*:

> Till our author hath resolved all the doubts that may arise about the next heir, and shewed that they are plainly determined by the law of nature, or the revealed law of God, all his suppositions of a monarchical, absolute, supreme, paternal power in Adam, and the descent of that power to his heir [...] would not be of the least use to establish the authority, or make out the title, of any one prince now on earth.[9]

Because God's will to donate power can be discerned through only the divine law or the natural law, and divine law is revealed in scripture while the natural law is apparent to reason, Locke's *First Treatise* is concerned mainly with scriptural interpretation and exegesis, whereas the *Second Treatise* looks at natural law and what is purportedly manifest to reason.

The arguments of the *First Treatise* are along the following lines: a grant of authority over the earth and beasts, such as was given to Adam, was not a grant of political power, and not a grant to rule over other

6. John Ponet, *A shorte treatise of politike pouuer [...]* (Strasbourg: Printed by the heirs of W. Köpfel, 1556), transcription by Text Creation Partnership, 2004-03 (EEBO-TCP Phase 1), available at http://name.umdl.umich.edu/A09916.0001.001.

7. Locke, *Essays,* 182.

8. Ibid., 187.

9. Chap. 11, §124.

human beings generally; both father and mother have authority by scripture ("honor your mother and your father"), and so patriarchal rule is essentially limited and cannot be the basis of absolute power; and, even on the assumption that God granted political power to Adam and that it was passed down by heredity, we would have no way of knowing now who are the rightful heirs of Adam. The argument of the *Second Treatise* is the celebrated argument that the government gets no power except what is delegated to it by the members of the body politic, who have an original grant of power in the state of nature.

I will look at the celebrated argument in a little more detail later. Here I wish only to observe that there is no transition from natural law to natural rights seen in the *Second Treatise*, because the very presupposition of the *Second Treatise* is that a claim of political power by right has to be substantiated by tracing that claimed power back to the natural law, which tracing back serves to establish someone's title to that power.

Admittedly, a claim of natural right in this sense can tilt toward a procedural and legalistic outlook, because the claim to hold a power by right is established by looking to the law rather than to the merits of the person claiming the right. Compare the law of inheritance, which is a central notion examined in Locke's *First Treatise*, since Locke is there concerned to refute Filmer's claim that by divine law a power originally granted to Adam was somehow conveyed to certain of his heirs through the relationship of paternity. It is notorious that title as established by the law of inheritance can be strikingly at odds with what might seem right if the assignment of property were awarded on the merits. But the property goes to the person who has a legal title, not the person who most deserves it or can make the best use of it. We shall see that the ease of giving a legalistic interpretation of a right in this first sense contributes to Locke's introducing "rights" of an entirely new sort.

I claimed that the second sense of natural right, as referring to rights always or never due to others in virtue of their nature, plays no significant role in Locke's political philosophy. It is understandable that one might want to claim that it does, given what Locke says about equality and our being the "workmanship" of God in chapter 2 of the *Second Treatise*, as for instance in the remark there that

> men being all the workmanship of one omnipotent, and infinitely wise maker; all the servants of one sovereign master, sent into the world by his order, and

about his business; they are his property, whose workmanship they are, made to last during his, not one another's pleasure: and being furnished with like faculties, sharing all in one community of nature, there cannot be supposed any such subordination among us, that may authorize us to destroy one another, as if we were made for one another's uses, as the inferior ranks of creatures are for our's.[10]

However, clearly the claim that human beings are the workmanship of God does nothing to establish any special treatment for them, because mosquitoes are the workmanship of God, too, and we smash them when they annoy us. If I may destroy a brute creature for my purposes, although it is the workmanship of God, then why not a man? There is nothing said by Locke in the *Second Treatise*—whether about human dignity, human rationality, or human beings as made in the image of God—that could serve to explain the different treatment we should accord human beings rather than brute animals. Nor is anything added by saying that a man is "about God's business," if nothing at all is said about what that business can be. But those who are familiar with how Locke deals with the notions of "human being" and person in his *Essay* would hardly find any of this surprising.

Rather, all the work is done by the merely formal notion of equality: Locke's view, clearly, is that it is because each man is equal to every other that none can treat another as subordinate to his own interests. But what makes us equal, and how are we so? Locke never explains; he only asserts that "creatures of the same species and rank, promiscuously born to all the same advantages of nature, and the use of the same faculties, should also be equal one amongst another without subordination or subjection."[11] But we do not have the same advantages and faculties, and what if by nature the human species was meant to show rank and hierarchy such as are found in other social animals, for instance, in insects or wolf packs? It is unclear why the subordination of children to parents or the natural authority of old over young does not prove that we are not all of the same rank. As mentioned, equality is a derivative notion and must be based on something that constitutes the equality, just as two things cannot be similar unless they first have the same quality. But Locke offers no account of our equality along those lines.

10. Chap. 2, §6.
11. Chap. 2, §4.

It is difficult not to view Locke's remarks about workmanship as *ad hoc*, and the location of the remarks in the text is consistent with their having been spliced in later. Locke's argument requires that an individual not have the power to sell himself into slavery—because if he can, then he might in principle alienate his freedom to an absolute ruler, which Locke needs to deny—but to sell oneself into slavery is as good as killing oneself, Locke holds, since a slave continues to live only at the whim of his master; hence Locke needs to rule out suicide, and according to a venerable tradition beginning with Plato's *Phaedo,* the consideration that we are the workmanship of God or the gods has been taken to rule out suicide.

NATURAL RIGHT AS POLITICAL POWER

As I said, there is a third sense of natural right in Locke, natural right as a power vested in an individual, equivalent to the power that the government possesses in political society. This sense is distinct from the first two senses of right we have considered; it constitutes Locke's distinctive contribution to the modern turn in political philosophy.

Locke defines political power, when it is possessed by the magistrate, as "a RIGHT of making laws with penalties of death, and consequently all less penalties, for the regulating and preserving of property, and of employing the force of the community, in the execution of such laws, [...] all this only for the public good."[12] Since Locke believes all power is derived from God's power, and by nature all human beings are equal, how then does the magistrate come to such power? He is delegated that power by individuals who contract into political society, says Locke. But these individuals cannot give power that they do not have themselves. Thus Locke's argument requires that the same power that the magistrate possesses in political society is the power that individuals possess in the state of nature.

According to Locke's argument, individuals begin in the state of nature (*individuals*, for all we know, and if their families are somehow counted as well, then presumably as falling within the "property" of individuals, as counted, that is, among their life, liberty, and goods). These

12. Chap. 1, §3.

individuals are under the law of nature, which, says Locke, is evident to all of them by reason. Materially, their life is good within the state of nature. Because of the fecund and fructifying character of cultivated nature, the inhabitants of the state of nature are easily able to provide for themselves. Note that the market, bartering, and commercial activity play no essential role in moving individuals into political society, according to Locke. Plato and Aristotle have political society forming originally around the market; Locke seems to imagine happy subsistence farmers. Note too that Locke is not concerned with leisure or the use of leisure. In the classical conception, one of the chief goods that comes with political society is some amount of relief from the toil and necessity of taking care of daily needs, in order to devote time to worship and broadly contemplative activity. Locke seems entirely unconcerned with this. Thus neither the market, nor cult, nor the development of knowledge is at the basis of political society, for Locke.

What is, then? Some of these individuals in the state of nature, who by reason discern the law of nature and, presumably, too, discern that the law of nature is the highest authority for them, nonetheless transgress against the law of nature, which tells us to preserve ourselves and the human race, and therefore not to harm ourselves or others. Some individuals steal from others, injure others without cause, and murder. Why do they do so? Locke says that when someone breaks the law of nature even in a slight matter, he shows that he is unwilling to live according to reason and makes himself into a beast. But why do reasonable beings turn themselves into beasts? Locke never explains. Nor does he say whether this falling away from reason is shown only by some individuals, namely, those who actually rob, maim, and murder, or by all of us, but that it is simply not manifested for us all—which makes a big difference. It makes all the difference in the world whether most basically we are all murderers in principle, or only some of us are. Since Locke is a great proponent of equality—we are all of the same stock and kind, and all that—one would think that the murderer tells us something about every human being. Again, do those who rob, maim, and murder do so despite their seeing that the law of nature forbids it, or rather because they have somehow lost sight of human equality and think themselves entitled to subordinate the interests of others to their own, or for some other reason? Depending upon how we answer these important questions, laws in civil society would presumably need to be tailored differently. But, again, Locke does not say. His political philosophy is not founded on a philosophical anthropology, as were the classical accounts. The closest he comes to explaining transgression of the natural law is his idea that the invention of money causes greed, because for the first time it becomes worth someone's while to store up more than he can reasonably use for good purposes. This idea of Locke's seems to be the first expression of the distinctively modern view that an instrument can elicit its bad use. So there is one modern turn, at least, but I will not dwell on it.

Anyway, given that some individuals in the state of nature do start harming others, what comes next? Is the fact that some or all of us harm or are disposed to harm others the reason that we leave the state of nature, according to Locke? Actually, no. Locke gives us little reason to think that people in the state of nature will not be well enough able to protect themselves, or that the burdens of establishing political society and its government would not be greater than any expected gain in protection. It is not the harms that are a menace, for Locke, but the response of individuals to these harms, in the state of nature. According to Locke, everyone can see by reason that a law without a punishment attached is vain and, really, no law at all. Likewise, everyone can see that the law of nature gives proscriptions, but it carries with it no punishments for transgressions. Therefore, says Locke, the only reasonable conclusion to be drawn, and which would be drawn by reasonable individuals in the state of nature, is that they themselves are authorized to execute the law of nature by punishing transgressors. Locke refers to this authorization as the natural right to exact punishment for transgressions of the law of nature, and, as I said, the postulation of this right is Locke's distinctive contribution.

One might object that the law of nature does have punishments attached: drunkards get cirrhosis, adulterers destroy their own happiness, and so on: "Vengeance is mine; I will repay, saith the Lord," according to the verse from Deuteronomy quoted as the motto for *Anna Karenina*. One might insist that the proper view is that human punishments attached to violations of the natural law only complete natural punishments and confirm them externally. However, because Locke rejects teleology, posits no afterlife, and recognizes no damage to the soul (as Plato did), he cannot conceive that the law of nature actually is largely enforced by God's providence shown in created nature, dealt out by the same authority who set down the law of nature in the first place. Oddly, Locke imagines a supreme lawgiver who is impotent when it comes to executing his own laws.

We might also wish to object that surely if anything is to be deduced about our exacting punishments for transgressions to the law of nature, then one should deduce a duty, not a power. Is it not better to say that the lawbreaker *must* be punished, and that therefore we have a duty, not simply a power, or the option, to punish him? Locke gives no explanation for our reasonably deducing merely a power. It is clear from his argumentative purpose why he needs it to be a power rather than a duty. As mentioned, he thinks that the power of the government in political society is exactly the same sort of power as the power of individuals in the state of nature, because the government gets that from individuals by contract; hence if the government has only the power and not a duty to punish transgressions, Locke's argument requires that he ascribe no more to individuals in the first place—otherwise the difference between the two powers would still be reserved by individuals, and then presumably they would be authorized to punish transgressors if, in their opinion, the government should have done so but failed to do so.

THE RIGHT TO PUNISH THE OFFENDER

Let us say more about the scope of this power, because it is on account of its vast scope that individuals prefer to leave the state of nature. Understand first that the law of nature cannot be enforced corporately, by mankind as a whole, but only by individuals; the reason is that there is no such entity as "mankind as a whole." There are only free, equal, and—Locke insists—"independent" individuals. To suppose corporate action is to suppose that individuals have already contracted out of the state of nature, at least to form a body politic. So everyone has this right: each individual possesses this power, to be exercised at his own digression. Moreover, the right has a universal object and scope: an individual in the state of nature has the power to punish any transgression of the law of nature, anywhere, anytime. If he learns of a transgression in a distant place, he has the power and authority to travel to that place and punish the transgressor. There need be no relation, pretext, condition, or previous relationship for him to interpose himself. According to Locke, the reason that the scope of this right is universal is that the law of nature is universal in what it commands. The law of nature obliges us to preserve humankind. In this connection Locke understands "humankind" distributively, not collectively, as according to the Golden Rule: each other person is such that we should treat him as we would treat ourselves. But since in our own case we would regard ourselves as authorized by the law of nature to exact punishment for transgressions against us, so, by the Golden Rule, we can take the place of any other aggrieved person and conclude rightly that we are authorized to exact punishment for any transgressions against him. An odd use of Golden Rule reasoning, that: not as we would like to be forgiven, so should we forgive others, but rather, as we would like to get revenge for ourselves, so should we punish others.

Again, the right is universal in its occasion and remedy. The reason is that even the slightest infraction, as mentioned, shows that someone is prepared to depart from the order of reason. Locke's example is a man who would rob us even of something small, say a purse with a few coins. It was English law then that the person accosted could kill the robber, if necessary, to remove the attempt at coercion. Locke does not question the justice of that law but assumes rather that it gives insight into the state of nature. Even someone's slight attempt to coerce me shows that he is prepared to have his way with me against my will, which is equivalent to enslaving, which is equivalent to murder, since anyone who enslaves is prepared to kill the person he enslaves if it suits him:

> Using force, where he has no right to get me into his power, let his pretence be what it will, I have no reason to suppose that he who would take away my liberty would not, when he had me in his power, take away everything else. And, therefore, it is lawful for me to treat him as one who has put himself into a state of war with me—i.e., kill him if I can.[13]

> I should have a right to destroy that which threatens me with destruction: for, by the fundamental law of nature, man being to be preserved as much as possible, when all cannot be preserved, the safety of the innocent is to be preferred. [...] And hence it is, that he who attempts to get another man into his absolute power, does thereby put himself into a state of war with him; it being to be un-

13. Chap. 3, §18.

derstood as a declaration of a design upon his life: for I have reason to conclude, that he who would get me into his power without my consent, would use me as he pleased when he had got me there, and destroy me too when he had a fancy to it; for no body can desire to have me in his absolute power, unless it be to compel me by force to that which is against the right of my freedom, i.e. make me a slave.[14]

So the right to punish is held by everyone, for everyone, for every transgression, and up to every possible punishment, that is, the highest possible punishment, which is death. It is a completely unrestricted power—unrestricted, that is, except that it is not triggered until someone transgresses against the law of nature. It should be emphasized that according to Locke the power is not limited by the merit of what someone deserves for his transgression. Locke says explicitly that the purpose of punishment is to suppress future wrongdoing by the transgressor and to deter wrongdoing in others, up to the point of death in any case, if necessary to achieve those ends. Death presumably is necessary for any transgressor who is unrepentant.

Although Locke does say in passing that human nature is such that we are hot-headed and biased in our own case—again, he does not explain why reasonable beings become thus irrational, or why this irrationality shown in the course of punishing does not remove from them the authorization to punish—the unrestricted character of the right to punish seems enough on its own to ensure that punishments will be greater in number and intensity than the crimes that inspired them, leading to a circle of violence, where it becomes difficult if not impossible to tell whose original transgression started it all in the first place. A single crime could lead to an unending sequence of putative punishments and counter punishments. (Note that, although such a condition might look like a state of war, Locke does not give it that name; rather, it is the state of nature, but with the inconveniences that attend to it. To punish is to observe the law of nature and still be in the state of nature—since the state of nature simply is the state we are in when we are following the law of nature. Only the original transgression, and any settled disposition to rob, maim, and murder, would be a state of war.) The menace posed by righteousness, not unrighteousness, is Locke's motive for political

14. Chap. 3, §§16–17.

society. A kind of peace could be attained in the state of nature, if only men did not overreach in attempting to enforce the law of nature. The *pleonexia* for justice, not for material goods, is what disturbs the peace.

So individuals in the state of nature seeing the endless and irresoluble conflicts that arise precisely from their exercising the natural right to punish will determine that it is better to give up the universal possession of this power and instead confer a monopoly of this power on a single entity, which is exactly what the government is, viz., that entity which has a monopoly on the power to punish transgressions through inflicting punishments, as necessary, up to the point of death.

We can only agree to what is better for us. Hence, Locke says, no one in the state of nature would agree to form a political society that was governed by a king with absolute rule. The reason is that citizens are defenseless against the attacks of such a king. He can take away their property, maim them, or put them to death, and they have no recourse, either individually or collectively in self-defense. The situation of citizens under an absolute king is even worse than in the state of nature, since at least in the state of nature each person can defend himself from attackers. Hence, no king could hold a natural right to rule as an absolute ruler—no king could hold absolute power by right of the law of nature—because persons in the state of nature could not responsibly give up their power of punishing transgressions of the law of nature in that way.

The power of individuals to punish in the state of nature is both the same as and different from the government's power to punish in political society. Locke defines political power as "a RIGHT of making laws with penalties of death, and consequently all less penalties, for the regulating and preserving of property, and of employing the force of the community, in the execution of such laws, … all this only for the public good."[15] Although in the definition he mentions making laws and regulating property, it is clear from the argument of the *Treatise* that the essential mark of political power is this matter of coercion and lethal punishment, "employing the force of the community" and "with penalties of death." In an obvious and straightforward sense, the government of the body politic is regarded as entitled to coerce and punish in ways that the government of the local chess club cannot. Locke, following in the

15. Chap. 1, §3.

tradition going back to St. Paul's mention of the "power of the sword," regards justified coercion and justified application of the death penalty as both puzzling and distinctive marks of political power. As mentioned, he holds that the government's power is derived from that of individuals in the state of nature. The argument of Locke's *Second Treatise* resembles the arguments of Locke's *Essay* in wanting to show how something complex and apparently abstract is derived from particulars that are similar in kind. However, note this difference. In political society, the magistrate exercises the power of punishment, Locke says, "for the public good." That is, he is not entitled to punish any transgression he wants. The mere fact of something's being a transgression does not itself justify the magistrate's punishment of it; somehow it must additionally be the case that the punishment of that transgression will contribute to the public good. But in the state of nature, as we saw, there is no such limitation. So what is the same about this power, for individuals in the state of nature and for the magistrate, is that it is a power to punish any transgression of the law of nature up to the point of death, if necessary, to suppress and deter, but in the state of nature the exercise of this power is not limited by reference to its contribution to any common good.

It should be clear by this point that the power which individuals possess to punish in the state of nature—the natural right with which Locke is mainly concerned, perhaps the only fundamental natural right he recognizes—is a right in neither of the two senses in which natural rights are compatible with natural law. It is not a right which is a mere creature of law, because law is directed to a common good, but this right as exercised in the state of nature, as we saw, has no such direction. Neither is it a right which involves what is due to something, because, as we also saw, Locke rejects retribution as a basis for punishment and does not believe that the reason to punish is to give the transgressor his due; rather, punishment is for suppression and deterrence. The power to punish is an unrestricted power of vengeance, restricted neither by considerations of the common good nor by consideration of merit.

A right in this third sense is an individual's having a power or authority, in his domain, which is the same in kind as the power or authority of the government of a commonwealth. It is as if one took the separate states of the world and shrunk each of them down so that only one person was left, and that person had a share of the highest political authority in that state, so that he retains it still and as it were becomes a sovereign nation consisting of just himself: then the power which he has, equivalent to the power of those others, each constituting a sovereign authority, would constitute his "right," or what he was authorized to do "by right," in this third sense. The right of an individual would be the sovereignty that he has. Obviously a right in this third sense, insofar as it is not contracted away, would limit the sovereignty of government, in the way that the sovereignty of any government limits the sovereignty of any other. The purpose for which this right is exercised, how it orders and disposes of what is under its domain, presumably is set by the holder of that right himself, just as a sovereign power determines the ends toward which he will direct everything in his domain.

THE MODERN TURN

Obviously, Locke's philosophy is modern rather than classical according to the differences mentioned at the beginning. Locke thinks that not merely government but also political society itself is artificial and the result of agreement; by nature, each individual is independent. Also, if Locke by "individual" means actually the male who is head of a household, then any relationships he has within his household are irrelevant to those he establishes with other heads of household, through compact and agreement. The nature of happiness is irrelevant to Locke's political philosophy; all that Locke says along these lines is that we are the workmanship of God and about God's business, but what that business is, Locke does not say. Similarly, just as persons want to leave the state of nature only because of transgressions of others against their property, so the laws of government in political society are aimed only at "preserving," that is, defending the property of each against everyone else—although, as we saw, this is not to say that defense against injustice is the main motive for leaving the state of nature, but rather relief from excesses of *justice*.

These attributes of Locke's philosophy are largely familiar. But other more particular aspects of the modern turn are directly related to Locke's postulate of the equivalent of sovereignty for individuals by nature. Locke's attribution of sovereignty to individuals is the direct ancestor and cause of a variety of aspects of liberalism today, of which I shall mention three: liberalism's inability to sustain a public philosophy which supports liberalism itself; liberalism's easy acquiescence in seeming illiberal behavior, such as slavery and abortion; and an ease with which liberalism can turn from benign respect for perceived paternalism to a swift and savage attack on it.

First, liberalism's weakness in sustaining a public philosophy that supports liberalism itself. Locke had already observed in his *Third Letter on Toleration* that his social contract argument implied that no laws designed to uphold a religious belief were justified:

> The end of a commonwealth constituted can be supposed no other, than what men in the constitution of, and entering into it, proposed; [...] since no man, or society of men, can by their opinions in religion, or ways of worship, do any man who differed from them any injury, which he could not avoid or redress, if he desired it, without the help of force; the punishing any opinion in religion, or ways of worship by the force given the magistrate, could not be intended by those who constituted or entered into the commonwealth; and so could be no end of it.[16]

It is obvious that the same argument applies to thought and expression generally, so that the viewpoint of Mill's *On Liberty* is no true innovation but follows trivially. However, Locke's argument here is only negative, pertaining to what government may not do. Positively, we may also say the following about what individuals alone are entitled to do: since individuals have the equivalent of political power in the state of nature, and they give up only that aspect of power which pertains to defense and punishment as regards the transgressions of others against them—and whatever they do not delegate, they retain—then they retain exclusive control in matters pertaining to themselves over what they deem good, what they should think, and what they should pursue. That is to say, a kind of practical relativism is the consequence of Locke's view—which he failed to see, I think, because of his great confidence in the light of natural reason and the obviousness of the natural law, characteristic of his day. But more pertinent for our purposes is that government is not permitted through the laws it passes to encourage, provide for, or sustain any of the philosophical views that underwrite Locke's liberal-

16. John Locke, *The Works of John Locke in Nine Volumes* (London: C. and J. Rivington et al., 1824), 5:212.

ism—which includes the original equality of human beings, our being the workmanship of God, that there is a law of nature, that we cannot consent to be enslaved, and so on. That is, government can pass no law whatsoever on these matters, not merely criminal law, because law in its essence is coercive.

Second, liberalism's easy acquiescence in seemingly illiberal behavior, such as slavery and abortion. This consideration can be approached in the following way. Suppose that persons were not the workmanship of God. Then on Locke's grounds they would have unhindered freedom to dispose of their bodies and their lives as they see fit—because their being the workmanship of God was the only bulwark against that. Then their sovereignty would extend to suicide, for any cause they saw fit; that is, they would have a "right to suicide," in our sense. Again, any power they hold can be delegated: so they would have a right to assisted suicide as well. This all follows once the premise that we are the workmanship of God is waived. But that is not my point yet, but the following. We can ask: can they also corporately delegate power to the government to kill citizens, say, on certain well-understood grounds, such as in the case of terminal patients in great pain? It is difficult to see why not. On Lockean grounds it would seem that they could justifiably decide to do so even through a simple majority vote, because Locke holds that, once persons constitute themselves as a body politic, then they implicitly allow future decisions to be determined by majority vote.

Be that as it may, once the workmanship argument is rejected, then, so far, with one caveat, there seems to be an essential connection between the views that individuals can with right kill themselves, and that the government can with right kill them. The caveat is this: if they could establish in some other way that the power cannot or had not been delegated, then they could establish that the government did not have this right. But how is this to be established? The only available grounds on which the argument can be based is the sovereignty of individuals: insist either that doing it oneself is crucial in certain matters, say, those pertaining to one's "property" in some sense, or that the grounds on which one might do so oneself are inscrutable to others. Alternatively one might corroborate the claim that the power never had been delegated by pointing to individuals, either historically or in the present, who decide to do so on their own grounds. That is, since the sovereignty of one entity surely places a limit on the sovereignty of another, one establishes the government's incompetence to decide a certain thing by insisting on one's sole competence. So a limit of the government's power to kill would be established by an individual's taking it upon himself to kill according to the justification that he sees fit; a limit on the government's power to enslave is established by an individual's taking it upon himself to enslave according to the justification he sees fit; and so on.

Hence we see the position that looks so puzzling today to those who take a human right to be a matter of due treatment based on the merit of the thing. Such persons, understandably enough, consider that the same reasons that hold against the government's killing or enslaving hold also against an individual's killing or enslaving. However, someone who takes a right to be sovereignty, equivalent to political power, is concerned only with which entity in a particular matter has sovereignty, the government, or the individual ("who decides?"); and the claim that the government may not properly decide the matter is established by the individual's properly doing it for whatever reason seems good to him.

In the absence of the recognition of an authority above both individuals and government, which sets limits to the authority of both, it is inevitable, on Lockean premises, that what formerly was protected by appeal to that authority looks like it can be preserved from government domination only by reasserting the power of the individual akin to that which he possesses in the state of nature, and that is the force today of appeals to the "right to privacy." The "right to privacy" today is not an aberration in liberal political philosophy but rather what remains of Locke's notion of the individual's original sovereignty in the state of nature, once the workmanship argument and similar seeming considerations based on human dignity have been abandoned.

Third, the ease with which liberalism can turn from benign respect for perceived paternalism to a swift and savage attack on it. This is the other illiberal aspect of Lockean liberalism, which I have been wanting to emphasize in saying that it was righteousness rather than unrighteousness that precipitates the move from the state of nature to political society for Locke. The shocking illiberalism of Lockean liberalism is a consequence of a series of equivalences which Locke accepts. Law is coercion; therefore, the attempt to pass a law is an attempt to coerce. But any attempt improperly to coerce, however slight, is in effect an attempt to enslave another. To enslave another is as it were to take his life, since a master can kill his slave at will. In particular, anyone who attempts to use the law improperly to coerce in effect makes himself the equivalent of an absolute ruler, who would enslave the people. Such a person in effect returns himself in relation to others to the state of nature; he takes himself out of political society, and can be dealt with as a beast that is a threat to humanity. But paternalistic legislation is improper, for the reasons given above. Hence, although someone adhering to Locke's liberalism may initially smile fondly upon fellow citizens who aim to pass measures which he regards as paternalistic, perhaps admiring their idealism and moral concern, if he holds to a view in the Lockean tradition, then the logic of that position will require him in the end to respond to such a person with the full force and ferocity he would use against beasts, that is, with the full conviction of course that he is suppressing those who are enemies of the human race.

Insofar as we look to Locke as our philosophical ancestor, then all of the worrying oddities of contemporary liberalism, its weakness toward enemies and harshness toward those who believe themselves to be liberalism's friends, and its periodic embrace of apparently the most illiberal actions, such as enslavement and the killing of unborn human beings, should be regarded not as unfortunate lapses from principled liberalism, but as natural developments of a view of natural right as a quasi-divine power possessed by individuals, which seems intended by those who constituted or entered into the commonwealth.

Nicholas Jolley

6 Leibniz

Modern or Premodern Philosopher?

In a number of autobiographical passages in his works, Leibniz describes the discovery of the moderns as one of the turning points in his life. In the *New System*, Leibniz writes:

> I have constantly meditated on philosophy from my youth up, for it has always seemed to me that in philosophy there was a way of establishing something solid by means of clear proofs. I had traveled far into the world of the Scholastics when mathematics and modern writers [*auteurs modernes*] lured me out again, while still a young man. I was charmed with their beautiful way of explaining nature mechanically and scorned, with justice, the method of those who make use of forms and faculties from which we learn nothing.[1]

Later in the same work Leibniz remarks that he is "as willing as any man to give the moderns their due."[2] It can hardly be said, however, that Leibniz's enthusiasm for the philosophy of the moderns is unqualified in the *New System*, for he goes on to insist on the need to revive the medieval doctrine of substantial forms. If Leibniz recounts his discovery of modern philosophy, it is because he is primarily intent on reassuring a French and largely Cartesian readership of his credentials; he is not a provincial German ignorant of the advantages of the mechanical philosophy.

1. C. I. Gerhardt, ed., *Die Philosophischen Schriften von G. W. Leibniz* (Berlin: Weidmann, 1875–90), IV:478 [hereafter "G"], in G. H. R. Parkinson , ed., *G. W. Leibniz: Philosophical Writings* (London: Dent, 1973), 116 ["P"]; cf. G III:606, in L. E. Loemker, trans. and ed., *G. W. Leibniz: Philosophical Papers and Letters,* 2nd ed. (Dordrecht: Reidel, 1969), 654–55 ["L"].

2. G IV:481 (P 119).

The sense that Leibniz's philosophical identity is hard to pin down is nicely captured in the title of Stuart Brown's paper, "Leibniz: Modern, Scholastic, or Renaissance Philosopher?"[3] Brown goes on to answer his own question by saying that he is all of these at once. In view of the multifaceted nature of Leibniz's genius there is much to be said for this answer. In this paper, however, I shall depart from Brown's claim in two main ways. First, I shall take more seriously than Brown does the question of what is meant by describing a seventeenth-century figure as one of the modern philosophers. I shall distinguish two standard senses of the term "modern" and argue that Leibniz is not a fully modern philosopher in either sense. Nonetheless, I shall recognize a restricted sense in which Leibniz can be counted as one of the moderns. In the second half of the paper I shall argue that, though they are not always on the surface, Leibniz's deepest philosophical affinities are with the Renaissance tradition by virtue of his Neoplatonism and his syncretism or eclecticism. In the concluding section I shall argue that there is a conceptual link between these two aspects of his Renaissance legacy.

I

Leibniz's contrast between the moderns and the premoderns, or scholastics, shows that there is one issue that does not arise in discussion concerning his philosophical identity or allegiance. Some standard philosophical taxonomies run the risk of being anachronistic; this is notoriously the case with regard to the division of early modern philosophers into opposing camps of rationalists and empiricists. This division, while useful for pedagogical purposes, seems to be the product of nineteenth-century historiography; certainly none of the philosophers who are classified in this way ever self-identified as rationalist or empiricist. But if the division of seventeenth-century philosophers into modern and premodern is not anachronistic, it does run the risk of equivocation or ambiguity, for we can distinguish between a seventeenth-century and a more recent sense of "modern." When Leibniz writes of his discovery of modern

3. Tom Sorell, ed., *The Rise of Modern Philosophy: The Tension between the New and Traditional Philosophies from Machiavelli to Leibniz* (Oxford: Clarendon, 1993), 213–30. I am grateful to Michael Rohlf and other members of the audience at the Catholic University of America for helpful comments.

philosophy as a young man, he is thinking above all of the mechanical philosophy; in Leibniz's words, "the hypothesis of the moderns [*hypothesis recentiorum*] ... conceives no incorporeal entities within bodies but assumes nothing beyond magnitude, figure, and motion."[4] By contrast, our understanding of what it is to be a modern philosopher is captured in the textbook dictum, now strongly disputed in some quarters, that Descartes is the father of modern philosophy. My polling of colleagues on what we mean by this famous claim has yielded somewhat different answers, but I take it that we can distinguish at least two elements. In the first place, the opening of the *Meditations* captures much of what people have in mind. To say that Descartes is the father of modern philosophy is to say that he will accept nothing on the basis of tradition, authority, education, or preconceived opinion; he will seek to rebuild the edifice of knowledge on absolutely secure foundations. Indeed, Descartes is the father of modern philosophy in the sense that the theory of knowledge assumes a methodological priority and importance that it had not enjoyed before. Secondly, to say that Descartes is the father of modern philosophy may imply that he is the discoverer or inventor of the so-called mind-body problem. Thus the textbook claim can be seen as having both an epistemological and a metaphysical dimension. In what follows I shall speak of the seventeenth-century and textbook senses.

We can bring out the difference between the two senses in the following way. It is possible to be a modern in the seventeenth-century sense of the term without being a modern in the textbook sense. To be a modern in the first sense is to be committed to the principles of mechanical or corpuscularian philosophy: thus Boyle is a modern in this sense but not in the textbook one, since he has no commitment to epistemological foundationalism of the kind found in Descartes nor any special interest in the mind-body problem. Conversely, it is possible to be a modern philosopher in the textbook sense without being a modern philosopher in the seventeenth-century sense; thus one might be interested in both foundationalist epistemology and the mind-body problem without having any commitment to the mechanical model of scientific explanation. (Consider a philosopher, say, who seeks to establish secure foundations

4. German Academy of Sciences, ed., *G. W. Leibniz: Sämtliche Schriften und Briefe* (Darmstadt, 1923–), VI.i:164 [hereafter "A"] (L 95). This passage is discussed by Brown, "Leibniz: Modern Philosopher?," in Sorell, *Rise of Modern Philosophy*, 217.

for a commonsensical picture of the physical world.) Descartes himself of course is a modern philosopher in both senses of the term, but that in a way is a matter of historical contingency rather than of logic.

It may be objected that the contrast between the two senses is drawn too starkly. Surely, it may be said, there is at least some degree of overlap between the two senses, for both imply a rejection of scholasticism. But we can, I think, concede the justice of this observation without really undermining the case for the importance of distinguishing sharply between two senses of "modern." For even with respect to the rejection of scholasticism, there is a clear difference of emphasis. When Leibniz contrasts modern philosophers with their predecessors, especially the scholastics, he has something rather limited in mind: he is thinking of the restricted goal of substituting mechanical explanations for explanations in terms of substantial forms. By contrast, when Descartes is called the father of modern philosophy, what is at issue is his rejection of the entire scholastic philosophical methodology. Let us begin by seeing why Leibniz is not a modern philosopher in the textbook sense.

II

The most obvious reason for denying that Leibniz is a modern philosopher in the textbook sense is his lack of sympathy with foundationalist epistemology. This lack of sympathy with the foundationalist project of the *Meditations* and the *Principles of Philosophy* is nowhere more apparent than in his response to the method of doubt. For Leibniz, the method of doubt is more like a theatrical device designed to win the applause of the ignorant than an indispensable methodological tool for making progress in philosophy.[5] Perhaps because of his conviction, which we shall discuss later, that the human mind is a mirror of God, Leibniz is not able to take seriously what is sometimes called "defective nature doubt"; that is, he dismisses the concern, articulated in the First Meditation, that we may have a nature that makes us incapable of knowledge. For Leibniz, the only reasonable grounds for worrying that we may have fallen into error are the commonplace ones that our mind is tired, distracted, or insufficiently attentive.[6] Leibniz further raises the objection that Cartesian

5. G IV:355 (L 384).
6. G IV:361 (L 388).

methodological doubt is not serious; as he remarks in the *New Essays*, to doubt in earnest is to doubt in a practical way.[7] Cartesian doubt, by contrast, is self-consciously designed to have no implications for practice.

Leibniz may be an unsympathetic critic of Descartes's method of doubt, but he is also in some ways a characteristically shrewd one. Like some modern commentators Leibniz is sharply critical of Descartes's less careful formulations of the method. Notoriously Descartes sometimes describes the method of doubt in terms of considering that one's former opinions are all false.[8] As Leibniz notes, when described in these terms the method is a recipe not for freeing ourselves from prejudices but rather for changing them.[9] Suppose that among my former opinions are at least some true ones; if I then reject all my previous opinions as false, I have simply added to my stock of false beliefs. Obviously Descartes's method of doubt is more carefully characterized as explaining the rejection of previous beliefs in terms of suspension of judgment about them rather than as believing that they are all false.

Leibniz's attitude toward Descartes's famous Archimedean point—the *cogito*—is not similarly dismissive, but it is lukewarm and perhaps somewhat insensitive. Certainly Leibniz shows no tendency to accord the *cogito* the privileged status that Descartes claims for it. Leibniz insists that "Various things are thought by me" is no less certain than "I think, therefore I am."[10] Here Leibniz is no doubt alluding to his own metaphysical doctrine that the human mind is a simple substance that perceives many things; indeed, it perceives the whole universe according to its point of view. Leibniz's readiness to put these two principles on a par as primary truths of knowledge suggests a certain blindness to the distinctive features of the *cogito*. As many commentators have noticed, the *cogito* is not merely an incorrigible judgment in the sense that necessarily, if I believe it, it is true; it is also self-verifying. To deny one's own thinking and one's

7. *New Essays on Human Understanding (Nouveaux Essais sur l'Entendement Humain)*, IV.xi [hereafter "NE"], A VI.vi, in P. Remnant and J. Bennett, trans. and ed., *G. W. Leibniz: New Essays on Human Understanding*, 2nd ed. (Cambridge: Cambridge University Press, 1996), 444–45 [hereafter "RB"].

8. C. Adam and P. Tannery, ed., *Oeuvres de Descartes* (Paris: Vrin, 1964–76), VIIIA 5 [hereafter "AT"]: J. Cottingham, R. Stoothoff, and D. Murdoch, trans., *The Philosophical Writings of Descartes* (Cambridge: Cambridge University Press, 1985), 1:193 [hereafter "CSM"]; cf. AT VI 31 (CSM I 126–27).

9. G IV 355–56 (L 384).

10. G IV 357 (L 385).

own existence is not to say something that is necessarily false in the logical sense, but it is pragmatically self-defeating. Curiously, Leibniz never shows any signs of appreciating these features of the *cogito*.

Leibniz's lack of enthusiasm for foundationalist epistemology is clear; thus if we insist that such foundationalism is a necessary condition of being a modern philosopher in the textbook sense, then we could simply rest our case. But it would be wrong to close the discussion without taking up the issue of Leibniz's attitude to the mind-body problem; here those who would claim that Leibniz is a modern in the textbook sense are apparently on stronger ground. It is true of course that, consistently with his negative attitude to the method of doubt, Leibniz rejects the argument for substantial dualism that Descartes advances in the *Discourse on Method*; indeed, since Leibniz fails to see anything of philosophical value in this method, his attitude entails this rejection. But on the face of it, he not only feels the force of the problem; he also puts forward his own arguments to solve it. Thus in the *Monadology* Leibniz advances his famous "mill" argument apparently to show that no materialist reduction of the mental to the physical can possibly be right.[11] Such an argument is not only prominent in Leibniz scholarship; it is also still discussed by contemporary philosophers such as Paul Churchland writing about the mind-body problem as it comes down to us from Descartes.[12]

But Leibniz's relationship to the mind-body problem in its Cartesian form is not a straightforward matter. For one thing, the mind-body problem as it is discussed by Descartes and his twentieth-century heirs is paradigmatically a problem about the relationship between matter and consciousness. It cannot be said, however, that Leibniz is specifically interested in a problem of this form. As Alison Simmons has argued, it is not consciousness that constitutes the essence of the mental for Leibniz; it is rather representationality of a certain kind.[13] Leibniz defines perception as "the expression of the many in the one."[14] Secondly, his

11. G VI:609 (P 181).

12. See Paul Churchland, *The Engine of Reason, The Seat of the Soul* (Cambridge, Mass.: MIT Press, 1995), 191–92. See also Paul Lodge and Marc Bobro, "Stepping Back Inside Leibniz's Mill," *Monist* 81 (1998): 553–72, for a helpful review of other modern discussions of Leibniz's argument.

13. Alison Simmons, "Changing the Cartesian Mind: Leibniz on Sensation, Representation, and Consciousness," *Philosophical Review* 110 (2001): 31–75.

14. G II 311.

account of the relationship between the human soul and its body retains elements from the Aristotelian scholastic tradition. Consider this passage from "Notes on Some Comments by Michael Angelo Fardella": "the soul, properly speaking, is not a substance but a substantial form, or the primitive form existing in substance, the first act, the first active faculty."[15] It may seem unfair to put too much weight on this passage, for it is something of an anomaly in Leibniz's mature writings; for this one passage where Leibniz denies the soul the status of a substance, many others could be adduced where he affirms it. But if in general the human soul, for Leibniz, is a substance in its own right, it still plays the role that was traditionally assigned to the substantial form; thus it is the presence of a soul that transforms a physical aggregate into a substantial unity. Indeed, this account of its role survives changes in his underlying metaphysical commitments. Even when Leibniz makes the transition from a theory of corporeal substances to full-blooded monadology, the fact that he conceives of the soul as the dominant monad with respect to the body shows that he still assigns it the role of a substantial form. Moreover, Leibniz remains faithful to the scholastic tradition by virtue of his insistence that the soul is the principle of life in an organism, human or otherwise; he resists the Cartesian attempt to sever the connection between soul and vitality. It is in this way that Leibniz can extend souls to animals and other organisms while denying them consciousness.

Leibniz, then, is not a modern philosopher in the textbook sense since he has no commitment to epistemological foundationalism; his interest in the mind-body problem, at least in its classic Cartesian form, is open to challenge. Is he a modern in the sense of the term that he himself deployed? Remember that Leibniz's characterization of the moderns is in terms of their conceiving no incorporeal entities and assuming nothing for the purposes of explanation beyond magnitude, figure, and motion.[16] As Stuart Brown has noted, Leibniz's most enthusiastic endorsements of the principles of the moderns tend to come from near the end of his life when in his view these very principles were under attack from the Newtonians; in particular, the Newtonians seemed to be abandoning

15. A. Foucher de Careil, ed., *Nouvelles lettres et opuscules inédits de Leibniz* (Paris: Durand, 1857), 323 [hereafter "FC"]: R. Ariew and D. Garber, ed. and trans., *G. W. Leibniz: Philosophical Essays* (Indianapolis, Ind.: Hackett, 1989), 105.

16. A VI.i 164.

the principle that all interaction between bodies takes place by way of contact action in favor of the theory that they tend toward each other by virtue of a primitive attractive force.[17] If we are to take Leibniz at his word, then in his maturity he had never been anything but a modern; he consistently offered physical explanations that appealed only to intelligible notions such as size, shape, and number, and he had always thought that nothing is moved naturally except through contact action. But Leibniz's history of his thought here is somewhat disingenuous. Perhaps because he is attacking the Newtonians, for whom a concept of force is supposed to be central, Leibniz makes no mention of the role that force had played in his own natural philosophy; thus it is simply not true that Leibniz had consistently been a modern in the sense of seeking to explain all natural phenomena in terms of intelligible notions such as number, size, and shape. Secondly, Leibniz is similarly disingenuous in his claim that he had always been a strict mechanist in the sense of holding that all physical interaction is by way of contact action. On the contrary, Leibniz had affirmed in many passages that collision is simply the occasion on which the elastic force of bodies is exercised: "No impetus is transferred from one body to another, but each body is moved by its innate force, which is determined only by the occasion or relation of another. For eminent men have already recognized that the cause of the impulse one body receives from another is the body's elasticity itself, by which it recoils from the other."[18] In this way Leibniz seeks at least to bring his dynamics into line with his metaphysical principle of the denial of causal interaction. Indeed, Leibniz sometimes writes as if the denial of strict contact action between bodies were simply a consequence of his metaphysics. But this cannot be correct. For Leibniz's metaphysical doctrine is a thesis about the absence of causal interaction between substances, and this thesis does not warrant the denial of strict causal interaction between inanimate bodies, which are not substances but aggregates of substances; at no time in his philosophical career does Leibniz hold that such bodies are substances. As Russell suggested long ago, the relationship between Leibniz's dynamics and his metaphysics, far from being one of the strong points of his philosophy, is in fact one of its weaknesses.[19]

17. Brown, "Leibniz: Modern Philosopher?," 222.

18. G VII:313 (P 79).

19. Bertrand Russell, *A Critical Examination of the Philosophy of Leibniz*, 2nd ed. (London: Allen and Unwin, 1937), 93.

Despite his claims in his polemics against Newton, the mature Leibniz was never a paradigmatic modern in the sense of recognizing explanations solely in terms of intelligible notions and contact action. We may also approach the issue from a somewhat different angle. Consider Stuart Brown's claim that Leibniz is a modern by virtue of his commitment to what we might call "the secularization or, perhaps better, the de-spiritualization of natural philosophy."[20] In one way this claim is correct inasmuch as Leibniz insists on the explanatory autonomy of science. Just as in the *New System* he argues that no appeal to substantial forms should be made when doing physics, so in the later theory of monads he argues that no appeal should be made to the primitive force, or appetition, of monads. But from a more metaphysical perspective Brown's claim is misleading, for the bodies at the phenomenal level that is the subject matter of physics are anchored in, and derivative from, substances at the ground floor metaphysical level that are not at all despiritualized. The substances from which the force in bodies derives are not spirits in Leibniz's sense, for they lack self-consciousness, reflection, and the capacity for knowing the eternal truths; but they are spiritual in the sense of being immaterial, soul-like entities.

Brown's claim that Leibniz is one of the moderns by virtue of his despiritualization of natural philosophy is a little misleading, but there is indeed one respect in which Leibniz may be counted as a modern philosopher: he shares the characteristic seventeenth-century ambition of providing a metaphysical framework for the new science. Such an ambition is clearly present in Descartes, who in a famous passage writes that "the whole of philosophy is like a tree. The roots are metaphysics, the trunk is physics, and the branches emerging from the trunk are all the other sciences."[21] Leibniz of course holds that Descartes wholly failed in his attempt to realize his ambition, and he articulates his own program in large measure as a critique of Descartes's project. For Leibniz, not only is Descartes's physics flawed by the falsity of its conservation principles, but also his metaphysics is flawed by its failure to formulate a concept of substance that is adequate for understanding the physical world. According to Leibniz, no entity whose essence is constituted by extension can be a genuine substance, for any such entity must be an aggregate,

20. Brown, "Leibniz: Modern Philosopher?," 218.

21. AT IXB 14 (CSM I 186).

and aggregates are not true unities; hence since "unity" and "being" are convertible terms, no such entity can be a genuine substance or ultimate subject of predication. Moreover, Descartes and his disciples not only lack an adequate concept of active force in physics; they fail to recognize that activity is of the essence of substance in general: to conceive of substances as devoid of activity is to reduce them to the status of Spinozistic modes.[22] As we have seen, for Leibniz, the active force in bodies, which is the subject of dynamics, derives from the primitive force or appetition in monads.

III

Although Leibniz is not a modern philosopher in either of the two rather standard senses identified at the beginning of this essay, he shares Descartes's ambition of creating a metaphysical framework for the new science; to this extent he may be regarded as one of the moderns. But of course there is much in Leibniz's overall philosophical project that cannot be captured in these terms. Consider, for instance, his lifelong preoccupation with the problem of theodicy. His strategy for solving this problem is not wholly irrelevant to the project of providing a metaphysical framework for science; for the thesis that God chooses a world that maximizes variety of phenomena and simplicity of laws is designed to serve as a heuristic device for identifying those laws that are actually instantiated by this world. But *pace* Rescher, Leibniz's insistence on the variety/simplicity criterion, as it is often called, constitutes only one part of his theodicy.[23] Leibniz is at least as much concerned to solve the problem by showing that the actual world is the one in which the happiness of spirits is at a maximum. Thus in order to answer the question of Leibniz's overall philosophical identity, we need to turn to the other possibilities canvassed by Stuart Brown in his paper "Leibniz: Modern, Scholastic, or Renaissance Philosopher?"

A good case can be made for saying that Leibniz is in large measure the last of the great scholastic philosophers; certainly no characterization of his philosophical identity would be correct that did not emphasize the strong residual element of scholasticism in his philosophy. Leib-

22. G IV:515 (L 507).

23. Nicholas Rescher, *The Philosophy of Leibniz* (Englewood Cliffs, N.J.: Prentice Hall), 19.

niz famously distances himself from his great contemporaries among the moderns by insisting that there is much of philosophical value in scholastic thought that ought to be retained; as he characteristically says, "there is gold buried in the dross."[24] Indeed, Leibniz may have been more indebted to the scholastic tradition than he himself realized. Such a debt would not be surprising in a philosopher who was trained in the intellectually conservative Germany of his age.

Leibniz's residual scholasticism is evident in various ways. Most obviously, it emerges in his attempt to accommodate and rehabilitate particular Aristotelian scholastic doctrines wherever possible. Unlike Descartes and Spinoza, he insists that teleological explanations still have a role to play in science (for example, optics), and he seeks to accommodate the Aristotelian doctrine of prime matter even in contexts where such an appeal seems rather strained; it is in terms of this doctrine, for instance, that Leibniz characterizes the passive element in monads, even though what is at issue is the confusion of perceptual states.

Leibniz's scholastic inheritance is evident not just in his reinterpretation of particular doctrines; it is evident also in his very choice of problems to place at the forefront of the philosophical agenda and the angle from which he approaches problems of moment to his contemporaries. Consider, for instance, Leibniz's approach to issues about contingency and human freedom. In the early modern period, the problem characteristically arose from the scientific picture of the world as a vast machine governed by causal laws. Leibniz is indeed aware of the apparent problem posed by what he calls "the series of causes," and he attempts to incorporate causal determinism in his philosophy in a compatibilist spirit.[25] But Leibniz is highly unusual among the philosophers of his age inasmuch as the challenge to human freedom and contingency that most interests him comes not from "the series of causes" but from the nature of truth; if future contingents have a determinate truth value, as Leibniz believes, then how can I be free in respect of traveling from New York to California next Sunday? In the centrality that he accords to problems about truth in his philosophy Leibniz is very much the heir of Aristotle and his scholastic successors. Arguably too the logical sophistication that he brings to such discussions, as indeed his interest in logical problems for

24. E.g., NE IV.viii, A VI.vi (RB 431).
25. FC 178 (P 106).

their own sake, aligns him with the medievals rather than with his contemporaries.

The case for emphasizing the residual scholasticism of Leibniz's thought is a strong one, but scholasticism, I believe, is not the core of his philosophical identity. On the contrary, in my view Leibniz's deepest philosophical allegiance is not to modern philosophy or to scholasticism; it is rather to the thought of the Renaissance. At first sight this may seem a surprising claim. For one thing, we do not normally think of the Renaissance as one of the great ages of philosophy; indeed, there is a sense in which Leibniz did not think so either, for allusions to Renaissance philosophers tend to be easily outnumbered by allusions to classical giants such as Plato and Aristotle and the major figures of the seventeenth century such as Descartes, Hobbes, Malebranche, and Locke. Moreover, there is one theme in Renaissance thought that seems to find little or no echo in Leibniz's philosophy, and that is the problem of skepticism. As Popkin and others have shown, for various historical reasons the ancient problem of skepticism takes on a new lease of life in the Renaissance, and forms an essential part of the background to the father of modern philosophy.[26] Descartes was neither a Renaissance philosopher nor a skeptic, but skepticism apparently mattered more to him than it did to Leibniz.

The case for saying that the spirit of Renaissance thought is the key to Leibniz's philosophical identity rests on two prominent features of his philosophy. In the first place, there can be little doubt that the leading metaphysical themes of his philosophy owe much to the Neoplatonism that was revived in the Renaissance. Thus Leibniz's two most famous metaphysical doctrines—the thesis that the actual world is the best of all possible worlds and the doctrine that the universe ultimately consists of monads—are both of Neoplatonic inspiration. The doctrine that this is the best of all possible worlds is a descendant of Plato's claim in the *Timaeus* (30a) that the highest can produce nothing but the best. In what follows, however, I wish to focus rather on two Neoplatonic claims about mirroring that are central to Leibniz's theory of monads: each spirit is a mirror of God and every substance is a microcosm or mirror of the universe.

There is no doubt that Leibniz is strongly committed to each of these

26. Richard Popkin, *The History of Scepticism from Erasmus to Spinoza* (Berkeley: University of California Press, 1979), esp. chap. 1.

doctrines from the *Discourse on Metaphysics*, the first work of his maturity, to his last works such as the *Monadology* and *Principles of Nature and of Grace*. But there is room for disagreement over whether Leibniz seeks to extend the "mirror of God" doctrine to all substances, or confine it to spirits, that is, rational, self-conscious souls. In a previous work I have argued for attributing the stronger thesis to Leibniz, and have cited the *Discourse on Metaphysics* in support of such an attribution: "Further, every substance is like an entire world and like a mirror of God, or of the whole universe, which each one expresses in its own way, very much as one and the same town is variously represented in accordance with different positions of the observer."[27]

Now there are clearly ways in which even the humblest monads instantiate godlike properties; for instance, every monad is immaterial and enjoys unrestricted causal self-sufficiency. But I now think that, though suggestive, the attribution of the stronger thesis to Leibniz may be mistaken. For one thing, at least in his later works Leibniz seems to wish to confine the "mirror of God" doctrine to spirits; his standard claim is that while minds or spirits are images of God or little gods (that is, they mirror the divine perfections), other substances are mirrors only of the universe. Moreover, the passage from the *Discourse* can be read in a way that is consistent with such a claim, for Leibniz formulates his thesis about substances disjunctively: every substance is like a mirror of God or like a mirror of the whole universe. Such a formulation is consistent with recognizing that not all substances are like mirrors of God; souls below the rank of spirits satisfy the condition in the second disjunct but not the first.

But suppose, for the sake of argument, that in the *Discourse on Metaphysics* Leibniz is committed to saying that every substance is a mirror of God. It is still possible to claim that Leibniz is not committed to extending the "mirror of God" thesis to souls below the rank of spirits. The key point is that at the time of the *Discourse on Metaphysics* Leibniz has not finally settled basic issues of ontology; although he is clear throughout his maturity about the intension of the term "substance," he is less clear about its extension. As the drafts reveal, in the *Discourse on Metaphysics* Leibniz is still flirting with the idea that spirits are the only substances in the universe; that is, in contrast to the later monadology, he has not yet

27. G IV:434 (P 19–20). Nicholas Jolley, *Leibniz* (London: Routledge, 2005).

definitively ruled out a Berkeleian-style ontology according to which all substances are of the nature of spirits. To say, then, that all substances are mirrors of God is simply to make a claim about spirits. Thus it is possible that at no point during the period of his philosophical maturity is Leibniz committed to the conjunction of the following two theses: (1) all substances are mirrors of God; (2) there are substances below the rank of spirits. At the time of the *Discourse on Metaphysics* Leibniz may be committed to (1) but not to (2); in the writings of the monadological period Leibniz seems to be committed to (2) but not to (1). Thus though we can see how the "mirror of God" thesis could be extended to all substances, even in the later ontology of monads, there is reason to be cautious about attributing such a doctrine to Leibniz as an explicit commitment.

Neoplatonism may have been revived in the Renaissance, but of course it does not originate with it. The other leading characteristic of Leibniz's philosophy is arguably a Renaissance invention: this is the pervasive syncretism or eclecticism of his philosophy that sets him apart from his great contemporaries. Consider, for instance, the opening statement by Theophilus, Leibniz's spokesman in the *New Essays on Human Understanding*: "I have been impressed by a new system, of which I have read something n the learned journals of Paris, Leipzig and Holland and in M. Bayle's marvelous *Dictionary*, in the article entitled 'Rorarius'; and I now think I see a new aspect of the inner nature of things. This system appears to unite Plato with Democritus, Aristotle with Descartes, the Scholastics with the moderns, theology and morality with reason."[28] For Leibniz in this passage, the ability to accommodate the insights of opposed philosophical traditions is clearly a presumption in favor of the truth of his own system; this is one of the advantages that it enjoys over Locke's philosophy. Indeed, the syncretic aspect of Leibniz's philosophy is so important that he gives it top billing in his response to Philalethes's opening statement. It is this characteristically Renaissance commitment to syncretism or eclecticism that finds expression in Leibniz's oft-quoted remark that the majority of philosophical sects are right in much of what they affirm, but not so much in what they deny.[29]

28. NE Preface, A VI.vi (RB 71).
29. G III:607.

IV

Leibniz, then, is a Renaissance philosopher by virtue of his commitment to Neoplatonic doctrines and his thoroughly syncretic approach to philosophy. At first sight it may seem that these two characteristics of his philosophy pull him in different directions, for to say that Leibniz is a Neoplatonist is to say that he privileges one philosophical sect over another, whereas to say that he is a syncretist is to say that he holds that there is truth in the tenets of every philosophical sect. But in fact his Neoplatonism and syncretism are linked in interesting ways, for his Neoplatonism informs and governs the interpretation of the doctrines of philosophical sects which his syncretism leads him to accommodate.

To see just how this is so, let us return to the objection that there is one characteristic of Renaissance philosophy that Leibniz does not share: an interest in skepticism. It is true, as we have seen, that Leibniz is not attracted to the method of doubt, and is prepared to admit as much. But it would be wrong to say that Leibniz sees himself as lacking an interest in skepticism or dismissing it as of no philosophical value. Indeed, as his syncretism would lead us to expect, in the *New Essays* Leibniz insists through his mouthpiece Theophilus that his own system can find a place for skeptical ideas and arguments: "I now see what Plato had in mind when he took matter to be an imperfect and transitory being; what Aristotle meant by his 'entelechy'; in what sense even Democritus could promise another life [...]; how far the sceptics were right in decrying the senses."[30] As a syncretist, then, Leibniz believes that the ideas and arguments of the skeptics should be incorporated in the true system of philosophy, provided they are given a good sense or reasonable interpretation.

But if Leibniz is apparently so uninterested in such epistemological issues, in what does a reasonable interpretation of the skeptics consist? In Book I of the *New Essays* Leibniz seems to attribute to the skeptics the rather commonplace insight that the senses are not a reliable guide to the nature of physical reality, let alone the ground floor metaphysical level. In other contexts, however, Leibniz develops a more interesting, if also more eccentric, "reasonable interpretation" of skeptical arguments:

30. NE Preface, A VI.vi (RB 71).

> The Academics were not completely wrong to argue (although they have either been misinterpreted or they made bad use of good arguments) against those things, which are imagined to exist outside us.[31]

> The Academics have doubted whether material things were outside us; which can be given a reasonable interpretation, by saying that they would be nothing outside of perceptions, and that they have their reality from the agreement of the perceptions of apperceiving substances.[32]

The first thing that may strike us about such passages is that Leibniz's way of giving a good sense or reasonable interpretation to skeptical ideas seems to consist in converting their epistemic concerns into positive metaphysical claims; according to Leibniz, the truth in skepticism is the reductive phenomenalist thesis that bodies are nothing over and above perceptions. To us today this may seem to miss the point of skeptical arguments, for it is surely a key premise of such arguments that bodies are essentially mind-independent entities; without such an assumption skeptical arguments can hardly get started. Indeed, Leibniz's project of giving a reasonable interpretation of their arguments sounds more like Berkeley's strategy for refuting skepticism than a statement of their views. Certainly Leibniz's way of doing justice to skeptical arguments is consistent with the lack of any real engagement with epistemological issues that we touched on earlier in the essay in connection with his response to Descartes's method of doubt. But for our purposes the important point is not that Leibniz's supposedly reasonable interpretation of skepticism is eccentric to the point of perversity; it is rather that it is informed by the idealism that is the heart of his later metaphysics. And Leibniz's idealist metaphysical thesis that there are no substances over and above souls or monads is clearly a reflection of his Neoplatonist thesis that an immaterial God will produce only immaterial substances. Even if the later Leibniz is not prepared to say outright that all substances are mirrors of God, he still holds that God's creation mirrors his nature as an immaterial being.

Leibniz's Neoplatonism, then, informs the interpretation of the skeptical arguments that, as a syncretic philosopher, he seeks to accommodate in his system. But there is at least one other major way in which

31. G II:275–76.
32. G III:623.

Leibniz's Neoplatonism is linked to his syncretic approach to philosophy. Whether or not Leibniz holds that all substances are mirrors of God may be disputed, but there is no question that he holds that all minds or spirits are both mirrors of God and microcosms of the universe, even though their perceptions are in varying degrees obscure and confused.[33] For Leibniz the doctrine clearly underwrites his syncretic conviction that there is truth to be found in every philosophical system; every philosopher perceives the eternal truths in God as well as the whole universe, according to his point of view. It is natural to object that the connection between Leibniz's Neoplatonic doctrines about mirroring and his syncretic approach to philosophy is rather a loose one. For consistently with the mirroring principles of Leibniz's Neoplatonism it might be the case that some philosophers' perception of the truth is so confused—so distorted—that it is lost labor trying to uncover it and incorporate it in the true system. But arguably Leibniz would not have seen matters in these terms. Here it may be helpful to consider, by way of analogy, Leibniz's famous simile concerning innate ideas and truths in the *New Essays*:

> For if the soul were like such a blank tablet then truths would be in us as the shape of Hercules is in a piece of marble when the marble is entirely neutral as to whether it assumes this shape or some other. However, if there were veins in the block which marked out the shape of Hercules rather than other shapes, then that block would be more determined to that shape and Hercules would be innate in it, in a way, even though labour would be required to expose the veins and to polish them into clarity, removing everything that prevents their being seen.[34]

Thus the figure of Hercules, in the second case, is indeed fully present in the block of marble, even though labor is required to bring it to the light of day. In the same way philosophical truth is indeed present in the systems of each of the sects, even though labor—that is, the labor of interpretation—is required to unearth it. There is surely no question in Leibniz's mind that such interpretive labor is worth the effort. Of course, as in the case of Leibniz's treatment of the skeptics, we may be inclined to think that the resulting interpretations are sometimes philosophically perverse, but that is a different matter.

33. E.g., *Monadology*, 83, G VI:621 (P 192).
34. NE Preface, A VI.vi (RB 52).

The thesis that Leibniz is fundamentally a Renaissance philosopher is no doubt controversial. In the first place, it might be argued that Leibniz is at least as much a Baroque philosopher as a Renaissance one: Deleuze's *The Fold: Leibniz and the Baroque* is dedicated to this theme. For readers trained in the Anglo-American analytic tradition, Deleuze's argument is obscure, but it is possible to see at least in broad terms what he has in mind; he is concerned with such distinctively Leibnizian doctrines as that every corporeal substance is endowed with a soul that unifies a body that consists of an aggregate of corporeal substances, each of which is in turn endowed with a soul that unifies an aggregate of corporeal substances, and so on to infinity. Turning to the work of a scholar who is more familiar to many of us, we might say that the Leibniz who emerges from Donald Rutherford's well-known study, *Leibniz and the Rational Order of Nature*, is a strikingly Baroque thinker inasmuch as his system exhibits fantastic complexity; Rutherford emphasizes the multiplicity of ontological levels in Leibniz, and argues that this very multiplicity is one of the features that make the actual world the best of all possible worlds.

To describe a philosopher's identity in terms that have artistic and architectural connotations or resonances is of course a somewhat dangerous enterprise. In order to counter possible misunderstandings, it should be emphasized that when Leibniz is called a Renaissance philosopher, the term is used in a rather strict sense to identify certain leading characteristics of the philosophy of a certain period; it is not intended to conjure up vague, if suggestive, analogies with the art and architecture of the age. The fact, if it is one, that Neoplatonism and syncretism are not confined to the thought of the Renaissance but have artistic and architectural analogues is not strictly relevant to the claim about Leibniz's philosophical identity.

The other objection comes from a different quarter: it is that by omitting Kant from the discussion I have understated the case for Leibniz's credentials as a modern philosopher. No one is likely to question Kant's own credentials as a modern philosopher, and from a certain vantage point the parallels between Kant and Leibniz can seem quite striking; there is of course the shared commitment to idealism and the distinction between appearance and reality. The fundamental continuity between Leibniz and Kant is the theme of Eberhard's polemic against the critical philosophy. Even Kant responded, not by dismissing the charge altogether, but rather by claiming that his *Critique of Pure Reason* may well be "the genuine apology for Leibniz."[35]

To do justice to this objection would require a book-length discussion rather than the closing paragraph of an essay. But we can at least sketch the outlines of a response, one that in a sense brings us back to our starting point. It is indeed possible to characterize at least some of the central doctrines of the two philosophers in a way that suggests strong continuity between them. But the appearance of continuity is actually misleading. For though Kant and Leibniz are both in a sense idealists, they reach their idealist conclusions by entirely different routes. Leibniz's idealism is founded in metaphysical considerations about the unity of substances, infinity, and the composition of the continuum; by contrast, as is well known, Kant reaches his conclusions by an epistemological route that was pioneered by Descartes, Locke, and Hume. Once again it is Leibniz's failure to appreciate the epistemological turn that makes it inappropriate to describe him as a modern philosopher in the sense in which that term is most widely used today.

35. H. E. Allison, trans., *The Kant-Eberhard Controversy* (Baltimore, Md.: Johns Hopkins University Press, 1973), 160.

Richard F. Hassing

7 Modern Turns in Mathematics and Physics

PREFACE: NATURAL SCIENCE AND ETHICAL DISPOSITION

The boundary between wishing and choosing is defined by the limits of our power. As Aristotle says, we can wish "for impossible things, like [bodily] immortality," but we actively choose what we judge to be within our power.[1] Differing accounts of physical nature—specifically, differing accounts of the relation between the sensible and the intelligible—convey different implications concerning what is within our power, and thus different implications for our pattern of choices in life and related dispositions of will and appetite.[2] Here lies the moral significance of early modern philosophy, and its offspring, classical physics. In Bacon and Descartes, culminating in Newton, *laws of nature* replace natural forms and ends as the fundamental intelligibles of physical science, and

1. "[Choice] is not wish, although it seems near to it; for choice cannot relate to impossible things ... but there can be wish for impossible things, like immortality .... But no one chooses such things, but only what he thinks can be brought about through his own efforts.... In general, choice seems to be concerned with the things that are up to us." *Nicomachean Ethics*, trans. Terence Irwin (Indianapolis, Ind.: Hackett, 1999), III.2.1111b20–30 (33–34), translation slightly modified [hereafter "*NE*"].

2. "The origin of action ... is choice, and that of choice is desire and reasoning with a view to an end. Hence choice cannot exist either without intellect and thinking, or without ethical disposition; for good action and its opposite cannot exist without thinking and character" (*NE* VI.2.1139a31–35 [87]). "Each state of character has its own ideas of the noble and the pleasant" (*NE* III.4.1113a32 [37]). Irwin translation slightly modified in both quotations. "Do you suppose that the regimes arise 'from an oak or rocks' and not from the types of character of the men in the cities, which, tipping the scale as it were, draw the rest along with them?" Plato, *Republic* 544d–e, trans. Allan Bloom, *The Republic of Plato* (New York: Basic, 1991), 222.

imply a vast expansion of human power to predict, control, and transform natural processes and bodies—for the prolongation of life and "the relief of the human estate."[3] The latest phase of this project is synthetic biology and its apparently radical possibilities for the transformation of human life. There is even talk of achieving bodily immortality—something impossible on grounds of Aristotle's natural science of organic form, or soul, and its correlative, necessarily corruptible matter.[4]

Because of these connections, between accounts of physical nature and their implications—real or imagined—for the limits of our power, our patterns of choice, and resulting dispositions of will, desire and imagination, I doubt that it is possible to separate completely natural philosophy and metaphysics from ethics.[5] This is especially problematic today due to the difficulty of accurately discerning the range and limitations of modern science. Accordingly, the following presentation and comparison of three accounts of nature (Aristotelian, classical, and quantum) owes much to the thought of William A. Wallace on Aristotelian physics, Richard Kennington on early modern philosophy, and Jacob Klein on modern symbolic mathematics.[6]

3. Bacon, *New Organon*, ed. Fulton H. Anderson (Indianapolis, Ind.: Bobbs-Merrill, 1960), II.52 (267); see also I.88, I.129, II.1–6 (86, 118–19, 121–27). See *Wisdom of the Ancients* XIII, Proteus, in *The Works of Francis Bacon*, ed. J. Spedding, R. L. Ellis, and D. Heath (London: Longmans and Co., 1857–70; reprinted in Stuttgart-Bad Canstatt: Frohmann-Holzboog, 1963), 6:725–26. In *The Advancement of Learning*, Bacon refers to "the dignity and excellency of knowledge and learning in that whereunto man's nature doth most aspire, which is immortality or continuance" (*Works* 3:318). See also Descartes, *Discourse on the Method*, Part 6 (AT VI 61–62, CSM I 142–43), and *Principles* (French) III.44 (AT IXB 155, CSM I 255).

4. Stanley Shostak, *Becoming Immortal: Combining Cloning and Stem-Cell Therapy* (Albany: State University of New York Press, 2002).

5. "Every desire [*orexis*] … is for the object of desire [*orekton*], which is the starting point of the practical intellect. . . .But desire or imagination [may be] right and [may be] not right. . . .What always causes motion is the object of desire [*orekton*]; but this object may be either the good or the apparent good" (*De Anima* III.10.433a16–29; author's translation).

6. The philosophical comprehension of modern science in relation to premodern physics and mathematics is a central focus of their work. See especially William A. Wallace, *From a Realist Point of View* (Lanham, Md.: University Press of America, 1983); Richard Kennington, *On Modern Origins: Essays in Early Modern Philosophy*, ed. Pamela Kraus and Frank Hunt (Lanham, Md.: Lexington, 2004); Jacob Klein, *Greek Mathematical Thought and the Origin of Algebra*, trans. Eva Brann (Cambridge, Mass.: MIT Press, 1968).

INTRODUCTION: TECHNICAL ANALYSIS AND PHILOSOPHICAL INTERPRETATION OF PHYSICS

The principal device employed in this essay is a comparison between classical physics, on the one hand, and Aristotelian physics, on the other. From the contrast between them, two fundamental features of classical physics are brought out: species-neutrality, which concerns the relation between the intelligible and the sensible—a standard topic in philosophy—and physico-mathematical secularism, which concerns the relation between mathematics and natural science, is not a standard topic, and is explained in the following.[7] In keeping with the Preface on ethics, I note as well an immoderate disposition or attitude to nature—we could call it *transformism*—that arises in connection with early modern philosophy and classical physics, and that continues on into genetic science today, despite great differences between contemporary biology and classical physics.

Classical physics and its associated conception of the material world are conveniently exemplified by Newton's theory of the solar system and its generalization to the forces-and-particles model of the universe, a vast mental construct at the heart of which is the concept of *trajectory*—the path in space of a body moved according to laws of motion and force, starting from a given position with a given velocity.[8] Certain basic and very general characteristics of this Newtonian account are found throughout all of prequantum physics, including thermodynamics, the field physics of Maxwell, the relativity physics of Einstein, and the recently developed non-linear dynamics or "chaos theory" originally discovered by Poincaré.[9] These characteristics are well described by Louis de Broglie,

7. I take the term "species-neutrality" from Kennington, *Modern Origins*, 25, and private conversations. I take the term "secularism" in relation to mathematical physics from François De Gandt: "Newton claimed to treat forces in a purely mathematical mode; by deferral, which in a sense turned out to be final, he left in suspense the properly philosophical or physical questions concerning the causes of gravitation and the ontological reality of force. This neutrality (or 'secularism') of centripetal force in face of the controversies on the cause of gravitation is the essential characteristic of the new science." *Force and Geometry in Newton's* Principia, trans. Curtis Wilson (Princeton, N.J.: Princeton University Press, 1995), x–xi. Physico-mathematical secularism concerns the question whether mathematical objects and physical objects differ and, specifically, whether it matters.

8. The starting position and velocity of the body are "given" in two senses: first, as stipulated or set down by the theoretical physicists in order to initiate the calculation of the trajectory under the equations of motion (to see how it behaves); second, as measured by the experimental physicists using instruments (like meter sticks and clocks).

9. Henri Poincaré, *Science and Method*, trans. Francis Maitland (New York: Dover, 1952),

as discussed in part 1, below, in which the basic theme of mathematics and nature, ancient and modern, is introduced. Part 2 presents the Newtonian trajectory calculation for gravitational force as a concrete example of de Broglie's general description of classical physics. Part 3 then elaborates the species-neutrality of Newton's law of gravitational force. Part 4 treats Newton's proposed generalization of the gravitational theory of the solar system to the forces-and-particles model of the universe, a mental construct with radical implications for the meaning of nature, one of which is transformism, discussed in part 5. Part 6 then turns to an alternative understanding of nature, Aristotelian physics, and presents the sharp contrast between it and classical physics. Throughout, by "classical physics" I mean all post-Aristotelian, mathematical, and experimental physics, with the exception of quantum theory. I treat the latter mainly indirectly, in part 7, by means of brief comparisons to Aristotelian and classical physics. Against the background of classical physics, quantum physics appears indeed to be a radical departure. But, as I argue in the following, classical physics is itself a radical departure from the preceding Aristotelian understanding of nature.[10] This is hardly to say that Aristotelian natural philosophy can provide the adequate philosophical compre-

---

67–69. Chaotic dynamics falls within classical physics because the mathematical models (non-linear differential or difference equations) hypothesized to account for certain unpredictable physical phenomena (e.g., a forced pendulum, turbulent flow, weather patterns) yield deterministic trajectories, as discussed in part 1, below. What distinguishes chaotic dynamics within classical physics is the following secondary but significant point concerning the initial data, i.e., the numerical values inputted to the model (the first sense of "given" in note 8) that specify a particular deterministic trajectory: due to sensitive dependence on initial conditions—a feature of non-linear equations—no matter how close the numerical values with which two modeled trajectories begin, they (the two trajectories) diverge so rapidly that even the most precise *empirical* measurement of initial data, e.g., on turbulent flow, a weather system, a forced pendulum (the second sense of "given" in note 8) would still contain within its tiny but necessarily finite error interval differences in numerical value that would determine trajectories so rapidly diverging that the physical process would *appear* random, i.e., under the same empirically measured conditions, very different physical changes occur no matter how precise the measurements. Thus, any systems in nature governed by non-linear interactions of this type (subject to sensitive dependence on initial conditions) would be fully deterministic but quite unpredictable in their behavior. Hence the name "deterministic chaos" is often used to describe the field of non-linear dynamics; see Heinz Georg Schuster, *Deterministic Chaos* (Weinheim: VCH Verlagsgesellschaft, 1989), 1–5. For a good nontechnical presentation, see David Ruelle, *Chance and Chaos* (Princeton, N.J.: Princeton University Press, 1991), also James Gleick, *Chaos: Making a New Science* (New York: Viking Penguin, 1987). See note 85, below, on the philosophical significance of chaos theory.

10. "The design of reality in classical physics contains greater enigmas than your so-called quantum mystery." Kurt Riezler, *Physics and Reality: Lectures of Aristotle on Modern Physics at an International Congress of Science* (New Haven, Conn.: Yale University Press, 1940), 25.

hension of quantum physics. The quantum phenomenon of non-locality or entanglement is a challenge for any philosophy of nature today, and, historically, the Aristotelian doctrine of the essential heterogeneity of terrestrial and celestial matter and motion was an error that impeded the progress of science.[11] Nevertheless, I believe that the Aristotelian back-

11. Non-locality or entanglement refers to a remarkable effect—instantaneous action at a distance to arbitrary range—predicted by quantum physics and highlighted in the famous 1935 exchange between Bohr and Einstein, Podolsky, and Rosen (EPR), over the completeness of the Copenhagen Interpretation. Einstein, Podolsky, and Rosen, "Can Quantum-Mechanical Description of Physical Reality Be Considered Complete?" *Physical Review* 47 (May 15, 1935): 777–80; Bohr, "Can Quantum-Mechanical Description of Physical Reality be Considered Complete?" *Physical Review* 48 (October 15, 1935): 696–702. We can get a sense of the issue against the background of Einstein's firmly classical conception of what physics is and ought to be: "I cannot seriously believe in [quantum mechanics] because the theory cannot be reconciled with the idea that physics should represent a reality in time and space, free from spooky actions at a distance." Einstein to Born, 1947, in Max Born, *The Born-Einstein Letters* (New York: Walker and Co., 1971), 158. "But on one supposition we should, in my opinion, hold absolutely fast: the real factual situation of system S_2 is independent of what is done with the system S_1, which is spatially separated from the former .... (One can escape from this conclusion only by either assuming that the measurement of S_1 (telepathically) changes the real situation of S_2 or by denying independent real situations as such to things which are spatially separated from each other. Both alternatives appear to me entirely unacceptable." Einstein, "Autobiographical Notes" (1949), in Paul Arthur Schilpp, *Albert Einstein Philosopher-Scientist* (La Salle, Ill.: Open Court, 1969), 1:85. What Einstein means is that physical influences from one position in space (that of S_1) can produce an effect at another position (that of S_2) only by propagating temporally through the intervening space. Einstein's special relativity limits the propagation speed to that of light. For Einstein (as for many), instantaneous action at a distance is by nature impossible. Schroedinger clearly foresaw the prediction of "spooky actions at a distance" entailed by his equation for the wave function. Writing shortly after the EPR-Bohr exchange, he introduced the term "entanglement": "When two systems, of which we know the states by the respective representatives, enter into temporary physical interaction due to known forces between them, and when after a time of mutual influence the systems separate again, then they can no longer be described in the same way as before, viz. by endowing each of them with a representative of its own [independent of the other]. I would not call that *one* but rather *the* characteristic trait of quantum mechanics, the one that enforces its entire departure from classical lines of thought. By the interaction, the two representatives (or ψ-functions) have become entangled. To disentangle them we must gather further information by experiment .... After reestablishing one representative by observation, the other one can be inferred simultaneously. In what follows the whole of this procedure will be called *the disentanglement*. Its sinister importance is due to its being involved in every measuring process .... Attention has recently been called [Einstein, Podolsky, and Rosen, *Phys. Rev.* 47 (1935): 777] to the obvious but very disconcerting fact that even though we restrict the disentangling measurements to *one* system, the representative obtained for the *other* system is by no means independent of the particular choice of observations which we select for that purpose and which by the way are *entirely* arbitrary. It is rather discomforting that the theory should allow a system to be steered or piloted into one or the other type of state at the experimenter's mercy in spite of his having no access to it. This paper does not aim at a solution of the paradox, it rather adds to it, if possible." Schroedinger, "Discussion of Probability Relations between Separated Systems," *Proceedings of the Cambridge Philosophical Society* 31, no. 1 (January 1936): 555–56. EPR correlations were confirmed by the Aspect

ground is valuable, perhaps indispensable, for the philosophical interpretation of physics, both classical and quantum. An example is presented in part 8, on physico-mathematical secularism.

PART 1—BASIC CHARACTERISTICS OF CLASSICAL PHYSICS: DE BROGLIE'S SYNOPTIC DESCRIPTION

Louis de Broglie provides a remarkable overview of classical physics in his 1955 *Physics and Microphysics*. The lengthy passage quoted below describes basic characteristics common to the three great theories of classical physics—mechanics, electromagnetism, and thermodynamics—as well as Einsteinian relativity and chaotic dynamics.

With [Cartesian] coordinates of space and time [x, y, z, t], classical mathematical physics was in a condition to represent in a precise way the succession of phenomena which our senses allow us to verify around us.

From that moment a way opened quite naturally before theoretical physics and it boldly entered upon it. It was thought that all evolution of the physical world must be represented by quantities [e.g., the position and velocity of a discrete particle, or the intensity of a continuous field] localized in space and varying in the course of time. These quantities must render it possible to describe completely the state of the physical world at every instant, and the description of the whole of nature could thus be given by figures and by motions in accordance with Descartes's programme. This description would be entirely carried out with the aid of differential equations ... enabling us to follow the localization and the evolution in the course of time of all the quantities defining the state of the physical world. A magnificent conception for its simplicity and confirmed by the successes which it has achieved for a long time! It sustained and orientated all the efforts of the great schools of mathematical physics of the nineteenth century.

Assuredly not all scientists agreed to this description of the world by figures and movements exactly in the same way. Some with lively and concrete imagination sought to picture the elements of the material world so as to make the phenomena observed by our senses flow from the existence and movements of

---

experiments in 1982. As of 2008, they have been detected to a range of 18 km with a speed that could be no less than ten thousand times that of light. D. Salart, A. Baas, C. Branciard, N. Gisin, H. Zbinden, "Testing Spooky Action at a Distance," *Nature* 454 (August 14, 2008): 861–64. On the now-problematic relation between this amazing effect and special relativity, see Tim Maudlin, *Quantum Non-Locality and Relativity* (Malden, Mass.: Blackwell, 2002).

atoms or of corpuscles too small to be directly observed; they wanted to dismantle the machine to see all the wheels functioning. Others, more cautious and above all endowed with a more abstract mind, wanted to content themselves by uniquely representing phenomena by means of directly measurable quantities, and mistrusted the hypotheses—in their eyes too speculative and useless—of the atomists. And whereas the atomists were thus boldly advancing, opening new ways and allowing science to make astonishing progress, the energeti[ci]sts, impeded by their more formal and timid methods, retained a certain advantage from the conceptional point of view when they denounced what was simple and a little naïve in the pictures invoked by their bold rivals. But, without being aware of it, both [the atomists and the energeticists] admitted a ... number of common postulates of which the future was to prove the frailty.

They were, in fact, agreed in admitting the validity of the abstract framework of space and time, the possibility of following the evolution of the physical world with the aid of quantities well located in space and varying continuously in the course of time, and the legitimacy of describing all phenomena by groups of differential equations. If the energeti[ci]sts, like Pierre Duhem, refused to allow the intervention everywhere of the "local movement" which could be represented by a displacement of parts, they fully admitted the consideration of "general movements" defined more abstractly by the variations of quantities in the course of time. In spite of their differences of view on the manner of carrying out this program, all theorists were then in agreement in representing the physical universe by well-defined quantities in the framework of space and time and subject to differential equations.

The differential equations ... of classical mathematical physics have the common character of allowing us to follow rigorously the whole evolution of the phenomena which they describe, if we suppose that there are certain known data relative to an initial state corresponding to a particular value of time. From this there was deduced the possibility of establishing a kind of inevitable interconnexion of all the phenomena, and thus was reached the conception of a universal determinism of physical phenomena. It is not my purpose to examine from the philosophical point of view the idea of universal determinism, and I have not to ask myself, for example, if the mind, which, after all is said and done, is the creator of mathematical physics, could recover its place in a nature conceived of in such a rigid manner. What is certain is that physical phenomena, in so far as they were exactly represented by the differential equations of classical physics, were submitted to a very precisely defined determinism.

Classical physics thus represented the whole physical universe as projected with absolute precision into the framework of space and time, evolving from it according to the laws of an inexorable necessity. It completely set aside the means used to arrive at a knowledge of the different parts of this vast mechanism for, if it recognized the existence of experimental errors, it only saw in them a result of the lack of precision of our senses and of the imperfection of our techniques, and accepted the possibility of reducing them indefinitely, at least in principle, by an adequate improvement in our methods. All these representations rested essentially on the classical ideas of space and time; for a long time they appeared sufficient for a description of the evolution of the material world.[12]

From this long passage, I distill three basic characteristics of all classical physics. Implicit therein is a notion of the relation between human mind in its knowing activity and the physical world that is to be known. The three characteristics and the associated mind-world relation stand opposed, on the one hand and in one way, to Aristotelian physics, and, on the other and in a different way, to quantum physics. The three are *continuity of space, time, and motion*; *spatio-temporal imageability of fundamental processes*; and *universal determinism*. Let us consider each in turn.

First, *continuity of space, time, and motion* is a shorthand formula for what de Broglie more accurately describes: continuity in the spatio-temporal variation of physical quantities such as the position, r(t), and velocity, v(t), of a discrete particle, or the intensity of a continuous (say, electrical) field, E(r,t).[13] As an apt example of what is physically meant by continuity, consider a body in motion that suddenly disappears from its present position and instantaneously reappears at a different position; this would be absurd, as in a dream. A planet, for example, does not change its distance from the sun by suddenly disappearing from its present position and instantaneously reappearing on an orbit with a different radius. The motions of planets and,

12. Louis de Broglie, *Physics and Microphysics*, trans. Martin Davidson (New York: Harper Torchbooks, 1960), 116–18. "Descartes's programme" refers, as de Broglie puts it, to "the possibility of describing natural phenomena by figures and by motion in the framework of space and time ... capable of allowing, always and everywhere the establishment of rigid and precise ties of inevitable succession amongst all natural phenomena" (110). This project is clearly set out by Descartes in *World* and *Principles of Philosophy*; *Principles* 2.64 provides an especially compact formulation: "The only principles that I accept or require in physics are those of geometry and pure mathematics; these principles explain all natural phenomena, and enable us to provide quite certain demonstrations regarding them" (AT VIIIA 78, CSM I 247), taking "geometry" here to mean his own analytical geometry applied to numerical magnitudes possessing physical dimensions, as described in Rule 14 (AT X 447–50, CSM I 62–64), and familiar today as length, mass, time, charge, etc.

13. On discrete particles; or, for most applications, positions and velocities of many particles, $r_1, \ldots r_N, v_1, \ldots v_N$. As N increases, probability theory is then brought to bear, e.g., in kinetic theory of gases and statistical mechanics.

more generally, the local motions of bodies, are continuous; there are no jumps. But jumps do occur among the electronic states or orbitals of atoms and molecules; it is part of their distinctive form of stability, as discussed in part 7, below. The classical continuity of space, time, and motion thus contrasts sharply with the state transitions of quantum physics.

What about Aristotle; does he deny continuity of local motion in favor of some sort of quantum jumps? He does not. For, in *Physics* IV.11, Aristotle says: "Since a moving thing is moved from something to something and every magnitude is continuous, the motion follows the magnitude; for through the magnitude's being continuous, the motion too is continuous, and through the motion the time." And again in *Physics* VI.1: "It is impossible for anything continuous to be made of indivisible things; for example, a line cannot be made of points, if the line is continuous and the point indivisible [*Metaphysics* 1016b27]. And it belongs to the same argument for a magnitude, a time, and a motion to be composed of and divided into indivisibles, or none of them."[14] Finally, in *Physics* VI.2: "every magnitude is divisible into magnitudes (for it has been shown that it is impossible for anything continuous to be made of uncut-able parts, and every magnitude is continuous)."[15] Therefore, the opposition between classical physics and that of Aristotle concerning space, time, and motion must be on a different level, namely, that of the relation between human mind in its knowing activity and the physical world that is to be known.

What must be appreciated in de Broglie's exemplary expression of the self-understanding of classical physics is that mind is there looking not directly at the world but rather at the products of its own constructive activity: elaborate structures of real-numerical variable magnitudes of which the variables, x, y, z, and constants, a, b, c, etc., of Descartes's *Geometry*, essentially our analytic geometry, are the prototype. The material world external to this sophisticated mental artifice is admitted as *known* only guardedly, under the carefully controlled conditions of the experiment: does the numerical result of the empirical measurement *match* the mathematically predicted numerical value to within current limits of experimental precision (the error intervals)? If so, then the conceptual structure of variable quantities possessing physical dimensions, the equations and graphs derived from the laws of physics, that is, the

14. *Physics* IV.11.219a11–13, VI.1.231a24–25, b18–20; trans. Joe Sachs, *Aristotle's* Physics: *A Guided Study* (New Brunswick, N.J.: Rutgers University Press, 1995), 121, 147–48.

15. *Physics* VI.2.232a23–25 (149).

model that has been proposed by us to nature is accepted as corroborated.[16] If not, then more adequate models based on revised equations or new laws are to be constructed; we are on our way into the standard philosophy of hypothetico-deductive science that is available in many textbooks. For our purposes here, let us note that the mind-world relation characteristic of physics has two components, the mathematical model and the extra-mathematical reality to be modeled: they "transact" in the "common currency" of number, calculated and measured.

The world-conception of classical physics described by de Broglie assumes the progressive improvement of the numerical precision of experimental measurements, and thus of the match between filtering mind and the filtered ("true") world. It thus assumes the complete adequacy of real number to nature, as discussed in part 8, below. The point for now is simply that this is not the type of mind-world relation that is found in Aristotle's *Physics*. There, intellect looks directly through the senses at the kinds of beings that make up the world: the elements (the land, the waters, the weather), plants, animals, artifacts and the human beings that produce them, and, above it all, the celestial bodies, which appear to move so differently from all the rest. Each of these beings is a whole whose parts are related in various ways, and all are subject to being moved, to acting and being acted upon, in various ways according to the causes judged to be necessary in order to fit speech to the phenomena, beginning with ourselves who bespeak the phenomena.[17] Aristotle's way of thinking together the objects of his science of nature is as follows: "what moves is a mover of something moved, and what is moved is moved by something moving it, and there is no motion apart from things

16. "Mathematical physics ... is bent on *matching* the consequences derived mathematically from hypotheses with observations dictated by these hypotheses.... It is not its business to say what, for example, gravitation, or electromagnetism, or energy *is*, except by establishing in a symbolic-mathematical formula the relations that bind these entities (if it is at all permissible to use this word) to observable and mathematically describable magnitudes." Jacob Klein, "On Precision," in *Jacob Klein: Lectures and Essays*, ed. Robert B. Williamson and Elliott Zuckerman (Annapolis, Md.: St. John's College Press, 1985), 305–6, and, above all, Kant: "reason has insight only into that which it produces after a plan of its own, and ... it must not allow itself to be kept, as it were, in nature's leading-strings but must itself show the way with principles of judgment based upon fixed laws, constraining nature to give answer to questions of reason's own determining." *Critique of Pure Reason*, trans. Norman Kemp Smith (New York: St. Martin's Press, 1965), B xiii (20).

17. See especially *Parts of Animals* I.1.639a1–41a18 for the self-referential character of Aristotle's natural philosophy.

[*ouk esti de tis kinêsis para ta pragmata*]."[18] Motion, that which is mobile, and causes of motion must be thought together, along with the time and (in local motion, increase and decrease) the magnitude traversed. Finally, for Aristotle, the meaning of physical motion (*kinêsis*) cannot be adequately expressed without using the words most characteristic of his understanding of nature: act and potency, *energeia* and *dunamis*:

> motion is the actuality of the potentially being as such [*hê tou dynamei ontos entelecheia hê toiouton kinêsis estin*].... it cannot be placed in an unqualified way either under the potentiality or under the actuality of things [*oute eis dunamin tôn ontôn oute eis energeian*].... a motion [then] is sort of an actuality [*energeian men tina einai*] ... such as we have stated, difficult to grasp but capable of existing.[19]

This is far from the representation of motion as position, x(t), velocity, v(t) = dx/dt, etc. There, the symbols (x, v, t, dx, dt) possess a kind of objectivity, or being in their own right, deriving sense or meaning through their membership in the system of signs constituted by the axioms and binary operations of algebra prior to, and independently of, any possible application to the material and mobile beings that we see with our eyes and point at with our fingers.[20] For us, there *is* motion—mathematical "motion"—apart from things.[21]

18. *Physics* III.1.200b32–34 (73). The passage goes on to say that there is no change or motion outside the categories of substance, quantity, quality, or place. See also *Physics* II.2.193b23–194a15 and *Metaphysics* VI.1.1025b29–26a4: mathematical objects are separable from motion (*kinêsis*) and matter, but motion is not separable from matter.

19. *Physics* III.1.201a11–12, III.2.201b29–30, 202a2; trans. Hippocrates G. Apostle, *Aristotle's* Physics (Grinnell, Iowa: Peripatetic Press, 1980), 43–45.

20. "Nothing but the internal connection of all the concepts, their mutual relatedness, their subordination to the total edifice of science, determines for each of them a *univocal* sense [cf. *Metaphysics* IX.6.1048a37-b10, on the analogical sense of *energeia*] and makes accessible to the understanding their only relevant, specifically scientific content.... Two things ... constitute the heart of the symbolic procedure: ... identify[ing] the object represented [e.g., "two"] with the means of its representation ["2"], and ... replac[ing] the real determinateness of an object with a *possibility* of making it determinate, such as would be expressed by a sign [e.g., x] which, instead of *illustrating* a determinate object [e.g., thirty units], would *signify* possible determinacy [e.g., in an equation, 2x + a = b]." Klein, *Greek Mathematical Thought*, 121, 123. "Because the mere perceptual content of the signs involved in symbolic mathematics [e.g., 2, x] is insufficient to establish their mathematical significance, this significance must somehow be stipulated by the calculative method employed [the rule-governed method of designating and manipulating sense perceptible signs to perform 'calculations' with general mathematical objects], only after which the sense-perceptible signs can become known as 'symbols.'" Burt Hopkins, *The Origin of the Logic of Symbolic Mathematics: Edmund Husserl and Jacob Klein*, §140. An excellent summary of algebra for physicists is provided by Richard P. Feynman, Robert B. Leighton, and Matthew Sands, *The Feynman Lectures on Physics* (Reading, Mass.: Addison-Wesley, 1963), vol. 1, chap. 22.

21. "We commence with a chapter on *Motion*, a subject totally independent of the

Being detached or separate from material being, the mental apparatus of our formal-symbolic mathematics is like a universal and demiurgic tool that, as such, is separate from (not bound into, not a part of) the material to be worked on and, therefore, is available in advance for application to any material. In his review of Jacob Klein's *Lectures and Essays*, with its distinctive emphasis on the Greek understanding of number, *arithmos*, Richard Kennington provided the following apt formulation: "The Cartesian *numerus*, in contrast to the *arithmos*, cannot function as the bond of our world-relatedness; or rather its lack of such relatedness permits what is other than man to be understood as 'world' and Cartesian man to be world-less."[22] Thus, whatever we are, we are free and powerful. I note that, according to Klein, it is Plato for whom *arithmos* is the bond of our world-relatedness; for Aristotle, it is soul.[23] But Descartes transforms soul, too.

A sign of the difference between Aristotle's physics and classical physics is de Broglie's reference to "coordinates [x, y, z, t . . .] the abstract framework [the classical ideas] of space and time." As Klein states it at the conclusion of his account of the concept of number in Descartes:

> In Descartes' thinking, the dignity of representing the substantial "being" of the corporeal world accrues to extension precisely by reason of its *symbolic* objectivity within the framework of the *mathesis universalis*. Only at this point [Descartes's invention of general magnitude as the fundamental term of physics] has the conceptual basis of "classical" physics, which has since been called "Euclidean space," been created. This is the foundation on which Newton will raise the structure of his mathematical science of nature.[24]

---

existence of *Matter* and *Force*." William Thomson and Peter Guthrie Tait, *Treatise on Natural Philosophy* (Oxford: Clarendon Press, 1857), v. Thomson and Tait was a standard textbook of physics in the nineteenth century. A contemporary textbook is that of David Halliday and Robert Resnick, *Physics* (New York: John Wiley and Sons, 1978): "Mechanics, the oldest of the physical sciences, is the study of the motion of objects. . . . When we describe motion we are dealing with that part of mechanics called *kinematics*. When we relate motion to the forces associated with it and to the properties of the moving objects, we are dealing with *dynamics*" (30).

22. Richard Kennington, book review of Jacob Klein, *Lectures and Essays*, *Review of Metaphysics* 41, no. 1 (September 1987): 144–49, here 147. According to Klein, it is Plato for whom *arithmos* is the bond of our world-relatedness (*Lectures and Essays*, chap. 3). For Aristotle, rational soul is the bond, e.g., *De Anima* III.5.429a27, III.8.431b21.

23. E.g., *De Anima* III.5.429a27, III.8.431b21.

24. Klein, *Greek Mathematical Thought*, 211. The quotation marks indicate that "Euclidean space" is inaccurately so called in the sense that Euclidean geometry is not coordinate

This concludes my comment on the first of the three basic characteristics of classical physics: continuity of space, time, and motion.

The second basic characteristic is *spatio-temporal imageability of fundamental processes.* It means that we can always project in our mathematical imagination and express on paper Cartesian spatial coordinate axes (x, y, z) and then picture the relevant physical quantities—magnitudes with dimensions of length, mass, charge, time, and their combinations—varying in that space with time, t. In particular, we can know, from the data and the model, what is going on *inside* any physical system—an atom, an organism, a laboratory (e.g., two-slit interference) apparatus—even though the mind is looking mainly at the products of its own activity![25] We can imagine, for example, a particle with a precise position given by its Cartesian coordinates, x(t), y(t), z(t), and precise velocity with components, $v_x(t)$, $v_y(t)$, $v_z(t)$, for any time, t, moving on what is thereby defined as its *trajectory.* Or we can imagine (slightly more abstractly) the intensity of an electric field, **E**(x, y, z, t), varying in both spatial position, x, y, z, and time, t. This way of using the mind is assumed to be fully adequate to the nature of things; the common currency of number or, more precisely, numerical magnitude is taken as sufficient for all transactions between the mathematics (equations and calculation) and the physics (measurement and matching). This assumption does not entail the rather crude Cartesian *identification* of physical objects with mathematical objects, but rather the more sophisticated assumption that, whatever may be the differences between mathematicals and physicals, such differences can make no difference for the conduct of our (now thoroughly mathematical) physics.[26] In

(numerical) geometry—that is the achievement of Descartes (and Fermat). See Klein, "The World of Physics and the 'Natural' World," in *Lectures and Essays*, 21. In post-Newtonian physics, however, "Euclidean space" is often used in contradistinction to coordinate spaces with other metrics or distance functions, e.g., the Minkowski space of special relativity and the Riemannian space of general relativity. Descartes's coordinatization of geometry thus opens doors to remarkable physical theories whose development would be difficult to imagine without the enabling Cartesian foundation.

25. De Broglie's description of the atomists is apt: "they wanted to dismantle the machine to see all the wheels functioning." With the turn of the nineteenth century, the more phenomenological and cautious energeticists (Mach, Duhem, Poincaré, Ostwald) were vanquished by the rapidly mounting body of molecular theory corroborated by experimental evidence, e.g., Einstein on Brownian motion. See Jean Perrin, *Les Atomes* (Paris: Librarie Felix Alcan, 1913).

26. "I conceive its [matter's] extension . . . not as an accident, but as its true form and essence." Descartes, *The World*, chap. 6, (AT XI 36, CSM I 92). "I recognize no matter in corpo-

other words, the natural-philosophic question of the difference between mathematical objects and physical objects can be suspended; let it be a private matter. This is what I mean by "physico-mathematical secularism," the subject of part 8, below.

The third basic characteristic, *universal determinism*, means that, through the equations of motion, the numerical values of the relevant quantities at one instant of time, t, or position, x, in space enable us to calculate the values of those quantities at the next instant of time, t + Δt, or adjacent position in space, x + Δx, and the next, on into future time and distant space. No other type of causality, beyond initial data or boundary conditions and equations of motion, is needed to account for all natural phenomena. But, as should now be clear, this determinism—first made explicit by Laplace—is based in the mathematics, that is, it is a feature of the mathematical description.[27] Its alleged universality in physics is a philosophical claim inspired by particular instances of success, to wit, *to the extent that* the behavior of a physical system, for example, the solar system, is found by observation or experiment to match the mathematical predictions of the model to within given limits of precision, we say that the physical system thereby modeled is deterministic. The successes of classical physics on various classes of deterministic phenomena (celestial mechanics, electromagnetism, thermodynamics, vibrations and waves in material media) were stunning, but they were always empirical and particular. And so the claim for *universal* determinism (of *all* natural phenomena) was a matter of the disposition and imagination of scientists and philosophers, not scientific warrant.

To state essential conclusions thus far: within the self-understanding of classical physics, strong claims (for continuity, imageability, determinism) about the transparency and, as we shall see, the malleability of nature are made based on (1) the mind's view of its own conceptual constructions and (2) a disposition to ascend from particular scientific results to universal philosophic claims. Let us illustrate the classical conception of the physical world by reviewing the basic logic of the Newtonian calculation of the trajectory of a body moved under gravitational force. This will exemplify de Broglie's account, enable us to understand species-neutrality,

real things apart from that which the geometers call quantity." *Principles* 2.64 (AT VIIIA 78–79, CSM I 247); also *Principles* 4.187 (AT VIIIA 314–15, CSM I 279).

27. Laplace, *A Philosophical Essay on Probabilities*, trans. F. W. Truscott and F. L. Emory (New York: Dover, 1951), 4, 6.

and prepare the generalization from the Newtonian theory of the solar system to the forces-and-particles model of the entire universe.

PART 2—EXAMPLE: ESSENTIAL LOGIC OF THE NEWTONIAN TRAJECTORY CALCULATION

Our goal in this section is not to become proficient classical celestial "mechanics" (able to solve actual problems of motion in the solar system) but rather to be able to *see the reason* for Newton's key achievement: the predictive calculation of the trajectory of a body in motion under gravitational force, for example, a planet or a comet around the sun. To this end, I follow not the current textbook approach (oriented to the training of successful researchers) but the more insightful description of Einstein and Infeld.[28]

The problem to be solved is this: given by empirical observation the position, $\mathbf{r}_0$, and velocity, $\mathbf{v}_0$, of a planet or comet relative to the sun at a given initial time, t_0, to derive the position and velocity, $\mathbf{r}_1$, $\mathbf{v}_1$, at a later time, t_1, without further recourse to observation.[29] The principles governing the calculation are two: Newton's second law of motion, and his law of universal gravitational force. We must examine the role played by each and recognize the crucial significance of the gravitational force law.

The conceptual framework of space is, in this case, the two- dimensional plane with the sun, of mass M, represented at the origin of coordinates.[30] We represent the initial position and velocity vectors, $\mathbf{r}_0$, $\mathbf{v}_0$, of the planet or comet, of mass m, as shown in figure 1. Can anything at all be predicted from our two pieces of initial data? The answer is, yes, approximately. Knowing $\mathbf{v}_0$, the initial velocity, we can *estimate* the

28. Albert Einstein and Leopold Infeld, *The Evolution of Physics* (New York: Simon and Schuster, 1968), 9–30. This derivation will be essential for part 7, on the breakdown of the trajectory concept.

29. We use the standard vector notation for position and velocity in Cartesian coordinates, x, y, z, and time, t: $\mathbf{r}(t) = x(t)\mathbf{i} + y(t)\mathbf{j} + z(t)\mathbf{k}$, and $\mathbf{v}(t) = (dx/dt)\mathbf{i} + (dy/dt)\mathbf{j} + (dz/dt)\mathbf{k}$, where $\mathbf{i}$, $\mathbf{j}$, $\mathbf{k}$ are unit vectors along the x, y, z axes. The initial position and velocity, $\mathbf{r}(t_0) \equiv \mathbf{r}_0$, $\mathbf{v}(t_0) \equiv \mathbf{v}_0$, are the "known data relative to an initial state corresponding to a particular [initial] value of time [t_0]" referred to by de Broglie.

30. Angular momentum, $\mathbf{L} = \mathbf{r} \times m\mathbf{v}$, is conserved in the motion of a body of mass, m, under any central force, thus for an inverse-square gravitational force. Therefore, the position, $\mathbf{r}$, and the velocity, $\mathbf{v}$, of the moved body must lie in a fixed plane. (I am assuming the masses are known, a big assumption, in order to focus on the most essential point.)

FIG. 1

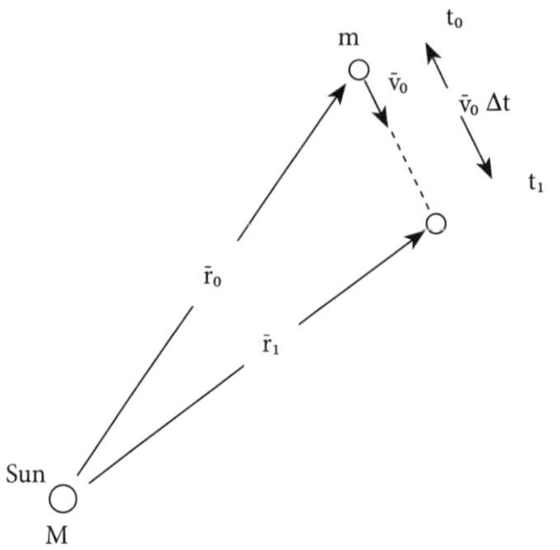

position, $\mathbf{r}_1$, of the planet or comet a short time later, at time t_1, by taking its motion as rectilinear (even though it is necessarily curvilinear due to the gravitational force of the sun). This is erroneous, but we can make the error as small as we like by making the time interval, $\Delta t = t_1 - t_0$, smaller and smaller. So we "move" the planet or comet, that is, we move the point that represents it in our figure, in the direction of $\mathbf{v}_0$ a distance that represents $\mathbf{v}_0\Delta t$ in the solar system. For example, if we are studying the motion of Mars, whose mean orbital speed is 24.1 km/sec, then, picking $\Delta t = 1$ sec, we would plot its new position at a distance in the direction of vo representing 24.1 km in space from its initial position. We have now derived from the initial data, $\mathbf{r}_0$, $\mathbf{v}_0$, the approximate position, $\mathbf{r}_1$, of the body at time t_1.

But what is the new velocity, $\mathbf{v}_1$? As noted, a planet or comet under the gravitational attraction of the sun moves on a curved path (it must, by Newton's first law). Thus the direction of the velocity vector that we use to represent its motion is constantly changing. To estimate the new velocity, $\mathbf{v}_1$, at time t_1, we must find the change in velocity of the body, $\Delta\mathbf{v}_{01}$, that occurs during the first time interval, Δt, from t_0 to t_1. Then we can construct, by vector addition, $\mathbf{v}_1 = \mathbf{v}_0 + \Delta\mathbf{v}_{01}$. This would complete our prediction of the new position *and* velocity of the planet or comet a short time, Δt, into the future. This may seem like a small step, because

Δt is small, for example, one second, but if we can repeat this procedure for the next time interval, from t_1 to t_2, deriving $\mathbf{r}_2$ and $\mathbf{v}_2$ from $\mathbf{r}_1$ and $\mathbf{v}_1$, and so on, then we will have made a world-historic revolution in human thought. The focus of our attention is, therefore, on $\Delta\mathbf{v}_{01}$: how is it determined? This is where Newton's law of universal gravitation comes into play; it is the crucial link in the logic of the trajectory calculation—linking $\Delta\mathbf{v}_{01}$ to $\mathbf{r}_0$—without which our procedure would stop dead after the estimate of r1.

The second law of motion relates the net force on a body of mass m to its resulting acceleration or time rate of change of velocity: $\mathbf{F} = m\Delta\mathbf{v}/\Delta t$, in the limit as $\Delta t \rightarrow 0$. But what *is* the net force on the planet or comet under study? It is the law of gravitation that relates the known distance, $\mathbf{r}_0$, to the net force exerted by the sun on the planet or comet at time t_0.[31] Thus combining the law of gravitation with the second law of motion enables the determination of the (approximate) change in velocity, $\Delta\mathbf{v}_{01}$. The direction of $\Delta\mathbf{v}_{01}$ is that of the force, toward the sun, and its magnitude is calculated as follows (figure 2): $-GMm/r_0^2 = m\Delta v_{01}/\Delta t$. Therefore, $\Delta v_{01} = -GM\Delta t/r_0^2$, in which all the quantities on the right hand side are known. Having thus determined $\Delta\mathbf{v}_{01}$, we have by vector addition, $\mathbf{v}_1 = \mathbf{v}_0 + \Delta\mathbf{v}_{01}$.

The last step in the calculational procedure is to transfer ("move") the vector $\mathbf{v}_1$ parallel to itself (preserving both its magnitude and its direction) from position $\mathbf{r}_0$ to position $\mathbf{r}_1$. We have completed our task: we have derived $\mathbf{r}_1$, $\mathbf{v}_1$ from $\mathbf{r}_0$, $\mathbf{v}_0$. We can repeat this algorithm: From $F_1 = -GMm/r_1^2$ derive $\Delta\mathbf{v}_{12}$, and then construct $\mathbf{v}_2 = \mathbf{v}_1 + \Delta\mathbf{v}_{12}$, plotting $\mathbf{r}_2$, $\mathbf{v}_2$, at time t_2, etc. *Thereby we trace out the orbit or trajectory of the body* moving under the gravitational force of the sun, without further recourse to observational data. After performing the calculations, we ask, does the prediction match future observation? For example, does the planet Mars or Halley's comet in fact appear in the night sky when and where we predicted it would? Within the limits of observational precision, yes, it does.[32]

31. In present-day notation, $\mathbf{F}(t_0) = -\mathbf{r}_0 GMm/r_0^3$. For a discussion of Newton's own distinctive kinematic-infinitesimal geometry in relation to the analytic-algebraic mathematics that quickly followed see my "The Exemplary Career of Newton's Mathematics," *The St. John's Review* 44, no. 1 (1997): 73–93. The differences between the two are not relevant for present purposes.

32. Thus our calculations have something to do with what is going on in the heavens. But

FIG. 2

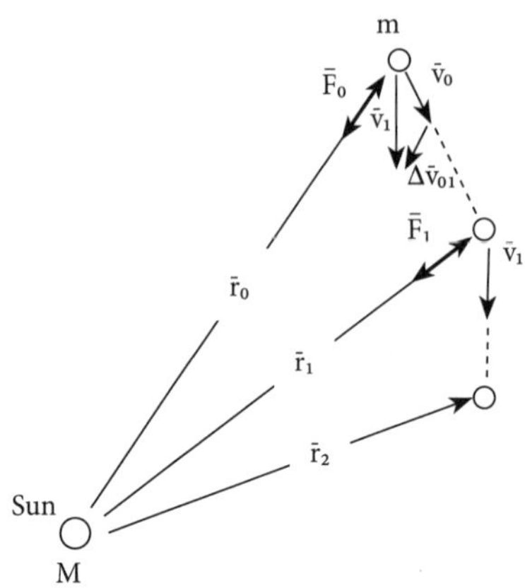

In this account of the concept of *trajectory*, I have suppressed technical details (energy and angular-momentum considerations, non-linearity, the many-body problem, and calculus) involved in actual trajectory analysis in order to display what is essential to the kind of thinking characteristic of classical physics. In the following, I bring out two features of this Newtonian account that are not explicitly discussed by de Broglie, and that are of great importance from the side of the philosophy of nature, namely, (1) species-neutrality and (2) physico-mathematical secularism. With a view to the latter, let us look at the last step of the above procedure (in figure 2): the velocity vector (defined by its magnitude, i.e., speed, and its direction) can be detached from one position, $\mathbf{r}_0$ (where we performed the vector sum, $\mathbf{v}_0 + \Delta\mathbf{v}_{01}$), and "moved" on our plotting paper (always parallel to itself to keep it the same vector) to another position, $\mathbf{r}_1$. This is vivid testimony to our ability to conceive "motion apart from things" and our possession of an ingenious art of solving certain problems of local motion and force. Let us note, however, that this physico-mathematical art knows neither of Aristotle's act and potency, nor of Heisenberg's uncertainty principle.

"the heaven, even the heavens are the Lord's" (Ps 115:16). Have we (following Newton) entered into the mind of God? Is this belief the inspiration for the remarkable claims that we see in the following?

PART 3—SPECIES-NEUTRALITY: A NEW TYPE OF RELATION BETWEEN SENSIBLE AND INTELLIGIBLE

It is important to appreciate the remarkable character of Newton's law of gravitational force. In his own words, "there is a power of gravity pertaining to all bodies, proportional to the several quantities of matter which they contain … [and] inversely as the square of the distance."[33] Normally, the way a body moves or behaves is intimately related to what kind or species of body it is, as known through ordinary sense perception. Pigs do not fly, sparrows do not oink. Accordingly, the way in which two bodies interact depends on what kind each is. A dog and a cat interact in a certain way (the dog approaches to a critical distance at which the cat scratches its nose, then it rapidly recedes), a cat and a mouse in another (the cat approaches, the mouse recedes, but maybe not fast enough, and it gets caught and suffers a painful death). The traditional (Aristotelian and scholastic) name for the essential relation between the source of activity (form) and the supporting structure (matter) in a body is hylomorphism. It is reflected in assertions like the following in Aristotle: "Matter is among the relative things: for a different form, a different matter." "All things that change have matter, but there is distinct matter in distinct things."[34] Quite generally, in Aristotle's science of nature, the intelligible principles—natural form and common sensible matter—that account for the behavior of the sensed particulars (a cat, a tree, a stone) are species-typical or species-specific. Form, matter, and privation are indeed universal principles of natural things, but they are predicated of the different kinds (e.g., plants, animals, human beings) analogically, not univocally: "We cannot say that all things have the same elements and principles, except by analogy, just as if one were to say that there are three principles: form, privation, and matter. But each of these is different as it concerns each class of things."[35]

Newton's law of gravitation does not exemplify the Aristotelian, species-specific type of relation between sensible and intelligible.[36] The

33. Newton, *Mathematical Principles of Natural Philosophy*, trans. Andrew Motte and Florian Cajori (New York: Greenwood Press, 1962), Book III, Prop. 7 and Cor. 2.

34. *Physics* II.2.194b9 (53), *Metaphysics* XII.2.1069b25 (198); see also *Physics* VIII.1.251a12–13.

35. *Metaphysics* XII.4.1070b17–20 (200), translation slightly modified. The term "body" is thus, for Aristotle, not univocal, as it is for us, but analogical.

36. The general idea of laws of nature as species-neutral principles was pioneered by Bacon; see *New Organon*, I.51, I.66, I.88, II.3, II.35 (53, 63, 86, 122, 186).

equation "F = –GMm/r²" expresses an intelligible principle of local motion in nature that is indifferent or neutral to the kind, size, shape, internal structure, and function of the two interacting bodies. Newton's gravitational law is thus species-neutral, as are the terms (mass, distance) of which it is composed. For all bodies—celestial and terrestrial, natural and artificial, living and nonliving—possess mass and relative position, also velocity, acceleration, momentum, kinetic energy, etc.[37] All the algebraic terms of classical mechanics are species-neutral. They are understood univocally, not, like form and matter, analogically. The algebraicization of science thus entails the homogenization of our thoughts and therewith a certain detachment of the resulting concepts from things. Klein describes this in an important passage of *Greek Mathematical Thought and the Origin of Algebra*:

[In the] "new" science ... nothing but the internal connection of all the concepts, their mutual relatedness, their subordination to the total edifice of science, determines for each of them a *univocal* [*eindeutig*] sense and makes accessible to the understanding their only relevant, specifically scientific content.... Thus every one of the newly obtained concepts [e.g., quantity, body, mass, motion, velocity, acceleration, momentum, force, work, energy] is determined by *reflection on the total context of that concept*. Every concept of the "new" science belongs to a new conceptual dimension. The special intentionality of each such concept is no longer a problem: it is indifferently the same for all concepts; it is a medium beyond reflection [*sie ist das allgemeine, von der Reflexion nicht mehr erreichte Medium*], in which the development of the scientific world takes place.[38]

Klein speaks here of the new concepts as being determined by reflection on their "internal connection . . . their mutual relatedness," namely, according to those axioms and operations of algebra, then according to the physical dimensions that they bear (e.g., mass, length, time, charge), and finally—an external connection—according to the operations of

37. Spinoza expresses succinctly the sense of the common (species-neutral) properties of what will become classical physics: "That which is common to all [bodies] ... and which is equally in a part and in the whole [e.g., Cartesian extension, Newtonian mass], does not constitute the essence [the Aristotelian natural form; *Metaphysics* 1030a12] of any particular thing.... Those things which are common to all ... cannot be conceived except adequately." *Ethics*, II.37, 38 (87, translation slightly modified).

38. Klein, *Greek Mathematical Thought*, 120–21.

measurement (e.g., our handling of scales, meter sticks, clocks) whereby they can be specified as, for example, 110 kilograms, 330 meters, 33 seconds. This is a new conceptual medium beyond the old (ancient and medieval) type of reflection on the "special intentionality" of each word. Consider, for example, the word "quantity," Greek *to poson*, Latin *quantum*, thus, more accurately (because more concretely), "the quantified," which expression points beyond itself and outside our thought to the quantified things. This ("quantified," *poson*, *quantum*) cannot be said univocally of the two kinds, discrete number, *arithmos*, and continuous magnitude, *megethos*, but only analogically. These two kinds of the quantified fall in one and the same category of being because they are both divisible into parts in such a way that both (*arithmos* and *megethos*) accept the equal and unequal (greater than, less than); but, whereas magnitude is infinitely divisible into parts having boundaries that can touch, number is finitely divisible into indivisibles—the units—lacking boundaries that can touch.[39]

This old type of reflection, on the ways "our thought, and also our words, signify or intend their [different kinds of] objects" would preclude the homogenization of the heterogeneity of discrete and continuous into the one univocal concept of the arithmetical continuum, or the real number system.[40] Similarly, for the old versus the new reflection on the words "body" (*soma*) and "motion" (*kinêsis*), and so forth, in natural science.[41]

We have gone from the species-neutrality of classical physics, to the univocalization of analogies, and homogenization of heterogeneities, in both mathematics and physics. We thus return to an important result first noted in our reading of de Broglie: mind's detachment from the world through the algebraicization of thinking.

A further implication derivable from Newton's gravitational law is the use of points to model physical processes. Since all bodies and their

39. Aristotle, *Metaphysics* V.13, *Categories* VI. The even and the odd belong to number, but not to magnitude. A square magnitude can always be divided into two equal square magnitudes, but a square number can never be divided into two equal square numbers.

40. Klein, *Greek Mathematical Thought*, 118.

41. In "The World of Physics and the 'Natural' World," Klein seems to say that in fact the late scholastics had drifted into this new conceptual medium without knowing it and thus without knowing how to use it to maximum effect, which involves turning the mind in a new direction and questioning in a new way. *Lectures and Essays*, 3, 6–7.

parts, regardless of kind, size, internal structure, and function, have mass and attract each other pairwise according to $F = -GMm/r^2$, as long as the spatially extended bodies in a gravitational system do not bump into each other, they can be represented mathematically as unextended points: *mass* points. Recall that, according to Aristotle, in *Physics* VI.4, "every changing thing is necessarily divisible."[42] An unextended, indivisible point, therefore, could be moved only *per accidens* by being in or on something that is itself *per se* movable (movable through itself), which, therefore, has an interior and is necessarily extended. A physical-material point is, on this account, a contradiction in terms. But for the solution of many problems in the physics of gravitational systems, this piece of natural philosophy is not needed. In these cases, the spatial extendedness, the coherent shapes and sizes of bodies do not matter. And, in other cases (e.g., the study of gases, liquids, and solid bodies), where they do matter, perhaps they can be accounted for by reasoning that is in some way analogous to the treatment of the solar system. Indeed Newton says, "Nature is exceedingly simple and conformable to herself. Whatever reasoning holds for greater motions [e.g., of the solar system] should hold for lesser ones [of the particles of bodies] as well."[43] This postulate—of the multi-level identity of nature whereby there is no natural scale of size—makes possible Newton's remarkable generalization of his gravitational theory.[44]

42. *Physics* VI.4.234b10 (153).

43. "Unpublished Conclusion of the *Principia*," in A. R. and M. B. Hall, *Unpublished Scientific Papers of Isaac Newton*, 333. A more compressed formulation (that omits explicit reference to greater and lesser motions) is given in Rule III of the Rules of Reasoning in Philosophy: "nor are we to recede from the analogy of Nature, which is wont to be simple, and always consonant to itself." Since we find that sensible bodies possess hardness, impenetrability, mobility, and inertia, "we conclude the least particles of all bodies to be also all extended, and hard, and impenetrable, and movable, and endowed with their proper inertia. And this is the foundation of all philosophy.... Lastly ... we must ... universally allow that all bodies whatsoever [both big visible planets and tiny invisible particles] are endowed with a principle of mutual gravitation." *Mathematical Principles*, Book III, 398–400. Finally, *Opticks*, Query 31 (New York: Dover, 1952), 375–406, esp. 394 and 397. For the Cartesian version of "the analogy of Nature," see Descartes, *Principles of Philosophy*, 4.20: "No one who uses his reason will, I think, deny the advantage of using what happens in large bodies, as perceived by our senses, as a model for our ideas about what happens in tiny bodies which elude our senses merely because of their small size. This is much better than explaining matters by inventing all sorts of strange objects which have no resemblance to what is perceived by the senses <such as 'prime matter,' 'substantial forms' ...>. " (CSM I 287).

44. The phrase "multi-level identity of nature" is Laurens Laudan's. See Laudan, "The

PART 4—REDUCTIONIST GENERALIZATION: NEWTON'S UNIVERSAL FORCES-AND-PARTICLES MODEL

The species-neutrality of the law of gravitational force facilitates Newton's remarkable generalization from his particular gravitational theory to the universal forces-and-particles model, a mental image of everything physical in the whole universe. Newton proposes this in the preface to the *Principia*:

> I derive from the celestial phenomena the forces of gravity with which bodies tend to the sun and the several planets. Then from these forces ... I deduce the motions of the planets, the comets, the moon, and the sea. I wish we could derive the rest of the phenomena of Nature by the same kind of reasoning from mechanical principles, for I am induced by many reasons to suspect that they may all [!] depend upon certain forces by which the particles of bodies, by some causes hitherto unknown, are either mutually impelled towards one another, and cohere ... or are repelled and recede.... These forces being unknown, philosophers have hitherto attempted the search of Nature in vain.[45]

Here, every body is like a solar system writ small. This is a grand analogy, but not of ancient or medieval type (conveying ontological sameness and difference). Rather, it is conceptually homogeneous, like "big circles are analogous to small circles." All the sensible, composite bodies are mentally conceived as clouds of subsensible particles, which move in space on in-principle calculable trajectories. It is assumed here that the intelligible principles of natural phenomena will, like the gravitational force law, be expressible in species-neutral terms like mass, and the spatial relations of particles, point-like centers of attraction and repulsion. The discovery of electric charge and Coulomb's law of electrical attraction and repulsion, similar in its algebraic form to Newton's, gave the Newtonian program great impetus. Thus in 1847 Helmholtz proclaimed the goal of physical science as the complete intellectual penetration of nature by human mind:

Clock Metaphor and Probabilism: The Impact of Descartes on English Methodological Thought, 1650–65," *Annals of Science* 22, no. 2 (June 1966): 73–104, esp. 91–92. The postulate of the multi-level identity of nature clashes with ordinary experience, is therefore incompatible with Aristotle's physics, and is refuted by quantum physics.

45. Newton, *Mathematical Principles*, 1686 Preface, xviii.

> Natural phenomena are to be related to the motions of matter possessing unchanging forces of motion, which forces depend only on spatial relations.... The force, however, which two whole masses exert on each other must be resolved into the forces of all their parts on one another; thereby mechanics goes back to the forces of material points, that is, to the points of space filled with matter.... Finally, then, the task of the physical natural sciences is specified thus: to reduce natural phenomena to unchanging attractive and repulsive forces, whose strength depends on the distance. The realizability of this task is, at the same time, the condition of *the complete comprehensibility of nature.*[46]

De Broglie's general description is here, in the words of Newton and Helmholtz, exemplified for classical mechanics. According to this world-conception, all the properties and activities of all the wholes in nature are derivable from, or somehow entailed by the local motions and quantitative properties of their constituent particles. Thus mass, charge, associated force laws, particle position, velocity, momentum, energy, associated densities, distributions, and flows are taken to be the terms adequate for the explanation of all natural phenomena.

What does the forces-and-particles model of the universe imply, according to its own inner logic, about nature as we prescientifically encounter it, specifically, as articulated into visible kinds or species, for example, "lion, eagle, rose, gold, and the like"?[47] The following paradoxical implications clash with our ordinary sense-perception-based experience of, and belief about natural things, both living (a lion, an eagle, a rose) and nonliving (gold), but especially about living things.

Wholes are reducible to sufficiently simple parts or particles. Thus there are no holistic systems—compounds that are irreducible to their parts—in nature. Wholes that, unlike artifacts, strike us as irreducible to parts (they seem to be more than aggregates) are the ones we call "alive," because of their intrinsic unity (if we try to pull an animal apart it bites and scratches, works hard to keep itself together) and characteristic stability of their kind (cats have kittens, dogs have puppies). Biological

46. "On the Conservation of Force," *Wissenschaftliche Abhandlungen* (Leipzig, 1882), 1:15–16; author's translation (emphasis added).

47. Bacon, *New Organon* II.17 (152). Bacon is well aware of the dualism of subsensible particles and laws, on the one hand, and sense-perceptible compounds, on the other—a dualism of "the homogeneity of laws and the heterogeneity of kinds" in Thomas Prufer's apt phrase—and thus of the need to explain how the former give rise to the later. But no such explanation is provided in the *New Organon.*

phenomena fuel Aristotle's account of form as a holistic principle, discussed in part 6, below.

"Sufficiently simple" in the first sentence of the preceding paragraph means *with respect to a force law*; that is, in the quantitative division of bodies, we come to a level of smallness such that the particles (bearing properties like mass and electrical charge) obey one or more mathematically expressible force laws enabling the calculation of trajectories from initial data, on the Newtonian model as described in part 2, above. It is the assumed availability of such laws ("certain forces by which the particles of bodies [interact]") and resulting equations of motion that grounds this type of reductionism, not the existence of ultimate or metaphysically first particles, like the unbreakable atoms of Democritus. Indeed, a particle that is taken as an indivisible whole at one stage of theory can be further reduced to subparticles at a later stage if corresponding forces and force laws are discovered. In this sense, the first principles of nature are laws, not beings.[48] I resume my list of paradoxical implications.

There is no true genesis, no real novelty in nature, no substantial change, because the only real motion in nature is the local motion of particles under unchanging laws of force. Sense-perceptible qualities and their changes, for example, alteration, must then be intramental representations arising through some sort of psychophysical association with extramental particle motions.

There are no privileged moments or states, no ends in nature. A configuration of particles moves under the equations of motion as determined by initial data (e.g., positions and velocities) at any given time.[49] There is no "room" in the basic logic of the trajectory calculation for a future state, for example, health (something we all experience to be a natural end), to be a cause of present motion, for example, healing, as discussed in part 7, below. Furthermore, the equations of particle

48. See Kennington, *Modern Origins*, 33–56. The unity of nature would then be grounded in the most general laws, Bacon's *summa lex* or *magna forma* (*Advancement of Learning*, *Works* 3.265, *New Organon*, II.26, II.52), or, in contemporary parlance, the Theory of Everything. But practical success—prediction and control of natural processes and the creation of remarkable technologies—does not require knowledge of the ultimate laws.

49. "We ought then to regard the present state of the universe as the effect of its anterior state and as the cause of the one which is to follow. . . . The regularity which astronomy shows us in the movements of the comets doubtless exists in all phenomena. . . . The only difference is that which comes from our ignorance" of the present positions and velocities of all the particles and the forces by which they interact. Laplace, *Probabilities*, 6.

motion are invariant under time reversal (replacing t and v with –t and –v), which implies that the arrow of time conspicuously evident to us all has no basis in (what are here conceived to be) the fundamental principles of nature.[50]

Finally, nature is completely malleable: one kind of body can be transformed into another. In Newton's own words, "every body can be transformed into another, of whatever kind, and all the intermediary degrees of qualities can be successively induced in it."[51] Newton is not simply saying here, in Hypothesis III, what ancient materialists said, that is, that nature is in flux, that any body will at some time go back to its elements, which will then enter into the composition of some other body.[52] Newton's remarkable assertion of *transformism* follows the inspiration of Bacon: "On a given body to generate and superinduce a new nature or new natures is the work and aim of human power."[53] The transformation of bodies takes place according to human will.

PART 5—TRANSFORMISM: AN IMMODERATE DISPOSITION TOWARD NATURE

How does transformism follow from the universal forces-and-particles model? I believe it follows quite simply, and present a deduction of it that Newton never explicitly presented but which is faithful to the logic of the forces-and-particles model.

If the intelligible principles are species-neutral, then the heterogeneity of species, so evident to our senses, for example, eagle, rose, gold, must not result *per se* from those intelligible principles, but must rather be, somehow, accidental. That is: the sensible species are not the effects of

50. The problem of irreversibility in the foundations of physics persists to this day: "At the level of particles [more precisely, wavicles], things can happen in reverse, because particles obey time-symmetric laws of mechanics. But then why does matter, which is made up of these building blocks, behave irreversibly?" Oliver Penrose, "An asymmetric world," *Nature* 438 (December 15, 2005): 919.

51. Newton, *Principia*, First Edition, Hypothesis III.

52. Nor is Newton's assertion an echo of Aristotle's doctrine of the transmutation of the elements through the open-ended potency of primary matter (under the four elemental forms, earth, air, fire, water) and the agency of the sun. As discussed in Part 6, on Aristotle, the higher natural forms, e.g., squirrel-form, are *per se* unchangeable and strongly limit the malleability of composite natural substances.

53. Bacon, *New Organon* II.1 (121).

causes aimed *per se* at those effects (like Aristotelian form and matter), and so their heterogeneity is not rooted in the essential nature of things, and, furthermore, might not be a barrier to our operation.

For example: in light of Newton's law of universal gravitation, we learn that there is no essential difference or heterogeneity of celestial and terrestrial bodies. In fact, in light of Newton's laws of motion and gravitational force, humanly controlled space flight is discovered to be possible, to be within our power, so that we can choose to do it. By launching a body from earth, namely, a rocket, with enough velocity, engineers can make it go up into the heavens and, metaphorically speaking, transform a terrestrial body into a celestial body. This is in fact shown at the end of Newton's *Principia.*[54] Moreover, by means of rocket stages and appropriate midcourse burns, following the same physics, the engineers can control the trajectory of the rocket and make it go, to a significant extent, wherever we desire. Now this is a wonderful but particular piece of physics and engineering; we have not mastered all physical phenomena but only one type, those of gravitational systems. But look what happens to this particular case when, in our imagination, we apply to it Newton's universalizing analogy: "Whatever reasoning holds for greater motions [the earth, the rocket, the solar system] should hold for lesser ones [the tiny particles of a body] as well."[55] Therefore, one imagines, just as engineers can shape the trajectory of a rocket in the solar system, so also they should be able in the future to control the trajectories of the minute particles in a cloud that we have traditionally called, say, "a cat" and thereby shape that cloud into one that we have traditionally called "a dog." This may be *practically* difficult today, due to the smallness of the particles and their large number, but there is nothing in the *nature of things* to prevent this—nothing about material being and its principles, or the process of sense perception, or, as de Broglie describes, the use of experimental apparatus that might limit our knowledge and control of the phenomena.[56] By this logic, then, transformism is demonstrated.

54. *Principia* (Motte-Cajori, 551).

55. "Unpublished Conclusion of the *Principia*," in A. R. and M. B. Hall, *Unpublished Scientific Papers of Isaac Newton*, 333.

56. It is a basic feature of quantum phenomena that the act of measurement disturbs and alters the entities under study in an essential (thus quantitatively irreducible) way. Whereas a planet is what it is independently of the reflected light whereby we observe it, the same cannot be said of an electron. "The impossibility of a closer analysis of the reactions between the

Newton's Hypothesis III of the first edition of the *Principia* is extreme. It clearly implies the ability to transform a dead body into a living one, and would thereby bring bodily immortality within human power. It is not part of the warranted (mathematical and hypothetico-deductive physical) reasoning of the *Principia*, and Newton removed it from the second and later editions. But the outlook it expresses is not unique to Newton; it is a disposition characteristic of early modern philosophy and the accompanying new science of nature.[57] Here are Bacon (also above), Descartes, and Spinoza on the same theme:

> Therefore a separation and solution of bodies must be effected, not by fire indeed, but by reasoning and true induction, with experiments to aid [...]. In a word, we must pass from Vulcan to Minerva if we intend to bring to light the true textures and configurations of bodies on which all the occult and, as they are called, specific properties and virtues in things depend, and from which, too, the rule of every powerful alteration and transformation is derived.[58]

> I took pains to make everything belonging to the nature of fire very clearly understandable.... Thus I made clear how it is formed and fueled, how sometimes it possesses only heat without light, and sometimes light without heat; how it can produce different colors and various other qualities in different bodies; how

particle and the measuring instrument is indeed no peculiarity of the experimental procedure described, but is rather an essential property of any arrangement suited to the study of the phenomena of the type concerned, where we have to do with a feature of *individuality* [the entity studied and the instrument that studies it form an indivisible whole] completely foreign to classical physics." Neils Bohr, "Can Quantum-Mechanical Description of Physical Reality Be Considered Complete?," *Physical Review* 48 (October 15, 1935): 696–702, here 697. "Phenomena in atomic physics possess a new property of wholeness, in that they cannot be dissected into part-phenomena without changing the entire phenomenon substantially every time [a measurement] is attempted." Wolfgang Pauli, "Naturwissenschaftliche und Erkenntnistheoretische Aspekte der Ideen vom Unbewussten," *Dialectica* 8 (1954): 285. In terms of classical physics itself, there is a fundamental problem in my demonstration of transformism: the ability to effect extraordinarily delicate manipulations of minute particles that I have attributed to future engineers (they can transform a cat into a dog) would enable them as well to perform the operations of Maxwell's demon whereby heat is made to flow from cold to hot without expending energy, in violation of the second law of thermodynamics, of which Newton did not know. See James Clark Maxwell, *Theory of Heat* (New York: Dover, 2001), 328–29.

57. As noted in the Preface and Introduction, the belief in and desire for the unlimited mastery of nature abides. It is a disposition incompatible with any understanding of nature as normative: "Everything is in principle open to intervention; because all is alterable, nothing is deemed either respectably natural or unwelcomely unnatural" (Leon Kass, *Toward a More Natural Science*, 11).

58. Bacon, *New Organon*, II.7 (128).

it melts some bodies and hardens others; how it can consume almost all bodies, or turn them into ashes and smoke; and finally how it can, by the mere violence of its action, form glass from these ashes—something I took particular pleasure in describing since it seems to me as wonderful a transmutation as any that takes place in nature.[59]

Nothing comes to pass in nature, which can be set down to a flaw therein [cf. Aristotle, *Physics* 199b4]; for nature is always the same, and everywhere one and the same in her efficacy and power of action; that is, nature's laws and rules, whereby all things come to pass and change from one form to another, are everywhere and always the same; so that there should be one and the same understanding of the nature of all things whatsoever, namely, through nature's universal laws and rules.[60]

Not form, but transformation is the point. Such transformation is the focus of will, reason, and imagination in each of these passages.

In developing the theme of transformism, I began with the species-neutrality of the law of gravitation. I did not end there, for Newton's forces and particles model is not only species-neutral but, as clearly noted, reductionist: wholes are reducible to parts or particles; parts are prior to wholes, ontologically and thus epistemologically. The absolute priority of parts to wholes is necessary for Newton's radical thesis of universal transformism. It is because the (sufficiently simple) parts of one species of whole, such as a cat, are indifferent to, or unmodified by their membership in that whole that they can be removed from it and put into some other kind of whole, such as a dog, or used to compose a new kind of whole altogether. If this were not the case—that is, if the parts or particles of certain kinds of wholes, and the force laws by which they interact, were somehow affected or modified or limited in their being by their membership in that kind of whole—then it would not be possible to use those particles as universal building blocks that could be disassembled and reaggregated in the transformation and synthesis of other kinds of wholes.

Let us now reverse course to take a further look at the Aristotelian alternative, an understanding of nature that is species-specific and holistic, and accordingly less technologically potent.

59. Descartes, *Discourse on the Method*, Part 5 (AT VI 44–45, CSM I 133).
60. Spinoza, *Ethics* III, Introduction (129).

PART 6—ON ARISTOTLE'S SCIENCE OF NATURE: FORM PRIOR TO MATTER, WHOLES PRIOR TO PARTS

We have two distinctions: (1) between species-neutral and species-specific principles of nature and science; (2) between reductionist and holist whole-part relations. I have used Newton's law of gravitation and the forces-and-particles model to exemplify the first terms in these distinctions (species-neutral, reductionist). Aristotle's doctrine of natural form (*morphê, eidos*) and natural substance (*ousia*) exemplify the second terms (species-specific, holist).

Physics II.1 provides the argument for form as principle and cause of change and stability in a natural substance: "The things existing by nature [not by art] all appear to have *within themselves* a principle of motion and rest. … [So] nature is a certain principle and cause of being moved and of coming to rest *in* that to which it belongs, primarily and essentially and not accidentally."[61] Nature is both form and matter, and "the form is nature more than the matter."[62] The complicated adverbial phrase, "primarily and essentially and not accidentally," means (among other things) that natural form is internal to the moved thing, such as an animal, in a way that cannot be fully derived from, or completely reduced to its material parts: "[Natural] things will be neither without matter nor determined by their matter."[63] Form is thus a holistic principle; the parts of a naturally informed compound are what they are and act as they do only in terms of the whole they compose. If separated by dissection from the whole, they cease to be what they were:

> The whole must of necessity be prior to the part; for if the whole [body] is destroyed there will not be a foot or a hand, except in the sense that the term is similar (as when one speaks of a hand made of stone).... For it is not in any manner whatsoever that a hand is a part of the body, but only when it can perform its function, so it must be alive; if not, it is not a part.[64]

61. "*Ta men gar phusei onta panta phainetai echonta* en heautois *archên kinêseôs kai staseôs.* [...] *hôs ousês tês phuseôs archês tinos kai aitias tou kinesthai kai êremein* en *hô huparchei prôtôs kath'auto kai mê kata sumbebêkos.*" *Physics* II.1.192b14–15, 21–23 (25); emphasis added. The *appearance* of having an irreducibly internal source of motion is accepted by Aristotle as reliable.

62. *Physics* II.1.193b7 (27, translation slightly modified).

63. *Physics* II.2.194a14–15 (52, translation slightly modified).

64. *Politics* I.2.1253a20–22, trans. Carnes Lord, *Aristotle's* Politics (Chicago: University of

Therefore, one whole informed material substance, such as a squirrel, cannot be adequately understood in terms of its parts. Rather, since the whole is ontologically prior to the parts, the parts cede some of their being to the unifying authority of the form. Thus, for Aristotle, the parts of a natural substance exist only potentially (*dunamei*) in the whole; they are not fully actual in the whole: "And the continuous and limited is said to be a whole when it is some one thing consisting of many constituents, most of all when these exist potentially, but if not, actually.... Whenever the parts [of an animal] are one and continuous by nature ... they will exist potentially."[65] In fundamental contrast, the parts of an artifact, such as a clock, are what they are independently of the whole; they are fully actual, and thus in their being are neutral or indifferent to the whole. Therefore, a watch, which lacks the substantial unity of that squirrel, can be taken apart, its parts can be analyzed in isolation from each other, and then both the parts and our knowledge of the parts can be reaggregated in the whole, or even rearranged in a new and different "species" of whole.[66] Here, the parts are prior, ontologically and epistemologically, to the whole. The clock—in which we can literally "see all the wheels functioning"—is thus a paradigm for the reductionist and anti-Aristotelian conception of the whole-part relation. In general,

---

Chicago Press, 2013), 4; *Metaphysics* VII.11.1036b31–32 (126); see also VII.10.1035b23–25. Hegel's (post-Newtonian) formulation of the whole-part relation in a living thing accords with that of Aristotle: "The notion of the whole is to contain parts: but if the whole is taken and made what its notion implies, i.e., if it is divided, it at once ceases to be a whole. Things there are, no doubt, which correspond to this relation: but for that very reason they are low existences [...]. The relation of whole and parts comes very easy to reflective understanding; and for that reason it often satisfies when the question really turns on profounder ties. The limbs and organs, for instance, of an organic body are not merely parts of it: it is only in their unity that they are what they are, and they are unquestionably affected by that unity, as they also in turn affect it. These limbs and organs become [mere] parts, only when they pass under the hands of the anatomist, whose occupation, be it remembered, is not with the living body but with the corpse. Not that such analysis is illegitimate: we only mean that the external and mechanical relation of whole and parts is not sufficient for us, if we want to study organic life in its truth." Hegel, *Encyclopedia Logic*, §135, note; see also §38, note.

65. *Metaphysics* V.26.1023b33–35, VII.16.1040b14–17 (98, 133, translation slightly modified); see also *De Anima* II.2.414a20–28.

66. Within Newtonian physics, the reductionist or mechanical relation of whole and part (parts unaffected by the whole) is implicit in the parallelogram rule for composition of forces, Corollary II of Newton's *Principia*, whereby the conjoint action of the particles composing a compound body is assumed to be the sum of the actions (forces) of each particle taken separately. See my "Wholes, Parts, and Laws of Motion," *Nature and System* 6 (1984): 195–215, and "Animals versus the Laws of Inertia," *Review of Metaphysics* 46 (1992): 29–61.

reductionism is a sufficient but not necessary condition of species neutrality. For example, Darwin's biology is species-neutral but not reductionist in the strong (material) sense used here.[67] Conversely, a species-specific account, like Aristotle's doctrine of natural substance, is, to a significant extent, necessarily holist.

Aristotle's doctrine of parts being potentially in the whole is admittedly obscure. We can get a sense of it only by consideration of his examples, which are almost all biological.[68] I argue in part 7, below, that it has relevance as well for the quantum physics of atoms and molecules. In any case, despite the obscurities, it is fair to say that, in the Aristotelian account, the relativity and subordination of the being of the parts of a natural compound to its unifying form necessarily implies limits to the alteration, manipulation, and transformation of bodies by separation and recombination of their parts. To separate the part from the whole is not only to mutilate the whole but, unlike the gear removed from the clock, to alter the part so that it cannot "perform its function." Within this understanding, then, the form is not only a source but also a limit to our knowledge and control of nature: "Limit means … the substance of each thing, and the essence [*to ti ên einai*] of each thing, for this is a limit of knowledge, and if of knowledge then of the thing also.… Essence will belong to nothing which is not a species [*eidos*] of a genus, but only to a species of a genus.… By form [*eidos*] I mean the essence of each thing."[69] In particular, our ability to know what is going on inside a natural substance is limited. Aquinas expresses the Aristotelian teaching succinctly: "natural forms are not *per se* subject to motion […] they are, moreover, the perfections of mutable things."[70]

Aristotle's species-specific, form-limited holism stands at the oppo-

67. Random variation and natural selection are governing principles common to all living species, but (to my knowledge) Darwin never claimed that an animal is nothing but an aggregate of particles. On the species-neutrality of Darwinian biology, see my "Darwinian Natural Right?," *Interpretation* 27, no. 2 (2000): 129–60; Larry Arnhart, "Defending Darwinian Natural Right," *Interpretation* 27, no. 3 (2000): 263–77; and my "Reply to Arnhart," *Interpretation* 28, no. 1 (2000): 35–43.

68. The exception is parts (intervals) of a line potentially present in the line, *Physics* VIII.8.263a28.

69. Aristotle, *Metaphysics* V.17.1022a5–10, VII.4.1030a12–13, VII.7.1032b2 (93, 112, 117).

70. Aquinas, *In de trinitate*, q. 5, a. 2, ad 6; translated by Armand Maurer in Thomas Aquinas, *The Division and Methods of the Sciences* (Toronto: Pontifical Institute of Medieval Studies, 1986), 31.

site extreme to Newtonian species-neutral and reductionist transformism. Is there a reasonable mean? The reality of laws of nature and the particular successes of reductionist explanation make clear that nature is less Aristotelian than Aristotle thought. But classical physics suffered its own great embarrassment on the problem of the stability of matter, the problem of how to account for the specific properties of atoms and molecules, that is, of the chemical species. This is discussed in the following section. Preparatory to that discussion, consider the following by J. S. Mill in 1843, "On the Composition of Causes":

The preceding discussions have rendered us familiar with the case in which several agents, or causes, concur as conditions to the production of an effect. [...] Suppose, then, that two different agents, operating jointly, are followed, under a given set of collateral conditions, by a given effect.... Now, if we happen to know what would be the effect of each cause when acting separately from the other, we are often able to arrive deductively, or *a priori*, at a correct prediction of what will arise from their conjunct agency. To render this possible, it is only necessary that the same law which expresses the effect of each cause acting by itself shall also correctly express that part due to that cause of the effect which follows from the two together. This condition is realized in the extensive and important class of phenomena commonly called mechanical [which are based on] the principle of the [parallelogram rule for] Composition of [Newtonian] Forces: and, in imitation of that well chosen expression, I shall give the name of the Composition of Causes to the principle which is exemplified in all cases in which the joint effect of several causes is identical with the sum of their separate effects.

This principle, however, by no means prevails in all departments of the field of nature. The chemical combination of two substances produces, as is well known, a third substance with properties different from those of either of the two substances separately, or of both of them taken together. Not a trace of the properties of hydrogen or of oxygen is observable in those of their compound, water. ... This explains why mechanics is a deductive or demonstrative science, and chemistry is not....

This difference between the case in which the joint effect of causes is the sum of their separate effects, and the case in which it is heterogeneous to them; between laws which work together without alteration, and laws which, when called upon to work together, cease and give place to others; is one of the fundamental distinctions in nature.[71]

71. John Stuart Mill, *A System of Logic*, Book III, Chapter VI (London: Longmans, Green

Chemistry can become "a deductive or demonstrative science" only on grounds of a new type of physics in which the principle of the composition of causes does not hold.

PART 7—STABILITY OF MATTER: RADICAL FAILURE OF CLASSICAL PHYSICS

The species-neutral reductionism of classical physics is so radical that it directly contributes to one of the great scientific revolutions of the twentieth century, quantum physics. Rutherford's analysis of scattering experiments in 1911 led to the nuclear or "planetary" model of the atom: a dense, positively charged nucleus surrounded by smaller electrons in a much larger environing space. It seems, at first (conceptual) glance, like a tiny solar system (hence the name "planetary") and thus like a vindication of Newton's universal forces and particles model.[72] But will the postulate of the multi-level identity of nature hold, that is, will "the same kind of reasoning from mechanical principles" work on the atomic scale of size as it does on the astronomical and terrestrial-engineering scale? It will not. The classical conception of the nuclear atom poses the problem of the stability of matter. It is a problem with two parts, internal and external, as follows.

The problem of internal atomic stability. Consider an isolated atom. Negatively charged electrons must be strongly attracted (by the Coulomb force) to the positively charged nucleus (containing protons and neutrons). What maintains the electrons in place around the nucleus—either at fixed positions or, if we conceive them to circulate like tiny planets, in orbits of fixed radii—against the electrical force that pulls them in to the nucleus? For, unlike an orbiting planet in Newtonian gravitational theory, an orbiting charged particle in classical electromagnetic theory must emit electromagnetic radiation, which depletes its kinetic energy;

and Co., 1941), 242–44. See note 64 (above), on the composition of forces. Newton well appreciated the significance of the parallelogram rule: "the use of this Corollary [II] spreads far and wide, and by that diffuse extent the truth thereof is further confirmed. For on what has been said depends the whole doctrine of mechanics" (*Principia*, 17).

72. E. Rutherford, "The Scattering of α and β Particles by Matter and the Structure of the Atom," *Philos. Mag.* 21 (April 1911): 669–88. The characteristic radius of the solar system is 10^{12} meters, of a hydrogen atom 10^{-10} meters. The assumption that the same principles should hold on both scales is extraordinary.

continuous acceleration along its classical trajectory entails continuous energy loss by the moving particle. What then happens?

The problem of external atomic stability. Consider the many atoms composing a liquid or a solid, atoms so closely packed that, unlike a gas, the materials they compose resist compression. What enables each atom to maintain its shape and integrity, and thus its specific characteristics, against the strong external disturbances (crunching against the other atoms or, if they are on the surface of the liquid or solid, being buffeted by light) to which it must be continually exposed?

Classical physical theory cannot provide answers to these questions. Classical theory makes the stability of atoms—wholes composed of nuclei and electrons—unintelligible, and therewith the properties of the chemical species composed of atoms. We prescientifically experience these properties all the time in, for example, the solidity of our bones and of the chair we are sitting on, and we scientifically observe them in sophisticated laboratory experiments, for example, the color spectra of light emitted from gases under electrical stimulation (a strong external disturbance). This is the world-historic failure of classical physical theory: it cannot account from its own first principles for the evident specificity of the material world.[73]

The failure of classical physics on the internal atomic stability problem is described in standard textbooks. There is no stable equilibrium configuration of static, electrically charged particles, a theorem originally attributed to Samuel Earnshaw and immediately derivable from Laplace's equation, $\nabla^2\varphi = 0$, for the electric potential in free space.[74] For electrons circulating around the nucleus, there is no stable configuration

73. To be sure, for about two centuries, classical physics solved all sorts of engineering problems in which the stable properties of liquids and solids were taken for granted and incorporated in the equations as boundary conditions or empirically determined constants. For example, water is incompressible and has a given viscosity, while cement is solid, unlike butter, and will contain the water in a swimming pool, whose surface will be horizontal in equilibrium in the earth's gravitational field. If disturbed, the water will propagate surface waves and eventually return to its stable equilibrium state with a flat surface. This does not, however, explain the respective characteristics of water and concrete in terms of their atomic and molecular constituents, or nuclei and electrons. For this, quantum physics is required.

74. See William Thomson and P. G. Tait, *Treatise on Natural Philosophy* (Oxford: Clarendon Press, 1857), 372–73; L. D. Landau and E. M. Lifshitz, *The Classical Theory of Fields* (Reading, Mass.: Addison-Wesley, 1962), 100; Feynman, *Lectures*, vol. 2, §5–2, especially "Stability of Atoms."

of orbits due to radiative energy loss, whereby the electron would spiral into the nucleus in a tiny fraction of a second.[75] In other words, executing the trajectory calculation of part 2, above, using Coulomb's law for the electrical force of the nucleus on an electron (of mass, me, and charge, e) beginning from initial position and velocity, ro, vo, just as we did using Newton's law for the gravitational force of the sun on a planet (of mass, m), leads, not to a spectacular success, but a radical failure. An electron in an atom does not behave according to the properties that define it classically—mass and charge—and that would determine classically its local motion in an electric field. Rather, the phenomena of atomic stability require that the electron be altered, modified, in some way limited by its membership in the whole atom (were this not the case, the atom could be explained through Mill's "Composition of Causes"). Is this not a distant echo of Aristotle's obscure doctrine of material parts potential in the informed whole?[76] As Wallace describes it:

> The organization or formal arrangement of these components [electrons, protons, and neutrons], and not the components themselves, makes [e.g.,] sodium be what it is.... None of the three components of the sodium atom acts simply as an electron, proton, or neutron, ... each functions instead as a part of sodium.... On its own, each electron would be indifferent to the particular energy state it might occupy within the atom; within the atom, according to the Pauli exclusion principle, each electron is assigned to a unique state occupied by no other.[77]

Aristotle's obscurity will be removed by the mathematical theory of quantum states, their superpositions and transformations, but that theory removes as well the central concepts of classical physics: particle

75. R. M. Eisberg, *Fundamentals of Modern Physics* (New York: John Wiley and Sons, 1961), 108–9; see also 366–69 on the great importance of the Pauli exclusion principle, namely, "in a multi-electron atom there can never be more than one electron in a given quantum state" (366); without this, "atoms, and therefore the entire universe, would be *radically different*" (368).

76. The notion of parts existing potentially in the whole is complemented by the doctrine of parts being virtually present in the whole: the electron retains its mass, m_e, and charge, q_e, in an atom (this is the unmodified presence), but the function of the electron is not given by the classical equations for a particle of mass, m_e, and charge, q_e, in the field of the nucleus; what the particle is when it is inside the atom is thus modified relative to its nature as classically conceived.

77. William A. Wallace, *The Modeling of Nature* (Washington, D.C.: The Catholic University of America Press, 1996), 46–47.

trajectory and field magnitude (spatio-temporally continuous and deterministic); they are not adequate to nature. Let us continue the story of the stability of matter. It remains to discuss the stability of atoms against external disturbances.

The failure of classical physics on the external stability problem is succinctly described by Niels Bohr as paraphrased by Werner Heisenberg in the following excerpt, which situates the difficulty precisely in the notion of deterministic particle trajectory:

> My starting point was not at all the idea that an atom is a small-scale planetary system and as such governed by the laws [like those] of astronomy. I never took things as literally as that. My starting point was rather the stability of matter, a pure miracle when considered from the standpoint of classical physics.
>
> By "stability" I mean that the same substances always have the same properties, that the same crystals recur, the same chemical compounds, etc. In other words, even after a host of changes due to external influences, an iron atom will always remain an iron atom, with exactly the same properties as before. This cannot be explained by the principles of classical mechanics, certainly not if the atom resembles a planetary system. Nature clearly has a tendency to produce certain forms ... and to recreate these forms even when they are disturbed or destroyed. You may even think of biology: the stability of living organisms, the propagation of the most complicated forms which, after all, can exist only in their entirety. But in biology we are dealing with highly complex structures, subject to characteristic, temporary transformations of a kind that need not detain us here. Let us rather stick to the simpler forms we study in physics and chemistry. The existence of uniform substances, of solid bodies, depends on the stability of atoms; that is precisely why an electron tube filled with a certain gas will always emit light of the same color, a spectrum with exactly the same lines. All this, far from being self-evident, is quite inexplicable in terms of the basic principles of Newtonian physics, according to which all effects have precisely determined causes, *and according to which the present state of a phenomenon or process is fully determined by the one that immediately preceded it.* This fact used to disturb me a great deal when I first began to look into atomic physics.[78]

On grounds of classical theory, then, there is no way in which a future state could be a cause of present motion.[79] This makes unintelligible (or

78. Heisenberg, *Physics and Beyond*, trans. A. J. Pomerans (New York: Harper Torchbooks, 1972), 39; emphasis added.

79. This is an imprecise but didactically useful formulation of final causality.

a matter of extraordinary improbability, “a pure miracle”) health and healing (“the stability of living organisms”), and, more to the point, the *ground state* characteristic of a given species of atom, to which the atom returns by emission of specific frequencies of light after it is disturbed by an external influence.

We can see exactly what Bohr is getting at by means of the trajectory calculation, in part 2, above: imagine that a typical classical system, the solar system, suffers a strong external disturbance. Say a large comet or asteroid passes through the solar system, not colliding with any planets, but pulling them off of their previous orbits through its own gravitational force. Is there anything in the fundamental principles of Newtonian physics—the principles that we used to calculate a trajectory from given initial conditions—that would cause the planets to recover their previous orbits? The answer is, no, for the effect of the comet or asteroid is simply to “reset” the initial conditions, the positions and velocities of the planets, which then *fully* determine the future trajectories under the laws of motion and force. There is no room in this classical kind of reasoning for the solar system somehow to remember, as it were, its past configuration and get back to it.

The radical species-neutrality and reductionism of the classical world conception make nature completely indifferent to itself, thus without privileged states that are specific to the kind and self-reconstitutive—like the ground states of the atoms of the chemical elements. As elemental, a given kind of atom enters into and is common to many species of more composite bodies; for example, carbon is an essential element in all living bodies. As such, the chemical elements are species-neutral principles of nature and natural science. More fundamentally, however, the quantum physics that accounts for the specific stability (ground state, allowed transitions, chemical bonds, and reactivity) of atoms is species-specific and thus holistic, unlike classical physics.[80]

80. A great question is posed: as we ascend from the more elementary and potential to the more composite and actual levels of nature (from nuclei and electrons to atoms, to molecules, to gases, liquids, solids, cells, tissues, organs, organisms) where does the holism “top out,” i.e., at what level do we have a whole complete in itself and independent of some larger whole; at what level do we have a *substance*? Aristotle’s answer is commonsensical: “a human being or a plant or something of that sort ... we most of all call substances.” *Metaphysics* VII.7.1032a20 (128). But there is much more to the story as, e.g., Plato, Spinoza, Hegel make clear, not to mention Aristotle’s own account of the substance that is most fully actual.

In sum: in view of the twofold problem of atomic stability, it is not surprising that the new type of theory required to account for the phenomena does not possess the three fundamental characteristics of all classical physics: (1) continuity of space, time, and motion, (2) spatio-temporal imageability of elementary processes, and (3) deterministic causality. The next step—logical and chronological—in the story would be quantum physics and its non-classical characteristics.[81] This vast topic is very well covered in many works, and lies outside the natural-philosophic and phenomenological intention of the present essay.[82] Accordingly, I return to the mathematization of nature, which obviously extends to both classical and quantum physics.

PART 8—PHYSICO-MATHEMATICAL SECULARISM: WORKING AROUND THE QUESTION OF THE DIFFERENCE BETWEEN MATHEMATICAL OBJECTS AND PHYSICAL OBJECTS

Are mathematical objects different in some fundamental way from physical objects? Plato says, yes: as intelligible, mathematical objects must exist independently of all sensible (material and changeable) things. Aristotle says, yes, but not in the way that Plato thinks: mathematical objects do not exist independently of sensible things but they can be understood independently of them through abstraction.[83] Descartes says, no, the object of physics, matter in motion, *is* the object of geometry, figurate extension.[84] My point is simply that there are well-known major disagree-

81. The continuous but non-spatio-temporal time-evolution of the wave function punctuated by its discontinuous "collapse" in the act of measurement; superposition and interference, Heisenberg indeterminacy and Bohr complementarity, non-locality or entanglement. See note 10 (above).

82. For an extensive bibliography (covering all interpretations, not just Copenhagen) see Bryce S. Dewitt and R. Neill Graham, "Resource Letter IQM–1 on the Interpretation of Quantum Mechanics," *American Journal of Physics* 39 (July 1971): 724–36; and John A. Wheeler and Woyciech H. Zurek, eds., *Quantum Theory and Measurement* (Princeton, N.J.: Princeton University Press, 1993). For a good account written for laymen, see David Lindley, *Where Does the Weirdness Go?* (New York: Basic, 1996), esp. 129–68. For a useful article-length overview, see Max Tegmark and John A. Wheeler, "100 Years of Quantum Mysteries," *Scientific American* (February 2001): 68–75.

83. For example, Plato, *Republic* 510c–e, 525de, 529b; Aristotle, *Physics* 193b23–194a2, and *De Anima* 431b13–18.

84. See note 25 (above).

ments in the history of philosophy about the being of mathematical objects and their relation to physical objects. In the face of these long-standing disagreements, Newton represents a new position: let us set aside these philosophical disputes, and *assume that any difference between mathematical objects and physical objects makes no difference for the conduct of our mathematical physics.* Henceforth, one can have one's private beliefs about the modes of being of mathematical and physical objects, such as central forces, but no scientific attention will be paid to the question. It will suffice to focus on the mathematical principles of natural philosophy; other principles (and causes) need not be discussed. Newton does not explicitly assert the italicized words, above, but his posture is fairly clear from the content (not to mention the title) of the *Principia*, beginning with the Preface, and it is especially well brought out by de Gandt who introduces the term "secularism" to characterize it.[85] (One sees the analogy to secularism in early modern political theory: one's religious beliefs will be a private matter; the differences between, say, Catholics and Protestants will not be allowed to affect the conduct of government.) In the following, I explicate the meaning of physico-mathematical secularism in terms of (1) Cartesian coordinates in the classical framework of space and time, (2) the Heisenberg uncertainty principle in quantum physics, and (3) act and potency in the physics of Aristotle.

Physico-mathematical secularism is embedded in the use of Cartesian coordinates (x, y, z, t) to represent *physical* space and time, and physical properties of bodies, particles, and fields, as described in the opening lines of de Broglie's description. Consider the particle trajectory that we then calculated and represented on paper in part 2: at each instant of time, t, the particle is conceived to possess a real-numerically precise value of position, x, y, z, and a real-numerically precise value of

85. *Force and Geometry*; see note 7 (above). In Def. VIII, concerning central forces, Newton says, "I here design only to give a mathematical notion of those forces, without considering their physical causes and seats" (*Principia*, 5). The preface of the *Principia* is more subtle (and remarkable): the first third explains that both mechanics and geometry should be understood in terms of (and subsumed under) *accuracy*. Accuracy means the fit or match (see note 16, above) between (1) a perfect figure ("perfectly accurate") and one drawn less perfectly, as well as (2) the closeness of a calculated to a measured number of units ("accurately proposes and demonstrates the art of measuring"), i.e., numerical precision in terms of decimal digits, e.g., accurate to the fifth decimal place. Thus when Newton (remarkably) says, "the errors are not in the art, but in the artificers," I take him to mean that there is no mismatch between the mathematical and the physical *that is rooted in the nature of the physical itself.*

momentum, mv_x, mv_y, mv_z, relative to the center of force. In general, it is assumed that such variable magnitudes can faithfully represent anything measurable in the physical world. It is thus presupposed that the properties of physical objects are conformable to the real-number line, or that the real-number line is perfectly adequate to the properties of physical objects.[86] Our measurements (using instruments of increasing precision) will match (with increasing accuracy) our calculations (solving the equations that express the laws of nature). We can then predict, and, to the extent possible, control the physical quantities that we conceive as objectively existing in space and time, e.g., particle position and momentum. Or are we confusing mathematical objects with physical objects? No matter (pun intended); it is not a problem: unwitting reification of mathematical objects can do no harm (lead to no fundamental error) in physics—this follows from the original (seventeenth-century) assumption of physico-mathematical secularism.[87]

This assumption is dubious, the more so in view of the highly constructed character of the Cartesian, numerical-variable magnitudes that

86. The real number system was brought to explicit definition in the nineteenth century through the work of Dedekind and Cantor, and so Descartes and Newton did not use the terms "real number" or "arithmetical continuum." The absence in their work of any concern for the longstanding premodern doctrine of the essential heterogeneity of discrete number and continuous magnitude makes clear that their conception of number and magnitude was implicitly real-numerical, e.g., the variable, x, is both a number and a line segment, thus the expression, $1 + x + x^2 + x^3 + x^4 + \ldots (x<1)$, as in Newton's analyses of infinite series, makes sense not only arithmetically but also geometrically as it could not in classical geometry.

87. The significance of non-linear dynamics or "chaos theory" is that, while leaving the classical concept of deterministic trajectory intact, it corrects the assumption of the unconditional conformability of measurable properties of physical objects to the mathematical real number line. *As measurable*, physical properties can be numerically specified only approximately, e.g., to within Δx, finite no matter how small. Therefore, if a non-linear physical system is in the regime of sensitive dependence on initial conditions, then, due to the rapid divergence of initially adjacent (within Δx) trajectories, no actual measurement, e.g., of initial position, $x(t_0) \pm \Delta x$, can determine a unique trajectory. "Newtonian dynamics has, over the centuries, twice foundered on the assumption that something was infinite when in fact it was not: the speed of light, c, and the reciprocal of Planck's constant, 1/h. Reformulations omitting these infinities led first to special relativity and then to quantum mechanics. Complexity theory now reveals a third tacitly assumed infinity in classical dynamics, namely the assumption of infinite computational and observational precision." Joseph Ford, "How Random Is a Coin Toss?," *Physics Today* (April 1983): 40–47, here 46. Another point, more centrally relevant to my purpose: If physico-mathematical secularism arose in the seventeenth century, what about the preceding Aristotelian-scholastic physics and mathematics, which spoke of mixed sciences; what is the relation between the mixed-science tradition and physico-mathematical secularism? This important question is discussed in the conclusion.

FIG. 3

we use in our physics. To see what I mean by "highly constructed character," look at the two magnitudes (lines) shown in boldface:
Are the two equal or unequal? The answer is, yes. As Euclidean geometrical magnitudes, they are obviously unequal, since I can lay the left one adjacent to the right one, cut off a part of the right one equal to the left one, and exhibit the remainder.[88] But as Cartesian variable magnitudes, taken in our minds as possessing (unlike Euclidean magnitudes) *numerical* value, point by point, based on our arbitrary choice of a unit length, they are obviously equal, since they both have the same numerical value, c. We, unlike premodern mathematicians, have two different concepts of magnitude in our mental toolbox. The difference between them is considerable.

The continuous magnitudes of Euclidean geometry are "put before us" in a direct way.[89] A line, for example, is delimited by its two endpoints (each designated by a letter) within a given figure, and it is the definition or *logos* of the figure from which the intelligibility or meaning, thus the *being* of the line—how it is related (by equality, proportionality, parallelism, perpendicularity, etc.) to the other parts of the figure—*begins*. The line has no numerical character; it is not a *length*, that is, a number of units of measurement. Nor are two points separated by a *distance* (the length of the line they delimit). Accordingly, Euclidean demonstrations do not involve the operations (+, –, ×, ÷, √) to which numbers are subject.[90] Finally, we must continually look with our eyes at the drawn

88. *Elements*, common notions 4 and 5.

89. I owe to Andrew Romiti the very helpful phrase "put before us."

90. More precisely: Euclidean magnitudes of the same kind can be added unconditionally. They can be subtracted on condition that the one removed does not exceed that from which it is taken. "Multiplication" (called "application") is limited to construction of a rectangle from two lines or a solid from a line and a plane figure. Division of heterogeneous magnitudes (a

figure in front of us and examine it, but we know that our thinking is not about that figure but about an ideal, intelligible one, of which the visible one is an imperfect image.

The numerical-variable magnitudes or *coordinates* of Cartesian analytic geometry are quite different. Here, everything begins (consider plane problems) from the x and y *axes*. A point on an axis, say, the x-axis, is conceived as having, not a particular numerical value, such as 53.74, but numerical value in general, x, which stands for the distance from the origin that it would have if a unit of length were chosen on the axis. The origin does have a particular value: 0. Since a unit length can always be chosen (place a mark on the axis to the right of 0) whereby any line acquires a numerical value in terms of that unit (ratios of incommensurable lines having been conceived as irrational numbers), we need not choose a unit prior to performing calculational operations, +, −, ×, ÷, √, on the letter signs, x, y, a, b, etc. A unit can be specified later, if needed. We are working with generic numbers (increasing to the right on the x-axis or upward on the y-axis from the origin). The x-y plane is then brought into being by our mental conception of its points as ordered pairs, that is, as coordinates (x, y), where x means the distance the point would have from the y-axis measured parallel to the x-axis, and y means the distance it would have from the x-axis measured parallel to the y-axis upon choice of a unit. Most relevant and useful: the coordinates, x and y, are conceived *to vary* (lengthen and shorten) relative to the origin at (0, 0). We can stipulate and express how, say, y varies with x in a *functional relation*, such as $y(x) = ax + b$. This *equation* is usefully expressed by the curve (here a line) whose points possess the coordinates (x, y(x)) thereby defined. Curves and their equations can be studied, and problems can be solved by operating on the letter-signs and finding the algebraic expressions for the functional relation between coordinates of interest, for example, the position and momentum of a particle in relation to time, x(t), p(t). The Cartesian letter signs, or symbols, x, y, t, a, b, etc., for variables and constants do not image ideal objects as do the figures of Euclidean geometry. Nor do they stand for the definite numbers of pure units (monads) or their fractional parts as in the Diophantine arithmetic.

rectangle by a line) is impossible. Ratio can exist only between two magnitudes of the same kind; accordingly, a proportion involving heterogeneous magnitudes cannot be alternated.

My point in all of this is that the mind's constructive activity contributes much to the structure of Cartesian geometry—to the intelligibility or meaning of its thus conceptually complex objects. (Note the appearance of the words "conceived" and "conception" in the preceding paragraph; they have the sense defined in Descartes's *Rules for the Direction of the Mind*.)[91] The Cartesian plane, and the coordinate axes that bring it into being are not "put before us" in the direct manner of Euclidean magnitudes.[92] Now can we *identify* the spatio-temporal objects of physics with these conceptually constructed objects of mathematics? Is the conformability of the former to the latter, or the adequacy of the latter to the former unconditional—as was assumed by the physico-mathematical secularism of classical physics? My repeated reference, above, to the position and velocity or momentum, thus the trajectory of a particle should make the answer to this question quite clear. The Heisenberg uncertainty principle is emblematic of the failure of physico-mathematical secularism.

In 1927 Werner Heisenberg set out what has since been known as the uncertainty principle of quantum physics: "The more accurately the position [of a particle] is determined, the less accurately the momentum is known and conversely."[93] More specifically: the product of the uncertainty in the measurement of particle position, x, at time, t, and the uncertainty in the measurement of its momentum, Δp, at time, t, cannot be reduced below (approximately) the numerical value of $\hbar$, Planck's constant divided by 2π: $\Delta x \Delta p \geq \hbar$. The reciprocal relation of the uncertainties means that, as position, x(t), is measured with increasing accuracy—approaching the classical ideal, $\Delta x = 0$—all values of the momentum, p(t), become equally possible, and conversely, as $\Delta p \rightarrow 0$, $\Delta x \rightarrow \infty$. The Δx and Δp are not observational errors of classical type resulting from the imprecision of present-day instruments, to be progressively sharpened in the future. Most importantly, the Δx and Δp are not merely expressions

91. Rule 12 (AT X 416, CSM I 42). The concept of general magnitude—the progenitor of real-numerical variable magnitude or coordinate axis—is then elaborated in Rules 13–16.

92. Using the scholastic terminology of first and second intentions, Klein characterizes Cartesian magnitudes as second intentions taken by the intellect as first intentions by means of the visible letter sign, which thereby becomes an algebraic *symbol*, and analytic geometry an algebra of line segments. See *Greek Mathematical Thought*, 208, and *Lectures and Essays*, 17–21.

93. "Je genauer der Ort bestimmt ist, desto ungenauer ist der Impuls bekannt und umgekehrt." Heisenberg, "Über den anschaulichen Inhalt der quantentheoretischen Kinematic und Mechanik," *Zeitschrift für Physik* 43 (1927): 127–98, here 175.

of an unpredictable disturbance of the tiny particle's, such as the electron's, local motion due to the unavoidably much larger (and energetic) observational apparatus. This is the "uncontrollable disturbance" interpretation of the uncertainty principle. It leaves the central concept of classical mechanics—particle trajectory, that is, simultaneously well defined values of position and momentum—intact, maintaining only that the trajectory is made unpredictable in the future by our unavoidably intrusive efforts to observe the particle right now (it gets uncontrollably deflected by the light used to detect it), so that the trajectory is uncertain only to us, not indeterminate in itself. Rather, the uncertainty principle is ontological, such that, "the term 'uncertainty principle' is, therefore, somewhat of a misnomer. A better term would be 'the principle of limited determinism in the structure of matter,'" or the Heisenberg indeterminacy principle.[94]

Heisenberg's principle means, among other things, that the being and knowability of spatio-temporal properties, like particle position, x, at time, t, are intertwined with the being and knowability of dynamical properties, like momentum, p, and energy, E. Here, again, is de Broglie:

94. David Bohm, *Quantum Theory* (New York: Dover, 1979), 101. The following is from Max Jammer, *The Conceptual Development of Quantum Mechanics* (New York: McGraw-Hill, 1966), 329–30: "[A] notion like 'path' or 'trajectory' ('Bahn'), which presupposes a sharp knowledge of both position and momentum, can be retained in quantum mechanics, contended Heisenberg. For 'the path comes into existence only when we observe it,' he declared. This contention, one of the most provocative statements ever made in physics, was justified by him as follows. If an atom which, say, is in its 1000th excited state is illuminated by light of relatively long waves [...] the electron, owing to the Compton effect [photon-electron scattering], may be found after the interaction somewhere between the 950th and the 1050th state, the particular orbit being indeterminate. The electron will therefore be represented by a wave packet in configuration space, composed of the eigenfunctions of the states just mentioned, and of a size determined by the precision of the position measurement, that is, by the wavelength of the illuminating light. The packet describes an orbit analogous to that of a classical particle, but spreads with time. Every new observation by which a certain [position, x] is selected out of a multitude of possibilities reduces the otherwise spreading wave packet again to the dimensions of the wavelength of the incident light. The constant replacement in each consecutive observation of the wave packet, which has spread out, by a smaller packet gives rise to the orbit as the temporal sequence of the locations where the wave packet has been observed." For the quantum mechanical explanation of a track in a cloud chamber, see Bohm, *Quantum Theory*, 137–40. Heisenberg indeterminacy and Bohr complementarity are the essential features of the Copenhagen Interpretation of quantum mechanics. Alternative interpretations that accord with the classical conception of mind and world are, after Bell's theorem and the Aspect experiments, necessarily non-local and, in the case of Bohm theory, holistic with a vengeance; see D. Bohm and B. J. Hiley, *The Undivided Universe* (London: Routledge, 1993).

> What is now [e]specially important for us to understand is the profound meaning of this rather mysterious idea of the quantum of action [Planck's constant, $h = 6.62 \times 10^{-27}$ erg-sec]. Up till [the early twentieth century] the space and time of classical physics, or its successor—the space-time of the relativity physics—had appeared to us as a framework given *a priori* and [being] quite independent of what one could put into it, [being] quite independent particularly of the movements and evolution of the bodies which were localized in it. [...]
>
> The real significance of the quantum of action has been disclosed to us notably by the discovery of Heisenberg's uncertainties [...]. It seems certain today that the existence of the quantum of action expresses a formerly totally unsuspected union between the framework of space and time and the dynamical phenomena which take place in it. The picture of space and time [in classical physics] is essentially static; a body, a physical entity, which has an exact location in space and in time is, by this very fact, deprived of all evolutionary property; [but] on the contrary, a body which is developing, which is endowed with dynamic properties, cannot really be attached to any point of space and time. These are philosophical remarks which go back to Zeno [and so to Aristotle, *Physics* VIII.8]. [...] Heisenberg's uncertainty relations appear akin to these remarks; they teach us, in effect, that it is impossible to attribute simultaneously to a body a well-defined motion and a well-determined place in space and time.[95]

There is no way in the classical conception of mind and world, space and time, mathematics and physics, measurement and calculation, in which our knowledge of one physical quantity, say, position or time, could affect or interfere with, or limit our knowledge of another such quantity, say, momentum or energy. They are all just Cartesian magnitudes, real numbers of appropriate units. They can be thought conjointly and put together on paper (the position and velocity vectors in the trajectory calculation); or separated in our thought and on paper. As Cartesian mathematical objects, each is unmodified by, and indifferent to its membership in any whole. There is no "holism" of motion, mobile, place, and time. But, as de Broglie reminds us, pointing back to Aristotle, a moving body—as opposed to a mathematical point "moving" in our imagination—is not *actually* in a place or at a fixed position; if it were, it would not be in motion. Matt Crawford puts it nicely:

95. De Broglie, *Physics and Microphysics*, 120–22

The identification of natural beings, having first intentional magnitudes (as Klein says), with Cartesian real-numerical magnitudes (by which identification they are also reduced to a collection of decoupled, quantity-holding attributes, abstracting from other [...] characteristics that depend on the coupled whole), is no longer tenable given that, as we now know, the framework of space and time is only putatively determinate in the way real numbers are, and this putative determinateness is an artifact of its abstract conception.[96]

Aristotle, of course, did not quantify the indeterminacy in the position of a body moving with a given speed; he did not discover Planck's constant. But Aristotle does prepare us for the ideas of indeterminacy and potentiality—of some things having less being than others—and thus of limits to the intelligibility of the potentially being. Heisenberg used Aristotle as an aid in attempting to explain the obscure reality of the wave function: it is "a quantitative formulation of the concept of δύναμις, possibility, or in the later Latin version, *potentia*, in Aristotle's philosophy."[97] The actualization of this potentiality is the act of measurement whereby the wave function is reduced, or "collapses" to one of the eigenstates of which it is a superposition (a type of sum) and to which corresponds a possible (potential) result of the measurement, for example, the particle has spin up or spin down. Heisenberg's analogy to Aristotle is right in this sense: the process of wave-function collapse cannot be expressed mathematically, it cannot be modeled (imaged) as the spatio-temporal variation of some Cartesian magnitudes as in a classical equation of motion. Wave function collapse from a set of many possible outcomes to one actual outcome escapes the grasp of mathematics. With a notable exception, discussed below, the reduction of *dunamis* to *energeia* in Aristotle's physics likewise escapes the grasp of mathematics. Unlike Aristotle's act and potency, however, the possible outcomes

96. Matt Crawford, private communication, July 30, 2006.

97. The full quotation is that the probability amplitude, $\psi(x, t)$, is "a quantitative formulation of the concept of δύναμις, possibility, or in the later Latin version, *potentia*, in Aristotle's philosophy. The concept that events are not determined in a peremptory manner, but that the possibility or 'tendency' for an event to take place has a kind of reality—a certain intermediate layer of reality, halfway between the massive reality of matter and the intellectual reality of the idea or the image—this concept plays a decisive role in Aristotle's philosophy. In modern quantum theory this concept takes on a new form; it is formulated quantitatively as probability and subjected to mathematically expressible laws of nature [e.g., the Schroedinger equation]." Heisenberg, *On Modern Physics* (New York: Clarkson Potter, 1961), 9–10.

of a quantum measurement occur with numerical probabilities that can be calculated from the wave function, such as .75 for spin up, .25 for spin down. More generally (since every analogy is imperfect), of the various senses of the potentially being and its actualization in Aristotle, none fits quantum processes exactly.[98]

Let us state the essential conclusion of this section: because act and potency, thus actualization of potentiality and material parts potential in the whole, do not belong to mathematical objects—whether ancient or modern—modern physico-mathematical secularism entails their banishment from physics. This decision was adequate for classical physics, but not for quantum physics.

CONCLUSION: SEEING HETEROGENEITY, MAKING HOMOGENEITY

The preceding paragraph poses a final question on which to collect our thoughts and finish this essay: premodern (ancient and medieval) physics had a significant mathematical component, namely, the four mixed or intermediate sciences, optics, harmonics, mechanics, and astronomy, which employed premodern mathematics, namely, arithmetic, geometry (also trigonometry), and proportion theory.[99] For example, Aquinas speaks of "reckoning the courses of the stars" (*cursus siderum computare*) in mathematical astronomy, for "mobile and incorruptible beings, owing to their uniformity and regularity, can be determined in their movements by mathematical principles."[100] But there is nothing in premodern

98. I find five senses (some overlapping) of potentiality with respect to material structure and change in Aristotle: (1) motion (*kinêsis*) in the categories of quantity, quality, and place, and (2) change (*metabolê*) in the category of substance (*Physics* III.1.201a11, 210a29, 201b5, III.2.202a7; *Metaphysics* V.12.1019a21–23, VII.9.1034a35–b1, IX.7.1049a14–17); actualization of (3) first and (4) second potency (*Physics* VIII.4.255a32–b14, *De Anima* II.1.412a22–29); (5) body parts being potentially in a whole living substance (*Metaphysics* V.26.1023b33–35, VII.16.1040b5–17; *De Anima* II.2.414a20–28). With respect to mathematical objects, points and intervals can be potentially in a line (*Physics* VIII.8.262a22–24, 263a28). For a detailed and clear explanation of the sense of potentiality in quantum physics, see Bohm, *Quantum Physics*, 132–33, 138–40, 166–67. This is not to be confused with the quantum potential of Bohm's later hidden-variables (specifically pilot-wave) theory; "A Suggested Interpretation of the Quantum Theory in Terms of 'Hidden' Variables," *Physical Review* 85, no. 2 (January 15, 1952): 166–93.

99. Aristotle, *Posterior Analytics* I.13.78b35–79a16; *Physics* II.2.193b32–194a12.

100. Aquinas, *In de trinitate*, q. 5, a. 1, ad 3, and a. 3, ad 8 (18, 46). In "reckoning the courses of the stars," geometrical figures (Ptolemaic circles) would image their paths while numbers

science like physico-mathematical secularism, no suspension of judgment concerning the difference between mathematical objects and physical objects, thus no ruling (methodological) assumption that the difference between them could make no difference for the science of nature. What accounts for this? The answer to this question becomes clear to the extent that we can remove ourselves from the conceptual standpoint of modern mathematics and physics and recover that naively direct (and thus error-prone) way of receiving the world characteristic of Aristotle's philosophy. There, as noted in part 3, above, we see (literally and figuratively) *heterogeneity*—differences in kind—in both mathematical beings and physical beings. As long as we apprehend several different kinds of mathematical beings (continuous magnitudes, discrete numbers, and, where homogeneity restrictions permit, ratios and proportions of them) none of which is subject to *kinêsis*, along with several other different kinds of physical beings (celestial, terrestrial, and among the latter, nonliving and living, and among the latter, plants and animals, and among the latter, nonhuman and human) each of which is substance and subject to *kinêsis* in different analogous degrees—as long as this is the case, it is clearly impossible to think that the difference between mathematicals and physicals might not matter for the science of nature.

The most striking difference or heterogeneity in the physical world is that between celestial and terrestrial. Aquinas just mentioned the most perfect kind of physical beings, the celestial bodies, which are (by the erroneous science of his time) incorruptible, and whose local motions are, accordingly, so regular that arithmetic and geometry can be applied to them. But, therefore, among the celestial bodies, generation does not occur, but only local motion, in which the mobile "departs least from its substance" (*Physics* VIII.7.261a22). In striking contrast, among the terrestrial living things, there is a craftlike succession of stages in their generation from seed (*Physics* II.8.199a8–19); final cause and chance are evident there, but there is (to this day) no mathematical description of their natural local motions. In sum, celestial and terrestrial beings are vividly distinct: in the one kind, we have mathematical description but final cause is not evident; in the other, final cause is evident but we have no

and fractions of angular units (all discrete) would approximate the positions of the stars at a given time continuously moving on those paths.

mathematical description. Among mathematical beings, as opposed to physical, the fundamental difference in kind is not at all so evident.

The essential heterogeneity among mathematical beings is that of discrete number and continuous magnitude. It is very difficult for us today to understand sympathetically the reasons for this longstanding premodern distinction. We are, as it were, born to the real number line, the Cartesian numerical-variable magnitudes described above, and this mental formation begins with elementary-school arithmetic. Jacob Klein's work on the origins of algebra is about this, and thus about the removal of the distinction within human cognition between discrete and continuous mathematical beings in favor of algebraic *symbols* lying in "a new [homogeneous] conceptual dimension"—and all that this implies.[101]

I wish here simply to bring out the following basic point: it is only after homogenizing the heterogeneities of both physical and mathematical objects, and thus conceiving the possibility of an adequation, fit, or match of Cartesian numerical magnitudes to the properties of physical beings, that physico-mathematical secularism becomes possible. These two homogenizations are historically concurrent but very different. The one in physics or natural science is famous; it is the Scientific Revolution, culminating in Newton's physics and the accompanying forces-and-particles conception of the world in which species-specific forms and ends are replaced by species-neutral laws of nature. The one in mathematics remains all but invisible.[102] But both have this in common: they have more the character of making (construction, creation) than of seeing (intuition, intellection).[103] But whereas the homogenizing transition in mathematics is subtle and inconspicuous, that in physics seems conspicuously willful. Granted, it was surely right to remove the mis-

101. "[This] modification ... of ancient mathematics is *exemplary* for the total design of human knowledge in later times" (*Greek Mathematical Thought*, 120–21). "Therewith the most important tool of mathematical natural science, the 'formula,' first becomes possible ... but, above all, a new way of 'understanding,' [a different conception of the world, a different understanding of the world's being] inaccessible to ancient *episteme* is thus opened up" (ibid., 175, 152). See 184–85, 192, 213, on the awareness of fundamental problems that is thereby lost.

102. "It remains immensely difficult to leave that medium of ordinary intentionality which corresponds to our [modern] mode of thinking, a mode essentially established in the last four centuries" (*Greek Mathematical Thought*, 118).

103. For a remarkable and remarkably interesting development of the meaning of construction in the history of mathematics, see David R. Lachterman, *The Ethics of Geometry: A Genealogy of Modernity* (New York: Routledge, 1989).

taken heterogeneity of celestial and terrestrial, but was it right to remove *all* heterogeneity from nature (living and nonliving, *human and nonhuman*), thereby committing science to conceive nature as all one stuff, for example, forces and particles, or particles and fields—"material to work on" in Locke's memorable phrase?[104] As long noted by thoughtful commentators, this leaves human being, especially the scientist, in an odd position.[105] Perhaps the greatest value of Aristotle lies not his philosophy of nature, which is valuable, as I have tried to show, but in his ethics: "Precision ought not to be sought in the same way in all discourses.... For it belongs to an educated person [*pepaideumenou*] to seek just so much precision in each kind [of discourse] as the nature of the subject admits."[106] But Aristotle's educated person has a special disposition that enables perception and judgment of limits and boundaries, one that is difficult to reconcile with that of modern natural science. And so we return to the beginning of this essay. I give Heidegger almost the last word:

> Modern science's way of representing pursues and entraps nature as a calculable coherence of forces. Modern physics is not experimental physics because it applies apparatus to the questioning of nature. Rather the reverse is true. Because physics, indeed already as pure theory, sets nature up to exhibit itself as a coherence of forces calculable in advance, it therefore orders its experiments precisely for the purpose of asking whether and how nature reports itself when set up in this way.... If modern [quantum] physics must resign itself ever increasingly to the fact that its realm of representation remains inscrutable and incapable of being visualized, this resignation is not dictated by any committee of researchers. It is challenged forth by the rule of Enframing [*Ge-stell*], which demands that nature be orderable as standing-reserve. Hence physics, in all its retreating from the representation turned only towards objects [i.e., the classical conception of

104. Locke, *Second Treatise of Civil Government*, chap. 5, section 35.

105. In addition to the writings of Kennington and Riezler, cited above, see the reflections on natural science and human self-understanding in Hans Jonas, Leon Kass, Charles De Koninck, C. S. Lewis, and Leo Strauss.

106. Nicomachean Ethics I.3.1094b13, 24–25 (2, translation slightly modified). Rule 1 of Descartes's *Rules for the Direction of the Mind* is precisely targeted against this (AT X 359–60, CSM I 9). The remainder of that early, unfinished work is a key text for the twofold homogenization that is constitutive of the modern scientific mind. We can appreciate Heidegger's remark: "Only one who has really thought through this relentlessly sober volume long enough, down to its remotest and coldest corner, fulfils the prerequisite for getting an inkling of what is going on in modern science." *What Is a Thing?*, trans. W. B. Barton Jr. and Vera Deutsch (South Bend, Ind.: Regnery, 1967), 101.

mind and world] that has alone been standard till recently, will never be able to renounce this one thing: that nature reports itself in some way or other that is identifiable through calculation and that it remains orderable as a system of information [i.e., digit strings].[107]

This means that our physics has nothing to say about the unity of nature or creation.

107. Heidegger, *The Question concerning Technology*, trans. William Lovitt (New York: Harper and Row, 1977), 21, 23.

Thomas W. Merrill

8 Hume contra Humean Practical Reason

Philosophy as the Choice of Our Guide

For many commentators, "Humean practical reason" is one name of contemporary relativism or emotivism with regard to morality. Humean practical reason in this sense denotes the view that reason is, in practical matters, simply instrumental. While reason can tell us whether a given choice of means is efficient or inefficient, it cannot give us any guidance about whether the ends of our actions are praiseworthy or despicable, whether we can reasonably endorse those ends or not. The ends of our actions are, on this view, simply derived from the passions, or whims, or subjective taste. This standard view of Humean practical reason finds its textual support in a well known passage from the *Treatise of Human Nature*: "Reason is, and ought only to be the slave of the passions, and can never pretend to any other office than to serve and obey them" (2.3.3.4).[1] This view also seems to be exemplified in Hume's observation that "Where a passion is neither founded on false suppositions, nor chooses means insufficient for the end, the understanding can neither justify or condemn it" (2.3.3.6). Reason cannot even, it seems, condemn a person who prefers the trivial pleasure of scratching his finger to the destruction of the world (2.3.3.6). Not surprisingly, this view has been extremely unsatisfying to almost all commentators. We want to believe that our deepest commitments are rationally defensible, that they rest on something

1. Parenthetical references in the text and footnotes are to the book, part, section, and paragraph of the *Treatise of Human Nature*, ed. David Fate Norton and Mary J. Norton (New York: Oxford University Press, 2000).

more solid than mere caprice or brute passion. In this light, Humean practical reason appears to be the very definition of modern relativism or nihilism. Indeed, "Humean practical reason" has become a term of art to denote the view that reason is only instrumental and without the capacity to judge ends.[2]

Yet it may well be asked, is "Humean practical reason" *Hume's* practical reason? A significant body of literature interpreting Hume's thought in recent years says no.[3] These commentators argue that the "slave to the passions" passage misstates Hume's true views on moral and ethical matters. Hume's point, they suggest, is not that we ought to unreflectively endorse all and every passion, no matter how destructive its consequences. It is rather that reason in isolation does not motivate us and so cannot be the source of our moral sentiments, which do motivate us. On this view passion is an inseparable part of moral judgment and deliberation, and Hume's aim in the "slave of the passions" question is to underline the centrality of the passions in any deliberation, moral deliberation included. It does not follow from the indispensability of the passions, however, that some form of impartiality or ethical objectivity is impossible. Indeed, these commentators hold that the "slave to the passions" passage is radically misunderstood if we do not see that the passions in question are, for Hume, moral passions: the moral sentiments, on this view, have a kind of sovereignty for Hume that the standard account of "Humean practical reason" completely misses.

There is much to learn from this literature, especially insofar as it points to Hume's intention to support liberal political institutions, a project that necessarily includes a more than merely instrumentalist account

2. The term is so used, for example, by commentators who agree in rejecting "Humean practical reason" even though their own ultimate commitments are quite different and incompatible: cf. Christine Korsgaard, "Skepticism about Practical Reason," *Journal of Philosophy* 83, no. 1 (January 1986): 5–25; Alasdair MacIntyre, *After Virtue*, rev. ed. (South Bend, Ind.: Notre Dame Press, 2007); Robert Pippin, *Idealism as Modernism: Hegelian Variations* (Cambridge: Cambridge University Press, 1996); Robert George, *In Defense of Natural Law* (Oxford: Oxford University Press, 1999), 17n4.

3. See, for example, David Fate Norton, *David Hume: Common-Sense Moralist, Skeptical Metaphysician* (Princeton, N.J.: Princeton University Press, 1982); Annette Baier, *A Progress of Sentiments: Reflections on Hume's* Treatise (Cambridge, Mass.: Harvard University Press, 1991); Sharon Krause, *Civil Passions: Moral Sentiment and Democratic Deliberation* (Princeton, N.J.: Princeton University Press, 2008), chap. 3; and Michael Frazer, *The Enlightenment of Sympathy: Justice and the Moral Sentiments in the Eighteenth Century and Today* (Oxford: Oxford University Press, 2010).

of practical reason.[4] Yet there is a dimension of this question that has been largely overlooked by the literature on Hume's account of the moral sentiments. Consider the claim that Hume makes at 1.4.7.13:

> Since therefore 'tis almost impossible for the mind of man to rest, like those of beasts, in that narrow circle of objects, which are the subject of daily conversation and action, we ought only to deliberate concerning the choice of our guide, and ought to prefer that which is safest and most agreeable. And in this respect I make bold to recommend philosophy, and shall not scruple to give it the preference to superstition of every kind and denomination.

Human beings, it seems, face a fundamental choice about which we must deliberate: should philosophy or superstition be the "choice of our guide"? At this moment, at least, Hume shows no hesitation about the role of philosophy or reason in human life: philosophy, he makes bold to assert, should be the "choice of our guide." Yet this is paradoxical: can it really be that philosophy should be our guide but our reason ought to be a slave to the passions? At the very least, one might say, we cannot give an adequate account of Hume's thought on these matters without giving some explanation of how the two statements, the apparent assertion of the sovereignty of rationalism and the apparent assertion of reason's thoroughgoing subordination to passion, go together: those interested in *Hume's* practical reason cannot simply identify it with *Humean* practical reason.

In this essay, I argue that both the conventional reading of Hume's emotivism and the recent commentators who emphasize moral sentiment get Hume's views about reason and the passions wrong because they fail to take seriously enough Hume's reflections on his own stance as a thinker. As I show, the *Treatise* presents a kind of contest between different forms of rationality. The first may be very roughly described

4. I have in mind here claims such as these: that while most people may not be aware of the arguments supporting a right of resistance to tyranny, "all men have an implicit notion of it" (3.2.10), i.e., all men are in some way conscious of the fact that resisting tyrants is just; and that the institution of slavery in the ancient world or the modern is contrary to "the eternal laws of reason and equity." *Essays, Moral Political and Literary*, ed. Eugene F. Miller (Indianapolis, Ind.: Liberty Fund, 1987), 384. While I do not pursue these themes here, I note that the core of Hume's politics is effectively that of modern natural right and not far in its central moral intuitions from Locke or Jefferson (however much their judgments on particular matters may diverge). For further discussion, see Thomas W. Merrill, "The Rhetoric of Rebellion in Hume's Constitutional Thought," *Review of Politics* 67, no. 2 (Spring 2005): 257–82.

as a version of Cartesian science, which aspires to provide a systematic physics characterized by discursive clarity and epistemological precision on the model of mathematical demonstration. That science is, moreover, associated with a dualistic account of what it means to be a human being, such that it is possible to speak of reason and passion being masters and slaves. The second is a form of moral and political philosophy, understood as a set of reflections by human beings on human beings. This form of rationality, Hume tells us, is moved by a natural inclination to inquire into all things (including, most paradigmatically, the question of the first or sufficient cause) and it takes human nature as the central object of its inquiry. It is this rationality that Hume recommends to us as the "choice of our guide," and it begins from the nondualistic insight that reason is an activity of the passions, not something separate from the passions.

As I argue below, the pivotal drama of the *Treatise of Human Nature* as a whole is the replacement of the former form of rationality by the second. To understand what Hume meant when he said that reason ought to be slave to the passions, therefore, we need to understand how and why for Hume science must be superseded by political philosophy and how that supersession or replacement explains Hume's account of reason and the passions. In what follows, I begin by explaining how Hume understood modern, Cartesian science and why he thought that it had certain, deeply rooted limitations, especially with regard to crucial matters of self-accounting and self-justification (section 1). I then turn to the crucial turning point in the argument of the *Treatise of Human Nature*, the last section of Book I (1.4.7), where Hume shows how and why modern science must be supplemented and guided by a human reflection about human things or moral and political philosophy. It is in this context that Hume asserts that philosophy should be our guide, and I suggest that this turn is the ground of Hume's true account of practical reason (section 2). Yet Hume's moral-political turn, even reconstructed in the way I propose, is nonetheless enigmatic and requires interpretation. Guided by an illuminating and underappreciated essay on Hume by Thomas Prufer, I provide an interpretation of the philosophical (as opposed to merely political) meaning of Hume's assertion of the superiority of moral and political philosophy (section 3). I then examine the slave of the passions passage directly, and suggest that the distinction between science and philosophy helps to clarify what Hume meant. While modern, Cartesian science understands itself from the beginning as an instrument or slave of the passions, philosophy is for Hume, perhaps paradoxically, itself a passion, albeit a passion that reasons. These crucial qualifications to the slave of the passions passage, I argue, point to Hume's more fundamental rethinking of the dualistic premises of the modern scientific project (section 4). Finally, I briefly consider the significance of this reinterpretation of Hume's views of reason and the passions for morality. The moral sense, our awareness of our need for some objective justification of our actions, turns out to provide the crucial clue for Hume's post-scientific investigation of human nature (section 5). I conclude with some reflections on the role of reason in Hume's account of the human things.

THE PROBLEM OF SCIENCE

Modern science, understood along Baconian-Cartesian lines as the methodical study of nature for the sake of relieving man's estate, is the initial theme of the *Treatise of Human Nature*. Hume famously opens the book with a boast that he will put an end to the interminable wrangling of all previous philosophers by putting the "science of man" on a new footing, on the firm foundation of "experience and observation." One could easily get the impression that Hume simply means to apply the methods of modern science to a novel object, human nature itself. He seems at first to be merely extending the Baconian-Cartesian project, not rethinking it. Yet not all appeals to experience and observation are the same, and Hume soon makes an analogy that cuts in quite another direction. It should not be surprising, he remarks, that the application of experimental philosophy to moral subjects should come at the long interval of a century after the advent of modern science proper, since it so happens that the interval between the birth of natural philosophy and the beginning of moral and political philosophy proper in antiquity was about the same. "Reckoning from Thales to Socrates," he remarks, "the space of time is nearly equal to that betwixt my Lord Bacon and some late philosophers in England, who have begun to put the science of man on a new footing."[5] Let us overlook Hume's bashfulness in burying him-

5. Introduction to the *Treatise*, 7.

self in a crowd of "late philosophers in England" and restate his analogy more directly. Hume will do for the founders of modern science, especially Bacon, what Socrates did for Thales and the other Presocratics.

Readers of the Platonic dialogues will know that this is no small claim, and not at all equivalent to merely applying someone else's research project to a new set of objects. According to the account given in the *Phaedo*, Socrates started out being a natural philosopher or scientist but was compelled to recognize certain grave defects in the science of his time and perhaps of any time. Perhaps the most serious such defect was the inability of that science to account for its own activity. Socrates was thereby compelled to make his famous "second sailing in search of the cause." That Socratic enterprise, we are told, took our everyday moral and political opinions as its starting point and attempted to reflect on the whole in light of enduring problems of human self-accounting and self-knowledge. Everyone sees Hume's boast to be the first scientist of human nature; but buried within that boast is the even more startling boast to be the Socrates of modern times. This observation raises a question about what Hume really means by his "science of man." Does he intend to follow through on the Baconian project, as we are initially tempted to read him? Or does he mean something different, as the Socratic analogy implies, a science of human nature that begins from a recognition of the inadequacies of science in the Baconian sense?

I believe that the latter alternative is correct and provides the key to Hume's intention in the *Treatise*.[6] That intention is complex, since Hume by no means rejects science. To the end, he remains a friend of science. Yet a friend of science is not necessarily a scientist through and through. For Hume science remains embedded in a deeper set of perplexities that it can neither elucidate nor avoid. Science as a practice can and must go on, but self-aware scientists must come to terms with the limitations internal to science itself, not least with regard to self-accounting and self-justification. In the remainder of this section I sketch very briefly the outlines of Hume's treatment of this question as it unfolds across Book I of the *Treatise*.

Book I of the *Treatise* elaborates Hume's initial aspiration to an epis-

6. It is relevant to the question of Hume's Socratism that he describes his own position at the end of the *Enquiry Concerning Human Understanding* as Academic skepticism. The Academy, of course, was founded by Plato and represented the skeptical branch of Platonism.

temologically precise, systematic science of nature, understood in a broadly Cartesian fashion. That science has at least three main commitments, each of which can be traced to a Cartesian source. The first is a roughly Cartesian account of consciousness that holds that our primary access to the world is not to the world itself but to the "perceptions of the mind" (1.1.1.1).[7] Fully elaborated, Humean science would not be a science of beings in their own right, a squirrel, say, or a tree—but a science of the ideas and impressions that make up our image of a squirrel or a tree. More precisely, Humean science will seek genuine or well-founded constancies within our perceptions and cast aside merely spurious or accidental correlations. Second, Humean science or knowledge as initially elaborated rests on an ideal of discursive clarity understood on the model of mathematics, especially algebra and arithmetic.[8] These sciences, unlike geometry, which always has an irreducible messiness, allow us to "carry on a chain of reasoning to any degree of intricacy, and yet preserve a perfect exactness and certainty" (1.3.1.5). While perhaps not confined to unfolding analytic truths, knowledge in the full-fledged sense, as Hume understands it, would move from intuited simples to complex wholes through discursively clear and demonstrative inferences.

Hume's third commitment is to what is sometimes called the separability criterion.[9] The separability criterion holds that all perceptions of the mind can be separated in perceptual simples, and that all perceptions that we can conceive of as separated from one another may in fact be separated from each other in reality. Stated the other way around,

7. This commitment is visible in the opening lines of Book I, which begins by distinguishing "perceptions of the mind" (1.1.1.1) into ideas and impressions and is spelled out at 1.2.6.7–8: "nothing is ever really present with the mind but its perceptions or impressions or ideas [...]. To hate, to love, to think, to feel, to see: all this is nothing but to perceive." By starting with ideas and impressions Hume implicitly rules out starting with the beings themselves.

8. Descartes articulates the ideal of mathematical rationality for knowledge in the *Discourse on Method*: "Those long chains composed of very simple and easy reasonings, which geometers customarily use to arrive at their most difficult demonstrations, had given me occasion to suppose that all the things that fall under human knowledge are interconnected in the same way." *Philosophical Writings of Descartes*, ed. John Cottingham, Robert Stoothoff, and Dugald Murdoch (New York: Cambridge University Press, 1985), 1:120. See also the *Rules for the Direction of the Mind*.

9. It is so called by Don Garrett, for example, in *Cognition and Commitment in Hume's Philosophy* (New York: Oxford University Press, 1997), chap. 3. For examples in the *Treatise*, see 1.2.1.3, 1.2.3.10, 1.2.5.3, and 1.2.6.3–4. For the ancestor of this position in Descartes, see *Meditations*, Part 6.

only those ideas and impressions that are so integrally linked that we cannot even conceive of them as separated can be known, as opposed to opined, to be linked. The separability criterion, one might say, lays down the ground rules for a strict, "mathematical" account of knowledge, a discursively precise, wholly transparent account of things. In that account, ideas and impressions would work like pixels on your computer screen. Pixels are in themselves wholly discrete: added together in sufficient numbers, however, they can present complicated, lifelike images. That Hume has some such notion of what a successful science would be is confirmed by his otherwise inexplicable claim that there must be minima sensibilia, smallest possible perceptions (1.2.1.3; 1.2.3.14–15; 1.2.4.19). His insistence of such a most basic building block leads him to make the very strange argument that lines are not infinitely divisible. It is almost as if he has never heard of the diagonal of the square. Yet as absurd as it may seem, the quest (for Hume only argues that there must be such a thing, not that he has actually found it) for a minimum perception is a necessary part of a discursively precise epistemology.

Such is the dream of an epistemologically precise science as Hume sketches it in Book I. That science succeeds in some respects but fails in other, perhaps more important respects. It succeeds insofar as it provides a framework for distinguishing well-founded generalizations from poorly founded ones. In this vein, Hume's treatment of science culminates in his "rules to judge of causes and effects" and the ground those rules give Hume to criticize "unphilosophical probabilities," which have the epistemic status of what we call stereotypes. On this level, science prospers as an ongoing, self-correcting, iterative endeavor to reach clarity about the phenomena of nature. On a deeper level, however, Hume's science runs into serious problems. The general shape of these problems is already visible in the separability criterion itself. By applying that criterion relentlessly and analyzing everything into its constituent perceptions, Hume makes it all but inevitable that science will face a crisis of how and why things hang together. A science guided by the separability criterion can provide a precise analysis of anything in its purview; it cannot, however, explain why things are integral wholes. Indeed, a good first approximation of Hume's skepticism is that it is the flipside of the separability criterion. His skepticism, one might say, is the hangover left by his science.

This is not just a problem, it must be underlined, for wooly-headed

Aristotelians or romantics in love with some primal wholeness of things. The problem goes to the heart of what it means to know or to be a self at all, including most especially the knower himself. This problem plays out in two prominent ways in the *Treatise*: belief, on the one hand, and the identity of things, including that identity we care most about, personal identity, on the other. By belief Hume means anything we take to be true, especially when a perception of something present makes us think that something else not present also exists. In Hume's more technical formulation, belief is a "lively idea related to or associated with a present impression" (1.3.7.5). The problem is that the separability criterion enjoins us not to recognize any entities as real above the level of bare ideas and impressions. No wholes, no hidden connections, are to be admitted. Yet we do believe in such things—nothing fancy, just the sort of entities we navigate around every day. Our ideas and impressions do not show up in our experience as unconnected pixels, but as intertwined with one another, in motion and in train with others. The ontology implied by the separability criterion is far too severe for any world remotely like the one we live in. Our mental life for Hume is more accurately described as a kind of zoology in which ideas and impressions act out a more or less natural lifecycle. Hume's governing metaphor for this way of seeing things is vivacity. Vivacity is that thing that differentiates something we genuinely believe in from something that we idly entertain, as a thought experiment. And what is vivacity? It is literally a je-ne-sais-quoi (1.3.8.16); we cannot say precisely what it is, but "we know it when we see it." The dream of an epistemologically precise, discursively transparent science runs into its limit in the apparently nonanalyzable, nondefinable root of belief.

These issues come to a head in Hume's famous discussion of personal identity near the end of Book I. Hume asks why we believe in personal identity at all. Why, he asks, do we "suppose ourselves possest of an invariable and uninterrupted existence thro' the whole course of our lives" (1.4.6.5)? Hume notes that we do not, in fact, have any single impression that accounts for our idea of self. When we examine the self, we find only a series of impressions of other things and never a single impression that is always with us labeled "self." Hume goes on to draw a surprising conclusion: "The identity, which we ascribe to the mind of man, is only a fictitious one, and of like kind with that which we ascribe to vegetables and animal bodies" (1.4.6.15). The use of the separability criterion dissolves even the self. The belief we take most for granted, that we are enduring selves, seems to be nothing more than a fiction. We are close indeed to a full blown skeptical crisis. But note some odd aspects to this argument. First, the sense of personal identity in question seems vastly stronger than any notion of personal identity we use in everyday life: Hume repeatedly describes the notion in question as one of "invariable and uninterrupted" identity. It is almost as if the self is or could be a Platonic notion of the self, always the same and uninterrupted by the flux of the world. Let me suggest that Hume is describing, not why I believe myself to be the same person today I was yesterday, but why we might believe in something like a separate soul or a pure mind as Descartes might have it. Second, there is something off even about Hume's claims that our identities are fictional. He says, "the identity *we ascribe*," "*we attribute*," "*we feign*." *We* feign? Who is this *we* that is doing all this work to construct a fictitious sense of our own identity? Does this not mean that at some level there is a self, perhaps not an eternally simple and identical self but one stable enough for all practical purposes? It is hard not to find something humorous in the whole argument.

But there is a serious point behind the argument: the epistemologically precise science elaborated in the course of *Treatise* Book I cannot give a plausible account of the self. In the wake of the unrestrained application of the separability criterion, the self, like everything else, comes to seem no more than a bundle of only accidentally related ideas and impressions. But this compels us to recognize something we might otherwise have ignored. Science presupposes, but cannot account for, the integrity of the self of the scientific knower himself. Put differently, unless there is some self that can think things together as well as think them separately, science is impossible. Science is dependent on something it cannot itself clarify. Personal identity is one of those things we can neither reasonably deny nor explain using the analytic tools of the epistemology of Book I of the *Treatise*. But this is to raise the question, what do we presuppose when we think that scientific knowing is possible? The questioner is himself called into question. It should come as no surprise, then, that the chapter on personal identity is the immediate prelude to Hume's frankest description of the crisis of science itself.

PHILOSOPHICAL MELANCHOLY AND DELIRIUM

That crisis is expressed in dramatic and unforgettable form in the very last section of Book I of the *Treatise of Human Nature*. There Hume raises, in autobiographical terms, the question of the human significance of the theoretical problems we have been discussing. The world that science uncovers—or more accurately, perhaps, presupposes—turns out to be inimical to human life, including the life of the scientist himself. In Hume's phrase, the experience of nature as known by modern science produces "philosophical melancholy and delirium." This text is often read in surveys of the history of philosophy, usually out of context of the rest of the book and usually as a skeptical prelude to Kant. Yet this approach distracts us from appreciating what actually happens in the course of Hume's philosophical autobiography. In this section I describe what happens in 1.4.7; in the next section I speculate on what is at stake philosophically in Hume's turn.

This section of the *Treatise* has fifteen paragraphs that divide into two equal parts separated by a central paragraph. That paragraph, paragraph eight, is a direct expression of the human experience of the nature of nature as known by modern science. That experience, which Hume calls "philosophical melancholy and delirium," is central both in the arrangement of the paragraphs and the substance of the argument. Paragraphs one through seven describe what may be called the way down to "melancholy and delirium" and moves back and forth between our desire to know the "original and ultimate principle" and the Sisyphean character of our efforts to satisfy that desire. Paragraphs nine through fifteen, the way back up, gives an account of what it might mean to philosophize in the light of our ignorance of first causes and what difference it makes for political life.

In the downward sequence in the first seven paragraphs, Hume first presents himself as a battered sailor who is about to set out to sea again, despite having narrowly escaped shipwreck. Like Socrates, Hume's initial voyage has apparently failed, and yet he is about to try again. This sailor travels neither for commerce nor to reach a specific destination. His ambition is comprehensive: he means to "compass [...] the globe, even under these disadvantageous circumstances" (1.4.7.1). Yet the immensity of the sea, "that boundless expanse," is terrifying. The meaning of the image becomes clearer as the key question of Hume's crisis comes into view. Recall that the pressing question of Book I is why things hang together at all, a question that has several objects, including everyday things, persons, and the world as a whole. Having been successful in using causes to explain things in the world, the human mind finds it impossible to resist trying to find the causes of those causes, on up to the "original" or "ultimate" cause. Hume remarks, "Nothing is more curiously enquir'd after by the mind of man than the causes of every phenomenon; nor are we content knowing the immediate causes but push on our enquiries, till we reach the original and ultimate principle" (1.4.7.5). Hume's skepticism is unintelligible if it is not seen in the light of its guiding question, the question of the first cause or natural theology. Hume bears unforgettable witness to the fact and depth of philosophical desire.

Let us call those who try to answer this question metaphysicians. Hume describes metaphysicians in this sense as devotees of the "opinion of the double existence of perceptions and objects" (1.4.2.46). This doctrine of double existence holds that there must be true objects, perhaps accessible only to a few, that cause or stand behind the manifest variability in the world that we all see. Platonic Ideas or Aristotelian substances are ancient examples; the view that bedrock reality is made up of the objects of our mathematical physics (shape, motion, speed) is Hume's modern example. Yet all of these examples, according to Hume, including mathematical physics, present a contradiction (1.4.5.15). On the one hand, they dismiss the variable appearances as worthless in the light of the superior intelligibility of the true objects; on the other, they admit or must admit that our only access to those true objects is through the appearances. Hume's judgment on his philosophic predecessors is that they simultaneously deny any validity to the "vulgar" point of view, while surreptitiously relying on just that point of view. Of the metaphysicians Hume says that they are like "those angels whom the scripture represents as covering their eyes with their wings" (1.4.7.6). What leads them to ascend also blinds them to what is right in front of them. His predecessors were hypocrites and boasters. But this also means that first or ultimate principles are elusive and philosophical desire is Sisyphean.

This is the thought that precipitates Hume's crisis. Most of us live in happy ignorance of these questions. We go about our business with nary a thought to the possibility that we might be skating on thin ice.

Not the least of these are the scientists, who treat causality as though it were known to be simply true. Yet once the question about the first cause is raised, there is no going back. For if we do not have insight into the "original and ultimate principle," how do we know that the future will resemble the past? Why do we think that a cause is required at all? Science presupposes that reality is causal but never proves it. Yet really to think the possibility that the world is not held together by something is bewildering, even wholly disorienting. The immensity of the sea is nothing in comparison to the indeterminacy opened up by our ignorance of first causes. Those who do not turn away from, or hide from themselves, the abyss that lies behind modern science will not know up from down. Hume calls this experience one of being "inviron'd with the deepest darkness"; it is perhaps what the world would look like if the separability principle were simply true, a statement about the ontology of things rather than a demand of methodology. On the deepest level the world of modern science is marked by an ontological indeterminacy. Yet to live in accord with that indeterminacy threatens insanity or "philosophical melancholy and delirium."

For all his pathos, however, Hume's drama does not end in insanity or the rejection of philosophy. Far from it: the immediate sequel involves a relaunching of radical inquiry, this time with no apparent worry about delirium, and culminates in an unexpected endorsement of philosophy as our "guide." Where the first seven paragraphs show the threat to a stable human life posed by radical inquiry, the last seven suggest that philosophy is not only unavoidable for serious human beings but required by sound politics. The trajectory of the way up has three stages. First is nature's reassertion of its power. When reason fails to resolve the problems it has itself created, nature "cures me of this philosophical melancholy and delirium" (1.4.7.9). In the first instance, this means an expression of necessity. Hume finds himself "absolutely and necessarily determin'd to live, and talk, and act, like other people in the common affairs of life" (1.4.7.10). In one sense this is a return to the mode of existence of human beings prior to science and philosophy. It is the moment of Hume's backgammon game and the convivial enjoyment of food and drink. Necessity democratizes; and the philosophical elitists of the "double doctrine" are compelled to recognize their kinship with the hitherto despised vulgar. Yet this return to ordinary life is not a return to innocence. Hume's philosopher wishes to throw all his books and papers into the fire and renounce "reasoning and philosophy" altogether. Hume indicates, however, that this hedonistic moment is merely a cover for a smoldering resentment, an expression of his "spleen and indolence," not a reasoned conclusion (1.4.7.11). Like many hedonists, he seems to enjoy his pleasures not for their own sake but as a means of punishing a desire that cannot be fulfilled.

The second stage shows human nature to be more complex than it seems at first. Hume remarks that the initial turn to pleasure is the product of his "spleen and indolence," and before long another part of his nature reasserts itself. "At that time [...] that I am tired with amusement and company [...] I feel my mind all collected within itself and am naturally inclin'd to carry my view into all those subjects about which I have met with so many disputes in the course of my reading and conversation" (1.4.7.12). Hume tells us that he has a natural inclination to inquire, an inclination not visibly chastened by "melancholy and delirium." Nor is that inclination bounded in any immediately obvious way, since it extends into "all those subjects" about which Hume has met controversy, presumably including those metaphysical and theological questions that had so recently threatened his sanity. Horace famously remarked that you can throw nature out with a pitchfork, but it will always come back in.[10] Hume's inclination to radical inquiry has something of the same character.

Nonetheless, there is a clear shift in the third and final moment of Hume's re-ascent to sanity in both the object and mode of inquiry. Where questions of metaphysics and natural theology had dominated Hume's original inquiries, moral-political themes now become the central focus of Hume's philosopher: "I cannot forbear having a curiosity to be acquainted with the principles of moral good and evil, the nature and foundation of government, and the cause of those several passions and inclinations, which actuate and govern me" (1.4.7.12). Investigating morality ("the principles of good and evil") now goes hand in hand with the problem of self-knowledge ("the cause of those several passions [...] which [. . .] govern me.") But not even this turn to the political adequately prepares us for what comes next. Even if he were not led by a natural

10. Horace, *Satires, Epistles, and Ars Poetica*, trans. H. Ruston Fairclough (New York: G. P. Putnam's Sons, 1926), Book I, Epistle X, 24–25.

inclination to reopen all the questions that had so plagued him, Hume says, he or someone like him would be compelled to do so by the practical problem posed by superstition. Superstition is "much more bold in its systems and hypotheses than philosophy" and is able to "disturb us in the conduct of our lives and actions" (1.4.7.13). Hume alludes to the defining political experience of early modernity, the wars of religion that embroiled Europe in the sixteenth and seventeenth centuries. Like Hume's personal struggle, early modern European politics is characterized by disputes over the character of the first cause. It might well be said, then, that the wars of religion represent a political "melancholy and delirium" that echoes or images Hume's "philosophical melancholy and delirium." In depicting his personal crisis, Hume aims to uncover and excite reflection in his readers on the roots of the European political crisis: the personal and the political crises are linked insofar as they are both expressions of a theological crisis.

This political crisis elicits from Hume his strongest statement about philosophy's role in politics (1.4.7.13):

> Since therefore 'tis almost impossible for the mind of man to rest, like those of beasts, in that narrow circle of objects, which are the subject of daily conversations and action, we ought only to deliberate concerning the choice of our guide, and ought to prefer that which is safest and most agreeable. And in this respect I make bold to recommend philosophy, and shall not scruple to give it the preference to superstition of every kind and denomination.

Moments after almost convincing us he would have to be institutionalized, Hume tells us that philosophy ought to rule. He does not say philosophy can be a useful tool to those who are in fact ruling; he does not say that philosophy is a good thing to have studied in college before the real work of life gets started; he says that philosophy should be our guide. The assertion is so strong, and so out of accord with expectation, that it is no surprise that many readers have simply missed it. Hume has just told us that there a natural human inclination to inquire into all questions. Now he mounts a more political defense: philosophy is a necessary ingredient of sound politics, because superstition is a perennial possibility.

Nonetheless, this assertion of philosophic rule is almost immediately qualified, though not quite retracted. Political life is not exhausted by the philosophers and the superstitious. There are also those Hume calls the "honest gentlemen" and whom he describes as "being always employ'd in their domestic affairs or amusing themselves in common recreations" (1.4.7.14). These "gentlemen" are solid citizens and representatives of the private life untroubled by the dangerous or delirious desire for insight into ultimates. An important practical goal of this text is to lure the ordinary citizens into a political coalition with the philosophers and away from the superstitious; 1.4.7 is therefore the core of Hume's Enlightenment politics. Yet Hume's Enlightenment is not the French Enlightenment. Hume does not look forward to a simply enlightened society in which the distinction between ordinary citizen and philosopher is erased. In particular, Hume is quite clear that the gentlemen will not and ought not become philosophers. They will neither be "associates in these researches or auditors of these discoveries" (1.4.7.14). Indeed, it is the philosophers who must go to school with the gentlemen: Hume thinks the philosophers need to acquire "a share of this gross earthy mixture" as a means of tempering "those fiery particles, of which they are compos'd" (1.4.7.14). Hume suggests that in this coalition each party contributes a distinct good to the common enterprise. The ordinary citizens bring a sober common sense, without which the philosophers are liable to fly off, Icarus-like, toward questions of the first cause and the like. As we say, they keep the philosophers "grounded." Yet the philosophers do something for the citizens that they cannot do for themselves. Thanks to their harrowing experiences, searching after ultimate principles, so recently on display, they are able to shoot down unwarranted claims about those principles, especially those claims to rule made on the basis of claims about the first principles made by the superstitious. Hume offers to play epistemic cop for the liberal regime. But in light of this proposal what came before appears in a new light: what we thought was the existential angst of "melancholy and delirium" was Hume exhibiting his job qualifications.

Many commentators, less impressed with the sturdy virtue of English gentlemen than Hume is or seems to be, have a hard time sympathizing with this passage. Yet Hume may be talking less about the actual gentlemen of his time than attempting to describe a human type that does not yet quite exist. Consider how Hume describes the character of this type: they are sober and do not lose sight of their own interests. They seem to have no desire to rule others. Their only political desire, so far as we can tell from what is said here, is not to be tyrannized by others. Their primary desire, it seems, is to be left alone to lead their own private lives.[11] Although they seem not to be well-suited to ruling themselves, they are the perfect constituency for a politics of individual freedom. They are, I suggest, closer to a modern, democratic bourgeois than they are to an Aristotelian, aristocratic gentleman. Needless to say, philosophers of whatever sort also have a large interest in preserving a sphere of private life, and so an interest, Hume thinks, in encouraging the human type represented by the "honest gentlemen." That alliance between skeptical philosophers and citizens who want to be left alone to lead their lives in private, let me suggest, is the fundamental social contract of modern, liberal politics as Hume understands it.[12]

Note well, however, that there is some ambiguity about who exactly is going to rule in the society Hume sketches. Hume first tells us that philosophy must be the "choice of our guide" but then that philosophers must learn from the sober common sense of the "honest gentlemen." Perhaps the strength of the coalition requires some blurring of which has priority. Note also that in some decisive respects the philosophers have more in common with the now-exiled superstitious than with the sober citizens. Unlike the sober citizens, both the philosophers and the superstitious have an apparently irrepressible desire to inquire into whatever lies beyond the phenomena of everyday life. We may ask, for example, why is superstition a perennial danger? Because the superstitious raise *exactly* the same questions that Hume's philosophers do. The deepest human phenomenon brought to light in 1.4.7, then, is that same natural inclination to raise questions, especially questions about first principles and the like: "tis almost impossible for the mind of man to rest, like those of the beasts, in that narrow circle of objects, which are the subject

11. There is, for example, no reason in what Hume says why the "honest gentlemen" must be male.

12. The fruit in Hume's later thought of his assertion that philosophy should be our guide is the claim that the philosopher can be a kind of umpire or judge of the competing constitutional claims of the various factions, albeit without ever claiming to rule in his own name. This is the role of the historian as Hume understood it. "It belongs, therefore, to a philosopher alone, who is of neither party, to put all the circumstances in the scale, and assign to each of them its proper poise and influence. Such a one will readily, at first, acknowledge that all political questions are infinitely complicated, and that there scarcely ever occurs, in any deliberation, a choice, which is either purely good or purely ill [...]. Hesitation, and reserve, and suspence, are, therefore, the only sentiments, he brings to this essay or trial." *Essays*, 507.

of daily conversation and action" (1.4.7.13). From somewhere deep inside the human being comes a desire to which no known object measures up. While Hume shows us that that desire must be subordinated to the sober common sense of ordinary citizens, he also shows the irrepressibility of the human inclination to inquire into ultimates.

HUME'S TURN

Yet someone might object to the foregoing account of Hume's turn to moral-political things in the following way. Even if we grant the practical necessity of taming the natural human inclination to philosophical speculation, Hume's argument, at least as so far presented, only proposes a prudential strategy for managing that inclination, not a theoretical argument about the truth of these practices. Yet precisely if we take the natural human inclination to inquiry seriously, as Hume claims to do, such merely prudential answers cannot possibly be satisfying. For the prudential strategy can only work if the truth about things is not simply incompatible with that strategy. If reality simply is the "deepest darkness" that Hume seems to find at the nadir of his trajectory, for example, the political strategy of promoting peace and liberty must fail. However sympathetic to Hume's politics we may be on prudential grounds, then, we need some further theoretical argument to persuade us of their soundness. Otherwise, Hume will be vulnerable to the objection that he is promoting what he believes to be a fiction in order to cover up what he takes to be a truth destructive to human life.

The objection is a good one and not easy to answer. Despite his demand for analytic clarity, on this crucial point Hume abandons straightforward argument and presents his insight in poetic images. The philosopher, at least the systematic philosopher, is characterized by "fiery particles" that must be tempered by the "gross earthy mixture" of ordinary common sense. The image is immediately intelligible, yet its very intelligibility can easily obscure the question it raises: what, exactly, is the "gross earthy mixture" that the philosophers are to take on? What can the philosophers possibly learn from the "honest gentlemen"? Many commentators, impressed with the threat of modern nihilism, have thought that Hume has no answer to this question and is simply covering up the absence of any substantive teaching. Yet by Hume's own lights he understood himself to be articulating a fundamental reorientation of the philosophic enterprise, not its abandonment. He manifestly proposes a turn from one kind of philosophizing to another and replaces one set of questions—questions about the first principle or sufficient causation—with another: questions about human nature, especially our own natures, which brings in its course a host of moral-political topics. In this section I offer some speculations on what might be philosophically at stake in Hume's turn to moral-political topics, in light of his claim not to be abandoning genuine inquiry but reorienting it.

I begin with observations made by Thomas Prufer in an illuminating essay on the *Treatise of Human Nature.*[13] Prufer remarks that the structure of Hume's argument is a *modus tollens* argument, which has the following character. Given an if-then statement, negation of the consequence entails negation of the premise. Prufer seems to mean something like this. If science as Hume describes it in Book I of the *Treatise* is a simply accurate depiction of the world, then the world is in fact a "deepest darkness" and cognition is impossible. But the world is not a "deepest darkness" and cognition, at least in some contexts, is possible, so science cannot be the whole truth about the world. In particular, the initial premise of Hume's epistemology, the radical separability of things, cannot be a simply accurate description of the world we live in. That epistemology cannot explain why things hang together at all. Nor can it explain what it means to be a self or a knower at all, including what it means to be a scientific knower. In Prufer's helpful formulation, the radical nominalism of Hume's epistemology—completely free-floating, unconnected impressions—cannot be both lived and formulated. If that nominalism were simply true, we could not say that it were true. That we can say or entertain the possibility that it might be true suggests that something else is going on. Hume is, however, aware of this self-reflexive problem that arises on the basis of the epistemology. He intends to give us a reductio ad absurdum of the premises of the epistemology with which he begins. That epistemology cannot even make sense of its own activities, much less give a sufficient account of everything else.

This is not to say, of course, that Hume has, or indeed that we have,

13. Thomas Prufer, "A Reading of Hume's *A Treatise of Human Nature,*" in *Recapitulations: Essays in Philosophy* (Washington, D.C.: The Catholic University of America Press, 1993), 43–47.

some other account of what it means to be a self that is both epistemologically precise and theoretically sufficient. In fact, the point of Hume's working through the internal problems of Cartesian epistemology is to uncover a fundamental human experience of necessity and intelligibility that we always presuppose, even or especially when we do science. In the immediate aftermath of "philosophical melancholy and delirium," Hume discovers that nature has a kind of teaching that cannot be avoided: "Here then I find myself absolutely and necessarily determin'd to live, and talk, and act like other people in the common affairs of life" (1.4.7.10).[14] Nature as used here is not nature as known by Cartesian science; this nature is human nature, nature as experienced from the inside. Whatever the vicissitudes of science and metaphysics, there seem to be a pretheoretical experience of nature that we are all always relying on. That experience does not rest on any theoretical insight into the metaphysical natures of things and perhaps cannot be grounded in such an account. But neither does that experience require such "objective" grounding. It is of course logically possible to deny it, but only at the heavy price of not being able to say anything at all. All there is, if you refuse to begin from the pretheoretical evidence of nature, is the "deepest darkness." The human experience of the human has a primitive intelligibility on which we cannot help but rely. Put differently, we cannot start from whatever may be first in itself; we can only start from what is first for us, because the alternative is "philosophical melancholy and delirium." Our experience of the primitive intelligibility of things, it seems, is presupposed but not explained by science or by metaphysics. Indeed, the point of Hume's working through the internal problems of Cartesian epistemology is to turn us around and show us that we have been relying on that intelligibility all along, even when we thought we were doing pure science. To use a phrase often found in Hume, we can neither explain nor deny our reliance on some intelligibility in the world.

To be sure, there is a serious perplexity about the meaning of nature implicit in Hume's claim on this point. Here again Prufer makes a crucial observation. Prufer notes that Hume in effect distinguishes two senses of

14. In a classic essay, Richard Kennington showed that Descartes also relied on a pretheoretical and prescientific "teaching of nature." "The 'Teaching of Nature' in Descartes' Soul Doctrine," now republished in *Of Modern Origins: Essays in Early Modern Philosophy* (Lanham, Md.: Lexington, 2004), 161–86. It may well be that the origin of Hume's thought lies in a rethinking of what Descartes has to say on this score.

nature, nature as known by modern science, which Prufer refers to a nature$_1$, and nature as we live and know it pretheoretically, which he refers to as nature$_2$. Prufer remarks: "Nature hides itself; nature, taken in one sense (nature$_2$), hides nature taken in another sense (nature$_1$); nature is ambiguous."[15] The deepest perplexity of the *Treatise of Human Nature*, perhaps, is that both senses of nature are unavoidable, yet neither can be reduced to the other. Nature seems to be irreducibly twofold, as both human nature and nature as known by modern science. Perhaps the meaning of Prufer's remark can be put this way: as rational animals, we both live and try to make sense of things, including life. Yet life as we live it and life as we can make it intelligible are in no small tension. In principle, the two should match up. Yet if Hume's story in 1.4.7 shows anything, it shows that for us they do not.[16] Neither science nor metaphysics can make sense of life as we know it from the inside, even though they are activities that only living beings, so far as we know, can engage in. If we recall that Hume was only able to make his epistemology work by appealing to the "vivacity" of ideas, it looks as though the problem of life was *the* perplexity of his thought on several different levels.

The story of 1.4.7 is, I suggest, an image of this fundamental fact about the human condition. Hume's turn is the uncovering of our primary awareness of the intelligibility of things. Stated metaphorically, philosophers cannot be philosophers without first being "honest gentlemen." Even to begin questioning about the world, much less to give a scientific account of some piece of it, presupposes some awareness or trust that the world makes sense. That awareness is the presupposition, not the result, of reasoned inquiry into the world. It is a fundamental perplexity embedded in our experience of the world. It may even be a deeper perplexity than the question of the first cause, which is so prominent in Hume's account of his crisis. The question of the first cause as Hume treats it in Book I of the *Treatise* assumes that we can give the same kind of causal explanation for the world that we can give for this or that event within the world. But the world does not seem to be intelligible in that

15. Prufer, "A Reading of Hume's *A Treatise of Human Nature*," 45.

16. Leon Kass similarly suggests that the tension between life as it is lived and life as we can know it scientifically or theoretically may well be a permanent limitation of biology. Not even Aristotle, Kass suggests, can account for the true unity of living beings. "The Permanent Limitations of Biology," in *Life, Liberty, and the Defense of Dignity: The Challenge for Bioethics* (San Francisco, Calif.: Encounter, 2002), 277–97, esp. 293–97.

way. We have no causal explanation of causality. Nonetheless, even to raise the question of the first cause presupposes some primary awareness of the world. We have no causal explanation of that awareness. Yet we cannot dispense with it except at the price of not being able to say anything at all. The crisis depicted so memorably in 1.4.7 has the effect of isolating that awareness and compelling us to see it as a question. In effect, Hume raises a question about the possibility of questioning at all: how is it possible that we are able to raise—and if Hume is right, cannot stop raising—questions about causality at all? It may well be the case that this question is more primary than the question about the first cause. Even were we able to answer that question, the puzzle posed by our primary awareness of things would remain. Seen in this light, Hume's turn is not a turn away from the philosophically important questions but a disclosure of the deeper question lurking behind them.

SLAVE OF THE PASSIONS

Hume's turn puts the investigation of human nature at the center of the reoriented life of philosophy. That investigation takes as its focus the topics and themes of moral and political philosophy: "the principles of moral good and evil, the nature and foundation of government, and the cause of those several passions and inclinations, which actuate and govern me" (1.4.7.12). Moved by a public-spirited passion to "contribut[e] to the instruction of mankind" and so to "acquire a name by my inventions and discoveries" (1.4.7.12), Hume now proposes a sympathetic treatment of the moral and political concerns of human beings as human beings. This statement buttresses and provides content to Hume's recommendation that we make philosophy "the choice of our guide" (1.4.7.13). It also appears to be in serious tension with Hume's famous statement later in the *Treatise* about reason's proper subordination to the passions (2.3.3.4).

At first glance, that statement seems to suggest that reason—that is, all forms of reason—are wholly impotent and that the passions or emotions (that is, all or any passions simply as passion) rightly dominate human life. From this understanding of the passage on reason and the passions, it is a short step to the standard view of "Humean practical reason" as a paradigmatic case of moral relativism or emotivism. Yet this view is manifestly inconsistent with the view that philosophy should be the "choice of our guide." How then are we to make sense of these apparently incompatible assertions?

Let us consider Hume's argument that leads up to the statement of reason's subordination (2.3.3.4):

Since reason alone can never produce any action, or give rise to volition, I infer that the same faculty is as incapable of preventing volition, or of disputing the preference with any passion or emotion. [...] Nothing can oppose or retard the impulse of passion, but a contrary impulse; and if this contrary impulse ever arises from reason, that latter faculty must have an original influence on the will, and must be able to cause, as well as hinder any act of volition. But if reason has no original influence, tis impossible it can withstand any principle, which has such efficacy, or ever keep the mind in suspense a moment. Thus it appears, that the principle, which opposes our passion, cannot be the same with reason, and is only so call'd in an improper sense. We speak not strictly and philosophically when we talk of the combat of passion and of reason. Reason is, and ought only to be the slave of the passions, and can never pretend to any other office than to serve and obey them.

Hume's main point here is not that reason is in competition with passion and that reason should lose. Nor does he deny that we experience conflicts within ourselves between what we think we should do and what we are merely attracted to doing out of gluttony, lust, or greed, conflicts that we traditionally describe as "reason" versus "passion." Hume's point is rather that we misunderstand these conflicts if we think of them as a battle between two wholly separate faculties, one of which is simply reason and the other simply passion. Because Hume thinks that reason simply cannot motivate us, both must be passions. Put differently, Hume's main opponent in this passage is some version of dualism, the view that human beings are somehow constituted by two separate and wholly distinct faculties, one of which must rule over the other. Note also that nothing in this passage implies relativism between the passions: it might well be the case that the all-important conflicts within the self are really conflicts between passions, and that we can legitimately judge, on moral or prudential grounds, that some resolutions of those conflicts are better than others. Indeed, the main theme of Hume's treatment of the passions in the sequel to this passage is how to do justice to the variety of, and tensions between, the passions.

These claims provide the crucial context for the "slave of the passions" passage, the usual source for the conventional view of Humean practical reason: "Reason is, and ought only to be the slave of the passions, and can never pretend to any other office than to serve and obey them." There are in fact two claims being made here, a factual claim that reason is the slave of the passions and a normative claim that reason ought to be slave of the passions. The factual claim simply restates the main thesis of the rest of the paragraph. It is the normative claim that is of interest, and is in important respects in some tension with the rest of the paragraph. If, as the main body of the paragraph holds, reason by itself as a matter of fact simply cannot motivate us and so cannot be the sort of thing that can rule the passions, what need is there for Hume to assert that it ought not rule? If reason never pretends to any other office than serving and obeying the passions, then why does Hume feel compelled to enforce a normative claim that reason should stay in its subordinate position? In the context of Hume's larger claim about reason and the passions, the meaning of the "slave of the passions" passage is enigmatic.

That meaning evidently depends on what Hume means by "reason" on the one hand and "passion" on the other. I suggest that Hume uses "reason" here as a synonym for Cartesian science, in the sense that he treats Cartesian science in Book I of the *Treatise*, as discussed earlier in this essay. Hume states in the immediate context of the "slave of the passions" claim that reason (or the "understanding") "exerts itself after two ways, as it judges from demonstration or probability" (2.3.3.2). The two forms of reason bear fruit in the "abstract relations of ideas," on the one hand, and "the relations of objects, of which experience only gives us information" (2.3.3.2). This is just Hume's standard account of what reason is. Not coincidentally, it also describes the two key elements of the modern scientific enterprise, theory-building on the one hand and empirical observations and judgments of probability on the other. The very art of modern science, understood as the methodical effort to discern well-founded generalizations about the world, lies in shrewdly using these two species of reasoning in combination in order to extend human insight and power as far as possible.

Hume's thesis about the subordination of reason to the passions has notable precedents in Descartes and others.[17] In the *Discourse on*

17. Hobbes, for example: "For the thoughts are to the desires as scouts and spies, to range abroad and find the way to the things desired." *Leviathan*, ed. Edwin Curley (Indianapolis, Ind.: Hackett, 1994), 41.

Method, Descartes tells us that "reason is a universal instrument," which suggests that the ends come from some source other than reason.[18] Of greater interest than mere verbal parallels, however, is the relationship between science and humanity that Descartes sketches in the sixth part of the *Discourse on Method*. There Descartes makes his case for the public tolerance and support of science on the Baconian grounds that science will provide goods that will ameliorate or even eliminate the evils of the human condition, including death. Descartes in effect sketches a social contract between science and political society in which unfettered inquiry can find public protection at the price of serving the fundamental human passion of the fear of death and disease.[19] Science wins public support by offering to become an instrument of human passions. Hume's subordination thesis restates this Cartesian and Hobbesian account of science's relation to the passions. More than that: one may say that Hume spells out the implicit self-understanding of modern science itself. From the beginning modern science—as expressed by Descartes, Bacon, and Hobbes—understood itself to be instrumental. It abstracts from the purposes and intentions of the inquirer by means of methodical rules in order to provide objective knowledge, knowledge that is valid regardless of point of view or metaphysical commitments. But since modern science does not put itself into action and does not tell us which questions are worth pursuing, it presupposes that some other entity or force within the scientist will orient the inquiry. Because science provides only the predictive power and thus in principle the means to any given ends, it relies on some other source to set the ends, to be responsible for knowing what the point of the whole endeavor is. Whatever that other, end-setting thing is, its relations with science are accurately described as mastery and slavery, *by modern science's own lights*.

Consider now how Hume understands the passions. Recall that Hume does not deny the fact of psychic moral conflict, but he does think that that conflict is not a conflict between two wholly separate faculties of pure and unimpassioned reason on the one hand and unreasoning passion on the other. That conflict is in reality a conflict between passions, specifically between calm and violent passions (2.3.4.8). Hume describes the calm passions as follows (2.3.4.9):

18. *Discourse on Method* (in *Philosophical Writings*), 140.

19. Ibid., 141–43.

> There are certain calm desires and tendencies, which, tho' they be real passions, produce little emotion in the mind, and are more known by their effects than by the immediate feeling or sensation. These desires are of two kinds; either certain instincts originally implanted in our natures, such as benevolence and resentment, the love of life, and kindness to children; or the general appetite to good, and aversion to evil, consider'd merely as such.

Because the calm passions have established themselves as the "predominant inclination of the soul" (2.3.4.1), human beings tend to fail to recognize them as passions and mistake them for reason pure and simple. What we call passion is better called a violent passion, one that threatens to overturn our settled habits. Hume's example of a violent passion is resentment or the desire to punish (2.3.4.9). Any given human being might give into his or her violent passions or align with the calm passions to resist the violent passions. Hume does not deny, rather he asserts, that the struggle between the calm and the violent passions is a, and perhaps even the, central moral drama for every human being: how that conflict is settled determines the whole diversity of human types (2.3.8.13). There is such a thing for Hume as "strength of mind," by which he means the "prevalence of the calm passions above the violent" (2.3.4.10), and which Hume praises as a necessary element of human excellence.

Now, much more needs to be said to fill in this crude sketch of Hume's account of the passions. In particular, we would need to know more about the legitimacy or justice of the rule of calm passions over the violent passions, a topic we will turn to in the next section. One passion, however, stands out in Hume's account of these matters. Some seven sections after the "slave of the passions" passage, Hume's treatment of the calm and violent passions culminates in a section entitled "Of curiosity, or the love of truth" (2.3.10). Hume there remarks that in reviewing all the passions he has hitherto been self-forgetful, for he has not given due consideration to "that love of truth, which was the first source of all our inquiries" (2.3.10.1). The love of truth, which has kept Hume in motion throughout this long book, is a passion, perhaps even for Hume the strongest passion. Strange as it may sound to say, philosophy for Hume is not on the side of reason but of the passions. It is a motion, a directed reaching out for something. It fuels and directs science without being reducible to science or perhaps being explainable by science. Recall that the deepest human phenomenon brought to light in 1.4.7 was the recurring, apparently irrepressible human desire to inquire, a desire whose paradigmatic example is the desire for insight into first causes. Whatever else the desire to inquire is for Hume, it is most definitely a passion, and not the bloodless abstract reason that discovers relations of ideas or relations of objects.

Let me draw these threads together to summarize what I take Hume to be saying in the slave of the passions passage. The reason that Hume says ought to be slave to the passions is not the philosophy that he recommends to us as the choice of our guide. The reason as used in the slave of the passions passage is a synonym for modern, Cartesian science, and when Hume asserts that it ought to be slave to the passions, he is simply articulating Cartesian science's understanding of itself. But this is the account of reason that led directly to Hume's skeptical crisis in 1.4.7, as we saw earlier. Hume argues throughout the *Treatise* that Cartesian science cannot account for itself, and for that reason is always surreptitiously borrowing from prescientific beliefs. Science of this sort does not set its own goals or establish its own fundamental presuppositions. In this sense science is accurately described as a slave. On the other side, the passions that Hume says ought to rule science are more complicated than they first appear. Those passions surely include the desire to know the truth about human things: Hume avows a natural inclination to investigate "the principles of moral good and evil, the nature and foundation of government, and the cause of those several passions and inclinations, which actuate and govern me" (1.4.7.12). Hume enslaves reason understood as Cartesian science but vindicates reasoning understood as the ongoing, informal investigation of human life by human beings. In fact, if we take seriously Hume's avowals, repeated in several different contexts, that curiosity or the love of truth is the "first source of all our inquiries" and for him the strongest passion, we will be tempted to read the slave of the passions passage quite differently than the normal interpretation of Humean practical reason.[20] The inner meaning of "Reason is and ought only to be slave of the passions" is, I suggest, "science is and ought to be slave of philosophy."

20. For such avowals, see *Treatise* 1.4.7.5, 12, 13; 2.3.10.1; *Essays*, 180: "Even to reason so carefully about [life], and to fix with accuracy its just idea, would be overvaluing [life], were it not that to some tempers, this occupation is one of the most amusing, in which life could possibly be employed."

THE MORAL SENSE

An alert reader might object at this point that, even if the interpretation of the slave of the passions passage given above is correct, it only establishes the necessary conditions for a nonrelativistic account of practical reason. It does not yet provide a full-fledged rational defense of our moral commitments. In the remainder of this essay, I shall not be able to provide anything like a full account of Hume's treatment of morals and politics in Book III of the *Treatise of Human Nature* and elsewhere. Instead, I shall provide a very brief sketch of Hume's treatment of the moral sense as it bears on the question of the relation of reason and the passions.

The moral sense is the initial and orienting theme of Book III of the *Treatise*. Hume begins that book by arguing that moral distinctions are not derived from reason but from a moral sense. Because this thesis is liable to be misunderstood in just the same way the slave to the passions passage is, it worthwhile to say something about what Hume means and does not mean. Hume uses reason here to mean exactly the same thing that it meant in the slave of the passions passage: reason signifies either the relations of ideas or the relations of objects. Neither branch of reason, however, gives us any reason to act or not act, and whatever else might be true about morality, morality must give us a reason to act. Our experience of morality is that it moves us, gives us some directedness toward action. Hume takes it for granted that this is in fact our experience of morality, accessible to us not as a matter of theoretical demonstration or of an empirical survey of objects outside of us, but as part of our everyday pretheoretical experience as human beings in a moral community. He therefore argues that, since morality does move us and reason does not, reason cannot be the source of moral distinctions. Or, stated more precisely, Cartesian science, because it does not move us, cannot be the source of moral distinctions.

This thesis is not identical with and does not imply the claim that morality cannot be rationally defended or is a matter of mere taste.[21]

21. Some readers may wonder how my reading squares with another well-known passage, Hume's apparent statement at 3.1.1.27 that no "ought" claim may be inferred from an "is" claim. I shall not provide an interpretation of the passage except to note that the consensus among Hume scholars seems to be that Hume was only providing a final note to his attack on those who believe that morality can be based simply on reason, *not* making a general impossibility claim about "is" and "ought." For examples of this reading, see Alasdair MacIntyre, "Hume

Hume's point is a phenomenological rather than a deflationary one: we do in fact experience the claims of morality, yet those claims cannot be accounted for on the basis of modern science. Hume's response to those who would deny the reality of moral distinctions is to simply point to the human experience of morality and virtue. Morality moves us; it draws us in and makes us fall in love with it and hate its opposite. We do not merely cognize it in the abstract, as a pure mind or a brain in a vat might do: "Here we cannot remain long in suspense, but must pronounce the impression arising from virtue, to be agreeable, and that proceeding from vice to be uneasy. Every moment's experience must convince us of this. There is no spectacle so fair and beautiful as a noble and generous action; nor any which gives us more abhorrence than one that is cruel and treacherous" (3.1.2.2). Whatever else it is, the moral sense is a passion and a feeling. Yet this is not to say that morality is merely a passion or feeling. To say that virtue pleases is not to say that virtue is virtue simply because it pleases (3.1.2.3):

> To have a sense of virtue, is nothing but to *feel* a satisfaction of a particular kind from the contemplation of a character. The very *feeling* constitutes our praise or admiration. We go no further; nor do we enquire into the cause of the satisfaction. We do not infer a character to be virtuous, because it pleases: But in feeling that it pleases after such a particular manner, we in effect feel that it is virtuous.

Not every pleasure, but only pleasure "after a particular manner," constitutes our approbation of virtue. The specific character of the pleasure produced by virtue is intimately connected with our ability to consider character in general, without regard to our own interests. We can and do, Hume remarks, recognize and esteem the virtues of an enemy, even when those virtues are "hurtful to us" (3.1.2.4), and we know that "virtue in rags is still virtue" (3.3.1.19). Hume's dismissal of reason or Cartesian science as the source of these moral distinctions does not entail a dismissal of the moral distinctions. In fact, the standard interpretation of these passages as leading to "Humean practical reason" or emotivism rests on an implicit assumption that reason and the passions are simply dichotomous

on 'Is' and 'Ought,'" *Philosophical Review* 68 (1959): 451–68; and Annette Baier, *A Progress of Sentiments: Reflections on Hume's* Treatise (Cambridge, Mass.: Harvard University Press, 1991), 177n2. It should also be noted that, whatever we finally make of the is-ought passage, Hume in fact does infer ethical claims from claims about nature quite often.

alternatives, such that to dismiss "reason" is to affirm unreasoning passion simply, that is, any and all passions. This is just the dualistic view at the bottom of Cartesian science. But not surprisingly, reading what Hume has to say about the moral sense with these assumptions misses Hume's point: "reason" and the "passions" are not simply separate things. The moral sense is a passion that already contains within itself a desire for objectivity.

To be sure, this account does not yet provide a full-fledged rational defense of the grounds of the moral sense. But this objection misunderstands the role of Hume's invocation of the moral sense in the overall structure of his argument. By showing that modern science cannot account for the moral sense, Hume aims to compel us to recognize a perplexity. At this point in his argument, the moral sense is the name of a question, not the name of an answer. Put differently, in dismissing reason (understood as Cartesian science) as the source of moral distinctions and making us wonder about the source or ground of our own moral opinions, Hume announces the question that orients Book III of the *Treatise*. Hume signals the priority of this question to the argument of Book III as a whole in his choice of epigraph to the book. That epigraph, taken from Lucan's *Civil Wars*, reads: "O lover of hardy virtue, ask what virtue is and demand an exemplar of an honest man." The epigraph expresses nicely the basic character of the human situation as Hume has so far brought it to light. To ask what virtue is, is the equivalent of asking what the moral sense is. That question is the guiding question of Hume's turn to moral and political philosophy, announced back in 1.4.7. Yet we cannot even begin to ask that question if we are not already somehow moved by the question. The question addresses itself to someone who is already a "lover of hardy virtue." It cannot be the case that we first investigate the question of morality abstractly as a mere theoretical matter and then later decide to be moved by virtue or not. The question of morality is a pressing question only because we are already in the grip of morality. Let me suggest that Cartesian science goes wrong, in Hume's view, because in taking itself as a mere instrument of goals set by some external entity, it closes off reflection on the fact that we are already moved by some morality or other. We cannot possibly come to terms with ourselves if we see ourselves as mere objects external to the inquiring gaze. We ourselves are already on the hook, in the middle of things, entangled in being both the subject and the object of our inquiry.

This is not the place for an account of Hume's attempt to tell the truth about the moral sense. Suffice it to say that he discovers that some habitually praised moral qualities are at bottom artificial virtues, the product of social utility, while others are natural and worthwhile regardless of social convention. That is, his investigation of the moral sense culminates in an account of natural virtues, those qualities of character that, unlike the artificial virtues, are self-rewarding and need no external supplement to make them good for the individual who exercises them (3.3).[22]

Let me conclude this sketch of the moral sense by reiterating what I take to be the crucial point underlying Hume's treatment of reason and the passions. The central error of the position on reason and the passions opposed by Hume is holding that reason and the passions are wholly distinct faculties whose relations must be mastery and slavery. The appropriate response to that erroneous claim is not to say that any and all passions as passions ought to be obeyed, the conventional interpretation of Humean practical reason. It is to point out that the passions are already involved in reasoning, and that reasoning is always motivated by some passion. That is, it is to deny that Cartesian dualism accurately describes the kind of beings we are. In a passage that brings to culmination Hume's treatment of reason and the passions, Hume remarks (3.2.2.14):

> Human nature being compos'd of two principal parts, which are requisite in all its actions, the affections and the understanding; 'tis certain, that the blind motions of the former, without the direction of the latter, incapacitate men for society: And it may be allow'd us to consider separately the effects, that result from the separate operations of these two component parts of the mind. The same liberty may be permitted to moral, which is allow'd to natural, philosophers; and 'tis usual with the latter to consider any motion as compounded and consisting of two parts separate from each other, tho' at the same time they acknowledge it to be in itself uncompounded and inseparable.

We can divide reason and passion in speech, and such division can clarify an otherwise messy reality. Yet such division is only in speech and for the sake of understanding: the truth of the matter is that the reality

22. In emphasizing the importance of the natural virtues, I differ from some important strands of Hume scholarship that see Hume's account of conventions, interpreted as Wittgensteinian language games, as Hume's distinctive contribution to moral and political philosophy. See, e.g., Frederick Whelan, *Order and Artifice in Hume's Political Philosophy* (Princeton, N.J.: Princeton University Press, 1985).

underlying reason and passion is "in itself uncompounded and inseparable." The analytic clarity provided by separating elements of larger wholes should not be allowed to obscure the ontological truth of irreducible complexity.[23]

CONCLUSION

"Humean practical reason" has become conventional shorthand for the view that reason is at best only instrumental reason and that it cannot adjudicate disputes over ends or purposes. It refers to a deeper moral relativism wherein serious moral disputes turn out to be based on unthinking passion, mere whim, or subjective taste. Yet this conventional usage may well say more about our anxieties about relativism or nihilism than about what Hume meant to say in the passages usually cited as the source of "Humean practical reason." In this essay I have argued that this view rests on a misunderstanding of those passages, and I have done so on two main grounds. First, "reason" as used in the slave of the passions passage is a synonym for modern science of a Cartesian inspiration and is the product of Hume's lengthy and relentless critique of that science if understood as a self-sufficient and self-justifying activity. Second, the standard reading of "Humean practical reason" rests on an obliviousness to Hume's endorsement of a life of reason, oriented not by an ideal of mathematical rationality and system-building but by the necessities of puzzling through the perplexities inherent in pretheoretical and prescientific life. It is this life of reason, I have argued, that Hume endorses when he recommends "philosophy" as the "choice of our guide" (1.4.7.13), and it is this life of reason that provides the ground of Hume's true account of practical reason.

Several aspects of this life of reason deserve mention by way of conclusion. Hume's life of philosophy is oriented above all by a natural desire or passion, apparently irrepressible even in the face of disappointment, to inquire into all things, especially the paradigmatic question of

23. The Aristotelian echoes should not be overlooked: Aristotle remarks that while the rational and irrational parts of our nature may be two in meaning, they are nonetheless "inseparable in nature, as are the convex and the concave in the circumference of the circle." *Nicomachean Ethics*, trans. Robert C. Bartlett and Susan D. Collins (Chicago: University of Chicago Press, 2011), 1102a28–32 (23).

the "original and ultimate principle" (1.4.7.5). The "mind of man" displays an inner restlessness and dissatisfaction that provides the deepest theme of Hume's anthropology. Yet this restlessness is the deep cause of the most serious political problem facing early modern Europe, the wars of religion. In proposing philosophy as the "choice of our guide," Hume announces his intention to give us a nonskeptical basis for sound political judgment. He suggests that we can know enough to govern ourselves on the basis of what we can know about human nature or human beings by starting from life as it is lived rather than the abstraction of human life as known by modern science. He proposes, that is, a quasi-Socratic human wisdom that takes questions of morality, politics, and self-knowledge as its guiding intention (1.4.7.12). Such a human wisdom, in his view, may even be more discerning about the fundamental human situation than either Cartesian science or a directly metaphysical inquiry into causation can be. Hume's turn to moral-political inquiries bears fruit in his analysis of the moral sense, our passionate awareness that our actions must be justified by something beyond our own impulses and desires. Yet the moral sense is not infallible: it requires investigation and grounding. In Hume's thought it serves as a guide or spur to inquiry, not as a definitive resolution to the problems of political life. In moral matters, as in political matters, there is for Hume no substitute for our own attempts to understand things in the light of our own reason.[24]

24. I have pursued the themes of this essay in greater detail in *Hume and the Politics of Enlightenment* (New York: Cambridge University Press, 2015).

Michael Rohlf

9 Happiness in Rousseau and Kant

Most modern philosophers understand happiness fundamentally in terms of the subjective states of pleasure or desire satisfaction, while premodern philosophers tend to understand happiness fundamentally in terms of possessing certain objective goods like virtue, which do not reduce to pleasure or desire satisfaction, or engaging in objectively worthwhile activities like doing philosophy.[1] This paper investigates two modern conceptions of happiness: namely, Kant's and Rousseau's. I argue that their subjectivist conceptions of happiness do not prevent them from recognizing certain objective goods that help us to become happy. In fact, I argue that they both hold that some of the same objective goods that Aristotle thinks happiness consists in—including virtue, the development of our rational powers, and love of others—are either necessary for or at least tend to promote one's own happiness.

THEORIES OF HAPPINESS

I begin by sketching three types of theories about happiness. First, *hedonism* is the view that happiness fundamentally consists in a feeling of pleasure and/or the absence of pain. The word "pleasure" tends to bring to mind a sort of episodic, physical buzz. But I include among hedonists those who identify happiness with a prolonged, pleasurable mental state. I interpret Rousseau to be this type of sophisticated hedonist.[2]

1. There are of course exceptions to these generalizations, such as Epicureans and modern natural law theorists.

2. For a sophisticated, contemporary discussion of hedonism, see Fred Feldman, *Pleasure*

Second, *desire theory* is the view, held by Kant, that happiness consists fundamentally in satisfying one's desires.[3] It is important to see that, although hedonism and desire theory may appear similar and they both define happiness in terms of subjective states, they are nevertheless different accounts of what happiness consists in. According to hedonism, it may be possible to live a happy life in which some of your most important desires remain unsatisfied, for example because satisfying these desires would actually be less pleasurable or lead to more pain than their remaining unsatisfied. By contrast, according to desire theory a happy life may be quite unpleasant or even painful, provided that one's important desires are satisfied.

Third, *objective goods theory* is the view that happiness consists in possessing certain objective goods or engaging in objectively worthwhile activities. Aristotle is an objective goods theorist because he holds that happiness consists primarily in the full development and exercise of the essentially human rational capacities, both practical and theoretical.[4] In the *Nicomachean Ethics*, Aristotle characterizes "the human good" as "activity of the soul in accord with virtue," where virtue is understood as what enables something to exercise its function well.[5] Since, for Aristotle, the human function is "activity of the soul in accord with reason or requiring reason," it follows that the human good or happiness consists in activity that requires reason and is done well, that is, in accord with virtue or excellence.[6] This requires developing and exercising both practical virtues of character such as bravery and temperance, and theoretical virtues of thought such as wisdom and prudence.[7] Given human nature, possessing and exercising these virtues—thus, the full development and exercise of practical and theoretical reason—is objectively good for

---

and the Good Life (Oxford: Oxford University Press, 2004), and *What Is This Thing Called Happiness?* (Oxford: Oxford University Press, 2010).

3. For sophisticated, contemporary discussion of desire theory, see James Griffin, *Well-Being* (Oxford: Oxford University Press, 1986). See also Derek Parfit, *Reasons and Persons* (Oxford: Oxford University Press, 1984), 493.

4. *Nicomachean Ethics* I.7–10. For sophisticated, contemporary discussion of objective goods theory, see Richard Kraut, *What Is Good and Why?* (Cambridge, Mass.: Harvard University Press, 2007).

5. *Nicomachean Ethics* I.7.1098a17–18. All quotations are drawn from *Nicomachean Ethics*, trans. Terence Irwin, 2nd ed. (Indianapolis, Ind.: Hackett, 2000).

6. *Nicomachean Ethics* I.7.1098a7–8.

7. *Nicomachean Ethics* I.13; II-V; and VI.1–7, 13.

us and essential to human happiness. And Aristotle also adds that happiness requires adequate external goods like friendship and wealth in a complete life.[8]

To distinguish objective goods theory from both hedonism and desire theory, consider again some cases in which these theories yield different verdicts. An objective goods theorist could hold that a happy life does not necessarily contain the most pleasure or desire satisfaction. Moreover, hedonists and desire theorists can maintain that happiness is possible even without some set of objectively good states or activities. But even in cases about which these theories yield the same verdict, they do so for different reasons. Aristotle, for example, holds that philosophy is the most pleasant activity and that a virtuous person fortunate enough to be able to spend much of his life doing philosophy will live a most pleasant life.[9] But what makes this person's life happy, according to Aristotle, is not primarily the pleasure he takes in it, but the objective value of the activity in which he takes pleasure.[10] By contrast, if a hedonist were to agree that the philosophical life is the happiest, then this would be primarily on the grounds that it is the most pleasant life and would not depend on claims about the objective worth of doing philosophy, independently of its tendency to produce pleasure.

Again, Aristotle may hold that a happy person will not have any (significant) unsatisfied desires, since he believes that exercising virtue is most important and desires this more than anything, and because he has adequate external goods to satisfy whatever moderate desires he has for these.[11] By contrast, a desire theorist would agree that this person is happy but could also hold that someone who desires only objectively worthless things, and satisfies these desires, is equally happy because what contributes to one's happiness, for the desire theorist, is not the objective worth of what one desires, but rather only the satisfaction of one's desires, regardless of what they are desires for. So, for a desire theorist, philosophy

8. See especially 1101a15–17: "the happy person is the one whose activities accord with complete virtue, with an adequate supply of external goods, . . . for a complete life."

9. *Nicomachean Ethics* X.7.1177a24–27.

10. Not every kind of pleasure is good, for Aristotle, but only pleasure in objectively valuable activities (or pleasure that completes those activities), that is, activities that accord with reason and exercise some virtue(s). *Nicomachean Ethics*, X.3–5.

11. This interpretation of Aristotle is defended by Richard Kraut in "Two Conceptions of Happiness," *The Philosophical Review* 88, no. 2 (April 1979): 170–71.

would contribute to your happiness only if and because you desire to do philosophy, or you have some other desire that philosophy satisfies, independently of claims about the objective worth of philosophy.

HAPPINESS IN ROUSSEAU

With these distinctions on the table, I turn now to Rousseau. It may seem controversial that I have characterized Rousseau as a kind of hedonist. In fact Rousseau's view of happiness is very complex and has elements that resemble the other two theories of happiness in some respects. Let me begin by looking at some of these elements.

Near the beginning of Book II of *Emile*, Rousseau explicitly offers an account of what happiness consists in. He initially employs hedonistic language to distinguish between what he calls "absolute happiness," which is not possible in this life but only in an afterlife, and "man's felicity on earth":

> We do not know what absolute happiness or unhappiness is. Everything is mixed in this life; in it one tastes no pure sentiment.... The affections of our souls, as well as the states of our bodies, are in a continual flux.... The happiest is he who suffers the least pain; the unhappiest is he who feels the least pleasure. Always more suffering than enjoyment; this relation between the two is common to all men. Man's felicity on earth is, hence, only a negative condition; the smallest number of ills he can suffer ought to constitute its measure.[12]

This passage seems to imply that absolute happiness would be a pure sentiment of pleasure, although in this life minimizing pain is the closest we can come to this. In both cases, happiness is understood in terms of pleasure and pain, that is, hedonistically.

But immediately after this, Rousseau appears, briefly, to translate this account into the language of desire theory. Pleasures and pains correlate with desires, he says: "Every feeling of pain is inseparable from the desire to be delivered from it; every idea of pleasure is inseparable from the desire to enjoy it; every desire supposes privation, and all sensed privations are painful." Therefore, Rousseau infers, the same substantive view of happiness can be expressed by saying that absolute happiness (in a "being endowed with senses") consists in equality between one's desires and

12. Rousseau, *Emile or On Education*, trans. Allan Bloom (New York: Basic, 1979), 80.

faculties, while unhappiness is a disproportion between desires and faculties. In other words, happiness consists, if not exactly in desire satisfaction, then in the feeling that one is strong enough to satisfy one's desires, while unhappiness consists in the feeling that one is too weak to satisfy one's needs and desires.[13]

The next paragraph adds one further element to Rousseau's account, however, which makes it quite clear that he is not a desire theorist. "The road of true happiness," Rousseau now says, lies

> not precisely in diminishing our desires, for if they were beneath our power, a part of our faculties would remain idle, and we would not enjoy our whole being. Neither is it in extending our whole faculties, for if, proportionate to them, our desires were more extended, we would as a result only become unhappier. But it is in diminishing the excess of the desires over the faculties and putting power and will in perfect equality. It is only then that, with all the powers in action, the soul will nevertheless remain peaceful and that man will be well-ordered.[14]

In other words, Rousseau now claims that "the road to true happiness" has two components: (1) achieving equality between our desires and faculties, and (2) putting all of our faculties into action. A desire theorist could make the first claim but not the second. Rousseau does not say that leaving faculties undeveloped would make us unhappy only if we felt it as a privation and desired to put these faculties into action. Rather, he says that this would make us unhappy because, with idle faculties, "we would not enjoy our whole being," and this would be the case even if we were entirely ignorant of the fact that we have undeveloped faculties and lacked any desire to develop them. For example, Rousseau's savage in the state of nature has no idea of the rational powers that lie dormant in his nature, and no desire to develop them; but on this account, the savage lacks true happiness because his undeveloped faculties render him unable to "enjoy his whole being."[15] Thus Rousseau cannot be a desire theo-

13. Ibid.

14. Ibid.

15. "This transition from the state of nature to the civil state produces a most remarkable change in man by substituting justice for instinct in his conduct, and endowing his actions with the morality they previously lacked. Only then, when the voice of duty succeeds physical impulsion and right succeeds appetite, does man, who until then had looked only to himself, see himself forced to act on other principles, and to consult his reason before listening to his inclinations. Although in this state he deprives himself of several advantages he has from

rist; he must be either a hedonist or an objective goods theorist, depending on whether putting all of one's faculties into action, or enjoying one's whole being, is more fundamental to his account of happiness.

It is not clear that *Emile*, considered apart from Rousseau's other works, provides enough textual evidence to attribute one but not the other of these two views to Rousseau. The passage I quoted earlier supports treating him as a hedonist in *Emile*, but there are other passages in which he sounds instead like an objective goods theorist, some of which I will address in a moment. In a later work, however, *The Reveries of the Solitary Walker*, Rousseau clearly commits himself to a version of hedonism. Although this may reflect the development of his views about happiness, I suggest that his account in the *Reveries* not only is broadly compatible with *Emile* but also helps to impose coherence on the account of happiness in *Emile*.

In the Fifth Walk of the *Reveries*, Rousseau repeats the claim, familiar from *Emile*, that "supreme felicity" is not possible "here-below," on earth, where "everything is in continual flux."[16] In *Emile* Rousseau took the ubiquity of flux in this life to imply that happiness on earth is only a negative condition in which pain is minimized but we do not experience pure pleasure. In the *Reveries*, however, Rousseau infers from the ubiquity of flux on earth, not that we can experience no positive pleasure in this life, but rather that we cannot achieve a permanent state of pleasure. The pleasures of this life, some of which are sweet and intense, are all transitory and fleeting. But "the happiness for which my heart longs," Rousseau says, "is in no way made up of fleeting instants, but rather [is] a simple and permanent state which has nothing intense in itself, but whose duration increases its charm to the point that I finally find supreme felicity in it."[17] In this permanent state of happiness, Rousseau continues, one would enjoy nothing other than what he calls the "sentiment of ex-

---

nature, he gains such great advantages in return, his faculties are exercised and developed, his ideas enlarged, his sentiments ennobled, his entire soul is elevated to such an extent, that if the abuses of this new condition did not often degrade him to beneath the condition he has left, he should ceaselessly bless the happy moment which wrested him from it forever, and out of a stupid and bounded animal made an intelligent being and a man." *Of the Social Contract*, Book I, Chapter 8, in *Rousseau: The Social Contract and Other Late Political Writings*, trans. Victor Gourevitch (Cambridge: Cambridge University Press, 1997), 53.

16. Rousseau, *The Reveries of the Solitary Walker*, trans. Charles E. Butterworth (Indianapolis, Ind.: Hackett, 1992), 68; see also 122.

17. Ibid.

istence," which would fill the soul completely, "without any other sentiment of deprivation or enjoyment, pleasure or pain, desire or fear."[18] We can achieve this permanent state of happiness only in the afterlife. But Rousseau claims that it is possible to enjoy the same sentiment of existence even in this life, albeit not permanently, if one manages "to spurn all the sensual and earthly impressions which incessantly come to distract us from it and to trouble its sweetness here-below."[19] So, according to the *Reveries*, happiness in this life (or the closest we can come to it) has both positive and negative components: the positive component is enjoying the sentiment of existence, and the negative component is spurning the fleeting, sensual pleasures that distract us from the sentiment of existence.

Rousseau therefore distinguishes between two kinds of pleasures: sensual pleasures that are fleeting and do not fulfill us because they are always outweighed by pains; and pleasure in the sentiment of existence, which does fulfill us because it is positive and can be permanent (at least in the afterlife). The *Reveries* leaves no room for doubt that Rousseau understands the sentiment of existence as a kind of pleasurable feeling. A sentiment is a feeling, and Rousseau repeatedly characterizes the sentiment of existence as a pleasurable feeling, at one point glossing it as "feel[ing one's] existence with pleasure."[20] But to understand how Rousseau intends to distinguish this fulfilling kind of pleasure in the sentiment of existence from the other, unfulfilling kind of pleasure, we must turn back to *Emile*. The sentiment of existence, Rousseau says in Book I of *Emile*, comes from the active use of our powers and faculties: "To live is not to breathe; it is to act; it is to make use of our organs, our senses, our faculties, of all the parts of ourselves which give us the sentiment of our existence. The man who has lived the most is not he who has counted the most years but he who has most felt life."[21] By contrast, the sensual kind of pleasures that do not fulfill us comes from the passive satisfaction of desires and passions.[22] I will return to these passive, sensual plea-

18. *Reveries*, 68–69.

19. Ibid., 69.

20. Ibid., 67. On 69–71 alone, Rousseau describes the sentiment of existence eight times as a form of pleasure or enjoyment, not including his repeated praise of its charm.

21. *Emile*, 42.

22. Rousseau has the Savoyard vicar say: "In meditating on the nature of man, I believed I discovered in it two distinct principles; one of which raised him to the study of eternal truths,

sures shortly. First I will note some connections with Aristotle that are suggested by Rousseau's view that the active use of our powers gives us a sentiment of existence.

Both Rousseau and Aristotle hold that the kind of pleasure that characterizes the happy life is pleasure in the active use of our powers. But Rousseau's account may be described as more subjectivist than Aristotle's in two respects. First, pleasurable feelings are subjective states, and Rousseau's hedonist framework treats them as fundamental, while Aristotle does not. But this is a purely theoretical distinction without any substantive difference, because Rousseau and Aristotle agree that happiness requires this pleasurable subjective state: for Rousseau happiness consists (positively) in the feeling of pleasure that is caused by exercising our powers, whereas for Aristotle it consists in the exercise of our powers which causes this feeling of pleasure.

A second difference between them is more substantive, however. There is more flexibility in the kinds of lives that can be happy for Rousseau than there is for Aristotle. Aristotle holds that only one kind of ideal life is happy: the philosophical life, led by a virtuous man blessed with adequate external goods, including living in and participating in the governance of a well-run city-state. But Rousseau does not recognize only one ideal life, because he denies that human development has any (known) natural limits.[23] For him, happiness in this life comes in degrees: we are happy to the extent that we enjoy the sentiment of existence, but it may be possible for us to be happier by living in a different way that enables us to enjoy the sentiment of existence more. The closest Rousseau comes to proposing an ideal life is to offer several ideals, each of which is tailored to a specific social context (or lack thereof): the savage in a state of nature is happy in one way, the Roman citizen in another, and Rousseau the

to the love of justice and moral beauty, and to the regions of the intellectual world whose contemplation is the wise man's delight; while the other took him basely into himself, subjected him to the empire of the senses and to the passions which are their ministers, and by means of these hindered all that the sentiment of the former inspired in him. In sensing myself carried away and caught up in the combat of these two contrary notions, I said to myself, 'No, man is not one. I want and I do not want; I sense myself enslaved and free at the same time. I see the good, I love it, and I do the bad. I am active when I listen to reason, passive when my passions carry me away; and my worst torment, when I succumb, is to sense that I could have resisted." *Emile*, 278–79.

23. *Emile*, 62. See also the *Second Discourse*, in *The Discourses and Other Early Political Writings*, trans. Victor Gourevitch (Cambridge: Cambridge University Press, 1997), 141.

solitary outcast in yet another way. Each of these is an ideal of sorts that portrays the kind of life that best enables one to enjoy the sentiment of existence within a given social context. But none of these ideals is appropriate for us in modern society. Rather, Rousseau the social critic refers to these ideals to suggest ways that modern society could be reformed so that we can enjoy the sentiment of existence more fully. But to those of us living in modern society, as it is presently constituted, Rousseau offers a different ideal of the natural man in civil society, represented by Emile.[24] So it turns out that Rousseau is like Aristotle after all in offering *us* a single ideal of the happy life.

But Rousseau's ideal does not give philosophy the central role in Emile's education that Aristotle gives it in the happy life. When in *Emile* Rousseau discusses what he calls objective goods—by which he presumably means states or activities that enable one to enjoy the sentiment of existence, and perhaps that are necessary for it—he mentions strength, health, good witness of oneself, the (moral) virtues, love, and especially freedom, which he calls "the first of all goods."[25] But he does not mention philosophy or theoretical reasoning in this context. Indeed, in the *Reveries* Rousseau says of himself that "reflection tires and saddens me; thinking always was a painful and charmless occupation for me."[26] But it would be a mistake to conclude from this that Rousseau fails to give philosophical thought a key role in the ideal of the happy life that he offers for us. *Emile* does not give prominence to theoretical reasoning as a source of happiness because it is a book about educating children, and Rousseau believes that "purely speculative knowledge is hardly suitable for children."[27] It does not follow, however, that Rousseau disdains purely speculative knowledge as a source of happiness for adults. Indeed, when *Emile* strays from the topic of education, as in the Savoyard vicar's confession of faith, Rousseau calls "the study of eternal truths, ... the love of justice and moral beauty, and [contemplation of] the regions of the intellectual world ... the wise man's delight."[28] Rousseau's autobiographical reflection in the *Reveries* that he himself did not delight much in thinking

24. For discussion of these ideals, see Joseph R. Reisert, *Jean-Jacques Rousseau: A Friend of Virtue* (Ithaca, N.Y.: Cornell University Press, 2003), chap. 5, esp. 134–40.

25. *Emile*, 84. See also 81 and 324.

26. *Reveries*, 91.

27. *Emile*, 177.

28. *Emile*, 278; see also 283.

is consistent with this view if we interpret it as a confession that Rousseau is not a wise man, which in turn would be consistent with his confession earlier in the same work that he is not a virtuous man and is too weak to live together with others in society.[29] But Rousseau denies that his own life provides an appropriate ideal for those of us who can and do live in modern society. The ideal he offers for us of the natural man in civil society, represented by Emile, is consistent with Aristotle's ideal in giving centrality to theoretical study as a positive source of happiness, although Rousseau does not go so far as to privilege knowledge over action.[30]

Rousseau's main difference from Aristotle is his special emphasis on and account of sources of unhappiness that are unique to modern society, on account of which we have a greater need to remove sources of unhappiness than to seek out positive sources of happiness such as philosophy. Positive sources of the sentiment of existence are plentiful for us because the competitive rigors of modern society tend to develop our faculties to such a high degree. But the same conditions that promote the advanced development of our higher faculties also breed unnatural passions that enslave us and distract us from truly fulfilling pleasures. On Rousseau's account this problem originates in an unavoidable conflict that everyone in modern society experiences between our natural sentiments and the demands of society.[31] We have a natural passion of self-love (*amour-propre*), which drives us to compare ourselves with others in society and to see ourselves, through the eyes of others, as equal or superior to them.[32] But

29. *Reveries*, 77, 83.

30. Aristotle arrives at his view that the happy life is the philosophical life by initially defining happiness as the highest good and then arguing that theoretical study of what is eternal and unchanging (i.e., philosophical activity in that sense) has all the characteristics of the highest good, because it is the most complete end, choiceworthy for its own sake, self-sufficient, and uniquely human (*Nicomachean Ethics* I.7 and X.7). Rousseau does not follow this procedure, perhaps in part because he does not hold that happiness is the highest good; rather, he thinks that virtue is the highest good, or some combination of virtue and happiness, where these are treated as conceptually distinct from one another. See Laurence D. Cooper, *Rousseau, Nature, and the Problem of the Good Life* (University Park: Pennsylvania State University Press, 1999), 26. But he does hold that happiness is a pleasurable psychological state that has many of the very same characteristics that Aristotle requires of the highest good: the sentiment of existence is complete since we desire nothing more and want to remain in that state permanently, it is desirable for its own sake, it is self-sufficient in the sense that it does not depend too much on external goods, and we must engage our uniquely human capacities (if not only these capacities) in order to experience it.

31. *Emile*, 40, 213, 288, 291, 317.

32. For discussion of the desire to be the best, see Frederick Neuhouser, *Rousseau's Theodicy of Self-Love* (Oxford: Oxford University Press, 2008), 59.

in modern society, prevailing social standards have come to place value on things that are not natural needs, such as wealth, status, and technology. We internalize these prevailing standards of comparison because of self-love, which through imagination transforms our passions and gives us new needs to meet or exceed these artificial standards. We thus come to identify happiness with the fleeting pleasure of satisfying unnatural needs. But this sort of 'happiness' is almost entirely illusory. The desire for such happiness is better described as a need to avoid the unhappiness of seeing oneself as inferior to others. There is no stable and positive state of fulfillment to be found through comparing oneself to others according to shifting social standards that are not based on natural needs. Desires to compare favorably with others in this way, when satisfied, yield at best transitory pleasures that are quickly followed by new, stronger desires to maintain or improve that status, which are increasingly more difficult to satisfy, especially in a competitive social environment in which one person's success at being seen as superior to others motivates those others to redouble their efforts and come out on top next time.

This is why Rousseau holds that the path to true happiness requires concentrating above all on the negative task of avoiding the unnatural passions formed through social comparison under the influence of self-love, and spurning the false pleasures of satisfying such passions. But the same social conditions that make these unnatural passions so difficult for us to avoid also force us to develop other natural powers, sentiments, and passions that can be positive sources of true happiness for us. These include reason, moral sentiments (conscience), and the passion of love. I have discussed how Rousseau regards theoretical reasoning as a positive source of happiness. He also holds that moral goodness and love are essential to our happiness. Moral goodness is essential because, without it, we will feel pangs of conscience and be incapable of self-respect, and because satisfaction with ourselves for acting morally is also a positive source of pleasure. Virtue is essential to our happiness for the same reason that Rousseau describes freedom as "the first of all goods": because virtue involves the freedom of self-governance, which is necessary to control and satisfy our desires, as well as being a positive source of pleasure in the practical use of our rational powers.[33]

33. *Emile*, 84; see also 81 and 324. In the *Reveries*, Rousseau says that "virtue consists in overcoming [our inclinations] when duty commands in order to do what duty prescribes" (77).

What virtue and love have in common is that both are essential to the happiness of weak beings like us. But they differ in that virtue is the strength to overcome our weaknesses, to govern our needs, and to be self-sufficient, while love involves irreducible dependence on others.[34] Rousseau calls love "the supreme happiness of life" because, at least in modern societies, human beings unavoidably depend on one another and share "common needs" that "unite us by interest," as well as "common miseries" that "unite us by affection."[35] The ultimate reason why absolute happiness is not possible for us in modern society—even with the advanced development of our powers, and even if we manage to avoid unnatural passions and their illusory pleasures—is that "the source of true happiness is within us," but in modern society it is impossible to avoid depending on others.[36] Even Emile, with his exemplary education, develops a strong passion of love for Sophie and fails to avoid forming attachments that make his happiness depend on others. I take this to mean that, on Rousseau's view, we have no choice but to live outside ourselves or to depend on others to some extent for our happiness in this life, but we do have a choice about the form our dependence on others takes. Either we live outside ourselves by chasing an illusory happiness defined by unfulfilling social comparisons; or we live outside ourselves by forming attachments based on the moral sentiments and the natural passion of love, both of which enable us to feel the sentiment of our existence *in* others, by identifying our interests and uniting our affections.[37]

And in *Emile*, he says that "the virtuous man ... knows how to conquer his affections; for then he follows his reason and his conscience; he does his duty; he keeps himself in order, and [he alone is] really free" (444).

34. *Emile*, 444.

35. *Emile*, 327, 221. Even in the *Reveries*, Rousseau the solitary outcast indicates that love is necessary to complete his own happiness by recalling in the final, unfinished Tenth Walk—written shortly before he died—his youthful love affair with Mme. de Warens.

36. *Reveries*, 13. This is also how Rousseau distinguishes between us and the savage in a state of nature: "the Savage lives within himself"—although this is not enough to qualify him for true happiness, on account of his undeveloped faculties—but the "sociable man, always outside himself, is capable of living only in the opinion of others and, so to speak, derives the sentiment of existence solely from their judgment" (*Discourse on Inequality*, 187).

37. "When the strength of an expansive soul makes me identify myself with my fellow, and I feel that I am, so to speak, in him, it is in order not to suffer that I do not want him to suffer. I am interested in him for love of myself, and the reason for the precept [of doing to others as we would have them do unto us] is in nature itself, which inspires in me the desire of my well-being in whatever place I feel my existence.... Love of men derived from love of self is the principle of human justice" (*Emile*, 235n). This is also how Rousseau characterizes the sweet,

So Rousseau is a kind of hedonist who holds that virtue, the development of rational powers, and love of others are necessary for becoming happy, insofar as it is possible to become happy in this life. Having established this, I turn now to Kant, who (I will argue) holds similar views but expresses them in terms of a different subjectivist conception of happiness.

HAPPINESS IN KANT

It is not controversial to claim that Kant holds a desire theory of happiness. He says repeatedly and consistently in different works that happiness, on his view, is the idea of a state in which all of one's inclinations are satisfied, over the entire course of one's life; where an inclination is (for Kant) a habitual desire.[38]

natural sentiment of pity, which transports us out of ourselves and into the suffering of others (221). The reason that forming attachments based on love or moral sentiment does not bring absolute happiness is that it makes our happiness depend in part on factors outside of our control, and in this life—where everything is in flux—this amounts to courting disappointment. Moreover, it is possible for duty and happiness to conflict, and in that case duty takes precedence. In *Emile*, this conflict takes the form of the adult Emile's duties to his fatherland that may call him away from his rustic, family life with Sophie (*Emile*, 473). Since even the truest happiness possible for us in modern society thus depends in part on fortune and may be taken away from us by factors beyond our control, Rousseau has two final recommendations regarding the sort of attitudes that should accompany our pursuit of happiness. To avoid disappointment, we should practice a kind of psychological detachment when misfortune strikes. Realizing that happiness depends on attachments to people and things that are not in our control, when fortune takes these (and thus part of our happiness) from us, we can minimize our loss by eventually moving on (*Emile*, 472). But Rousseau tempers this stoic recommendation with another one that he puts in the mouth of the Savoyard vicar, who asks: "what felicity is sweeter than sensing that one is ordered in a system in which everything is good?" (292). Note that (266) the point of the vicar's speech, he says, is to explain why he's happy and the true value of life. In other words, for Rousseau this limited detachment is advisable only if it is accompanied by faith that—in the end, at least in the afterlife—everything necessary for our happiness that we cannot secure for ourselves will be provided.

38. *Metaphysics of Morals*, 6:212. For example, in the *Critique of Pure Reason*, Kant says: "Happiness is the satisfaction of all of our inclinations (*extensively*, with regard to their manifoldness, as well as *intensively*, with regard to degree, and also *protensively*, with regard to duration)" (A 806/B 834). In the *Groundwork*, he calls happiness "complete well-being and satisfaction with one's condition" and says that the idea of happiness sums up the entire satisfaction of all of our needs and inclinations (4:393, 399, 405). The *Critique of Practical Reason* defines happiness as "the state of a rational being in the world in the whole of whose existence *everything goes according to his wish and will*" (5:124; see also 5:22). See also, for example, *Critique of Practical Reason*, 5:22; and *Critique of Judgment*, 5:208, 430, 434. For a different interpretation, according to which Kant is instead a hedonist about the nature of happiness, see Iain P. D.

If this much is uncontroversial, however, it is more controversial to claim that, on Kant's view, certain objective goods, especially virtue, promote one's own happiness. This may seem surprising in part because Kant repeats nothing more frequently in his texts on moral philosophy than that both the moral law itself and the motive to act morally cannot be derived (directly or indirectly) from an interest in one's own happiness; rather, they have an a priori basis in pure reason, which must be distinguished with the utmost precision from the satisfaction of sensible inclinations and desires. Nevertheless, it would be entirely consistent with that view to hold that acting from a purely moral motive, without taking account of any interest in one's own happiness, can shape one's sensible nature in a way that tends to enhance one's prospects of becoming happy. The key to Kant's version of this view, I will argue, is the Rousseauian idea that the content of our desires and what we take pleasure in is not entirely fixed by our nature, but rather can be shaped both through social comparison and by moral ideas. Becoming virtuous for Kant has the effect of shaping our desires so that more and more they become desires for developing our rational capacities and promoting the happiness of others. Shaping our desires in this way enhances our own prospects of becoming happy because it puts our happiness more (but never entirely) within our own control; and because, insofar as our happiness remains dependent on factors outside of our control, it makes our happiness compatible with the happiness of others and so removes one of the chief obstacles to our happiness.

Consider first the evidence that Kant agrees with Rousseau that social comparison can shape our desires. In the *Idea for a universal history with a cosmopolitan aim*, Kant claims that nature's aim for the human species is not our happiness but the development of our reason, which, following Rousseau, he defines as the essentially limitless ability to extend our powers beyond natural instinct.[39] The means nature employs for achieving this end, Kant says, is social antagonism or "the *unsociable sociability* of human beings," which he characterizes as a combination of two opposing natural tendencies: first, the natural inclination to enter into society and to become socialized; and, second, "the unsociable

Morrisson, *Kant and the Role of Pleasure in Moral Action* (Athens: Ohio University Press, 2008), 114.

39. *Idea*, 8:18.

property of willing to direct everything so as to get [our] own way."[40] The combination of these two opposed forces in human nature "awakens all the powers of the human being, brings him to overcome his propensity to indolence, and, driven by ambition, tyranny, and greed, to obtain for himself a rank among his fellows, whom he cannot *stand*, but also cannot *leave alone*."[41] Kant again defines reason as the ability to extend our powers beyond instinct in the *Conjectural beginning of human history*, which mentions Rousseau explicitly; but in this essay he adds that "it is a property of reason that with the assistance of the power of imagination it can concoct desires not only *without* a natural drive directed to them but even *contrary to* it."[42] The way reason creates new desires is by making comparisons between objects of existing desires and other, similar objects, for which we then develop new desires. From here it is but a short step to using reason to make social comparisons that produce new desires in us, and then to deliberately manipulating the desires of both oneself and others in order "to influence others to respect ... us (through the concealment of that which could incite low esteem)."[43] The result in our current state of development is that now "restless reason ... drives [us] irresistibly toward the development of the capacities placed in [us] ..., to take upon [ourselves] the toil [we hate] and run after the bauble [we despise] ..., on account of all those trivialities [we are] even more afraid to lose."[44]

So when Kant defines happiness as the idea of a state in which all of our inclinations are satisfied, he is talking at least in part about desires that are formed through social comparison, and hence desires that may not reflect, and may even conflict with, our natural needs. The nature of human reason itself (i.e., our unsociable sociability) drives us to understand our happiness in this way, which has the effect of making happiness essentially impossible for us, at least in this life. This is what Kant means by calling happiness an idea: on his view ideas can never be fully instantiated in the sensible world.[45] It would be impossible to satisfy all of our desires if any of them conflicted with one another, and Kant holds

40. Ibid., 8:20.

41. Ibid., 8:21.

42. *Conjectural Beginning*, 8:111.

43. Ibid., 8:113.

44. Ibid., 8:115.

45. A 367/B 310. See Michael Rohlf, "The Ideas of Pure Reason," in *The Cambridge Companion to Kant's* Critique of Pure Reason, ed. Paul Guyer (Cambridge: Cambridge University Press, 2010), 190–209.

that desires formed through social comparison sometimes conflict with our natural drives.[46] Moreover, we do not even have a determinate idea of what would satisfy all of our desires, because our desires change and we could not know everything we will ever desire over the course of our entire lives, and because our finite minds could never calculate what would satisfy all of these desires even if we knew them and even if they were all mutually consistent.[47] Despite this, our nature drives us all the same to chase after this illusory idea of happiness, because it stimulates the development of our rational capacities, and nature's aim is not our happiness but the development of reason in the human species as a whole.

This sounds very similar to what Rousseau says about seeking happiness through unfulfilling pleasures based on social comparisons. But for Rousseau that is only one conception of happiness—and a false one—which he urges us to replace with another, true conception of happiness based on fulfilling pleasure in the sentiment of existence. Rousseau understands both of these conceptions of happiness hedonistically, but he distinguishes the kinds and sources of pleasure at the root of each. I suggest that, although Kant uses a desire theory instead of hedonism, he too distinguishes two chief sources of the desires in whose satisfaction we may place our happiness. Besides desires based on natural drives, for Kant our default condition is to understand our happiness mainly in terms of satisfying desires formed through social comparison, as just described. But it is also possible to shape our desires by moral ideas; and becoming virtuous, which is not our default condition, has the effect that our desires become shaped progressively less by social comparisons and more by moral ideas.

In the earlier moral writings of Kant's critical period, such as the *Groundwork* and *Critique of Practical Reason*, he assumes that people think first about their own happiness and only later about morality. In the *Groundwork* he says that maxims arise from desires and inclinations with the cooperation of reason, by which he means that we initially formulate maxims in order to satisfy our desires, where a maxim is a subjective principle of action that says how we propose to act and why.[48] Only later, after we have formulated maxims in this way, do we consider

46. *Critique of Judgment*, 5:430. See also *Critique of Practical Reason*, 5:118, where Kant says that happiness is impossible because satisfying desires only produces new desires.

47. *Groundwork*, 4:399, 417; *Critique of Practical Reason*, 5:26.

48. *Groundwork*, 4:427. See also *Critique of Practical Reason*, 5:73 and 74. On maxims, see 4:401n.

whether they are morally permissible.[49] However, later, in the *Doctrine of Virtue*, Kant no longer assumes that people think about morality only after their own happiness. Instead, he claims that we have an ethical duty to set certain ends: specifically, the ends of perfecting oneself and promoting the happiness of others.[50] Kant's claim that we have a duty to set these two general ends means that we can and ought to formulate maxims to act in ways that aim at achieving these ends.[51] So now maxims do not necessarily arise from desires and inclinations, but can arise directly from the idea of an ethical duty.[52]

This difference between the *Groundwork* and *Critique of Practical Reason*, on the one hand, and the *Doctrine of Virtue*, on the other, may reflect either a development in Kant's views on moral psychology in the interim or a change of emphasis on Kant's part from an agent's earlier to later stages of moral development.[53] Either way, the *Doctrine of Virtue* is unique in focusing on Kant's conception of virtue and what he calls duties of virtue. A duty of virtue is a duty to set oneself an end; all specific duties of virtue fall under the general duties to set the ends of perfecting oneself and promoting others' happiness. Because setting an end is essentially an act of freedom, duties of virtue are not subject to external enforcement, that is, others can constrain my external actions (i.e., the

49. We (should) decide by asking ourselves whether we can will those maxims as universal laws. In Kant's favorite example, a man "finds himself urged by need to borrow money" that he cannot repay; but since he knows that nobody will lend him money unless he promises to repay it, he formulates a maxim to tell a lying promise to repay money that he knows he will not repay (*Groundwork*, 4:402, 421). He formulates this maxim to satisfy his needs and only later stops to consider that it is not morally permissible because it cannot be willed as a universal law.

50. *Doctrine of Virtue*, 6:385.

51. See *Doctrine of Virtue*, 6:389: "the end that is also a duty can make it a law to have such a maxim."

52. For example, I may originally formulate the maxim to help a child learn to read simply because I believe that I have a duty to promote others' happiness and that helping this child learn to read will promote her happiness. I may genuinely take no account of my own happiness in formulating this maxim at any stage.

53. I do not wish to take a position here on which of these two explanations of differences between these texts is to be preferred. Note that on the latter explanation, according to which the differences reflect only a change of emphasis, Kant himself may have believed when he wrote the *Groundwork* and *Critique of Practical Reason* that maxims can arise directly from the idea of an ethical duty. But he does not say this in those works. Instead, he says that maxims arise directly from desires and inclinations, but he leaves room between proposing a maxim and acting on it for duty to motivate us to act only on morally permissible maxims, as if duty does not inspire us to propose maxims in the first place.

movements of my body) but only I can make something my end.[54] Duties of virtue are also imperfect or wide duties, which require us to set ends but give us "playroom" or latitude in deciding how and when to pursue these ends.[55] Finally, duties of virtue are quite permissive: it is possible to discharge them minimally simply by having the relevant ends without doing anything to pursue them or pursuing them minimally. For example, I may choose to fulfill the duty to promote others' happiness by teaching a child to read or by writing a paper about happiness; and I can genuinely have these ends without helping the child to read on any particular occasion, because I spend so much time writing about happiness. But ethics for Kant is not just about discharging duties. It is also about developing virtue, understood as the strength of will to govern oneself and to overcome internal obstacles to fulfilling one's duties.[56] Complete virtue, or what Kant sometimes calls holiness, is an unattainable ideal for human beings.[57] Our goal should be to progress continually toward this ideal by bringing "closer to *narrow* duty … the maxim of complying with wide duty (in [one's] disposition)."[58] In other words, to become virtuous we should not be content to comply minimally with our duties; instead, we should strive to treat the wide duties to perfect ourselves and to promote others' happiness more and more as if they were narrow duties that require us to perfect ourselves as much as possible, and to promote the happiness of as many others as much as we can.[59] Progressing toward the ideal of virtue involves taking these ends progressively more seriously, so that our maxims arise more and more from them instead of (solely) from our desires.[60]

Kant holds that progressing toward virtue in this way shapes our sensible nature so that we come more and more to desire our own perfection

54. *Doctrine of Virtue*, 6:381.

55. Ibid., 6:390. This excludes what Kant calls duties of respect (6:449, 462) as well as the duty to increase one's moral perfection (6:446).

56. See, for example, *Doctrine of Virtue*, 6:380, 383, 390, 394, 405.

57. *Critique of Practical Reason*, 5:83; *Doctrine of Virtue*, 6:409.

58. *Doctrine of Virtue*, 6:390.

59. Kant also says that to become virtuous we should strive to fulfill duties of right (which are narrow or perfect duties) from the motive of duty, which those duties themselves do not require (*Doctrine of Virtue*, 6:390, 392).

60. See Kant's language at *Groundwork*, 4:430, where he is discussing the duty to promote others' happiness: "the ends of a subject who is an end in itself must as far as possible be also *my* ends, if that representation is to have its *full* effect on me."

and the happiness of others. Virtue does not consist, for Kant, in shaping desires so that they follow reason; it consists in the strength of will to act morally by representing moral ideas to ourselves in a way that overpowers internal obstacles to doing our duty.[61] But one effect of developing virtue is that we come to desire the ends of duty and to take pleasure in signs of their achievement. Kant is committed to this view because he holds that reason creates new desires whenever we set ourselves an end and represent that end as something we can achieve. In the *Critique of Practical Reason*, Kant says that either the experience or the expectation of pleasure is what causes us to form desires: we come to desire an object whenever we expect obtaining it to give us pleasure.[62] But he defines "pleasure" as "the *representation of the agreement of an object or of an action with the* subjective *conditions of life*," and he includes the will among what he calls subjective conditions of life.[63] According to this definition, to represent an end that we have set ourselves as achievable, as possible through our will, is pleasurable and thus causes us to desire the achievement of that end. Kant's somewhat different definition of pleasure in the *Critique of Judgment* also supports this view. There he says that pleasure is a representation of the feeling of life or the promotion of the powers of life, while displeasure represents the inhibition of life.[64] This definition

61. This is why the *Groundwork* provides multiple formulations of the categorical imperative that aim to "bring an idea of reason [i.e., the moral law] closer to intuition (by a certain analogy) and thereby to feeling" (4:436).

62. *Critique of Practical Reason*, 5:23. See also *Groundwork*, 4:427; and *Metaphysics of Morals*, 6:211. This is related to Kant's claim in the *Idea* and *Conjectural Beginning* essays that reason forms desires by making comparisons with objects we already desire. If I desire ice cream, then I expect (perhaps from past experience) that ice cream will give me pleasure. Reasoning that frozen yogurt is similar to ice cream may then lead me to expect that it too will give me pleasure, which causes me to form a new desire for it.

63. *Critique of Practical Reason*, 5:9n. Kant's text here is complicated. The full passage reads: "Life is the faculty of a being to act in accordance with laws of the faculty of desire. The faculty of desire is a being's *faculty to be by means of its representations the cause of the reality of the objects of these representations.* Pleasure is the *representation of the agreement of an object or of an action with the* subjective *conditions of life*, i.e., with the faculty of the *causality of a representation with respect to the reality of its object* (or with respect to the determination of the powers of the subject to action in order to produce the object)." Later in the same text, Kant defines "the will" as "a faculty either of producing objects corresponding to representations or of determining itself to effect such objects" (5:15). So, while he does not simply identify the will with "the subjective conditions of life," clearly Kant means to include the will among the subjective conditions of life to which he refers here.

64. *Critique of Judgment*, 5:204, 278. See also 5:220; *First Introduction*, 20:230; and the editor's note 3 on page 366.

of pleasure is similar to Rousseau's characterization of the sentiment of existence as pleasure in the active use of one's powers. Together with Kant's assumption that desires arise from the expectation of pleasure, this definition implies that using reason to set oneself an end, and actively pursuing it, produces pleasure and thus causes us to desire that end.

So Kant holds that progressing toward the ideal of virtue, by taking the ends of perfecting oneself and promoting others' happiness more and more seriously, has the effect of shaping our sensible nature so that we progressively desire—and thus place our happiness in—the achievement of these ends more and more, while social comparison shapes our desires proportionately less.[65] The fact that Kant holds this view, however, can be obscured by his tendency to emphasize that moral motivation does not reduce directly or indirectly to any sort of desire for pleasure, not even pleasure in acting morally.[66] Kant insists that the only feeling that arises directly as an effect of determining one's will by the moral law is a feeling of pure respect for the moral law, which is not pleasurable but painful because the moral law "*infringes upon* self-love" and "*strikes down* self-conceit," while revealing how far we fall short of the ideal of virtue.[67] But this does not imply that in exercising our rational powers to set ends that are duties, and in pursuing or achieving these ends, we experience no pleasure. Kant draws a distinction here between acting from pure respect for the moral law and acting for the sake of some end. Acting from pure respect for the moral law does not itself involve or produce pleasure; but pursuing ends does cause us to desire and take pleasure in the achievement of those ends. The key point is that progressing toward virtue by setting and pursuing the ends that are also duties—that is, one's own perfection and the happiness of others—involves *both* acting from pure respect for the moral law *and* pursuing these ends. As a result, our sensible nature is shaped by moral ideas, as we come to desire the achievement of ends that we set from a purely moral motive.

Because Kant is at pains to distinguish the satisfaction of these and

65. In addition to the texts I focus on here, Kant also makes a strong case for the virtuous habitation of desires in the *Anthropology from a Pragmatic Point of View*. I discuss this text in Michael Rohlf, "Emotion and Evil in Kant," *Review of Metaphysics* 66 (June 2013): 749–73.

66. "In a practical law [i.e., of duty] reason determines the will immediately, not by means of an intervening feeling of pleasure or displeasure, not even in this law" (*Critique of Practical Reason*, 5:25).

67. Ibid., 5:73.

all other desires from moral motivation—that is, to distinguish moral motivation from the desire for one's own happiness—he is very careful to describe happiness as the passive satisfaction of desires, and to contrast happiness with what we actively do. Passages in which he draws this contrast typically also claim that the worth of our existence comes only from what we actively do and not from what we passively enjoy, that is, not from happiness. For example, in the third *Critique* he says: "It is easy to decide what sort of value life has for us if it is assessed merely by *what one enjoys* (the natural end of the sum of all inclinations, happiness). Less than zero."[68] Later he adds that the value of a human being's existence "consists in what he does, in how and in accordance with which principles he acts, not as a link in nature but in the *freedom* of his faculty of desire, i.e., a good will is that alone by means of which his existence can have an absolute value."[69] I take Kant to mean that even when we desire ends that are also duties—for example, if you desire to perfect your theoretical reasoning capacity by pursuing a philosophy degree—the satisfaction of these desires is conceptually distinguishable from the activity of pursuing and achieving those ends. Even though the activities of thinking, studying, writing papers, etc., are causally responsible for your achieving the end of receiving a degree, these activities can be distinguished from the passive satisfaction of your desire for this end. All satisfaction of desires is passive in this sense, even when it results from our own activity; and happiness consists strictly in the satisfaction of desires and thus is to be distinguished from what we actively do. Moreover, satisfying desires does not give our lives value, even when those desires are for morally necessary ends; only a morally good will, which hopefully will manifest itself in the free activity of setting and pursuing these ends, can give our lives value.

This aspect of Kant's conception of happiness puts him at odds with Rousseau on the surface but masks a deeper agreement between them. For Rousseau, true happiness consists in taking pleasure in the active use of one's powers, which requires spurning the unfulfilling pleasures of satisfying desires formed through social comparison. But for Kant all

68. *Critique of Judgment*, 5:434.

69. Ibid., 5:443. See also *Conjectural Beginning*, 8:122; *Groundwork*, 4:395; *Critique of Practical Reason*, 5:88; *Critique of Judgment*, 5:208; *Theory and Practice*, 8:283n; *Doctrine of Virtue*, 6:387.

happiness consists in the passive satisfaction of desires and is to be distinguished from the active use of our rational powers. So Rousseau and Kant disagree about whether happiness should be understood as active or passive. But underlying this disagreement is a deeper agreement on at least two points: first, that passively satisfying desires has no value in comparison with actively exercising our rational powers; and, second, that actively exercising our rational powers helps us to become happy. For Rousseau it is necessary for happiness, since pleasure in the sentiment of existence is pleasure in the active use of one's powers. But for Kant pursuing the ends of one's own perfection and the happiness of others is not strictly necessary for one's own happiness, since Kant does not wish to rule out the possibility that fortune may smile on the vicious and make them happier than the virtuous, at least in this life, where it is impossible to satisfy all of one's desires in any case and so judgments about happiness must be comparative. Nevertheless, Kant has Rousseauian reasons for holding that developing our rational powers, along with virtue and love of others, at least tends to promote one's own happiness. Insofar as progressing toward virtue involves perfecting oneself by developing one's rational powers and shapes us to desire this end, it places our happiness (i.e., the satisfaction of these desires) more within our control and thus makes us less dependent on others for our happiness. And insofar as progressing toward virtue involves promoting others' happiness by identifying one's own ends with the ends of others, it makes one's happiness more compatible with the happiness of others. Kant calls the general duty to promote others' happiness the duty of love to other human beings.[70] Love so understood, not as a feeling but "as the maxim of *benevolence* (practical love), which results in beneficence," plays the negative role of mitigating the harmful effects of social antagonism as well as the positive role of promoting ends that one shares with others.[71]

But Kant's admission that vicious people may be happier than the virtuous indicates a sense in which his conception of happiness is more subjectivist than both Aristotle's and Rousseau's, because it allows still more flexibility in what kinds of lives can be happy. This is also true to an extent of Kant's conception of virtue and imperfect or wide duties. The duty to perfect oneself, in particular, requires us to cultivate all of

70. *Doctrine of Virtue*, 6:448.
71. Ibid., 6:449.

our faculties, which Kant divides into natural powers that include understanding, memory, imagination, learning, taste, and powers of the body; and the moral powers of practical reason and a good will.[72] Kant allows, however, that each person may choose the order of precedence among the natural powers he cultivates "in accordance with his own rational reflection about what sort of life he would like to lead [...] (e.g., whether it should be a trade, commerce, or a learned profession)."[73] So I may choose a life that gives the cultivation of understanding lower priority than all other natural powers; and that life can be as virtuous as others. Kant does not allow us the same flexibility in cultivating our moral powers, though: the duty to perfect ourselves requires that we strive to progress as far as we can toward a virtuous disposition. As far as happiness is concerned, the happiness of those who choose to give high priority to theoretical reasoning will depend on and be greatly enhanced by satisfying their desires for cultivating and exercising theoretical reason. But Kant seems to hold that a life that gives the cultivation of theoretical reason lower priority than other natural powers can be just as happy. So developing our practically rational powers plays a more central role in becoming happy, for Kant, than developing theoretical reason does. Developing theoretical reason is still an objective good, however—along with practical reason, virtue, and love of others—because we have a duty to cultivate it, even if only an imperfect or wide duty. Any end that we have a duty to promote is an objective end, hence an objective good, whose value derives from the absolute value of our capacity for a morally good will.[74] What makes all of these objective goods is not that they contribute to our happiness, but rather that we are morally required to pursue them as ends. Kant holds that these objective goods do help us to become happy, although they are not necessary for happiness, and that happiness does not consist—as it did for Aristotle—in possession of these goods.

72. Ibid., 6:386, 444.
73. Ibid., 6:445.
74. *Groundwork*, 4:428, 435; *Doctrine of Virtue*, 6:380, 385.

Paul Guyer

10 Kant, Autonomy, and Modernity

What is truly modern in Kant's practical philosophy? The central idea of this philosophy is that of the fundamental and unconditional value of autonomy, which is defined at the outset of Section III of the *Groundwork for the Metaphysics of Morals* as "the will's property of being a law to itself."[1] So it seems natural to see Kant's conception of autonomy as what is most novel in his work and as his paradigmatic contribution to the Enlightenment as a self-conscious break with past conceptions of morality and the source of its authority. Kant himself certainly suggested that he saw his conception of autonomy as the key to what is new in his philosophy when, in the conclusion of the Introduction to the *Critique of the Power of Judgment*, the last of his three critiques, he summed up his entire system of philosophy as a theory of "the faculties of the soul in general, insofar as they are considered as higher faculties, i.e., as ones that contain an autonomy."[2]

No doubt there is something right about the assumption that it is Kant's conception of autonomy that is his distinctive contribution to mo-

1. Quotations from Kant's writings in moral philosophy are taken from *Practical Philosophy*, ed. and trans. Mary J. Gregor (Cambridge: Cambridge University Press, 1996). However, citations will be located by volume and page number of the Akademie edition, *Kant's gesammelte Schriften*, ed. the Royal Prussian (later German, then Berlin-Brandenburg) Academy of Sciences (Berlin: Georg Reimer, later Walter de Gruyter, 1900–), which are reproduced in the margins of the Cambridge editions. "*G*" will abbreviate *Groundwork for Metaphysics of Morals*, "*PracR*" the *Critique of Practical Reason*, and "*MM*" the *Metaphysics of Morals*. For the passage cited in this sentence, the source is *G*, 4:446.

2. Immanuel Kant, *Critique of the Power of Judgment*, ed. Paul Guyer, trans. Paul Guyer and Eric Matthews (Cambridge: Cambridge University Press, 2000), introduction, section IX (5:196).

dernity. But the claim must be stated carefully, for there are certainly elements of Kant's conception that go back to antiquity, and that might be considered characteristic not so much of modernity as of philosophy itself. The ideas that we should rule ourselves by laws of reason and that by so doing we free ourselves of the dominion of our own passions, as well as the anti-voluntaristic idea that God (if there is one) wills that we should obey moral laws because they are rational rather than that they are binding just because he wills them, all of which are parts of Kant's conception of autonomy but the last of which in particular might be taken as the defining idea of the Enlightenment, all also go back to Plato and the Stoics. So is there anything new and modern in Kant's conception of autonomy? I will suggest that there is, but that it lies in the "positive" rather than in the "negative" aspect of Kant's conception of the fundamental value of freedom, that is, it lies in his idea that our fundamental value is setting our own ends as opposed to being pushed around by our passions, coupled with his idea that each of us must recognize that every instance of such autonomy is as valuable as our own, and thus that autonomy is a universal value.

A second question that I will raise is whether there is anything distinctively modern in Kant's way of arguing for this position. Here I will suggest that when Kant began thinking about the value of freedom, he appealed to essentially empirical arguments that are continuous with ancient, especially Stoic styles of argument. In the *Groundwork*, Kant replaced all such empirical arguments with an a priori appeal to our noumenal nature that might be regarded as novel simply because the ancients did not have his clear distinctions between the empirical and the a priori and the phenomenal and the noumenal (although at least one prominent twentieth-century Kant scholar who argued for the decisive influence of Plato on Kant's mature moral philosophy might well have contested this claim).[3] But Kant quickly backed off from this style of argument for the validity of the fundamental principle of morality, presumably because for all that he was happy to argue for "practical faith" in the noumenal agency of both ourselves and God as the necessary conditions for the rationality of attempting to fulfill antecedently accepted moral obligations, he

3. See Klaus Reich, "Kant and Greek Ethics," trans. W. H. Walsh in *Mind* (New Series) 48 (1939): 338–54, 446–63, reprinted in Reich, *Gesammelte Schriften*, ed. Manfred Baum et al. (Hamburg: Felix Meiner, 2001), 425–59, esp. 427–40.

realized that an a priori argument about the noumenal source of the very validity of the moral law itself would violate the epistemological strictures of his own theoretical philosophy. This left him with the strategy of accepting the validity of the moral law and its consequences as a "fact of reason" that could be philosophically defended precisely by showing that within the epistemological strictures of his theoretical philosophy it could not be disproven (the same stance Kant takes toward the existence of God). Perhaps we should also see this defensive and non-foundational argumentative strategy for moral philosophy as something distinctively modern, perhaps an anticipation of the method of "reflective equilibrium" advocated by John Rawls.

The following discussion will therefore be divided into three parts. First, I will briefly establish the ancient origins of some of the characteristic elements of Kant's conception of autonomy. Second, I will describe what is distinctively modern in Kant's conception of autonomy. Third, I will briefly describe Kant's difficult path toward a new style of argument for this conception.

THE ANCIENT ASPECTS OF AUTONOMY

I suggested that we might take anti-voluntarism as a defining mark of the Enlightenment. We find it for example in Shaftesbury, who wrote at the start of the eighteenth century that "whoever thinks there is a god and pretends formally to believe that he is just and good must suppose that there is independently such a thing as justice and injustice, truth and falsehood, right and wrong, according to which he announces that God is just, righteous and true."[4] Christian Wolff lost his position at Halle and came into danger of losing his life for arguing that the Confucian Chinese, without belief in God, nevertheless insisted that "reason be properly developed" since by means of it "one must arrive at a distinct knowledge of good and evil without grounding virtue on fear of a lord and without the hope of receiving a reward from him."[5] As early as

4. Anthony Ashley Cooper, Third Earl of Shaftesbury, *An Inquiry concerning Virtue or Merit*, Book I, Part III, Section 2, in his *Characteristics of Men, Manners, Opinions, Times*, ed. Lawrence E. Klein (Cambridge: Cambridge University Press, 1999), 181. The *Inquiry concerning Virtue or Merit* was first published, without Shaftesbury's authorization, in 1699, but then included by him in the first edition of the *Characteristics* in 1711.

5. Christian Wolff, *Oratio de Sinarum philosophia practica/Rede über die praktische Phi-*

1759 Kant endorsed Leibniz's anti-voluntarist view that God chose this world to exist because he recognized that it is the best among all possible worlds against Crusius's voluntarist view that this is the best of all possible worlds simply because God chose it to exist.[6] And in his earliest recorded lectures on ethics, the notes taken by Herder between 1762 and 1764, Kant stated that "From the *arbitrium divinum* I cannot myself obtain the relevant concepts of the good, unless the concept of the morally good be assumed beforehand ... the judgment as to the perfection of God's *arbitrium* presupposes the investigation of moral perfection."[7]

So there is no question that the idea that the fundamental law or laws of reality must be capable of being recognized by unaided human reason antecedently to any revelation of the will of God and that any such claimed revelation must be tested against our own insight into the moral law is certainly a characteristic idea of the leading thinkers of the Enlightenment and a lifelong commitment of Kant himself. But this aspect of the idea of autonomy cannot be regarded as a novelty in Kant nor in the Enlightenment as a whole, for it goes back to Plato, and for that reason can be regarded as a defining idea of philosophy itself rather than of modernity. In the *Euthyphro*, the very first in the traditional ordering of Plato's dialogues, Plato has Socrates argue that the pious is loved by the gods "because it is pious, but it is not pious because it is [...] loved" by them.[8] Socrates argues against Euthyphro that we can discover what is pious only through our own rational inquiry into what is right and wrong, and have no independent access to the loves of the gods by means of which to discover what is right and wrong; indeed, trying to determine the will of the gods without the compass of our own insight into right and wrong will lead only to contradiction and confusion. The idea of using our own reason to discover what is right and wrong is virtually the starting point of philosophy.

---

losophie der Chinesen, ed. Michael Albrecht (Hamburg: Felix Meiner, 1985), 45 (author's translation).

6. See Kant, "An Attempt at Some Reflections on Optimism" (October 7, 1759), 2:29–35, translated in Kant, *Theoretical Philosophy 1755–1770*, ed. and trans. David Walford and Ralf Meerbote (Cambridge: Cambridge University Press, 1992), 71–75; see the discussion in J. B. Schneewind, *The Invention of Autonomy* (Cambridge: Cambridge University Press, 1998), 492–97.

7. Kant, *Lectures on Ethics*, ed. Peter Heath and J. B. Schneewind, trans. Peter Heath (Cambridge: Cambridge University Press, 1997), 5 (27:9); see Schneewind, *Invention of Autonomy*, 497.

8. Plato, *Euthyphro*, trans. G. M. A. Grube, in Plato, *Complete Works*, ed. John M. Cooper (Indianapolis, Ind.: Hackett, 1997), 10d.

The idea that we must regulate our conduct by the use of our reason and not be led by our passions is also an idea that goes back to Plato and that was particularly emphasized by the Stoics from the origins of their school in the century following Plato. Socrates introduces the model of the tripartite soul in which reason should rule spirit and appetite in Book IV of the *Republic* (439c–442d), subsequently analogizing reason to the philosophically trained guardians who should rule the lower orders in the just republic. "Fashioning an image of the soul in words" (588b), he compares reason to the human being who can rule over beasts like the lion and the snake (588c–590c), and concludes that "it is better for everyone to be ruled by divine reason, preferably within himself and his own, otherwise imposed from without" (590d): at least the best-educated humans can be ruled by reason alone, without reliance on external inducements. The early Stoics transformed Socrates's idea of the just soul into the idea of living in accordance with nature, where nature itself is law-governed and its laws can be discerned by human reason. Thus Diogenes Laertius described Zeno of Citium, Cleanthes, and Chrysippus as saying that the goal for man is "to live in agreement with nature," in accordance with our own nature but where our own nature is part of nature in general: "Therefore the goal becomes 'to live consistently with nature,' i.e., doing nothing which is forbidden by the common law, which is right reason, penetrating all things."[9] Chrysippus made the continuity between our own nature and nature in general explicit: "By nature, in consistency with which we must live, Chrysippus understands both the common and, specifically, the human nature."[10] And according to Arius Didymus, reported by Stobaeus, "Zeno defined the goal thus: 'living in agreement.' This means living according to a single and consonant rational principle, since those who live in conflict are unhappy."[11] The assumption is that it is our nature to be rational, so to live in accordance with our nature is to live in accordance with reason, and our own reason can tell us what this requires, that being above all the avoidance of internal and external conflict.

9. Diogenes Laertius, VII.87–88, quoted in Brad Inwood and Pierluigi Donini, "Stoic Ethics," in Keimpe Alegra, Jonathan Barnes, Jaap Mansfeld, and Malcolm Schofield, *The Cambridge History of Hellenistic Philosophy* (Cambridge: Cambridge University Press, 1999), 675–738, at 685.

10. Diogenes Laertius, VII.88, from Brad Inwood and Lloyd P. Gerson, eds., *The Stoic Reader: Selected Writings and Testimonia* (Indianapolis, Ind.: Hackett, 2008), 114.

11. Quoted by Stobaeus, II.75.11–76.15 (Inwood and Donini, "Stoic Ethics," 684).

The account of early Stoicism preserved by Stobaeus also makes it clear that, as in Plato, governance by reason means governance of the impulses. "Passion is an impulse which is excessive and disobedient to the reason which constrains, or an irrational, unnatural motion of the soul," but in the rational person impulses are constrained by reason, and so do not become passions.[12] Later, in Roman Stoicism, the idea of the rule of impulse by reason to prevent the development of passion is transformed into an image of the "happy life" as consisting in freedom from fear and desire realized through the use of reason. Seneca's essay *De vita beata* is one of the chief texts of later Stoicism. Here Seneca writes that "The happy life [...] is a life that is in harmony with its own nature, and it can be attained in only one way." It must begin with "a sound mind and one that is in constant possession of its sanity," accompanied with fortitude, and through the vigorous use of reason we can drive "away all that excites or affrights us," from which "ensues unbroken tranquility and enduring freedom."[13] Seneca continues: "the happy life is to have a mind that is free, lofty, fearless and steadfast—a mind that is placed beyond the reach of fear, beyond the reach of desire ... the happy man is one who is freed from both fear and desire because of the gift of reason."[14] Living in accord with reason frees us from domination by our own desires, which are the source of our fears, for all our fears might be collectively characterized as fear of the disappointment of our desires. Freed from such fear by reason's insight that these desires bring more trouble than pleasure, we can live in tranquility.

The ancients thus certainly anticipated some aspects of the idea of autonomy that seems to be Kant's distinctive contribution to modernity: Plato pioneered the idea that we must live in accordance with our own reason and argued that any external claim to moral authority must be tested by the lights of our own reason, and the Stoics developed the idea of reason's rule over impulse or desire into a conception of freedom, which brings a tranquility more satisfying than the fulfillment of any particular desire could ever be. So what, if anything, did Kant add in making a truly modern idea of autonomy?

12. Stobaeus II.10 (Inwood and Gerson, *The Stoic Reader*, 137).

13. Seneca, *De vita beata*, III.3–4; from Seneca, *Moral Essays*, trans. John W. Basore (Cambridge, Mass.: Harvard University Press, 1938), 2:107.

14. Seneca, *De vita beata*, IV.3–V.1, *Moral Essays*, 2:109–11.

KANT'S CONCEPTION OF AUTONOMY

Perhaps the simplest answer to this question is that the ancients anticipated Schopenhauer, not Kant. That is, the ancient conception of freedom and its value is negative, the idea of freedom from the fear of disappointment that comes with taking the satisfaction of desires to be the source of happiness and the point of life, while Kant introduces a positive conception of freedom and its value, the idea that setting our own ends is unconditionally valuable and intrinsically satisfying and that even while the pursuit of self-chosen ends will inevitably expose us to the frustration of failing to realize at least some of them, the satisfaction of having chosen those ends ourselves will outweigh such frustration. Kant's guiding image of freedom secured through reason is not that of simple freedom from desire and fear of frustration but rather the idea of a framework within which individuals, all of whom are equally worthy, can choose their own ends in ways that are intra- and interpersonally consistent.

Kant did not arrive at this conception of autonomy overnight. In his earliest surviving writings about the value of freedom, notes jotted in his own interleaved copy of his popular 1764 book *Observations on the Feeling of the Beautiful and Sublime*, Kant explored Stoic and Rousseauian conceptions of the value of freedom from domination by one's own desires and the impulses of others, but did not yet have a clear conception of the intrinsic value of setting one's own ends.[15] Some of the most impassioned and impressive of these notes focus on the dislike of anyone who has ever tasted freedom for domination by others, perhaps inspired by Kant's recent reading of Rousseau's *Du contrat sociale* and *Emile.* For example, "what is harder and more unnatural" than our dependence on external sources such as the air and the sun for the satisfaction of our needs "is the subjection of one human being under the will of another. No misfortune can be more terrifying to one who is accustomed to freedom, who has enjoyed the good of freedom, than to see himself delivered to a creature of his own kind who can compel him to do what he will."[16]

15. An even earlier publication, the 1755 *New Exposition of the First Principles of Metaphysical Cognition*, deals with the conundrum of freedom of the will, but not with the value of freedom of choice.

16. Kant, *Notes and Fragments*, ed. Paul Guyer, trans. Curtis Bowman, Paul Guyer, and

Other notes, which read as if they had been lifted directly out of an ancient text, emphasize the need to avoid domination and then frustration by the untrammeled growth of one's own desires. Thus Kant writes: "It is not compatible with happiness to let the inclinations become excessive, for since there are uncommonly many cases where circumstances are unfavourable for these inclinations, when things are not as desired, they become a source of oppression, misery, and worry."[17] More fully, "One could promote one's welfare by allowing one's desires to expand and striving to satisfy them; one could promote one's rectitude if one allowed the inclinations of whim and luxuriousness to grow and then tried to resist them for the sake of moral incentives. But there is another solution to these problems, namely, not allowing these inclinations to arise."[18]

The Stoic character of Kant's thought at this early stage is even more unmistakable in passages in which he essentially suggests that the solution to the problem of potential domination by one's own inclinations is to live in accordance with nature, that is, to use reason to distinguish between our minimal and unavoidable but easily satisfiable "natural" desires and our readily frustrated but also unnecessary "unnatural" desires, and to ensure ourselves happiness by aiming to satisfy only the former. Thus he writes that "virtue does not at all consist in overcoming acquired inclinations in particular cases, but in seeking to be free of such inclinations and then learning to do without them gladly. It does not consist in conflict with the natural inclinations, but rather in making it the case that one has none except for the natural ones, because these can always be satisfied."[19] Here Kant defines virtue as freeing ourselves from unnatural inclinations and confining ourselves to natural ones, the ready satisfaction of which in turn brings happiness. This is an idea that could have been found in Seneca (or for that matter in Epicurus or his followers).

However, we also find Kant experimenting with several further ideas in these early notes. One idea that we find repeated several times is that

---

Frederick Rauscher (Cambridge: Cambridge University Press, 2005), 11; in Kant, *Observations on the Feeling of the Beautiful and Sublime and Other Writings*, ed. Patrick Frierson and Paul Guyer (Cambridge: Cambridge University Press, 2011), 128. The translations of the notes in the *Observations* in this volume are by Uygar Abacı, Thomas Hilgers, and Mike Nance.

17. Kant, *Notes and Fragments*, 7; *Observations and Other Writings*, 96.

18. Kant, *Notes and Fragments*, 6; *Observations and Other Writings*, 93.

19. Kant, *Notes and Fragments*, 10; *Observations and Other Writings*, 118.

the test of moral acceptability is that intentional actions not contradict themselves or cancel each other out if universalized: "That will must be good which does not cancel itself out if it is taken universally and reciprocally; on this account the other will not take as his what I have worked upon, for otherwise he would presuppose that his will has moved my body."[20] The idea of one person's will moving the body of another might initially seem like a metaphysical absurdity, and thus the idea could be that we should act only in reciprocally acceptable ways to avoid conflict with the metaphysical character of human nature. But of course the idea of one person's will moving the body of another is not a metaphysical absurdity, but is rather the essence of interpersonal domination, so the suggestion would rather seem to be that using reason's criterion that an intention not contradict itself if universalized is the means to the avoidance of such domination. A fuller exposition of what would eventually become Kant's formula of universal law, the first formulation of the categorical imperative in the *Groundwork*, does not supply any additional context, and thus seems again to suggest that the moral function of reason is to enable us to avoid the hated domination of one person by another:

> An action considered from the point of view of the universal will of human beings, if it contradicts itself, is morally impossible (impermissible). Let me have the idea of taking possession of the fruits of another. As I then see no person would acquire anything under the condition that what he has acquired can be ripped from him, I would from a private point of view want that which belongs to another, but from a public point of view decline it.[21]

Wanting something from a private point of view while declining it from a public point of view might again seem like a logical impossibility, and thus it might seem as if the point of testing our proposed actions by the criterion of universalizability is to avoid purely metaphysical problems. But wanting privately what one abjures publicly is hardly impossible; it is rather the essence of duplicity, by which domination of others can be achieved, so once again it looks as if the role of reason's test for non-contradiction upon universalization is to assist us in the avoidance of interpersonal domination, which we hate.

20. Kant, *Notes and Fragments*, 10; *Observations and Other Writings*, 110.
21. Kant, *Notes and Fragments*, 21; *Observations and Other Writings*, 177.

Still, thus far it looks as if Kant's early introduction of the test of universalizability functions primarily to explicate the role of reason in achieving freedom from domination by others, a negative conception of freedom. If we were to amplify his sparse remarks with an argument that we can use the test of consistency among multiple actions to test for the conjoint satisfiability of our own desires and thus as a way to avoid conflict among them and the frustration that would entail, we would still be in the terrain of the ancient conception of the value of negative freedom, that is, the tranquility that ensues upon freedom from domination by our own desires.

However, Kant begins to suggest an alternative conception of the value of freedom in at least one of these early notes. He writes: "Since the greatest inner perfection and the perfection that arises from that consists in the subordination of all of our capacities and receptivities to the free capacity for choice, the feeling for the goodness of the free capacity for choice must immediately be much different and also greater than all of the good consequences that can thereby be effected." He adds: "Now this capacity for choice contains either the merely individual will as well as the universal will, or it considers the person at the same time in *consensu* with the universal will."[22] Here Kant at least hints that there is a satisfaction in making our own choices that is distinct from any satisfaction in the realization of what we choose, and thus that our satisfaction in exercising our freedom is not equivalent to the happiness that results from confining ourselves to a set of readily satisfiable desires. Thus he suggests that there is a positive and not just a negative value to freedom, a satisfaction in the exercise of freedom as such rather than merely the tranquility that results from avoiding unsatisfiable desires and confining ourselves to readily satisfied ones. He further hints that we may be able to see the universal value of such freedom, that is, that we recognize its value not only in our own case but in the case of everyone, from which it would follow that we would always want to act in a way that is consistent not only with our own "free capacity for choice" but with the free capacity for choice of everyone. However, it can hardly be said that in these early notes Kant has spelled out this idea very fully or made explicit how an entire moral theory could be constructed upon it.

22. Kant, *Notes and Fragments*, 16–17; *Observations and Other Writings*, 165.

Twenty years after he wrote these notes, however, Kant was clearly committed to the idea of the value of freedom for its own sake and in every human being, not just its value as a way to avoid frustration from uncontrolled desires. During the summer semester of 1784, at a time when he was working on the *Groundwork for the Metaphysics of Morals*, to be published the following spring, Kant gave a course of lectures on *Ius natura* or natural right, known as *Naturrecht Feyerabend*, in the introduction to which he introduced the idea of an end in itself.[23] He told his students that "It is just as necessary in the system of ends that something must exist as an end in itself and not everything can be merely a means as it is in the series of efficient causes that there must be an *ens a se*," something that exists on its own, and then identified this end in itself as the human being, who is "never merely a means, because that is against his nature." He then added that "If only rational beings can be the end in itself, they cannot be this because they have reason, but because they have freedom. Reason is merely a means [...]. Freedom, only freedom alone, makes it that we are ends in ourselves. Here we have the capacity to act in accordance with our own will."[24] Here Kant clearly indicates his intention to found his moral philosophy and particular applications of it, such as its application to political theory, on the idea that freedom is not merely the means to tranquility through escape from desire, but is a, and indeed the only, thing that is intrinsically valuable; correspondingly, the role of reason is not to guide us toward the preference of readily satisfiable rather than readily frustrated desires, but to guide us toward the realization of freedom as the capacity to have "our own will." If we can locate the commencement of Kant's mature moral philosophy and of the modern conception of autonomy itself in any one passage, this would be it.

But we must still ask what Kant means by saying that having our own will is the ultimate and unconditional end of morality, and also how he

23. *Naturrecht Feyerabend* is transcribed in the Akademie edition, vol. 27, part 2.2, 1317–94; in *Lectures and Drafts on Political Philosophy*, ed. and trans. Frederick Rauscher and Kenneth Westphal (Cambridge: Cambridge University Press, 2016). The manuscript is dated "Winterhalben Jahre 1784," although the catalogue of lectures for the University of Königsberg shows that the course was actually given in the summer semester of 1784; see Michael Oberhausen and Ricardo Pozzo, eds., *Vorlesungsverzeichnisse der Universität Königsberg (1720–1804)* (Stuttgart-Bad Canstatt: Fromman-Holzboog, 1999), Teilband 2, 500. Thanks to Norbert Hinske for pointing this discrepancy out to me; perhaps the discrepancy results from a later rather than simultaneous transcription of the notes.

24. Kant, *Naturrecht Feyerabend*, 27:1321–22.

proposes to argue for this striking claim. I will consider the first of these questions in the remainder of this section, and the latter in the next.

Kant's transformation of the ancient conception of freedom into the modern conception of autonomy begins with his distinction between the negative and positive definitions of freedom at the start of Section III of the *Groundwork*. The negative definition of freedom is the concept of freedom as the property of the causality of the will "that it can be efficient independently of alien causes *determining* it"; on this definition, freedom is the independence of the will from direct determination by desires. But since the will cannot be determined by nothing at all, Kant accompanies this negative definition with a positive one, namely autonomy, "the will's property of being a law to itself," where "the proposition, the will is in all its actions a law to itself, indicates only the principle, to act on no other maxim than that which can also have as object itself as a universal law."[25] This principle is the moral law that Kant has identified in the previous two sections of the *Groundwork*, which takes the form of the categorical imperative insofar as it presents itself as a constraint to creatures like us who do not automatically do or desire to do what it requires. This principle can be considered the principle of pure practical reason insofar as it applies reason's inherent requirement of universality to the domain of actions through their maxims. Thus Kant's distinction between negative and positive conceptions of freedom could be considered his statement of the view that freedom from the determination of the will by mere desires or inclinations is only to be achieved through the determination of the will by pure reason instead; and then one might ask whether he has really advanced beyond the ancient conception of freedom, which also supposed that the use of reason is the means to the tranquility of freedom from desires and their accompanying fears.

The answer to this question lies in the complexities of the second section of the *Groundwork*, where Kant introduces a variety of formulations of the categorical imperative, of which the requirement to act only on universalizable maxims is only the first. Specifically, in *Groundwork* II Kant links the requirement of universalizability to the concept of an end in itself or necessary end that he had introduced in the *Naturrecht Feyerabend*. In *Groundwork* I Kant had derived the requirement of the uni-

25. *G*, 4:446–47.

versalizability of maxims from the supposedly common-sense idea that acting out of mere inclination, no matter how beneficial, is never morally estimable.[26] In *Groundwork* II, Kant derives this requirement from the very concept of a categorical imperative, by means of the argument that accepting the requirement of acting only on universalizable maxims is the only alternative to acting out of inclinations that can never lead to anything more than hypothetical imperatives, that is, recommendations of means to ends that are merely contingently determined by inclination. But Kant then goes on to accompany this argument by elimination or, we might say, negative argument for the categorical imperative, with a positive characterization of a necessary end or end in itself that could serve as "the ground of a possible categorical imperative," an end to be served by it that can give a positive reason for its acceptance.[27] Here is where Kant's conception of morality as freedom really turns from negative to positive and where his advance over the ancient conception of freedom really takes place, for this positive ground for the initial formulation of the categorical imperative is nothing other than the idea that "the human being and in general every rational being *exists* as an end in itself, *not merely as a means* to be used by this or that will at its discretion," which in turn leads to the second main formulation of the categorical imperative, "*So act that you use humanity, whether in your own person or in the person of any other, always at the same time as an end, never merely as a means.*"[28] This leads to a new conception of autonomy because Kant's conception of that which is to be an end in itself and never treated merely as a means is nothing other than the capacity to set ends itself.

Kant makes this clear a few pages later in the *Groundwork* when he states that "Rational nature is distinguished from the rest of nature by this, that it sets itself an end."[29] He also states in the later *Metaphysics of Morals* (1797) that humanity is, in contrast to animality, the property of a human being "by which alone he is capable of setting himself ends," and repeats that "The capacity to set oneself an end—any end whatsoever—is what characterizes humanity (as distinguished from animality)."[30]

26. *G*, 4:400–402.
27. *G*, 4:428.
28. *G*, 4:428–29.
29. *G*, 4:437.
30. *MM*, Doctrine of Virtue, Introduction, Section V, 6:387; Section VII, 6:392.

Plugging these definitions into Kant's statement of the second formulation of the categorical imperative results in the conclusion that the necessary end that is to be the ground of any possible categorical imperative is nothing other than the capacity to set ends itself; that is the thing of fundamental and unconditional value that grounds all other values in the system of ends just as, at least in the eyes of pure reason, an *ens a se* or something that exists on its own must ground everything else in the system of efficient causes.[31]

Kant makes it clear that we are to regard the capacity to set ends as of unconditional value in every instantiation, not only in our own. This is the point of the following argument:

> If, then, there is to be a supreme practical principle, and, with respect to the human will, a categorical principle, it must be one such that, from the representation of what is necessarily an end for everyone because it is an *end in itself*, it constitutes an *objective* principle of the will and thus can serve as a universal practical law. The ground of this principle is: *rational nature exists as an end in itself*. The human being necessarily represents his own existence in this way; so far it is thus a *subjective* principle of human actions. But every other rational being also represents his existence in this way consequent on just the same rational ground that also holds for me: thus it is as the same time an *objective* principle from which, as a supreme practical ground, it must be possible to derive all laws of the will.[32]

This is not a fallacious argument that because *I* hold my own capacity to set ends as my most fundamental value I must therefore hold everyone's capacity to set ends as of equally fundamental value, nor a fallacious argument that because everyone holds *his own* capacity to set ends as his most fundamental value, everyone must hold *everyone's* capacity to set ends as of equally fundamental value. It is rather an assertion that each of us must hold *his own and everyone else's* capacity to set their own ends as of equally fundamental value because the capacity to set ends is of objectively intrinsic and unconditional value, equally valuable in every instance. That we may have an emotional attachment to our own capacity to set ends is morally irrelevant, or rather one of the inclinations that

31. I add this qualification, of course, because it is the main argument of the *Critique of Pure Reason* that such conceptions of pure reason are not actually confirmable by or consistent with the character of our senses and lead to metaphysical illusion unless understood as either merely regulative principles for theoretical inquiry or moral ideals for practical conduct.

32. *G*, 4:428–29.

may have to be regulated in the name of morality; and that we may often be in a better position to preserve or promote our own capacity to set ends rather than anyone else's is only a contingent fact about the implementation of our duty to treat humanity always as an end and never merely as a means, not an essential feature of the duty itself.

Of course, this passage leaves open the question of how Kant might argue for the thesis that the capacity to set ends is a universal or objective value. I will return to that question in the next section. What has been said so far also leaves open precisely how the first formulation of the categorical imperative, the requirement of the universalizability of maxims that can be regarded as the definition of practical rationality itself, can be seen as a means to the realization of the second formulation, the intrinsic value of humanity as the capacity to set ends as an end in itself, as *Naturrecht Feyerabend*'s claim that reason is only the means to freedom implies that it should.

I will return to that question shortly, but first I want to pursue the issue of the objectivity or universality of the value of freely setting ends a little further. This is the focus of Kant's third main formulation of the categorical imperative. Actually, Kant offers two versions of the third formulation. First he describes "the idea of the will of every rational being as a *will giving universal law*" as the "present third formula of the principle" (this can be reformulated as an imperative by saying "Act only on maxims consistent with the idea of the will of every rational being as a will giving universal law"), but then he presents the third way "of representing the principle of morality" as the formula "that all maxims from one's own lawgiving are to harmonize into a possible realm of ends, as a realm of nature" (this is already in the form of an imperative).[33] These two formulations may be regarded as making explicit the universal scope of each of the two previous formulations: the first makes explicit that everyone is to aim for universalizability in all his maxims taken together, thus that each maxim of each person is to be part of a single, universally consistent set of maxims; and the second formulation describes what would be the outcome of accepting the second formulation of the categorical imperative: treating everyone as an end in himself would bring about a natural order in which everyone is treated as an end in himself.[34]

33. *G*, 4:432, 4:436.

34. For a detailed presentation of this analysis, see my "The Form and Matter of the Cat-

Kant's initial description of the concept of the realm of ends makes clearer what his final formulation of the categorical imperative really requires of us. He says that "The concept of every rational being as one who must regard himself as giving universal law through all the maxims of his will . . . leads to a very fruitful concept dependent upon it, namely that of a *realm of ends*," and then explains:

> By a *realm* I understand a systematic union of different rational beings through common laws. Now since laws determine ends in terms of their universal validity, if we abstract from the personal differences of rational beings as well as from all content of their private ends, it will be possible to conceive of a whole of all ends in systematic connection (a whole both of rational beings as ends in themselves and of the ends of his own that each may set himself), that is, a realm of ends, which is possible in accordance with the above principles.[35]

On the one hand, the necessity of treating every rational being whom we can affect, that is, every human being, as an end in himself is independent of our feelings about any particular person or about the particular ends ("all content of their private ends") that either we or they set in the exercise of their capacity to set ends. On the other hand, the intrinsic, unconditional, and completely objective value of each person's capacity to set ends means that we must not only treat each person's capacity to set ends as an end in itself and never merely as a means to our own ends, but also that, just because they have been freely chosen, we must make the ends that each person sets for himself in the exercise of this capacity our own end insofar as those particular ends form a consistent whole, that is, insofar as they can be consistently promoted and realized. We are not to do so because of our preference or inclination for the particular ends that anyone has set, but rather because of the value that these ends, whatever they are, as long as they are mutually consistent, derive from having been freely chosen by beings that are ends in themselves.

Only if we so understand Kant's conception of the realm of ends can we understand the fourfold classification of duties that he uses to illustrate the application of the categorical imperative—now using that term to refer to what is required of us by all the formulations of this imper-

egorical Imperative," in *Kant und die Berliner Aufklärung: Akten des IX. Internationalen Kant Kongresses*, ed. Volker Gerhardt et al. (Berlin: Walter de Gruyter, 2001), 1:131–50, reprinted in my *Kant's System of Nature and Freedom* (Oxford: Clarendon Press, 2005), 146–68.

35. G, 4:433.

ative working together—in the *Groundwork*, the division of duties into perfect and imperfect duties to ourselves and to others.[36] The first class of duties, perfect duties to self, is illustrated by the prohibition of suicide, the prohibition of the destruction of an instance of the capacity to set ends regardless of what the current inclination of that agent to shorten its life might be. The second class, perfect duties to others, is illustrated by the requirement to act toward others only in ways to which they can consent, or to make sure that the ends we freely chose for ourselves in other-affecting actions could also be freely set by them too. The class of imperfect duties to self is illustrated by the duty to cultivate our talents, which is necessary for the effective pursuit of the ends that we freely set for ourselves, so that our free choice of ends will not be constrained by an avoidable limitation of our means for pursuing them. And the final class of imperfect duties to others is illustrated by the maxim of mutual aid or beneficence, the duty to promote the realization of the particular ends freely chosen by others when we are in a better position to do so than they are. The first two of these kinds of duty clearly illustrate the requirement to treat the capacity to set ends as an end in itself: we are not to destroy our own capacity to set ends merely in order to gratify a current inclination, nor are we to constrain the ability of others to exercise their capacity to set their own ends in order to use them as a means to the realization of our own ends. The fourth kind of duty clearly indicates that the realization of particular ends by anyone derives value from the value of their capacity to set ends, not from their or our own inclination toward those particular ends. The third duty, the duty to cultivate our own talents, might illustrate the value of both the capacity to set ends and of the particular ends set by the exercise of this capacity: cultivating our talents makes us effective in the pursuit of our particular ends (or in the task of helping others to realize their ends), but also, as suggested, enables us to avoid unnecessary constraints on our very choice of ends.

There are many issues that arise from these illustrations, and I have no time to pursue them here.[37] Before continuing, I will comment only

36. See Allen W. Wood, "The Supreme Principle of Morality," in Paul Guyer, ed., *The Cambridge Companion to Kant and Modern Philosophy* (Cambridge: Cambridge University Press, 2006), 342–80.

37. For a fuller discussion, see my "Kant's System of Duties" in *Kant's System of Nature and Freedom*, 243–74, and my *Kant* (London: Routledge, 2006; rev. ed. 2014), 239–61.

briefly on the relation between the requirement of universalizability and this explication of what is required by the imperative to treat humanity whether in one's own person or that of any other always as an end and never merely as a means. Kant attempts to ground his prohibition of suicide on the requirement of the universalizability of maxims, although he succeeds only in arguing, dubiously at that, that it could not be a law of nature that the love of life sometime lead to suicide, not that there is anything contradictory in the universalization of the maxim to commit suicide when life promises more pain than pleasure. By contrast, the requirement to act only in ways to which others could consent is an obvious application of the requirement to act only on universalizable maxims. Finally, the requirements to cultivate one's own talents and to be beneficent to others are supposed to be entailed by the requirement of universalizability as well as by the value that accrues to the particular ends chosen in exercise of the intrinsically valuable capacity to choose ends: no rational being could choose to deprive itself of the means necessary to realize its ends, whether through its own talents or the assistance of others, and thus the maxims not to cultivate talents or aid others could not be universally accepted. Thus the requirement of universalizability is supposed to be coextensive with the requirement to treat the capacity to set ends as an end in itself and a useful test for whether a proposed course of action does satisfy the second requirement, and with the possible exception of the prohibition of suicide Kant's examples of duties of omission and commission do illustrate this claim.

When we thus explicate Kant's conception of autonomy as the positive definition of freedom by means of his formulae of humanity as an end in itself and the realm of ends, we can see that he has indeed made an advance over the ancient conception of freedom. To be sure, one might argue that tranquility, the ultimate aim of the Stoic virtue of controlling our passions through reason, is in practice a necessary condition of freely setting our own ends. But neither Plato nor the Stoics ever explicitly recognized the intrinsic value of setting our own ends, whereas Kant has erected his complex analysis of the moral law and his fourfold classification of our duties entirely on the ground of the intrinsic value of setting our own ends and the value that accrues to our particular ends not through the fact of our inclination toward them but rather through the fact of our having freely chose them. This, I suggest, can be regarded as a distinctively modern conception of autonomy, although I cannot stress too much that because of the presumptive coextensiveness of universalizability and autonomy, for Kant autonomy is never a merely personal or "subjective" goal set by inclination but is always a universal and "objective" value that can be recognized by pure reason.

ARGUING FOR AUTONOMY

But does Kant have a distinctively modern way of arguing for the unconditional value of autonomy as he has conceived it? I will conclude with a necessarily brief discussion of this question.

The Stoics argued that reason is the guide to living in accordance with nature, where their conception of nature, or at least of human nature, seems empirical: they argued that it is natural for human beings to seek their own preservation and tranquility in or from their desires, and the assumptions about human nature on which these claims are based seem grounded in experience. In his earliest arguments about freedom, Kant also at least sometimes seems simply to appeal to experience. His claims that anyone who has experienced freedom hates subsequent domination and that one could best promote one's welfare by not allowing excessive desires to grow are not obviously grounded on anything other than experience. But once Kant had decided, as he did in his 1770 inaugural dissertation, that "*Moral philosophy* … in so far as it furnishes the first *principles of judgment* [*diiudicandi*], is only cognised by the pure understanding," that is, what he would subsequently call reason, "and itself belongs to pure philosophy," an appeal to experience could not suffice to ground the fundamental principle of morality.[38] Further, once he had accepted the principle that "if a judgment is thought in strict universality … then it is not derived from experience, but is rather valid absolutely *a priori*," the possibility of an empirical foundation for the fundamental principle of morality was likewise excluded.[39] So Kant became committed to the need for a style of argument that the ancient world had not

38. Kant, *On the Form and Principles of the Sensible and Intelligible World*, §9, 2:396; in *Theoretical Philosophy, 1755–1770*, 388. Klaus Reich in particular argued for the importance of the inaugural dissertation in Kant's turn toward an entirely a priori foundation for morality; see Reich, "Kant and Greek Ethics."

39. Kant, *Critique of Pure Reason*, B 4; trans. Paul Guyer and Allen W. Wood (Cambridge: Cambridge University Press, 1998), 137.

explicitly recognized, an entirely a priori argument for the fundamental principle of morality.

But what form was this new style of argument to take? In the *Groundwork*, Kant tried to argue for the binding validity of the moral law by the use of a distinction that was also not explicitly made in the ancient world, although he borrowed ancient terms for it, namely his distinction between phenomena and noumena. "Phenomena" means objects for the senses, and "noumena" literally means "objects for the intellect," but in the *Critique of Pure Reason* Kant had argued that we are entitled to use the concept of noumenon only in a "negative sense," that is, "of things that the understanding must think without … relation to our kind of intuitions" and thus can think only indeterminately.[40] In the second section of the *Groundwork*, Kant had arrived at an analysis of the moral law valid for any rational being, but he saw the task before him in the third section as establishing by means of an a priori but synthetic rather than analytic argument (another contrast not made explicitly in the ancient world) that *we are rational beings*; and he appealed to the phenomenon/noumenon distinction to establish this. He argued that reflection on any object of knowledge would lead to the distinction between appearances and things in themselves, or phenomena and noumena in the negative sense; that we would inevitably apply this distinction to ourselves, and thus draw a distinction between information about ourselves furnished by inner sense and concerning only our appearance and the reality that lies behind such appearances. However, instead of stopping with the claim that we must count ourselves "as belonging to the *intellectual world*, of which however [we have] no further experience," Kant immediately turned around and asserted that "a human being really finds in himself a capacity by which he distinguishes himself from all other things, even from himself insofar as he is affected by objects, and that is *reason*," "pure self-activity," and on this basis he asserted that the moral law is thus the law of our real selves, of ourselves "as belonging to the intelligible world, under laws which, being independent of nature, are not empirical but grounded merely in reason."[41] He thus derived the moral "ought" from a metaphysical "is," from an a priori claim about our noumenal nature.[42]

40. Kant, *Critique of Pure Reason*, B 307 (361).

41. G, 4:451–52.

42. See my "Ist und Soll, von Hume bis Kant und Heute," in Heiner F. Klemme, ed., *Kant und die Zukunft der europäischen Aufklärung* (Berlin: Walter de Gruyter, 2009), 210–31.

This is a truly novel argument for the binding validity of the moral law and the objectivity of its ground, humanity or the capacity of choice as an end in itself. Unfortunately, it both violates the epistemological stricture of Kant's original distinction between phenomena and noumena and also, insofar as it makes the moral law the universally valid causal law of our real selves, raises a question about how we could ever act contrary to the moral law in the phenomenal world, which should be the appearance of the noumenal world but not a competitor to it. Kant does not seem to have recognized the second problem immediately, but he must have recognized the first problem quickly. Indeed, it might be argued that his clear formulation of the distinction between the permissible negative sense and any positive sense of the concept of the noumenon in the second edition of the *Critique of Pure Reason*, cited above, is his own concession of the inadmissibility of his synthetic argument; but be that as it may, Kant clearly withdrew this argument in the *Critique of Practical Reason*, published three years after the *Groundwork* and one year after the second edition of the *Critique of Pure Reason*. There he replaced this argument with the "fact of reason" doctrine, the argument that instead of inferring the validity of the moral law from metaphysical insight into our noumenal self-activity we must begin from an immediate awareness of the validity of the moral law and then infer the freedom of our will to act in accordance with it as a necessary condition of its validity, the possibility of which cannot be excluded precisely because we can establish determinism as a necessary feature of the phenomenal world but must remain ignorant of the noumenal world and therefore cannot assert that causal determinism holds there. As Kant says,

> something different and quite paradoxical takes the place of [the] vainly sought deduction of the moral principle, namely that the moral principle conversely itself serves as the principle of the deduction of an inscrutable faculty which no experience could prove but which speculative reason had to assume as at least possible ... namely the faculty of freedom, of which the moral law, which itself has no need of justifying grounds, proves not only the possibility but the reality in beings who cognize this law as binding upon them. The moral law is, in fact, a law of causality through freedom and hence a law of the possibility of a supersensible nature.[43]

43. *PracR*, 5:47.

(The last sentence of this quotation shows that Kant had not yet realized the danger of making the moral law a causal law of the will at any level, namely that it makes the occurrence of immorality impossible to explain.) Now this whole argument might seem like an elaborate concession of the impossibility of any a priori argument for the validity of the moral law and thus for Kant's modern conception of autonomy as our fundamental value. But perhaps instead of seeing the argument as a concession of failure, we should instead see it as the avatar of a new conception of philosophical argumentation, one that recognizes the impossibility of proving foundational principles without prior assumptions (for if one did appeal to prior assumptions, then the foundational principles would not be foundational after all), and instead confines itself to reconciling contradictions among our fundamental commitments, in this example between our fundamental commitment to the value of autonomy and the moral law erected on that and our equally fundamental commitment to the truth of determinism in the natural world of which we are a part (at least above the level of microscopic quantum phenomena). In other words, while Kant goes beyond the ancient ideal of tranquility as the fundamental principle of normative ethics, perhaps he here introduces reflective equilibrium as the fundamental methodology of metaethics. This, I think, would be as much of a modernist innovation in the methodology of morals as Kant's positive conception of autonomy is in the content of morals.

Harvey C. Mansfield

11 Tocqueville on Religion and Liberty

"I stop the first American I meet . . . and I ask him if he believes religion to be useful to the stability of laws and to the good order of society; without hesitation he answers that a civilized society, but above all a free society, cannot subsist without religion. . . . Even those least versed in the science of government know that much."[1]

Alexis de Tocqueville was a liberal, but, as he once said, a "new kind of liberal."[2] "One of the noblest enterprises of our time," he added, would be to show that "morality, religion and order" do not need to be opposed to "liberty and the equality of men before the law." For us today, no feature of his new liberalism is more remarkable than the alliance between religion and liberty that he sees in America and proposes to be imitated, wherever it can, in every free society. That alliance is part of his attempt to make liberalism political. For in his view the early, original theory of liberalism, by beginning from outside politics through a concept of the state of nature, rather than from the practice of politics, was never able to find politics, or return to it, once its practice was left behind.

The reason for abstracting from politics was its potentiality for religious conflict, as revealed in the actual wars of the seventeenth century that convulsed Europe but not America. Tocqueville goes on to say that even though there is no country where the boldest political doctrines of

1. Alexis de Tocqueville, *The Ancien Régime and the Revolution*, trans. A. Goldhammer (Cambridge: Cambridge University Press, 2011), 3.2, 140.

2. "Un liberal d'une espèce nouvelle"; letter to Eugène Stoeffels, July 24, 1836, in *Tocqueville: Lettres Choisies, Souvenirs*, ed. Françoise Mélonio and Laurence Guellec (Paris: Gallimard, 2003), 352–55.

the eighteenth-century *philosophes* were applied more than in America, the anti-religious doctrines for which they were best known never appeared there. We learn from his writings that the wisdom of ordinary Americans, in this regard and in general, not only illustrates the science of government but indeed, through the self-government Americans practice, provides the source of that science. "That great science of government," apparently the same as the "new political science" said to be needed in the introduction to *Democracy in America*, is never elaborated by Tocqueville but rather left to be discerned by his readers. They will find it "only in the play [*jeu*] of free institutions," that is, in America, neither in theories nor in the Old Regime of France.[3]

In liberalism today, there is a debate over the question whether liberal theory needs or should avoid a "foundation."[4] Tocqueville is not surely on either side of this debate. He may seem to take the foundational side, as he uses the words "first foundation" (*premier fondement*) to say what an individual needs to "build the edifice" of his own thoughts. This foundation is not chosen by his will; rather, the "inflexible law of his condition" constrains him to it. This law for "man separately" is not explained. A society, *any* society, needs "dogmatic" beliefs, for without common ideas there could be no common action. Neither of these is an intelligible "foundation" in reason of the kind foundational liberals desire and supply. Neither mentions "nature."

Tocqueville never mentions the "state of nature," the standard foundation of seventeenth-century liberalism, and in *Democracy in America* he omits any reference to the Declaration of Independence with its ringing foundational assertion that "all men are created equal."[5] Yet, if he avoids laying a foundation in reason, he also thinks that religion is essential to political liberty because of certain "very fixed ideas" or "ready-made beliefs" that it offers to ground the practice of self-government.[6] These are

3. Tocqueville, *Ancien Régime*, 3.1, 132; Tocqueville, *Democracy in America*, trans. Harvey C. Mansfield and Delba Winthrop (Chicago: University of Chicago Press, 2000), introduction, 7.

4. In the following remarks on foundations, I borrow from a companion article: Mansfield, "Intimations of Philosophy in Tocqueville's Democracy in America," in *Tocqueville's Voyages; The Evolution of His Ideas and Their Journey beyond His Time*, ed. Christine Dunn Henderson (Indianapolis, Ind.: Liberty Fund, 2014), 202–5.

5. Delba Winthrop, "Rights: A Point of Honor," in *Interpreting Tocqueville's Democracy in America*, ed. K. Masugi (Savage, Md.: Rowman and Littlefield, 1988), 415–16.

6. Tocqueville, *Democracy in America*, 2.1.5, 417, 2.1.2, 408; *Ancien Régime*, 3.2, 132.

doctrines of faith, since for Tocqueville "religion" means revealed religion, not a rational or natural religion, such as "deism," which other liberals in the seventeenth and eighteenth centuries had proposed to replace revealed religion.[7]

If these doctrines of faith are not natural religion, they yet rest on "an immovable foundation in [human] nature," for the human soul has needs—a "taste of the infinite" and "a love of what is immortal"—that must be satisfied.[8] This foundation in nature leads directly away from the liberal state of nature that reveals the need to satisfy man's bodily self-preservation. It reveals the need for the supernatural—an "edifice" of faith that eclipses even while it satisfies man's natural desire for the spiritual as opposed to the material. Faith is in accord with human nature yet not rationally constructed upon it, as is liberal society according to the early liberals. There are, to be sure, articles of reason encompassed in religious faith. Tocqueville was a strong opponent of divine right and a strong proponent of the separation of church and state. Although he praised the Puritans highly as being the "point of departure" for democracy in America, he criticized its theocratic character.[9] Personally, he seems to have suffered a crisis early in life when, as he recounts it, he came upon the books of eighteenth-century materialists in his father's library and promptly lost his faith, as far as we know never recaptured. The loss was not confined to religion but extended to "all the truths" that supported his beliefs and his actions.[10]

Questions arise that are still with us: what does Tocqueville hold against the introduction of foundational philosophical principles in dem-

7. Tocqueville said in a Letter to Louis de Kergorlay, June 29, 1831 (*Lettres Choisies*, 197), that deism, or what is called "natural religion," might suffice for the upper classes of a society but that the people would see in it the absence of belief in the other world and would tumble directly into the sole doctrine of self-interest.

8. Tocqueville, *Democracy in America*, 2.2.12, 510–11. For "foundation" rooted in "nature" see also 1.2.10, 328; 2.3.12, 573; 2.4.7, 673. "Foundation" occurs nineteen times in *Democracy in America*.

9. Ibid., 1.1.2, 32–35; 1.2.9, 266–67; 2.1.19, 468; n. V, 680–83; n. VI, 688–89.

10. Letter to Sophie Swetchine, February 26, 1857 (*Lettres Choisies*, 1242–45). See also the letter to Arthur de Gobineau, October 2, 1843, where he says: "I am not a believer (which I am far from saying in order to boast)," in ibid., 525. On the incident of his youth see Doris Goldstein, *Trial of Faith: Religion and Politics in Tocqueville's Thought* (New York: Elsevier, 1975), chap. 1, who treats the loss of faith as only in religion; see also Cheryl Welch, *De Tocqueville* (New York: Oxford University Press, 2000), 178–80; Christian Bégin, "Tocqueville et la Fracture Religieuse," *The Tocqueville Review* 32 (2011): 170–72.

ocratic politics, and how can they be kept out? What is the relationship between philosophy and religion, given the hostility of modern philosophers (particularly the French *philosophes*) to religion and his desire to make an alliance between the two? Just what essential support does religion supply to political liberty—the essential liberty according to Tocqueville—so that despite the separation of church and state necessary to political liberty he can say that religion "should be considered the first of [the Americans'] political institutions"?[11]

MORES AND RELIGION

To see how Tocqueville understands religion one must look to his view of mores, for in *Democracy in America*—his main discussion of religion—he first treats religion as the most important of mores. Mores (*moeurs*), defined as "the whole moral and intellectual state of a people," comprise both morals and customs.[12] The definition comes from "the ancients," and is related to the ancient emphasis on virtue in human affairs, but it is virtue understood as typical, ordinary, or average, so that modern thinkers who seek laws or rules of social behavior could find the concept useful and congenial. Tocqueville could have found important discussion of mores in two of his favorite philosophers, Montesquieu and Rousseau—for whatever his doubts, he read broadly and deeply in philosophy.[13] In the nineteenth century the concept of mores was picked up by the founders of sociology and became fundamental for that new discipline because, contrary to the ancients, it separated society from politics, implying that politics was not essential to the identity of society. In our time the concept of mores is used as value-neutral, replacing "morals," to try to describe without judging, which was emphatically not Tocqueville's practice.

In Tocqueville's thought, mores are connected to another, newer concept of the "social state" (*état social*), the product of fact and laws, or the

11. Tocqueville, *Democracy in America*, 1.2.9, 280.

12. Ibid., 1.2.9, 275.

13. "Broadly" might be conceded by Tocqueville scholars, but "deeply" will be contested. Tocqueville tends to sum up philosophy in its political effect, as will be seen, but not because philosophy is mere shallow rationalization of deeper interests or urges. See Tocqueville's *Discourse to the Academy of Moral and Political Sciences*, 1852, in his *Oeuvres*, ed. A. Jardin (Paris: Gallimard, 1991), 1:1215–26.

two united, which then in turn one can consider the "first cause" of most of a society's laws, customs, and ideas.[14] Mores and the social state comprise what is chosen by a society and what is not chosen, the two elements confused together. The consequence is to blur the clear view of the social contract liberals that politics is best understood as primarily a human choice, one made to escape the state of nature, not chosen by us.

We see too that the difference between politics and the social state is similarly confused, as the social state would seem to come first if it is the first cause. But then we note that there are two social states called "aristocratic" and "democratic," political designations implying that politics exists already in the social state and could not be caused by it. If politics comes first, and is the first cause, we are reminded of Aristotle, for whom the regime (*politeia*) is the main cause of a society and its *nomos* (his equivalent of social state).[15] If politics comes after society, we are reminded of the liberal social contract theorists of the seventeenth century, for whom political rule is subsequent to the state of nature. As Tocqueville has it, the social state replaces Aristotle's regime as the first cause and ignores the state of nature as a pre-political condition that antedates both politics and society. Now the regime and the social contract are both taken to be chosen, though differently, by the philosophers who conceived them and by peoples who apply them. The regime is a choice of the kind of rule establishing and maintaining a certain way of life, and the social contract is the choice of an instrument necessary to all free choices of how to live. Tocqueville's conception blurs the view shared by Aristotle and the early liberals that politics is best understood as a human choice. It also blurs the distinction between Aristotle and the early liberals as to whether politics decides the way of life or merely makes it possible while leaving it open to the choice of society or the individual.

Exploring the reason for this, we note that Tocqueville declares in his introduction to *Democracy in America* that democracy is a "providential fact." It is a trend that began seven hundred years ago and that only in his time has come to notice as providential in the one country, America, that

14. Tocqueville, *Democracy in America*, 1.1.3, 45; Pierre Manent, *Modern Liberty and Its Discontents*, trans. D. Mahoney and P. Seaton (Lanham, Md.: Rowman and Littlefield, 1998), 65–77.

15. *Aristotle's* Politics, trans. Carnes Lord, 2nd ed. (Chicago: University of Chicago Press, 2013), III.3, 6.

has adopted it and applied it fully and successfully. To call it providential means to deny that it is a human choice or discovery, for example that of John Locke, the philosopher who inspired the Declaration of Independence. Instead of Locke and the Declaration, Tocqueville begins with the Puritans, whom he calls the "point of departure" for America. The Puritans indeed came to America with an idea, for "they wanted to make an *idea* triumph," but it was a religious and Christian idea, for which they called themselves pilgrims, and in which they were "obey[ing] a purely intellectual need." Yet the religious doctrine was blended with "the most absolute democratic and republican theories," and those not merely of equality but also of self-government and public education, both of which were first put into practice by the Puritans.[16] In a later letter Tocqueville speaks of the "religious passion" that drove the Puritans into the "political passion" of wanting to govern themselves.[17] The religious passion was not the same as the political passion, for the Puritans had received their political education in the "rough school" of English township government, but their particular religion confirmed it.[18]

In place of liberalism and its deistic or atheistic foundation in the state of nature Tocqueville sets the Puritans—their religious idea together with their practices. It was they who first brought democracy into "broad daylight," not as a foundation but active and complete as a way of life. They did not merely offer an idea but also were able to live by it, transforming it into the mores of a social state that could be considered the "first cause" of American democracy.

This much said on behalf of the Puritans, however, Tocqueville goes on to criticize them gently and without Puritan severity, but profoundly. They were after all "puritanical," as we use the term, in their "ardor for regulation" and their "narrow spirit of sect" to legislate against sin with abundant resort to penalties of death. Their excesses had to be corrected, and they were corrected in what James Ceaser has called "Tocqueville's second founding" at the time of the American Revolution when many states abandoned the establishment of religion in favor of the separation

16. Tocqueville, *Democracy in America*, 1.1.2, 32. In regard to public education, Tocqueville notes that in America it is religion (i.e., not philosophy) that has brought enlightenment (1.1.2, 42).

17. Letter to Louis de Kergorlay, October 18, 1847 (*Lettres Choisies*, 586–90).

18. Tocqueville, *Democracy in America*, 1.1.2, 29.

of church and state. Yet, since the correction of Puritanism was established by the sovereignty of the people that the Puritans created and exemplified, one could also say, with Pierre Manent, that these were two phases of the same process. The ardent faith of the Puritans gave way to the "grave but superficial respect" for religion of their descendants.[19]

The point of departure needed to be departed from, and it is replaced by the principle or dogma of the sovereignty of the people, established at the time of the American Revolution. Not wishing to offend religion or praise its enemies, Tocqueville mentions the abolition of aristocratic entail at this time but not the disestablishment of religion. He only says that according to this sovereignty, "the people reign over the American political world as God does over the universe"—as if somehow the people who are like God had replaced God.[20] In the implication of this declaration the first cause of America—now the people—becomes more visible than in Puritan democracy, or visible as God is not. The Puritan usage of ancestral religion in their names and modes of speech disappears, and we are directed to conclude that in America, religion in the form of theocracy was the cradle of liberty, but that liberty grew up and out of its cradle. Or one could say that the true theocracy is democracy that has transformed its undemocratic sectarian beginning into religion for all—by command of the people. For all Tocqueville says in support of the alliance between religion and liberty in the United States, the people have no authority above themselves. They set an authority above themselves when they establish the Constitution, and they could hardly retain the power to unseat God as they do the Constitution. Yet they would seem to be able to unseat what they can seat. Tocqueville asks "what makes a people master of itself if it has not submitted to God?"[21] A people, like

19. James Ceaser, *Designing a Polity: America's Constitution in Theory and Practice* (Lanham, Md.: Rowman and Littlefield, 2011), 23–43; Pierre Manent, *Tocqueville and the Nature of Democracy*, trans. John Waggoner (Lanham, Md.: Rowman and Littlefield, 1996), 94. Tocqueville himself does not speak of a second founding and he seems to understand the first one rather as a kind of birth, a "point of departure," than as a founding. Tocqueville, *Democracy in America*, 1.1.2, 28, 39–45.

20. Tocqueville, *Democracy in America*, 1.1.4, 55. This statement apparently exaggerates the power of the people, for if God reigns over the universe, and the universe includes the people and the American political world, then he reigns over both of these too. The people are like God but replace God, so that the principle of the whole—all things—is human, not divine. The statement declares an assumption of human responsibility for the whole.

21. Ibid., 1.2.9, 282.

an individual person, makes itself more powerful with self-restraint, not less—but self-restraint may be self-excused.

The people sustain that alliance in their mores in a way that improves upon Puritan theocracy. In discussing what sustains a democratic republic in the United States Tocqueville brings up three "principal causes," which are "accidental and providential causes," namely, its situation far from Europe, its laws, and its mores.[22] The laws have more force than the situation, the mores more than the laws, and among mores the first in importance is religion. We note that "religion considered as a political institution" has more influence than providence as an accidental cause, by *not* working through politics. If the people are sovereign, the religion over them is by their choice, shown in the way in which each religion seeks to "harmonize earth with Heaven."[23]

Since religion has its influence in America through mores, it works more indirectly than directly. The *philosophes* believed that religion would lose its force as freedom and enlightenment advanced; America proves that they were wrong. The fact they overlooked is that, even when considering religion "from a purely human point of view," it has an unfailing source of strength in human nature: "the desire for immortality that torments the hearts of all men equally."[24] Here is *eros*, the yearning part of the soul in Plato's presentation. When founded on this desire, religions can aim at universality, but when they become united with government, they apply only to certain peoples and temporarily. Religion should avoid attaching itself to earthly authority and forswear all reliance on divine right, using mores to regulate democracy rather than relying on laws as much as did the Puritans. Religion is more powerful if it is pure, and it is pure only if it avoids earthly attachments. The purity of religion arises from human nature: "among all the beings, man shows a natural disgust for existence and an immense desire to exist." Now we recognize the *thumos* that Plato discerned as the other part of

22. Ibid., 1.2.9, 265.

23. Ibid., 1.2.9, 275. Note "earth with heaven" rather than the reverse. Surely the harmonizing works both ways, and perhaps in reverse more than as it is said. But Tocqueville emphasizes the noble. One could agree with Sheldon Wolin that for Tocqueville religion is an earthly method of "social control," and even that it has a "repressive role," if it were equally stressed that it is self-imposed by the people. Sheldon Wolin, *Tocqueville between Two Worlds: The Making of a Political and Theoretical Life* (Princeton, N.J.: Princeton University Press, 2001), 324–25.

24. Tocqueville, *Democracy in America*, 1.2.9, 284.

the soul that simultaneously defends one's existence and risks it. *Thumos* risks the self in the very act of defending it by claiming a selfless rationality beyond individual existence. In self-defense one suddenly becomes willing to die for a cause that is both one's own and beyond one's own: God's cause.[25] Applying the point to Tocqueville, we see that religion is paradoxically more powerful politically if it stays out of politics, if it does not appear as an authority in its own regard but under cover of the mores that the people practice and hold to. Its universality can then remain pure, surely an advantage to religion, and at the same time be adapted to the democracy of the American people.

This paradox suggests two points of advantage for Tocqueville's conception of the alliance of religion and liberty. First, it is a qualified advantage to religion enabling it to sustain its otherworldliness without renouncing its influence on earthly affairs. This is a particular advantage to the Christian religion because it lacks or forswears a political doctrine and a law, such as the law of Judaism or Islam, either of which would compel it to enter into earthly politics. Tocqueville has harsh words for the conquering nature of Islam, and in a letter he says that after studying the Koran, he came out with the conviction that "few religions are as dire [*funeste*] to men as that of Mohammed."[26] He seems to take it for granted, and as given by Providence, that the religion of liberty is Christianity, which itself provides the distinction between church and state that he accepts and develops in the interest of both religion and liberty. His argument opposes the worldly ambition of both the church and its enemy, the *philosophes*, because he wants to benefit the pride and ambition of democracy. The qualification to this advantage is that the church must accept the necessity of accommodating its ambition to that of democracy.

The second point of his paradox is a theoretical advantage to the democratic idea itself. Always chary of making theoretical arguments, he does not make this second point himself, but it can be made on his behalf. It is a serious failing of the democratic theory he ignores that it never proves that all men are created equal. Hobbes says that men are

25. *Republic* 375a-e, 439e–441c.

26. Letter to Arthur de Gobineau, October 22, 1843 (*Lettres Choisies*, 533–36); see also Tocqueville, *Democracy in America*, 2.1.5, 419–20. See the comments in his writings on Algeria in Tocqueville, *Writings on Empire and Slavery*, trans. Jennifer Pitts (Baltimore, Md.: Johns Hopkins University Press, 2001), 27–35, 140–42; Goldstein, *Trial of Faith*, 110–12.

naturally equal, or equal in the state of nature, but this turns out to mean that each man, satisfied with his own share of prudence, and eager to place his own interest first, considers or presumes himself equal to others—if only by denying that anyone else is better than he.[27] Each man's vanity is foiled when he sees the same vanity in others, but that forced recognition does not raise tamed vanity to the level of truth. Similarly, Locke says that all men are equal in having the faculty of reason, but he never states clearly why this similarity in possessing the faculty is more important than the great inequalities in degree of possession. Tocqueville too, explaining the "equality of conditions" he found in America, says that all men there consider themselves similar (*semblables*) if not precisely equal to others: a poor man there can approach a rich man on an equal level without abasing himself. Here again, in his account of Americans' beliefs, one finds no convincing proof for the belief.[28]

The difficulty is that any quality or set of qualities that might define a human being is held very unequally by one human being *vis-à-vis* another, and only by a very few in full. That which humans share by contrast to all other beings—which would have to be reason or some quality mixed with reason—is also the basis of very great contrast among humans. But when the basis of equality is religion, and all men are held to be equal in the sight of God, equal in the immortal souls they possess, then the argument transcends the human point of view, and democratic theory is excused from its embarrassment at having no sufficient proof for its most fundamental assertion. Tocqueville says at this point, as noted above, that he is "considering religions from a purely human point of view," but precisely from that point of view, no human being is satisfied with the human point of view. In this way the usefulness of religion arises from human nature and does not abstract from its truth but raises the question of its truth.

Tocqueville speaks of "what ought to be, in our day, *the natural state*

27. Hobbes, *Leviathan*, ed. Richard Tuck (Cambridge: Cambridge University Press, 1996), chap. 13. Hobbes in effect admits that societies of men have no direct access to or unmixed perception of human nature; their opinions are always present, always in the way. By never mentioning the "state of nature," Tocqueville calls it into question, and by replacing it with the "social state" he indicates that democracy is based on opinion, but on justifiable human pride rather than indefensible vanity. Mansfield, "Intimations of Philosophy," 225; Mansfield, *Tocqueville: A Very Short Introduction* (Oxford: Oxford University Press, 2010), 19–20, 48–49.

28. Tocqueville, *Democracy in America*, 1.1.3, 51; 2.3.13–14.

of man in the matter of religion." This is the state of religion in America, not in some abstract state, where religion is not as powerful as it might be for short periods but more lasting because its strength is reduced to what inspires it in human nature.[29] Nature, for him, is a kind of foundation, but it is divided into the material, the source of self-interest, and the spiritual, which wants to rise above the material in the form of religion. Thus "nature" is not a simple, clarifying notion to which humans have direct access and by which they can guide their lives with certainty, as in the early liberal "state of nature." Americans go to religion rather than nature because nature is divided against itself, its influence overwhelmed by the conventions of democratic opinion. In the statement quoted above "natural state" is said to arise out of "our time," the democratic age that gives rise to democratic conventions. By these conventions Americans see religion as useful for democracy, even for their self-interest ("self-interest well understood"). But their religion must lack purity to the extent that it is maintained because it is useful. If it is useful for democracy, it suffers from the same connection with politics that weakened the church in France under the Old Regime. From this one could infer that Americans, because they are firmly and publicly religious, are also hypocrites who find it useful to be religious.[30] Yet clearly religion will not be useful unless it is believed to be true. There is no upper class of aristocrats in America to look down on the religious delusions of the multitude. Americans must therefore identify useful with true. The result is terrific pressure on society, *from society*, to believe that religion is true, all the while reducing religion to what is useful. As Manent puts it, the truth that religion is useful because it forbids belief in the unlimited power of society is itself imposed by the unlimited power of society, the sovereignty of the people, in America.[31] Religion is, after all, a part of politics, "the first of [the Americans'] political institutions."

These are Tocqueville's formulations, yet ever careful as he is to deprecate the role of philosophy and of the philosopher, he presents them as opinions of Americans, not of his own. The paradox of greater power for religion in politics with less involvement is the perception, he reports, of American priests. Not that they have much choice: they perceive that

29. Ibid., 1.2.9, 286–87. See Manent, *Nature of Democracy*, chap. 8.

30. Tocqueville, *Democracy in America*, 1.2.9, 281.

31. Manent, *Nature of Democracy*, 92.

the majority wants them to stay out of politics.[32] There is another power with whom American clergy share their indirect influence, and that is American women. Religion, he says, does little to restrain the American man from his ardor for self-enrichment, but it "reigns as a sovereign over the soul of woman, and it is woman who makes mores."[33] It was a commonplace of the *philosophes* that credulous women were willing victims of the manipulation of superstition by the clergy, but when we consult the five chapters on women in the third part (on mores) of *Democracy in America*, we find a contrary statement. Tocqueville says that Americans give girls an education in reason as well as religion, and that they resort to religion for defense of their virtue only when "they have reached the last limits of human force."[34]

Here, as with the clergy, one may suspect that Tocqueville's description is idealized, and that it masks a recommendation he would prefer not to give outright. He is as modest and as manly as the American women he pictures. These women, treated as equals, are content with the separation of roles that used to mark them as unequal. Tocqueville's treatment nicely illustrates his refusal to ground his thought on a foundational nature. He asks whether democracy would not act on "the great inequality of man and woman … which seemed to have its eternal foundations in nature?" In American democracy women's natural inferiority is being overcome, he says, but the difference between the sexes, whether natural or not he does not say, is retained in order that women may have authority to moderate democratic mores. This they could not do if they were not wives apart from the business of men. American women exercise their sovereignty over mores by freely accepting the bonds of marriage as equals, submitting by their own choice and not by nature's dictates. They moderate democracy not only without violating democracy but even while vindicating the power of democracy to govern itself. Yet Tocqueville would not have been surprised that women in our time, joining the onward march of democracy, have chosen to imitate men

32. Tocqueville, *Democracy in America*, 1.2.9, 280, 286; 2.1.5, 423; Bryan Garsten, "Seeing 'Not Differently, but Further, Than the Parties,'" in *The Arts of Rule*, ed. Sharon R. Krause and Mary Ann McGrail (Lanham, Md.: Rowman and Littlefield, 2009), 361–64.

33. Tocqueville, *Democracy in America*, 1.2.9, 278. Cf. Manent, *Nature of Democracy*, 83–87; Wolin, *Tocqueville between Two Worlds*, 330; Catherine Zuckert, "Not By Preaching: Tocqueville on the Role of Religion in American Democracy," *Review of Politics* 43 (1981): 264–66.

34. Tocqueville, *Democracy in America*, 2.3.9, 565; 2.3.12, 573–76.

and abandoned the defense and enforcement if not quite the practice of modesty.

RELIGION AGAINST MATERIALISM

In the second volume of *Democracy in America*, Tocqueville turns to the question of the truth of religion as opposed to, or in addition to, its usefulness. His approach to the question is still through the usefulness of religion, but now we get a better view of just how it is useful and why American democracy has a stake in its truth. We also see better why he distrusts ideas and why philosophy needs to be concealed under religion.[35] In the end we receive his best estimate, or report, of the general truth that God offers to mankind, which proves to support the alliance he sees from the first between religion and liberty.

Religion is useful mainly because it hinders the taste for material enjoyments that is endemic to American democracy, indeed in modern democracy as such. It is of course a brake on licentious liberty and on the sovereignty of the democratic majority. It opposes the "maxim that everything is permitted in the interest of society," an impious maxim, Tocqueville says, "that seems to have been invented in the century of freedom to legitimate all the tyrants to come."[36] As we have seen, the maxim is enforced by the power of the democratic society it is designed to limit. Yet the true danger is not in the occasional viciousness of democracy, but in the mediocrity of soul it teaches to law-abiding citizens through the taste for material pleasures. This taste, though surely bourgeois, in his view comes from democracy, not from what we call capitalism. "Capitalism," or in his phrase "the passion for material well-being," he believed to come from democracy.[37]

Tocqueville's reasoning is that when all are equal, no one has natu-

35. On philosophy and religion in Tocqueville, see Jean-Claude Lamberti, *Tocqueville and the Two Democracies,* trans. A. Goldhammer (Cambridge, Mass.: Harvard University Press, 1989), 155–65; Peter Lawler, *The Restless Mind: Alexis de Tocqueville on the Origin and Perpetuation of Human Liberty* (Lanham, Md.: Rowman and Littlefield, 1993), chap. 8; Mansfield, "Intimations of Philosophy."

36. Tocqueville, *Democracy in America*, 1.2.9, 280.

37. The objection that capitalism antedates the appearance of democracy is countered by Tocqueville's view that democracy incubated for centuries in the bosom of monarchies that brought it to birth to their surprise, without meaning to. Tocqueville, *Democracy in America*, introduction.

ral authority over anyone else, and that when a democratic citizen looks for a guide to life, he finds no superior in whom to trust and ends his search by settling on himself. To this person, on the basis of no authority but his own, there is no distant goal in life to which he can devote himself, for everything beyond the immediate is vague and beyond his ken. The only evident goods to him are palpable and available—material goods—and he devotes himself to goods that he and everyone like him (his *semblables*) can appreciate. This is why those living under democracy, trusting in their own reason above all, conclude that "everything in the world is explicable" and have "an almost invincible distaste for the supernatural."[38] In America, however, this distaste, natural to democracy, is counteracted if not defeated by the taste for the infinite in human nature.

Religion is a "form of hope" in human nature. Its most important practical teaching is that man has an immortal soul, which is therefore divine, and man's natural hope is that he will live forever.[39] To have an immortal soul is a possession of inestimable value to the perfection of which one can devote one's life, yet it is also universal and equal, hence democratic, its perfection not a goal of aristocratic honor that sets one above others. As a form of hope, religion is not primarily a form of fear (except insofar as one fears one's hope for salvation may be dashed), as the early liberal theorists, particularly Thomas Hobbes, supposed. The fear of invisible spirits (in Hobbes) and the uneasiness of the self (in Locke) turn one's attention to the present; hope appeals to the future. In the future lies accomplishment in which one can take pride. The early liberals set their hopes on human enlightenment that they promised would eventually replace religious fears and in the meanwhile keep them in check. Their enlightenment would rest on the premise that man must first of all consult his fear for his own self-preservation.

For this reason the early liberals believed human pride to be the source of trouble, especially from the prideful notion that human beings are special in the universe because of their immortal souls. To them this claim, which is so easy to make and so hard to specify, leads easily to the tyranny of religion and then to the miseries of civil war. They thought that religion feeds pride and pride feeds partisanship. But for

38. Ibid., 2.1.1, 404.

39. Ibid., 1.2.9, 284; 2.2.12, 510; 2.2.15, 520–21.

Tocqueville, the reliance on worldly passions such as fear and material gain produces abject souls more fit for despotism than liberty: the weaknesses of democracy are rather stability and stagnation than anarchy and rebelliousness. Thus the early liberals were defending against the lesser danger and inviting the greater one. So for him religion promotes liberty by teaching men that they are special and that they deserve to take pride in their accomplishments. His most significant apparent departure from Christianity is from Christian humility. It is in regard to pride that he says with apparently conflicting import that religion is "the most precious inheritance from aristocratic centuries," and yet that religion warms itself at the hearth of patriotism in America.[40]

The pride constituting the specialness of man emerges in Tocqueville's insistence on the greatness of man. He seeks to rally the "true friends of liberty and human greatness," and the two go together because liberty in mediocrity leads to the new sort of despotism he identifies at the end of *Democracy in America*, mild despotism.[41] Mediocre souls trapped in material enjoyments will readily trade their political liberty for peace and security in those enjoyments. Such people suffer from the new democratic ill he identifies as "individualism," a new sentiment conceived by Tocqueville, that occurs when democratic citizens believe and feel themselves to be passive victims of large, impersonal, historical forces they cannot control or influence. In reaction, they withdraw from the public, forgetting they are citizens, and concentrate their lives on family, friends, and themselves. Losing sight of the public, they become oblivious to any distant goal and welcome the benevolent aid of big government, "the immense being" that acts on their behalf with their passive consent because it knows better and offers to take over responsibility for the "trouble of thinking and the pain of living," Tocqueville says sarcastically.[42]

Thus the only true liberty is political liberty in which the goal and the result may sometimes be greatness but the activity of which always exercises the soul. He remarks on the Americans' veneration for Plymouth Rock, a piece of matter that matters to them: "Does this not show very clearly that the power and greatness of man are wholly in his soul?"[43]

40. Ibid., 1.1.2, 43–44; 1.1.5, 89; 1.2.6, 225; 1.2.9, 281; 2.2.15, 519.

41. Ibid., 2.4.7, 670; 2.4.6.

42. Ibid., 2.2.2; 2.4.3, 644; 2.4.6, 663.

43. Ibid., 1.1.2, 34n8.

Religion provides a confirmation that men are not mere pawns of fate or of chance forces hostile or indifferent to them; it is a guarantee of greatness in human spirituality as it connects men to God. Religion combats the short-sightedness and fecklessness of democracy, and gives it something to be proud of, above the mediocrity of material enjoyments.

When this mediocrity appears as the main enemy of democracy through the erosion of political liberty, we come upon the baleful influence of democratic ideas. We begin to appreciate the reason why Tocqueville is so suspicious of philosophy. What he often simply calls "doubt" as characteristic of democratic ages is philosophic doubt of religion that issues in the suspense of belief—or in practice, when suspense is no longer possible, in denial of belief, in materialism. The doubt in question amounts to a denial of the human soul and in consequence, of human agency (as we say today). The spiritual, not the material, is what is doubted—though in modern mathematical physics it turns out not to be so easy to define or grasp what matter is.

In the early liberalism Tocqueville opposes or rejects, men are liberated from prejudice and superstition only to be enthralled to the worldly passions of fear and gain; they are conquered or bullied into promising obedience (in Hobbes's theory) or "quickly driven into society" (in Locke's words) rather than freely choosing to do so.[44] The model for liberty is the abstract, pre-political state of nature, which is posited and may or may not exist, rather than the model of political liberty existing in practice that Tocqueville finds in the township of New England. Early liberalism is apolitical; it supports politics with non-political motives and it contradicts the goal of liberty with the passive and slavish means it specifies for achieving liberty. This is not liberalism with soul, like Tocqueville's, because it degrades souls by overwhelming them with fear and seducing them with incentives for material gain. It is not a liberalism that can sustain liberty. Liberalism needs motives for liberty that can be prompted by pride. If pride is evaded by the appeal to interest, deflected out of politics into moneymaking, or suppressed by denying the worth of honor, liberty becomes a gift of fortune or nature and man a mere agent in larger motions.

In the second volume of *Democracy in America*, Tocqueville specifies

44. Hobbes, *Leviathan*, chaps. 21, 25; cf. the milder "perform" in Locke's *Second Treatise*, chaps. 14–15 (§127).

two schools of idea-mongers he deplores, pantheists and democratic historians. Pantheism had its origin in Spinoza and in Tocqueville's time had its influence through German philosophy and French literature. It appeals to the democratic mind by its desire for generality and unity. It seeks to enclose God and the universe within a single whole that destroys human individuality, for if God can be enclosed, so *a fortiori* can man: "all who remain enamored of the genuine greatness of man should unite and do combat against [pantheism]."[45] By denying the special status of human beings within nature, it reveals itself as a democratic convention that falsely simplifies nature. Democratic historians he contrasts to aristocratic historians who look to the wills and humors of certain men as the causes of events; the former attribute no influence to the individual, almost as if society advanced by itself. They look for general causes that provide excuses both for mediocre politicians, whose faults are lost in the impersonal trends of history, and for mediocre historians, who shirk the difficult task of discovering individual influences within those trends.[46] Both pantheists and democratic historians have lazy minds; like the democratic peoples they think for, they are satisfied with, or insist upon, generalities to simplify the understanding of things.

Such thinkers deny to citizens the power to influence their own fate, and subject them to inflexible providence or blind fatality. They encourage the tendency toward the "individualism" Tocqueville conceived. As opposed to old-fashioned selfishness, a universal human vice, democratic individualism is "reflective and peaceable" rather than depraved; it is based on the "erroneous judgment" encouraged by democratic thinkers that individuals are impotent in the face of general causes and impersonal forces. It is caused or encouraged by democratic ideas of many sorts, all of which feed the appetite of democratic peoples for "general ideas."[47]

General ideas formulated in disregard of relevant differences are hostile to forms of thinking and behavior that are established with the intent to preserve those differences. Democratic peoples are hostile to forms; they demand informality in everything—in thought, mores, and politics.

45. Tocqueville, *Democracy in America*, 2.1.7, 426; see Manent, *Nature of Democracy*, 102–3.

46. Tocqueville, *Democracy in America*, 2.1.8, 469–72.

47. Tocqueville, *Democracy in America*, 2.1.3, 411; 2.2.2, 482. See James Schleiffer, *The Making of Tocqueville's* Democracy in America, 2nd ed. (Indianapolis, Ind.: Liberty Fund, 2000), chap. 18.

In thought they prefer unity to articulation, species to individuals, surface to depth and height; in mores, they want access over distance, inclusiveness over exclusiveness, friendliness over reserve; in politics, they seek direct action over due process, decision over deliberation, sensation over reflection. Respecting the forms and formalities in all human activity is fundamentally aristocratic rather than democratic, but Tocqueville thinks that it is vital to the orderliness and good sense of democratic life as well as to the protection of liberties, especially of the weak against the strong. With their impatience, often represented as a "can-do" attitude, "democratic peoples naturally have more need of forms than other peoples, and they naturally respect them less."[48] Hostile to forms, democratic peoples are particularly receptive to materialism, a group of ideas that tends to reduce difference of form to sameness of matter.

It may seem contrived or superficial to claim a connection between the philosophic doctrine of materialism and the popular taste for material well-being, but Tocqueville does just that. The ancient materialists were hardly partisans of democracy, as they made a distinction among kinds or forms of pleasure, the pleasures of philosophy for the few above bodily pleasures for the many. Still, the connection between the reduction of form to matter and of the good to pleasure is clear, and modern materialists who abandon the soul for the self might seem more consistent than Lucretius with his soul atoms tenuously held distinct from other atoms. And with both the ancient and the modern materialists, politics and public-spiritedness are dismissed as troublesome, inconvenient, and irrational. Tocqueville sees democracy, especially when carried to an extreme in democratic ideas, as fundamentally anti- or apolitical, hence fundamentally indisposed to liberty—not hostile to liberty, often even tolerant or welcoming of it, but definitely subordinating it to equality and private ease. Equality and private ease are best found in despotism, in mild, democratic despotism. That is why materialism is to him the main enemy in our democratic age. It is not that souls are so corrupted that men sink into criminality but that honest as opposed to criminal materialism "softens them and in the end quietly loosens all their tensions."[49] Democracy does not carry men away into forbidden pleasures, as one

48. Tocqueville, *Democracy in America*, 2.4.7, 669; cf. 1.1.4, 55; 1.2.6, 220; 2.1.1, 404; 2.1.5, 421.

49. Ibid., 2.2.11, 509.

sees in the criticisms of it in Plato and Aristotle, so much as it absorbs men in the relaxed enjoyment of permitted pleasures. Tensions within the soul are required for elevating the soul, for its striving toward greatness.[50] Tocqueville's criticism is directed at the enervation of the soul rather than its lack of harmony and he argues for greatness rather than goodness as its aim.

Materialism teaches democratic peoples that they have nothing special in them to be proud of, and that, in the form of scientific determinism—powerful in Tocqueville's time as well as ours—they are incapable of avoiding the fate that chance decrees and science uncovers. But since pride is in human nature, materialists are unable to avoid taking pride in themselves. Their system might be useful if it gave them and taught others to take a modest idea of oneself—all of us, including Nobel prize winners, being matter of little account—but they do not in fact draw or expound this lesson. When they believe they have proved that men are no better than brutes, Tocqueville says, they are "as proud as if they had demonstrated they were gods."[51] The scientific materialism that deprives citizens of their belief in the possibility of self-government is used to justify instead the rational control of citizens by experts with knowledge of that science.

The danger of materialist ideas in our democratic age induces Tocqueville's leery distrust of philosophical ideas and his selective trust in religious ideas. The religious ideas he presents have more to do with philosophy than with revelation. He approves of certain philosophical ideas, those advancing spiritualism, but without much discrimination. He would rather you believe that your soul can migrate to the body of a pig than that you have no soul.[52] He reserves his approval for whatever spiritual doctrine emerges from philosophy and criticizes the usual effects of philosophical inquiry in democracy. Philosophical inquiry begins with doubt, but in a democracy doubt of superior authority spreads from the

50. Ibid., 2.4.6, 665.

51. Ibid., 2.2.15, 519–20. See also Tocqueville's letter to Henry Reeve, February 3, 1840 (*Lettres Choisies*, 457), which speaks of "realists" rather than materialists.

52. Tocqueville implies that the Aristotelian notion that brutes have soul is some protection against the reduction of men to matter, which in fact results in merely reducing men to brutes. Materialists do not go as far or as deep as they promise; in fact, their reductionism only reaches the level of brutes with some appearance of commonality with humans (e.g., the greediness of a pig).

few who think carefully to the many who are reckless, leading to the assumption of authority by the doubters. Instead of truly doubting, people taught to doubt systematically by a dismissive method merely doubt the authority of others and then, since authority there must be, they turn to themselves and their own authority. That is why Tocqueville treats Descartes, the philosopher of doubt, as, in effect, and perhaps despite himself, a teacher of democracy.[53] This is a perceptive estimation one will not find in textbooks.

When Cartesian doubt is generalized and transferred from philosopher to citizen, the result is the democratic dogma that each individual has sufficient reason to run his own life. So Descartes's thought is most perfectly realized in America where nobody has read him because nobody needs to read him in a society where doubt of dogmatic authority has become the dogmatic authority of doubt.[54] Socrates and Plato, by contrast, enjoy their reputation from their spiritual doctrine of the immortality of the soul, which with its anchor in human nature, with its "sublime spark," keeps them attractive at all times.[55] In the modern age the democratic propensity for material well-being, with its mediocrity, its individualism, and its mild despotism, renders philosophical materialism dangerous, and all philosophy suspect because in that age philosophy is likely to be materialist. Tocqueville wants to make "spiritualist opinions" reign particularly in times of democracy but to do so through religion, not the opinions of Plato—which would be included in the truths he first doubted as a youth. It is a mistake to consider him a spiritualist or idealist, for he can see truth in both spiritualism and materialism, as in both aristocracy and democracy. In aristocratic times, love

53. Tocqueville, *Democracy in America*, 2.1.1, 405. Letter to Charles Stoeffels, October 22, 1831 (*Lettres Choisies*, 238–41): "I consider doubt as one of the greatest miseries of our nature"; also letter to Louis Bouchitté, January 8, 1858, in ibid., 1278–80. J. Judd Owen notes nicely that Tocqueville says that Descartes is "best followed" in America, but not "most faithfully"; Judd Owen, *Making Religion Safe for Democracy* (Cambridge: Cambridge University Press, 2015), 116.

54. The displacement of doubt by the assumption of authority is not the only instance of pride inconsistent with the democratic principle to be found in democratic peoples. See Tocqueville, *Democracy in America*, 2.1.21, the chapter on "On Parliamentary Eloquence in the United States," in which one learns that democratic representatives, typically obscure figures, try their best to make themselves and their constituents feel important.

55. Tocqueville, *Democracy in America*, 2.2.15, 520. Socrates and his school settle on the sole belief "that the soul has nothing in common with the body and that it survives it." This differs from immortality joined with the "opinion in favor of rewards and punishments," which is religious and Christian though Tocqueville does not say so.

of material enjoyments is a corruption expressed in brilliant vices not so harmful as honest mediocrity in democracy.[56]

It is a more fundamental mistake to overlook the importance of Tocqueville's hostility to materialism in his thought on religion.[57] He had no use for the "secularization thesis" widespread since Max Weber which alleges that modern society became secular as it were unwittingly and inevitably through the corruption of dissenting Protestantism. The love of material enjoyments did not come out of the dissenting sects of the Protestant religion, resulting from its encounter with worldly temptations, but against it and with a willing surrender to such temptations. Though always reluctant to discuss philosophy, Tocqueville makes it clear that the modern philosophy of doubt in Descartes and of pantheism in Spinoza expresses the materialism of democracy. He does indeed mention Luther as an innovator, a man who "comes to conceive in a single stroke a system of ideas," and who submits to individual reason "dogmas of the ancient faith" with "the same method" as Descartes and Voltaire.[58] It is an odd description of Luther, one better suited to Machiavelli, almost as if *per impossibile* Tocqueville had made a typographical error in his text and then repeated it.[59]

RELIGION IN PLACE OF PHILOSOPHY

The alliance between religion and liberty that Tocqueville adopts from the political lives of Americans to supply the basis for his liberalism arises from the new relationship between religion and philosophy that he

56. Ibid., 2.2.11, 508. It might be better to say that spiritualism aims at religion than that religion aims at spiritualism; cf. Bégin, "Tocqueville," 193.

57. Two recent works—James Schleiffer, "Tocqueville, Religion and Democracy in America: Some Essential Questions," *American Political Thought* 3 (2014): 254–72, and Mark Noll, "Tocqueville's America, Beaumont's Slavery, and the United States in 1831–32," *American Political Thought* 3 (2014): 273–302—make extensive use of Tocqueville's abundant marginalia and working papers for *Democracy in America*, and Schleifer remarks that Tocqueville sometimes "simply dropped" material he could (and, it is implied, should) have used in his text, which represents "only part" of his thought on religion (270). But this is to determine his thought by what he chose not to say. It is one thing to infer what he might have thought from what he said, as is often necessary and legitimate, and quite another to give rejected words equal or preferred standing to chosen words.

58. Tocqueville, *Democracy in America*, 2.1.1, 405; 2.3.21, 613.

59. For a different speculation, see Harvey Mansfield and Delba Winthrop, "Tocqueville's Machiavellianism," *Perspectives in Political Science* 43 (2014): 91.

also finds among them. The latter is a working relationship that he wishes to fashion into another alliance connected to the first. As to philosophy, Tocqueville says: "Americans have not needed to draw their philosophic method from books; they have found it in themselves." And as to religion, he says: "Men … have an immense interest in making very fixed ideas for themselves about God, their souls, their general duties."[60] The "very fixed ideas" do not arise from practice but precede and guide practice, and they must come from religion rather than philosophy.

In a letter written just before *Democracy in America* was published, Tocqueville calls it "the philosophico-political work" (*l'ouvrage philosophico-politique*) he was preparing. But he does not say that in his book. In a later letter to a writer of books on metaphysics, he allows: "I would have had a passionate taste for the philosophic studies that have occupied all your life if I could have drawn more profit from them." But whether it was the defect of his mind, or lack of courage in pursuing his design, or "the particular character of the material," he always found that the sciences never led him further than, and sometimes not as far as, "a few very simple ideas" that all men have more or less grasped. These ideas easily lead one to belief in a "first cause that is at the same time evident and inconceivable," the fixed laws one can see in the physical world and must suppose in the moral world. The most refined metaphysics, he adds, do not give him clearer notions than "the grossest good sense" (*le plus gros bon sens*). Then Tocqueville, using the word, refers to "what I have called the foundation that I cannot reach" (*le fonds que je ne peux pas toucher*), which is the plan of this "singular being" we call man. Having come to the bottom of his sheet, he closes his letter by joking that "the end of my paper warns me to finish my philosophy." Here is a man who prizes philosophy but keeps it under wraps or in its place.[61]

Those who try to rely on philosophy for the fixed ideas they need in their ordinary lives, Tocqueville says, do not find them but come to grief in doubt.[62] "Doubt takes hold of the highest portions of the intellect and half paralyses all the others." Each person becomes accustomed to hear-

60. Tocqueville, *Democracy in America*, 2.1.1, 404; 2.1.5, 417.

61. Letter to Gustave de Beaumont, December 3, 1836 (*Oeuvres Complètes*, 8:176); to Louis Blouchitté, January 8, 1858 (*Lettres Choisies*, 1278–80); and a similar letter to Arthur de Gobineau, October 22, 1843, in ibid., 533–35. Tocqueville disparages philosophy when writing to those he thinks are abusing it.

62. Here more borrowing from my essay, "Intimations of Philosophy," 204.

ing confused and changing opinions on matters of most interest to himself and people like him—vaguely troubling issues of the day in which it is hard to follow the arguments. We throw up our hands, feeling defeated, and in cowardly fashion refuse to think. If people will not think, doubt "cannot fail to enervate souls," thereby threatening the maintenance of liberty because enervated souls will not take the trouble to exercise liberty or defend it. Thus one of his memorable phrases: "I am brought to think that if [a man] has no faith, he must serve, and if he is free, he must believe."[63]

Here is a liberal rejecting liberal foundations in philosophy yet requiring them in religion. He seems to reject philosophy because it is not sufficiently or successfully dogmatic and to welcome religion because its dogmas support, or can support, human liberty. He turns to the practice of self-government in America—taking the anti-theoretical path of today's anti-foundationalism—yet claims to find precisely there the "philosophical method" that he avoids considering directly. His statement against doubt blames it for preventing people from thinking, that is, from thinking practically and usefully. Philosophical thinking leads to paralysis of practical thinking, in which overmatched would-be philosophers are led ultimately to passive acceptance of things as they are. Philosophy may begin from the questioning of authority, but when it appears that all the questioning leads to no answers, it stops and finds rest in the conclusion that nothing can be done. Faith, then, is not a substitute for reasoning simply but for philosophical reasoning; it is actually the basis for reasoning about one's closest interests.

Tocqueville says that religion imposes a "salutary yoke" on the intellect by preventing the use of individual reason to raise doubt and by establishing "general ideas" about God and human nature that permit men to recognize "an authority."[64] Such ideas, or dogmas, are necessary even to the practice of the sciences, where specialists must trust other specialists, and whose remote ideas are even more inaccessible to the majority. Tocqueville's objection to philosophy or metaphysics, unlike our postmodern anti-foundationalism, is not intended as an attack on reason, but as an aid to reason. It does for reason what reason cannot do for itself, which is to

63. Tocqueville, *Democracy in America*, 2.1.5, 417–18.

64. Ibid., 2.1.5, 418. Cf. "salutary servitude" leading to the "good use of … freedom," 2.1.2, 408.

establish an authority for itself by which reason can operate in daily life without having to become exhausted from chasing down solutions to unanswerable questions. The problem is that reason as philosophy gets in the way of reason as practice because the one attacks authority and the other requires it. Now what is the solution? Is it merely to declare that the two aspects of reason are antithetical, and that practice being more important than philosophy, the need for active practice must dominate the pleasure, if it is a pleasure, of speculating, and dogma must silence philosophy?

Tocqueville does not adopt that solution, though he may appear to do so because sometimes he seems to criticize all philosophy, philosophy itself. But in fact, or in practice, he particularly criticizes what one might call, though he does not, modern or liberal philosophy. He uses the word "foundation," when he notes that Americans adopt the "philosophic method" of Descartes as their "foundation" because just by living in a democratic social state they already know what he writes without having read his works.[65] For them their social state makes it unnecessary to read Descartes; without his help it does the work of his method, his foundation, which is to bring doubt to an end. The end is not the fundamental truth found by philosophy, but the fundamental truth that philosophy cannot supply a fundamental truth on which to ground practice. Yet Tocqueville shows appreciation for the contemplative life of the philosopher, praising the "ardent, haughty, and disinterested love of the true" one finds in Pascal and the lofty contempt for practice as "vile, low, and mercenary" in Archimedes, while distinguishing the science of the "most theoretical principles," that may flourish in aristocracy, from "general truths … [that] lead by a direct, short path to practice," which are characteristic of democracy. It is a weakness of democracy that it does not encourage "the contemplation of first causes." This is true even from the standpoint of applications of science, for when practice loses sight of the principles of science it becomes decayed and uninventive.[66] Tocqueville himself does not renounce philosophy. At the beginning of *Democracy in America* he warns his readers that he feels "obliged to push each of his ideas to all its theoretical consequences," and later in the book he does not hesitate to speak of "first causes."[67]

65. Tocqueville, *Democracy in America*, 2.1.1, 403.

66. Ibid., 2.1.10, 433–38.

67. Ibid., introduction, 15. On first causes, see especially 1.1.2, 28–29; 1.1.3, 45; Letter to

Religion, then, does not replace philosophy or science, but it serves as their public face and supplies the fixed ideas that men need not merely to live by but to live in freedom. Servility of soul is not the consequence of religion, as the *philosophes* asserted, but of anti-religious materialism, which denies the soul by demeaning man into matter or abases the soul by endorsing the democratic propensity to a life of material well-being. At the end of *Democracy in America* Tocqueville discloses something of the character of the religion he recommends. It is not just any religion, as he seemed to imply earlier when speaking of religion as part of democratic mores, but a reasonable religion that confirms the intelligibility of nature and of the world. In this it is unlike the religion recommended by the liberals he departs from, for whom a reasonable religion is one that compensates for the unintelligibility of nature and of the world, and not incidentally confirms that they are nothing but matter, while providing refuge for the weak.[68]

THE MIND OF GOD

In this climactic passage Tocqueville goes beyond the view of religion he took earlier as a "salutary yoke on the intellect," and beyond "the purely human point of view." At the end of the first volume, he had, in his own name, striven to achieve a "clear idea of the whole" of America like the voyager who climbs a hill outside a vast city to survey it. Now, at the end of the second volume, in his own name he strives, one may suppose like a philosopher, a youthful Pascal but with a view of the intelligible, to enter into the inclusive "point of view of God."[69] He had said at the beginning of the second volume that God does not have to use the "general ideas" that men, and particularly democratic men, find convenient for simplifying the perceptions of their weak intellects.[70] In accord with demo-

Louis Bouchitté, January 8, 1858 (*Lettres Choisies*, 1278–80); Mansfield, "Intimations of Philosophy," 219.

68. Thus for Hobbes, a reasonable religion corrects the fear of invisible spirits, not by reassuring humans that there are reasonable spirits but by appealing to the fear of the visible power of the sovereign's sword. Locke prescribes an appeal to heaven when parties conflict, which is to a more powerful judge, not to a just order. Rousseau's Savoyard vicar counsels reliance on reason, which is "my reason," not God's. My reason criticizes revealed religion instead of finding it orderly.

69. Tocqueville, *Democracy in America*, 2.1.5, 418–19; 1.2.10, 391; 2.4.8, 675.

70. Ibid., 2.1.3, 411–13.

cratic simplification, democratic poets prefer to appeal to the vastness of God, presiding over the destiny of humanity, rather than to flatter separate peoples or individuals.[71] But for Tocqueville, God is approachable to man through his (God's) mind, and God's point of view encompasses democracy and aristocracy, the permanent, ruling distinction among mankind that apparently declares the existence of "as it were [*comme*], two humanities." Here he justifies the comparisons he has made continuously throughout the book by referring them to one superhuman whole in which they are joined. "God" is apparently a person, and clearly distinct from his creation. Tocqueville does not insist on the difference between revealed and natural or rational religion, and earlier he had remarked that "it was necessary that Jesus Christ come to earth to make it understood that all members of the human species are naturally alike and equal."[72] Revealed truth is distinct from the truth of nature but revelation makes nature apparent to us in a way unassisted human reason cannot.[73] Thus, one could call religion "natural" because it fulfills yearnings of human nature, matching God's mind to human need, and one could also call it "civil" because it is part of self-government. But as religion it is revealed, and as the true or best religion, it is Christian. Philosophy is then under a duty not to overlook, but also neither to broadcast the difference between itself and Christian revelation nor to present itself as hostile to it. The order that Tocqueville sees in or imputes to God's mind leaves untouched the statements in scripture of God's hidden character without contradicting them.

Earlier, in the chapter on the tyranny of the majority in the first volume, Tocqueville had said that "only God … can be omnipotent without danger, because his wisdom and justice are always equal to his power."[74] This is not the case of any human authority, which always needs to be prevented from acting without control and dominating without meeting obstacles. Thus the perfect rule of God stands above all actual human rule as a necessary and desirable reproach and limitation rather than as inspiration to do God's work on earth. It is because we cannot success-

71. Ibid., 2.1.17, 461–62. Sanford Kessler, *Tocqueville's Civil Religion: American Christianity and the Prospects for Freedom* (Albany: State University of New York Press, 1994), 44–48.

72. Tocqueville, *Democracy in America*, 2.1.3, 413.

73. Cf. Aristide Tessitore, "Tocqueville's American Thesis and the New Science of Politics," *American Political Thought* 4 (2015): 85.

74. Tocqueville, *Democracy in America*, 1.2.7, 241.

fully imitate God that we must serve him. The mystery of his perfection encompasses his bodiless superiority to humanity, which prevents him from holding partisan attachments but also reminds us of our limitations. Tocqueville remains a liberal, if of a "new kind," because at least in a democratic age he wants to obstruct human tyranny as much as he wants to instruct it; hence in the first place he describes democracy as it is in America rather than discourses in political philosophy. Yet it is also true that liberty needs to be explained and defended as well as secured—or in order to be secured. So in the first volume he has to instruct democrats that they are limited and partisan and do not possess the God's wisdom and justice, but in the second he has to instruct them that, contrary to democratic theories, they are capable of acting freely. Religion hinders democrats from tyrannizing others by majority tyranny and also from being tyrannized by democratic doctrines, when majorities tyrannize themselves. For the first task, liberals must use religion to limit human authority, and for the second, liberals must use it to empower human authority: both negative and positive liberty are required.

To support positive liberty, religion must be understood as the order of God's mind, which Tocqueville now, at the end of his book, makes available to his readers. So understood, it repels "false and cowardly doctrines" that "men necessarily obey I do not know which insurmountable and unintelligent force born of previous events, such as the race, the soil, or the climate." Tocqueville renames this force "Providence" and describes it differently so that it leaves men leeway: "Providence has not created the human race either entirely independent or perfectly slave." Here are two extremes, implying two doctrines. The first, that man is entirely independent, appears in the aristocratic criticism of democracy as anarchic; the second, that man is perfectly slave, is the democratic idea to be found in pantheism and the democratic historians that peoples "necessarily obey … [an] insurmountable and unintelligent force born of previous events."[75] Both extremes may be found in the early liberal, social contract theories, the first in the state of nature in which men are anarchic and at war with one another, and the second in the means for escaping the state of nature, which play on fear and subject men to "in-

75. Tocqueville, *Democracy in America*, 2.4.8, 676. On the alternative of perfectly free and perfectly slave, see Tocqueville's remarkable chapter on the three races, in which the Indian represents perfect freedom, and the black, perfect slavery, 1.2.10.

surmountable and unintelligent force" consisting variously of laws of subrational motivation discovered by history and social science. Under Tocqueville's analysis, the state of nature in which men are independent of one another and the subjection of men in civil society combine in the apolitical individualism he finds in modern democracy. Under his program, as opposed to this danger, religion can cement its alliances with liberty and with reason, all three together in the politics of democracy.

The two contraries of entirely independent and perfectly slave stand for the two aspects of chance, unpredictability and subjection—chance fate—to which religion is opposed. The most fundamental democratic idea, as we learn from Aristotle, is that of the lottery. It is a system in which a decision is arrived at without a choice, in which every one, without discrimination, has an equal chance. No reason is exercised in making the decision and none is found in the result. No freedom exists, as one simply receives what befalls him. No virtue is required, and none is rewarded or expected. Opposite to a lottery is voting, which requires making a choice, and is aristocratic because one chooses for what one thinks is best, still according to Aristotle.[76] We moderns think that voting is the clearest sign of democracy, but we forget the aristocracy necessarily mixed in democracy. Even to institute a lottery requires choice, thought, and freedom—all items opposed to lottery, which is democracy in its raw, basic sense of mere chance. Religion as Tocqueville portrays it tries to make our life predictable, but not so predictable that we can succeed without trying. And it sets limits to our intellect, our freedom, and our choice—but not such narrow limits that we can never succeed no matter how hard we try.[77] The task of politics, which Tocqueville sometimes calls, in the manner of Plato and Aristotle, the task of the legislator, is to cooperate with religion and to guide our lives so that our virtue is rewarded and our freedom preserved.

"The legislator" in the singular has an art or science or theories or genius that is above democracy.[78] It rescues democracy from the grip of

76. Aristotle, *Politics* IV.16.

77. Tocqueville, *Democracy in America*, 2.2.17, 524.

78. For art, see ibid., 2.2.15, 518; science, 1.2.6, 222; theories, 1.1.2, 41; genius, 1.1.8, 129, 154. "The legislator" for Tocqueville is not "an extraordinary man in the state" apart from the "principles of political right," as for Rousseau, but an abstract person who combines the science of politics with the wisdom to apply it in circumstances. *The Major Political Writings of Jean-Jacques Rousseau*, trans. John T. Scott (Chicago: University of Chicago Press, 2014), 2.7.

chance by vindicating the contribution of intelligence to the common good.[79] Like God's mind, and like Tocqueville himself, it sees both the similarities and the differences of human beings while recognizing that either democracy or aristocracy must be chosen as a whole, each distinct from the other, a visible political whole that is partial in respect to the unseen whole of God's mind, where they are brought together. Thus the legislator combines the "as it were" two distinct humanities that Tocqueville makes available to his readers through his frequent, and always illuminating, contrasts of democracy to aristocracy. His political science is necessarily left scattered and uncollected because it cannot be set forth separately from its context in American politics in the form of a model without becoming excessively schematic, thus doing violence to its basis in practice. A schematic political science risks forgetting its basis in practice and claiming a false impartiality above practice—like our "democratic theory" today, which loses sight of the fact that democracy is not the whole of politics but a partial and partisan whole within the whole of politics. Our democratic theory is both less detailed and more parochial than Tocqueville's understanding.

Although being a democratic citizen is quite different from being "the legislator," Tocqueville's political science gives us an awareness of the connection between the two. To the task of the legislator our religion contributes "certain fixed ideas," which, though fixed are not arbitrary,

---

He stands for political science in practice, and one could assemble a survey of "political science" in *Democracy in America* by gathering the many (about forty) references to "the legislator." One of them, comparing him to a pilot, has a special classical redolence: "The legislator resembles a man who plots his course in the middle of the sea. Thus he can direct the vessel that carries him, but he cannot change its structure, create winds, or prevent the ocean from rising under his feet" (1.1.8, 155). Generally, "the legislators" means particular legislators, for example "the American legislators," but once Tocqueville speaks of "the American legislator" (1.1.7, 102), four times of "the legislator" as the majority (1.2.7, 237–38, 243). Deviating from wisdom, "the legislator" can keep blacks in slavery (1.2.10, 340, 343) and forget the principles of religious liberty (1.1.2, 39). See also the discussion of political science in Tocqueville, *Ancien Régime*, 3:1–3, 127–51, and Tocqueville's address of 1852 to the Academy of Moral and Political Sciences, in which he distinguishes political science from the "art of governing." Tocqueville, *Oeuvres Complètes*, 1:1217.

79. Unlike the democratic intellectual, the legislator is aware of his own inequality: "When the unequal is interpreted as random or arbitrary, as having no basis accessible to human understanding, then the natural can be understood only as the equal." Ralph Hancock, "The Uses and Hazards of Christianity in Tocqueville's Attempt to Save Democratic Souls," in *Interpreting Tocqueville's* Democracy in America, ed. K. Masugi (Savage, Md.: Rowman and Littlefield, 1988), 375; see also Owen, *Making Religion*, 138.

not unreasonable, not merely posited because we need them. The power that men must obey is not chance, or does not have to be chance. It permits "peoples [...] [to be] masters of themselves" if they take the legislator's wisdom to heart. Thereby the democratic dogma that each has sufficient reason to guide himself would be justified as the democratic principle: the intelligence of the legislator meeting the intelligibility of God's creation and communicated to the democratic citizen. It is then the task of citizens to make their accomplishments worthy of reasonable pride. Tocqueville does not have the legislator make up a religion (like Rousseau) or even propose that he revise an existing one (like Hobbes and Locke). The legislator works through the "American legislators," who accommodate the existing religion that Providence has supplied. By his multicultural analysis the best religion for the protection and fostering of democratic liberty is Christianity, but with apparent conditions—that it stay out of politics and that it compromise Christian humility.

Tocqueville presents himself initially as impressed with the strength of religion in America, but as he proceeds we see that he was exaggerating: religion is not strong enough and needs to be strengthened by the legislator.[80] That is why his book was written "under the pressure of a sort of religious terror in the author's soul," realizing as he did that religion is more friendly to human greatness than is philosophy.[81]

80. Owen, *Making Religion*, 142.
81. Tocqueville, *Democracy in America*, introduction, 6.

Rémi Brague

12 The Failure of the Modern Project

In this essay, I will argue in favor of the rather strong thesis that the modern project failed. In my opinion, it is high time we had the pluck to acknowledge this failure and to look for the adequate behavior that could enable us to cope with the situation that arises therefrom. The failure of such a project presupposes first that there was, or still is, such a thing as a modern project. As a consequence, I will have first to describe it. Scrutinizing the very idea of a project will yield what the modern project is driving at.

MODERNITY AS A PROJECT

I am far from being the first to speak of the "project of the Modern Age," the "modern project," and other phrases. I am afraid I would be at a loss to tell you who first coined this phrase. Anyway, it was launched in philosophical circles thirty-five years ago by Jürgen Habermas in a lecture he gave in 1980 and that was widely echoed. The theme was "Enlightenment as an unfulfilled project." This was part of the strategy of the German philosopher who sides with this project and looks forward to fulfilling it.[1] The observation that the Enlightenment remained a project that never was totally fulfilled is to be found not only as the provocative battle-cry of a philosopher, but as the sober result of research in the field of the history of ideas. This is the case in the United States (Louis Dupré) and in France (Pierre Manent).[2]

1. J. Habermas, "Die Moderne—ein unvollendetes Projekt," in his *Kleine politische Schriften, I–IV* (Frankfurt: Suhrkamp, 1981), 444–64, esp. 452–53.

2. See L. Dupré, *Passage to Modernity: An Essay in the Hermeneutics of Nature and Culture*

Yet, whereas the phrase crystallized only at a recent date, Europe did not have to wait too long to become the stage of a strange phenomenon. It took place precisely at the threshold of the age that we call "modern." Europe witnessed the rise, at strategic places, of words that designate the attempt, the experiment, the project. It is enough to name Montaigne with his *Essais* (1580) from which Bacon and in his wake so many others took up the title. As for the stress laid on experimentation, it is all the more conspicuous that the intention to experiment is earlier than its real implementation. Bacon's alleged experiments are for the most part mere fantasy. Even real scientists never were as talkative about the necessity of experimenting than when the facts on which they pretended to ground their hypotheses were mere thought experiments.[3] Galileo even lets the cat out of the bag in his *Dialogues on the Two Main World Systems* (1632), when he proudly confesses that he never tried to wage an experiment, since he is fully confident that the result will necessarily come out as he expects it to do.[4] Experimenting is more than a scientific ploy; it is a whole atmosphere. Nietzsche makes a far-reaching observation and writes that what characterizes the nineteenth century is not the triumph of science, but the triumph of method over sciences. The same author called his time "the age of attempts" (*Zeitalter der Versuche*).[5]

Furthermore, the fact that modernity as a whole is a project has been not only experienced but also reflected upon for a long time. Descartes initially wanted to start what was to become the *Discourse on Method*: "The project of a universal science that could lift our nature up to its highest degree of perfection."[6] Sixty years later, in one of the earliest among his many works, written in 1697, Daniel Defoe, who had still to

(New Haven, Conn.: Yale University Press, 1993), 101, 119, 126, 160; *The Enlightenment and the Intellectual Foundations of Modern Culture* (New Haven, Conn.: Yale University Press, 2004), 4; P. Manent, *Les Métamorphoses de la cité* (Paris: Flammarion, 2010), 9–11.

3. See A. Koyré, *Études d'histoire de la pensée scientifique* (Paris: Gallimard, 1966), 213–23 (on Galileo), 376–86 (on Pascal). Koyré's position is an extreme one that was later qualified.

4. Galileo, *Dialogo sopra i due massimi sistemi del mondo*, ed. F. Flora (Milan: Mondadori, 1996), 153.

5. Nietzsche, "Fragment 25 [290], Spring 1884," in *Kritische Studienausgabe* (Berlin: De Gruyter, 1980), 11:85 [hereafter "KSA"].

6. "Le projet d'une science universelle qui puisse élever notre nature à son plus haut degré de "perfection." Descartes, "Lettre à Mersenne, mars 1636," in *Œuvres Complètes*, ed. A. Adam and P. Tannery (Paris, 1897-), 1:339. Auguste Comte mentions the "great philosophical renovation, projected by Descartes and Bacon" in *Cours de philosophie positive, 58th Lesson*, ed. J. P. Enthoven (Paris: Hermann, 1975), 639.

wait for more than twenty years to become the famous author of Robinson Crusoe, wrote an "Essay upon Projects." He begins by pointing out that projects are fashionable, so that it would not be amiss to call the epoch "The Projecting Age." He thinks first and foremost of the speculations on great overseas trade, such as the one that had ruined him some years earlier. For overseas trade furnishes us with a privileged paradigm, because it is, says Defoe, "in its beginning, all project, contrivance, and invention."[7]

In 1726, Jonathan Swift caricatures the members of the Royal Society under the features of the absentminded passengers of the flying island of Laputa, to whom he gives the name of "projectors." He ascribes to them ludicrous inventions.[8] He thereby creates the type of the absentminded professor whose numerous popular incarnations are famous, from the Savant Cosinus to Professor Nimbus—two heroes of French comic strips. Yet, the word "projector" has nothing derogatory or ironic in itself. People can claim it as an adequate means to define their doings. It is to be found in Joseph Glanvill's tract of 1668 advertising for the Royal Society; and in Mary Shelley's novel, Frankenstein chooses it to designate himself.[9]

Late modern philosophical anthropology laid stress on the notion of project as defining the peculiar status of man among, and in contradistinction to, other beings. Sartre enlarged its use in an anthropological context and shifted it from "having" to "being." According to him, the project is part of the very definition of man, who is "nothing short of his project."[10] Let us stop a while and have a look at Sartre's formula: "I am my own project."[11] It was and is still touted by the whole Western intelligentsia, who repeatedly wields it as a weapon, whenever one attempts to invoke something like identity and tradition. The utterance makes sense as long as it remains a bombastic version of the platitude that we are not bound to carry on doing what was done up to now by our forebears. Yet,

7. D. Defoe, "An Essay upon Projects," in *The True-born Englishman and Other Writings*, ed. P. N. Furbank and W. R. Owens (Londres: Penguin, 1997), 186 and 188.

8. Swift, *Gulliver's Travels*, III, 4–6 (Oxford: Oxford University Press, 1948), 213–33.

9. Joseph Glanvill, *Plus ultra: or, The progress and advancement of knowledge since the days of Aristotle* . . . (London: James Collins, 1668; reprinted in Hildesheim: Olms, 1979), 8; M. Shelley, *Frankenstein*, chap. 24 (London: Penguin, 1994), 204.

10. J.-P. Sartre, *L'Existentialisme est un humanisme* (Paris: Nagel, 1946), 55; see also 23, 69–70.

11. J.-P. Sartre, *Cahiers pour une morale* (Paris: Gallimard, 1983), 267.

taken literally, the formula does not have a leg to stand on. For what makes it the case that the project is *mine*, that it is *my* project? If I am the result of a project, this project cannot be mine.

We will see later on that the idea of a project shifted from the active to the passive, from the project launched by man, to man being the project of some unknown and in any case unnamed agent. The history of ideas brings to the fore, and thereby confirms, the inner dialectics of concepts.

THE WORD "PROJECT"

The word "project" in itself is not devoid of meanings. Its Latin form does not correspond to any word in the Roman vocabulary. To be sure, ancient Latin was familiar with the adjective "projectus," which means "jutting"; used as an image, it more often than not has a derogatory undertone, for instance when speaking of an excessive ambition. But the substantive is not attested in Antiquity. A pro-ject is first of all, most obviously, what the etymology of the word suggests, that is, a throwing (*jacere*), that is, a motion in which the mobile body (*missile*) loses contact with the mover and forges ahead. This is the very phenomenon that ancient physics failed to account for, or that it could pigeonhole into its framework only through far-fetched theories that had little convincing force for intuition, like the so-called *antiperistasis*. Strangely, modernity, which can be and was considered as the age of the pro-ject, was at the same time the period in which physics began by making sense of throwing *tout court*, therefore introducing concepts that were to lead to the Newtonian idea of inertia.[12]

Choosing to describe an activity in the keynote of the project implies in any case a break between the subject and the object of the projecting. Furthermore, this choice implies a necessary forgetting of the subject that, precisely because he rests on himself, can hardly take himself as the object of his own reflection and must leave in the shade whatever is not his project. That this project is his own, that it stems from himself, that it expresses himself, including dimensions that remain hidden to himself—such are the elements that the subject must ignore if he only wants to be able to act.

12. See A. Maier, *Zwei Grundprobleme der scholastischen Naturphilosophie. Das Problem der intensiven Größe. Die Impetustheorie* (Rome: Storia e letteratura, 1951), 114–20.

As a consequence, one can elicit the three basic ideas of modernity as project from the mother-image of a throwing. For a project implies a new interpretation of the three dimensions of time: (1) toward the past, the idea of a new beginning, of a beginning from scratch, so that whatever came before will be forgotten; (2) toward the present, the idea of a self-determination of the acting subject; (3) toward the future, the idea of a environment that carries further action and guarantees its achievement (progress).

WHO IS THE PROJECTOR?

The question is: who projects? According to the premodern, that is, ancient and medieval worldview, there was something like a project of man's life. But it was not man's project, but the intention of a higher power, nature or God.

The oldest example of the idea, and of the word, may be the Ancient Egyptian *sẖr.* The word is interesting in itself, since it is the causative form ("to let somebody do something") of the verb *ẖr,* which means "to fall."[13] It is to be read in the famous *Story of Sinuhe,* which hails from the Twelfth Dynasty (ca. 1800 B.C.). The main character had to flee Egypt and spend a part of his life outside of the Nile valley, which amounted for an Egyptian to an exile, not to say a damnation. Yet, it turns out that this fact, a bad thing in itself, had positive consequences. The story has a happy end: Sinuhe is called back by the king, returns to Egypt and is sure to be buried there. Says the hero of his flight, at least according to a possible translation: "it was like the project of a god" *(yw my sẖr nṯr)*—although other translators have the more humdrum "as though it might be a god."[14]

Be that as it may, the idea of providence does not designate something posited in man's hands, but something higher. The Stoic *pronoia* has as its subject a nature that is not distinguished from the godly nature—or we may say the same thing in the other way, a god that is not distinguished from the eternal living fire that creates everything out of itself and periodically brings it back to its origin.

13. R. Hannig, *Grosses Handwörterbuch Ägyptisch-Deutsch* (Mainz: von Zabern, 1997), 748b.

14. "The Story of Si-Nuhe [Berlin 3022, 43]," §14, in J. B. Pritchard, *Ancient Near Eastern Texts Relating to the Old Testament* (Princeton, N.J.: Princeton University Press, 1955), 19b.

Biblical and Christian providence has as its subject a personal and loving God who cares for his creatures. Christians do not conceive of God's providence and man's prudence as excluding each other. On the contrary, they take seriously the deep linguistic identity between the two words. Classical thinkers of the Christian Latin West, such as Augustine and Aquinas, conceive prudence as being given by God to man, in the same way as providence endows each and every creature with the tools that enable it freely to reach its own goal, that is, the good that its own nature is striving for.

Providence and project are the two poles that could roughly define the difference between the premodern and the modern outlook.

THE PROJECT IS ITS CONTENT

There is an obvious question that I left unanswered up to now: what is the content of the modern project? I have been harping on the idea that modern times are a project, but I never said what exactly they project to do. Now, it is my contention that the content is already there in the very idea of a project. The project is its content.

There exist a great deal of works by historians and philosophers, some outstanding, which shed light on some aspects of the modern project. I have drawn heavily on their work, but I need not name them here. Whenever we follow those historians and philosophers, and try to describe the content of the modern project, we get a host of features: autonomy of mankind, becoming adult, emancipation from the bonds of external powers, etc., and hence a policy made able to rule itself without having to take its bearings from cosmology or theology.

In some extreme versions, we will even get the intention of inverting the relationship of man with whatever is above him (the natural and the divine), such as it obtained before modernity. Relying on nature becomes mastering nature. Depending on the divine as one's measure becomes defining one's own yardsticks—"creating values," and in some cases doing away with God. Yet all those aspects can be summarized in the idea of a project. This is all the more the case if we pay attention to the following fact.

PROJECT AND TASK

It is in no way necessary for human endeavours to understand themselves as being a project. I suggest that we should look at a genus that we could call "enterprise" and divide it into two species. One of those two species is the "project." But alongside it there is another species that I suggest we should call by the name of "task." The task possesses properties that oppose the three characteristics of the project that I have just been highlighting. Every aspect changes signs: in a task (1) I am entrusted to do something by an origin on which I have no hold, and which I do not always even know and must look for; (2) since I have received from elsewhere what I have to do, I must ask myself whether I am equal to my task, agreeing thereby to be dispossessed of what was, all the same, irrevocably entrusted to me; finally, (3) I am the only one responsible for what I am asked to fulfill, and I cannot possibly offload it onto another who could pledge for the success of my action.

It has been repeatedly pointed out that the whole gear of images and slogans that undergird modernity is biblical in origin: we inherited from the book of Genesis the idea of a domination of nature, and from Paul the metaphor of reaching adulthood, doing away with tutelage, and by so doing, emancipating. This requires qualification, by the way, especially the first claim.[15] Anyway, observations of this kind may either legitimize modernity or, on the contrary, compromise the Bible on which we foist the responsibility for the darker sides of modernity.

Now, with this concept of a task, we may be in possession of the criterion that enables us to distinguish modernity and its biblical heritage. For all the biblical images that are commonly called to our mind in this context, including the idea of a forward-tension (*epektasis*) in Paul (Phil 3:13), must be understood in the key of task rather than in the key of project.

MAKING EXPERIMENTS

Let me now take a second step and introduce a second basic idea of modernity. Where the idea of a project plays the lead, the very figure of truth changes. Truth becomes the result of an experiment. I already alluded to

15. See J. Cohen, *Be Fertile and Increase, Fill the Earth and Master It. The Ancient and Medieval Career of a Biblical Text* (Ithaca, N.Y.: Cornell University Press, 1989).

experimenting when mentioning the strange fashion of the vocabulary of "project," attempt, essay, etc., in early modern times. Now, the idea of experiment originated and spread in the ambit of natural science. But it took a metaphysical turn in German Idealism, and first of all with Kant, who reflects on the method favored by Bacon.[16] It begins to be some sort of confirmation of the idealistic postulate with the young Schelling who, in 1799, interprets the philosophy of Fichte, to which he still adheres, by taking up the metaphor used by Bacon, and later by Kant, according to which every experiment is a question put to nature, which she is compelled to answer. But he adds: "every question contains a hidden judgment a priori; every experiment that really is an experiment, is a prophecy; the very practice of experimentation [*das Experimentieren selbst*] is a production of phenomena."[17]

So the idea of experimentation goes beyond its original realm, which is the one in which it has a rigorous meaning, that is, the natural sciences, and invades the whole domain of life at large. For instance, and to begin with, in the realm of politics: according to the authors of the Federalist Papers, the young American republic is an "experiment."[18] Ernest Renan, in a work written in 1848, gets near to the idea of life as an experiment and gives as an example Saint-Simon, the utopian: "What would happen, if we could add to scientific experimentation the practical experimentation of life?"[19] Some ten years later, in Britain, John Stuart Mill's liberal ethics (1859) encourages what he called "experiments of living."[20] The idea of experimentation shifts thereby from theory to practice. This is the case in Nietzsche: philosophical effort is a series of attempts "to reach a form of life that we haven't yet reached."[21] It finds a cancerous, and even caricatural growth, in the realm of aesthetics.[22] And

16. Kant, *Kritik der reinen Vernunft*, Preface, B xii–xiv.

17. Schelling, *Einleitung zu dem Entwurf eines Systems der Naturphilosophie*, 4; in *Ausgewählte Werke, 1799–1801* (Darmstadt: Wissenschaftliche Buchgesellschaft, 1980), 276.

18. *The Federalist*, no. 14 (James Madison), ed. J. E. Cooke (Middletown, Conn.: Wesleyan University Press, 1961), 88–89.

19. Renan, *L'Avenir de la science*, 8n68; in *Œuvres Complètes*, ed. H. Psichari (Paris: Calmann-Levy, 1947–), 3:1133.

20. J. S. Mill, *On Liberty*, chap. 3, in *Utilitarianism, On Liberty, Representative Government*, ed. A. D. Lindsay (London: Dent, 1948), 115; see also 122 and 137.

21. Nietzsche, "Fragment 6 [48], Summer 1875" (KSA, 8:115–18).

22. See R. Shattuck, *The Innocent Eye: On Modern Literature and the Arts* (New York: Washington Square Press, 1986), 78–81.

still more, maybe, in the thirst for originality and eccentricity at all costs in the realm of everyday life.

BEING AN EXPERIMENT

A wholly different situation obtains when man is not considered as the subject, as the experimentator any longer, but rather as the object about which an experiment was mounted. The very existence of man is supposed to be nothing more than an attempt made by some impersonal power. The idea is not devoid of roots in the ancient world. A rather unclear verse in the Book of Job asked: "isn't there for man a service [*tsâvâ*] on earth?"[23] The Septuagint had translated this as: "is not the life of man on earth a trial [*peiratèrion*]?" And Augustine, who followed the ancient Latin translation, had "tentatio est vita humana super terram."[24] Maimonides interpreted the biblical story of Abraham's temptation (*nissayôn*) as a trial through which man's obedience toward God becomes manifest, not to God himself, who knows everything, but to man who thereby becomes conscious of his own abilities.[25]

Yet this all remains embedded in the representation of a benevolent God. And it has to be, for the very idea of enterprise, trial, endeavor, attempt, etc., implies that a failure is not excluded. If the experiment is a task, we may hope that it will be successful. But if it is a project, there is no warrant. Therefore, a sea change occurs when the subject that carries the experiment takes the impersonal aspect of nature as an indifferent force, such as she is conceived of by moderns. An intermediary step is represented by Villiers de l'Isle-Adam's novel *L'Ève Future*. Thomas Edison, on the verge of creating an artificial woman, reminds his sponsor: "Both of us are part of the experiment."[26] The attempt still has human beings as agents, but they are drawn into their own experiment and carried farther than they expected.

A further step is taken when man is conceived as being the merely

23. Job 7:1a. The classical Hebrew commentators all understand the passage as a reminder of the shortness of life. The translators of the Authorized Version do the same. The Vulgate (*militia*) and Luther (*im Dienst stehen*) choose the idea of "service."

24. Augustine, *Confessions*, X.28.39 (BA 14:210).

25. Maimonides, *Guide*, III.24, ed. Y. Joel (Jerusalem: Junovitch, 1929), 361; in *The Guide of the Perplexed*, trans. S. Pines (Chicago: University of Chicago Press, 1962), 189.

26. Villiers, *L'Ève Future*, ed. N. Satiat (Paris: Garnier-Flammarion, 1992), II.4 (187).

passive object of an experiment, the subject of which is nature. The idea appears, to the best of my knowledge, for the first time in Goethe. A friend of his reported a conversation held in the poet's garden in summer 1809:

> Let us think of nature as if she were sitting in front of a gaming-table and unceasingly shouting: "double!" That is, as if she luckily, nay infinitely played with what she had already won through all the realms of her action. Stone, animal, plant, everything is again put at stake after some lucky throws of that kind, and who knows whether man in his whole is not merely a throw towards a higher goal? [*wer weiß, ob nicht auch der ganze Mensch wieder nur ein Wurf nach einem höhern Ziele ist*].[27]

Goethe said this fifty years exactly before Darwin's pathbreaking masterpiece, *The Origin of Species*, but some forerunners of the idea of evolution already had adumbrated such ideas.

A whole tradition in anthropology conceives of man as being, not a fully achieved being, but a sketch of sorts. I already quoted Sartre's words to the effect that man is his project. But here, man is the object of a project that he does not control. Fichte writes: "all the animals are perfected and ready; man is only sketched and projected" (*angedeutet und entworfen*). Heidegger defines the life of what he calls Dasein as a "project" (*Entwurf*), and later on deepens the idea by making of the project not a whim or initiative of man any longer, but a fundamental feature of Being.[28] Mankind as a whole is an experiment of life. The idea is to be found in a poem that Rainer Maria Rilke wrote in Muzot on June 4, 1924, and that Heidegger placed at the center of his interpretation of the poet: we are a risk (*Wagnis*).[29] The song of the poet is echoed by the cold prose of the British biologist Julian Huxley: "[Humanity] is an experiment of the universe in rational self-consciousness.... The only significance we can see

27. Goethe, "Conversation with Johann Daniel Falk (no. 1185), June 14, 1809," in *Goethes Gespräche (Gesamtausgabe)*, ed. F. von Biedermann et al., vol. 2: *Vom Erfurter Kongress bis zum letzten böhmischen Aufenthalt* (Leipzig: Biedermann, 1909), 41 (emphasis added); for context, see P. Hadot, *Le Voile d'Isis. Essai sur l'histoire de l'idée de nature* (Paris: Gallimard, 2004), 263.

28. Fichte, *Grundlage des Naturrechts*, II, §6, η; *Ausgewählte Werke*, ed. F. Medicus (Darmstadt: Wissenschaftliche Buchgesellschaft, 1962), 2:83; Heidegger, *Sein und Zeit*, §30 (Tubingen: Niemeyer, 1963), 142; Heidegger, "Vom Wesen des Grundes," 59–64, and "Brief über den Humanismus," 169, both in *Wegmarken* (Frankfurt am Main: Klostermann, 1967).

29. R. M. Rilke, "Wie die Natur die Wesen überlässt," in *Gedichte 1910–1926*, ed. M. Engel and U. Fülleborn (Frankfort: Insel, 1996), 324. Heidegger, "Wozu Dichter?," in *Holzwege* (Frankfurt am Main: Klostermann, 1950), 248–95, esp. 255. The word "risk" is also in H. Jonas, *Das Prinzip Verantwortung* (Frankfurt: Insel, 1979), 247.

attaching to man's place in nature is that he is willy-nilly engaged in a gigantic evolutionary experiment by which life may attain to new levels of achievement and experience."[30] Finally, it is found at a very recent date in Hans Jonas's "Principle [of] Responsibility," although the whole point of his book is advocating prudence in the face of any utopian technological adventure. He mentions the "ontological experiment [*Versuch*] that Being launched with Man."[31]

THE DIALECTICS OF EXPERIMENTATION

Let us ponder a while the implicit logic of the idea. If man is the result of a throw of the dice, and if the agency that produced him (God, nature, being) can wager another throw, this means that the throw that resulted in the creation of man is not nature's last word. Hence its result, man, is a relative failure in comparison with what might come after him. In the words of Nietzsche's Zarathustra: man is to the Overman who is to come what monkeys are to human beings.[32]

The dialectics are the same as the ones that underlie the idea of progress. It was brought out very soon, even in the Middle Ages, for instance in the discussion between the Persian physician and freethinker Muhammad ibn Zakariya al-Rāzi and his contemporary the Ismaili propagandist Abu Hātim al-Rāzi.[33] If a continuous progress obtains, the present is, to be sure, supposed to be better than the past. Now, the past is the future of the future—and still more of the present. But, since the present is doomed to become the past of a better future, it is at the same time demoted to being nothing more than a preliminary stepping-stone.

Little wonder that the idea according to which man is an experiment was followed, some decades afterwards, by another, less pleasant idea: man is a failed attempt. I have not yet found its first use, but it was a hackneyed theme by the middle of the nineteenth century, probably because it was in keeping with the general Darwinian and Schopenhauerian atmosphere of this period of time.

30. J. Huxley, *What Dare I Think? The Challenge of Modern Science to Human Action and Belief* (London: Chatto and Windus, 1931), 150–51 and 177; see also 169.

31. Jonas, *Prinzip*, 188; see also 280.

32. Nietzsche, *Also sprach Zarathustra*, Prologue, 3 (KSA, 4:14).

33. See Razi, *Opera Philosophica fragmentaque quae supersunt*, ed. P. Kraus (Cairo, 1939), 301–2.

The idea of man as a failure occurs even in the private correspondence, although the general tone is urbane banter, of a Franco-Austrian diplomat with a smattering of Kant and Schopenhauer, Alexander von Villers. He writes in a letter of 1873: "I hold Man for a failed experiment [*misslungener Versuch*] of nature, that she is about to give up."[34] The idea hardly left Western consciousness. The German sculptor and playwright Ernst Barlach (d. 1938) is quoted to have said: "man is a failed attempt [*fehlgeschlagener Versuch*] of nature."[35]

This failure could take on a very concrete dimension. The empowerment of man, man taking his destiny in his own hands, was what the modern project was all about. Now, this sovereignty of man over himself very well could turn out to be the possibility for man definitely to put a stop to the experiment. The failure itself would thereby be entrusted to man. He would draw the negative conclusion and ratify its own condemnation by committing suicide.

Three years after Villers, in his "Diary of a Writer" (1876), the Russian novelist Dostoyevsky imagines a "materialist" committing suicide out of sheer boredom. He is supposed to have asked in his farewell letter the following question: "What, if Man was put on earth only for some sort of reckless experiment [*проба*], only in order to see whether a being made like him would succeed in living on earth or not?" The saddest thing is that "there isn't anybody who attempted the experiment, there is nobody whom we could curse, everything happened simply according to the inert laws of nature."[36] The same author discretely puts forth an analogous idea four years later, in the famous legend of the Grand Inquisitor, told by Ivan, one of the brothers Karamazov. He has his Grand Inquisitor characterize human beings as "unfinished, experimental [*пробные*] beings, created for derision."[37]

34. Alexander von Villers, "Letter to Warsberg, April 30th, 1873," in *Briefe eines Unbekannten*, ed. M. Gideon (Zurich: Manesse, n.d.), 245.

35. Ernst Barlach, quoted in H. Sedlmayr, *Verlust der Mitte. Die bildende Kunst des 19. und 20. Jahrhunderts als Symptom und Symbol der Zeit* (Salzburg: Otto Müller, 1948), 157.

36. Dostoevsky, *Дневник писателя 1876 год*, October 1876, I, 4; in *Собрание сочинений* (St. Petersburg: Nauka, 1994), 13:322.

37. Dostoevsky, *Братья Карамазовы*, II, v, 5 (Moscow: ACT, 2006), 265. The sentence looks like a quotation, and might allude to N. Strakhov's critique of the authors according to which man is only a transitory form, an essay of nature doomed to be superseded by a superior being. See D. Čyževskyj, "Literarische Lesefrüchte. IV," *Zeitschrift für Slavische Philologie* 13 (1936): 70. I owe this reference to Prof. Birgit Harress (Leipzig).

RISK

Modernity conceives of human history as an experiment. Yet there are not many people who face the consequence of this passage of human things under the yoke of the experimental, namely this utterly simple fact that if a laboratory experiment can have a conclusive result, it can have a negative one, too. In other words: an attempt can fail. It is as if a trace of a secularized faith in providence remained and fed confidence in experimentation.

Let me here quote the British scientist James Bernal: mankind, by increasing its own wisdom, by knowing more and wanting more, will risk more, and by so doing will risk its own destruction. But "this hardihood, this experimentation, is in fact the essential quality of life."[38] Bernal, who was a Marxist and even a staunch supporter of Stalin and of Lyssenko's bogus genetics, is thereby taking sides—strange bedfellows—with Nietzsche, who makes "attempt" (*Versuch*) into the very figure of truth.[39]

Nietzsche is among the few who considered the possibility of an irretrievable failure and honestly acknowledged it. Be that as it may, he has his Zarathustra say, in a passage that remained unpublished: "We are making an experiment [*Versuch*] with truth! Perhaps mankind will thereby founder! Never mind, go ahead [*wohlan*]!"[40] This is quite a brash formula. We might sober up and ask: what if, in fact, the experiment yields a negative result? What if mankind invents contrivances and/or adopts modes of behavior that endanger its own survival in the long run? The trouble is that if the experiment does fail, so that mankind as a whole walks the plank, who will have another try?

The modern project brought about the possibility of its own demise. It looked for an autonomous mankind. It wanted mankind to be set on its own ground, to be determined by itself and by itself only. Modernity, at least in its late form, say from the 1840s onward, endeavored to give up any external, transcendent reference point. This is, by the way, the

38. J. D. Bernal, *The World, the Flesh and the Devil: An Inquiry Into the Future of the Three Enemies of the Rational Soul* (London: Jonathan Cape, 1970), 64.

39. Nietzsche, *Morgenröte*, III, §187 (KSA, 3:160), V, §432 (266), §453 (274), §501 (294); *Die Fröhliche Wissenschaft*, I, §51 (415–16); III, §110 (471); IV, §324 (552); *Jenseits von Gut und Böse*, V, §203 (5:126).

40. Nietzsche, "Fragment 25 [305], Spring 1884" (KSA, 11:88). The exclamation *wohlan!* has in Nietzsche almost the value of a concept.

period of time in which the word "humanism" was coined and given its present-day shade of meaning, first in Germany, then in Britain and in France.

Suppose mankind can determine itself by itself and only by itself: why should it choose to be rather than not to be? Why should self-determination receive a positive interpretation? What reason could tip the scales in favour of being rather than not being? Since we cannot create ourselves, the choice is between accepting ourselves, hopefully while trying to improve ourselves, or destroying ourselves. And self-destruction is easier than self-acceptation and/or self-improvement.

THE UNANSWERED QUESTION

This is not an academic question any longer. That mankind did endanger and keeps endangering its very survival is now a matter of common knowledge. Two of the main dangers are obvious: atomic warfare and environmental destruction. I would add a third one, less glaring: the low birth-rates that could lead to a general shipwreck of mankind, beginning with the most "modern" countries. Many strategies are proposed for us to obviate some of these challenges, and some are being implemented.

On the other hand, one key question is not answered, and not even asked in proper terms: why should there be human beings? To quote one of the deepest British thinkers, Bertie Wooster: "Well, who wants to keep the human race going?"[41] Why is the existence of human beings better than their nonexistence or disappearance? I mean, to be sure, their peaceful extinction. A violent disappearance is not to be countenanced. We can find obvious moral objections against inflicting suffering and death on our fellow human beings. We can further level the same kind of objections against poisoning the earth and spoiling the life of other people. But how can we say that not having children is morally wrong? In the first two cases, we obviously harm other living beings. But whom do we harm by not having children? It might even be the case that begetting them is morally wrong, as argued by David Benatar, a South African philosopher, in a book published by Oxford University Press.

The endeavor to ground the humanity of man on man himself was

41. P. G. Wodehouse, *Jeeves in the Offing* (London: Penguin, 1963), 80.

successful as far as promoting a decent behaviour among people was concerned. Earlier types of mankind looked for a ground of social life and organization either in something suprahuman, nature or God, or in a mixture of both, in a divinized nature or in a God hardly distinguished from his creation. We do not need such a thing for us to organize our being-together, at least in principle. We must only negotiate how we will get on with each other on the basis of our interests. To be sure, this will happen provided we are clever enough to understand where our real interest lies and to take the long run into account. Yet, I repeat: at least in principle, for us to build a decent society, we need, to quote a famous, albeit imaginary, utterance of Alexander Hamilton, "no foreign aid." But a society, decent or not, has first to exist, and it is made of human beings. Now, to repeat: why should there be human beings?

What does the failure of modernity consist of? Modernity cannot answer the question about the legitimacy of mankind unless it gives up its own project. The title of this essay almost boils down to a tautology. Modernity failed because it understood itself as a project. If we stick to this project, we are at a loss about how to explain that mankind as a whole has to be. In order to do that, we need some fulcrum, an Archimedean point.

In other words: we can produce, and we do produce, a great deal of good things. I do not mean only material goods. Heaven forbid that I should indulge in one more version of the reactionary critique of consumerism, of so-called materialism, etc. But modernity can produce and does produce higher goods that are social and cultural in nature: the possibility for large masses to live decently under the rule of law, to have access to education and museums, to mention only some examples. Which is very much to its credit, and we must be thankful for that. On the other hand, modernity is unable to tell us why it is good that there be people to enjoy those goods. To give an answer, we need to shift to a higher, metaphysical, gear.

Selected Bibliography

Allison, Henry E. *The Kant-Eberhard Controversy*. Baltimore, Md.: Johns Hopkins University Press, 1973.

Aristotle. *Aristotle's* Metaphysics. Translated by Hippocrates Apostle. Grinnell, Iowa: Peripatetic Press, 1979.

———. *Aristotle's* Physics. Translated by Hippocrates Apostle. Grinnell, Iowa: Peripatetic Press, 1980.

———. *The Complete Works of Aristotle*. Edited by J. Barnes. 2 vols. Princeton, N.J.: Princeton University Press, 1984.

———. *Aristotle's* Physics. Translated by Joe Sachs. New Brunswick, N.J.: Rutgers University Press, 1995.

———. *Nicomachean Ethics*. Translated by Terence Irwin. Second edition. Indianapolis, Ind.: Hackett, 2000.

———. *Nicomachean Ethics*. Translated by Robert C. Bartlett and Susan D. Collins. Chicago: University of Chicago Press, 2011.

———. *Aristotle's* Politics. Translated by Carnes Lord. Second edition. Chicago: University of Chicago Press, 2013.

Arnhart, Larry. "Defending Darwinian Natural Right." *Interpretation* 27, no. 3 (2000): 263–77.

Bacon, Francis. *The New Organon and Related Writings*. Edited by Fulton H. Anderson. Indianapolis, Ind.: Bobbs-Merrill, 1960.

———. *The Works of Francis Bacon*. 14 vols. Edited by J. Spedding, R. L. Ellis, and D. Heath. London: Longmans and Co., 1857–70. Reprinted in Stuttgart-Bad Canstatt: Frohmann-Holzboog, 1963.

Bégin, Christian. "Tocqueville et la Fracture Religieuse." *The Tocqueville Review* 32 (2011): 167–99.

Baier, Annette. *A Progress of Sentiments: Reflections on Hume's* Treatise. Cambridge, Mass.: Harvard University Press, 1991.

Balibar, Etienne. *Spinoza and Politics*. London: Verso, 1998.

Berlin, Isaiah. "A Special Supplement: The Question of Machiavelli." *The New York Review of Books* 17, no. 7 (November 4, 1971).

Bohm, David. "A Suggested Interpretation of the Quantum Theory in Terms of 'Hidden' Variables." *Physical Review* 85, no. 2 (January 15, 1952): 166–93.

———. *Quantum Theory*. New York: Dover, 1979.

Bohm, D., and B. J. Hiley. *The Undivided Universe: An Ontological Interpretation of Quantum Theory*. London: Routledge, 1993.

Bohr, Niels. "Can Quantum-Mechanical Description of Physical Reality Be Considered Complete?" *Physical Review* 48 (October 15, 1935): 696–702.

Born, Max. *The Born-Einstein Letters*. New York: Walker and Co., 1971.

Boyle, Marjorie O'Rourke. "Machiavelli and the Politics of Grace." *MLN* 119 Supplement (2004): 224–46.

Brown, Stuart. "Leibniz: Modern, Scholastic, or Renaissance Philosopher?" In *The Rise of Modern Philosophy: The Tension between the New and Traditional Philosophies from Machiavelli to Leibniz*, edited by Tom Sorell. Oxford: Clarendon Press, 1993.

Calvin, Jean. *Institutes of the Christian Religion*. Translated by Henry Beveridge. Grand Rapids, Mich.: Eerdmans, 1959.

———. *Commentaries*, vol. 38: *Romans*. Translated by John King. Grand Rapids, Mich.: Baker Book House, 1993.

Ceaser, James W. *Designing a Polity: America's Constitution in Theory and Practice*. Lanham, Md.: Rowman and Littlefield, 2011.

Churchland, Paul. *The Engine of Reason, The Seat of the Soul*. Cambridge, Mass.: MIT Press, 1995.

Cohen, Jeremy. *Be Fertile and Increase, Fill the Earth and Master It: The Ancient and Medieval Career of a Biblical Text*. Ithaca, N.Y.: Cornell University Press, 1989.

Comte, Auguste. *Cours de philosophie positive*. Edited by J. P. Enthoven. Paris: Hermann, 1975.

Cooper, Laurence D. *Rousseau, Nature, and the Problem of the Good Life*. University Park: Pennsylvania State University Press, 1999.

Curley, Edwin. *Bayle vs. Spinoza on Toleration*. Mededelingen vanwege het Spinozahuis 95. Voorschoten: Uitgeverij Spinozahuis, 2009.

de Broglie, Louis. *Physics and Microphysics*. Translated by Martin Davidson. New York: Harper Torchbooks, 1960.

Defoe, Daniel. "An Essay upon Projects." In *The True-born Englishman and Other Writings*, edited by Philip Nicholas Furbank and W. R. Owens. London: Penguin Classics, 1997.

de Gandt, François. *Force and Geometry in Newton's* Principia. Translated by Curtis Wilson. Princeton, N.J.: Princeton University Press, 1995.

de Grazia, Sebastian. *Machiavelli in Hell*. Princeton, N.J.: Princeton University Press, 1989.

Deleuze, Gilles. *The Fold: Leibniz and the Baroque*. Translated by Tom Conley. Minneapolis: University of Minnesota Press, 1993.

Descartes, René. *Œuvres de Descartes*. Edited by Charles Adam and Paul Tannery. 11 vols. Paris: J. Vrin, 1964–74.

———. *Philosophical Writings of Descartes*. Edited by John Cottingham, Robert Stoothoff, and Dugald Murdoch. New York: Cambridge University Press, 1985.

Des Chene, Dennis. *Physiologia: Natural Philosophy in Late Aristotelian and Cartesian Thought*. Ithaca, N.Y.: Cornell University Press, 1996.

Dewitt, Bryce S., and R. Neill Graham. "Resource Letter IQM–1 on the Interpretation of Quantum Mechanics." *American Journal of Physics* 39 (July 1971): 724–36.

Dupré, Louis. *Passage to Modernity: An Essay in the Hermeneutics of Nature and Culture.* New Haven, Conn.: Yale University Press, 1993.

———. *The Enlightenment and the Intellectual Foundations of Modern Culture.* New Haven, Conn.: Yale University Press, 2004.

Einstein, A., B. Podolsky, and N. Rosen. "Can Quantum-Mechanical Description of Physical Reality Be Considered Complete?" *Physical Review* 47 (May 15, 1935): 777–80.

Einstein, Albert, and Leopold Infeld. *The Evolution of Physics.* New York: Simon and Schuster, 1968.

Eisberg, Robert. *Fundamentals of Modern Physics.* New York: John Wiley and Sons, 1961.

Feldman, Fred. *Pleasure and the Good Life.* Oxford: Oxford University Press, 2004.

———. *What Is This Thing Called Happiness?* Oxford: Oxford University Press, 2010.

Feynman, R., R. Leighton, and M. Sands. *The Feynman Lectures on Physics.* Vol. 1. Reading, Mass.: Addison-Wesley, 1963.

Fichte, J. G. *Grundlage des Naturrechts.* In Fichte, *Ausgewählte Werke*, edited by F. Medicus. Darmstadt: Wissenschaftliche Buchgesellschaft, 1962.

Ford, Joseph. "How Random Is a Coin Toss?" *Physics Today* (April 1983): 40–47.

Frazer, Michael. *The Enlightenment of Sympathy: Justice and the Moral Sentiments in the Eighteenth Century and Today.* Oxford: Oxford University Press, 2010.

Galilei, Galileo. *Dialogo sopra i due massimi sistemi del mondo.* Edited by F. Flora. Milan: Mondadori, 1996.

Garber, Daniel. *Descartes Embodied: Reading Cartesian Philosophy through Cartesian Science.* Cambridge: Cambridge University Press, 2001.

———. "Should Spinoza Have Published His Philosophy?" In *Interpreting Spinoza*, edited by Charles Huenemann. New York: Cambridge University Press, 2008.

Garrett, Don. *Cognition and Commitment in Hume's Philosophy.* New York: Oxford University Press, 1997.

Garsten, Bryan. "Seeing 'Not Differently, but Further, than the Parties.'" In *The Arts of Rule*, edited by Sharon R. Krause and Mary Ann McGrail. Lanham, Md.: Rowman and Littlefield, 2009.

George, Robert. *In Defense of Natural Law.* Oxford: Oxford University Press, 1999.

Glanvill, Joseph. *Plus ultra: or, The progress and advancement of knowledge since the days of Aristotle.* London: James Collins, 1668. Reprinted in Hildesheim: Georg Olms, 1979.

Gleick, James. *Chaos: Making a New Science.* New York: Viking Penguin, 1987.

Goethe, J. W. von. *Goethes Gespräche. Gesamtausgabe.* Edited by F. von Biedermann. Leipzig: Biedermann, 1909.

Goldstein, Doris S. *Trial of Faith: Religion and Politics in Tocqueville's Thought*. New York: Elsevier, 1975.

Goldstein, Rebecca. *Betraying Spinoza: The Renegade Jew Who Gave Us Modernity*. New York: Schocken, 2006.

Griffin, James. *Well-Being: Its Meaning, Measurement, and Moral Importance*. Oxford: Clarendon Press, 1986.

Guyer, Paul. "The Form and Matter of the Categorical Imperative." In *Kant und die Berliner Aufklärung: Akten des IX. Internationalen Kant Kongresses*, edited by V. Gerhardt et al. 5 vols. Berlin: Walter de Gruyter, 2001.

———. "Kant's System of Duties." In *Kant's System of Nature and Freedom*, edited by Paul Guyer. Oxford: Clarendon Press, 2005.

———. *Kant*. London: Routledge, 2006.

———. "Ist und Soll, von Hume bis Kant und Heute." In *Kant und die Zukunft der europäischen Aufklärung*, edited by Heiner F. Klemme. Berlin: Walter de Gruyter, 2009.

Habermas, Jürgen. *Die Moderne—ein unvollendetes Projekt*. In Habermas, *Kleine politische Schriften*. Frankfurt: Suhrkamp, 1981.

Hadot, P. *Le Voile d'Isis. Essai sur l'histoire de l'idée de nature*. Paris: Gallimard, 2004.

Halliday, David, and Robert Resnick. *Physics*. New York: John Wiley and Sons, 1978.

Hamilton, Alexander, James Madison, and John Jay. *The Federalist*. Edited by Jacob Cooke. New York: Meridian, 1965.

Hancock, Ralph C. "The Uses and Hazards of Christianity in Tocqueville's Attempt to Save Democratic Souls." In *Interpreting Tocqueville's Democracy in America*, edited by K. Masugi. Savage, Md.: Rowman and Littlefield, 1988.

Hassing, Richard F. "Wholes, Parts, and Laws of Motion." *Nature and System* 6 (1984): 195–215.

———. "Animals versus the Laws of Inertia." *Review of Metaphysics* 46 (1992): 29–61.

———. "The Exemplary Career of Newton's Mathematics." *The St. John's Review* 44, no. 1 (1997): 72–93.

———. "Darwinian Natural Right?" *Interpretation* 27, no. 2 (2000): 129–60.

———. "Reply to Arnhart." *Interpretation* 28, no. 1 (2000): 35–43.

Hegel, G. W. F. *The Encyclopedia Logic*. Translated by T. F. Geraets, W. A. Suchting, and H. S. Harris. Indianapolis, Ind.: Hackett, 1991.

Heidegger, Martin. *Holzwege*. Frankfurt am Main: Klostermann, 1950.

———. *Sein und Zeit*. Tubingen: Max Niemeyer, 1963.

———. *Wegmarken*. Frankfurt am Main: Klostermann, 1967.

———. *What Is a Thing?* Translated by W. B. Barton, Jr., and Vera Deutsch. South Bend, Ind.: Regnery, 1967.

———. *The Question concerning Technology*. Translated by William Lovitt. New York: Harper and Row, 1977.

Heisenberg, Werner. "Über den anschaulichen Inhalt der quantentheoretischen Kinematic und Mechanik." *Zeitschrift für Physik* 43 (1927): 172–98.

———. *On Modern Physics*. New York: Clarkson Potter, 1961.

———. *Physics and Beyond: Encounters and Conversations*. Translated by A. J. Pomerans. New York: Harper Torchbooks, 1972.

Helmholtz, Hermann von. "On the Conservation of Force." In *Wissenschaftliche Abhandlungen*, vol. 1. Leipzig: Johann Ambrosius Barth, 1882.

Hobbes, Thomas. *Man and Citizen*. Edited by Bernard Gert. Indianapolis, Ind.: Hackett, 1991.

———. *Leviathan*. Edited by Edwin Curley. Indianapolis, Ind.: Hackett, 1994.

———. *Leviathan*. Edited by Richard Tuck. Cambridge: Cambridge University Press, 1996.

Hopkins, Burt C. *The Origin of the Logic of Symbolic Mathematics: Edmund Husserl and Jacob Klein*. Bloomington: Indiana University Press, 2011.

Horace. *Satires, Epistles, and Ars Poetica*. Translated by H. Ruston Fairclough. New York: G. P. Putnam's Sons, 1926.

Hulliung, Mark. *Citizen Machiavelli*. Princeton, N.J.: Princeton University Press, 1984.

Hume, David. *Essays, Moral, Political, and Literary*. Edited by Eugene F. Miller. Revised edition. Indianapolis, Ind.: Liberty Fund, 1985.

———. *Enquiry concerning Human Understanding*. Edited by Eric Steinberg. Second edition. Indianapolis, Ind.: Hackett, 1993.

———. *Treatise of Human Nature*. Edited by David Fate Norton and Mary J. Norton. New York: Oxford University Press, 2000.

Huxley, Julian. *What Dare I Think? The Challenge of Modern Science to Human Action and Belief*. London: Chatto and Windus, 1931.

Inwood, Brad, and Pierluigi Donini. "Stoic Ethics." In *The Cambridge History of Hellenistic Philosophy*, edited by K. Alegra, J. Barnes, J. Mansfeld, and M. Schofield. Cambridge: Cambridge University Press, 1999.

Inwood, B., and L. P. Gerson, eds. *The Stoic Reader: Selected Writings and Testimonia*. Indianapolis, Ind.: Hackett, 2008.

Israel, Jonathan. *Radical Enlightenment: Philosophy and the Making of Modernity 1650–1750*. Oxford: Oxford University Press, 2001.

———. *Enlightenment Contested: Philosophy, Modernity and the Emancipation of Man 1670–1752*. Oxford: Oxford University Press, 2006.

Jammer, Max. *The Conceptual Development of Quantum Mechanics*. New York: McGraw-Hill, 1966.

Jolley, Nicholas. *Leibniz*. London: Routledge, 2005.

Jonas, Hans. *Das Prinzip Verantwortung: Versuch einer Ethik für die technologische Zivilisation*. Frankfurt am Main: Insel, 1979.

Kant, Immanuel. *Kant's gesammelte Schriften*. Edited by the Royal Prussian, later German, then Berlin-Brandenburg Academy of Sciences. 29 vols. Berlin: Georg Reimer, later Walter de Gruyter, 1900–.

———. *Critique of Pure Reason*. Translated by Norman Kemp Smith. New York: St. Martin's Press, 1965.

———. *Theoretical Philosophy 1755–1770*. Translated by David Walford and Ralf Meerbote. Cambridge: Cambridge University Press, 1992.

———. *Practical Philosophy*. Translated by Mary J. Gregor. Cambridge: Cambridge University Press, 1996.
———. *Religion and Rational Theology*. Translated by Allen W. Wood and George di Giovanni. Cambridge: Cambridge University Press, 1996.
———. *Lectures on Ethics*. Edited by P. Heath and J. B. Schneewind. Translated by Peter Heath. Cambridge: Cambridge University Press, 1997.
———. *Critique of Pure Reason*. Translated by Paul Guyer and Allen W. Wood. Cambridge: Cambridge University Press, 1998.
———. *Critique of the Power of Judgment*. Edited by Paul Guyer. Translated by P. Guyer and E. Matthews. Cambridge: Cambridge University Press, 2000.
———. *Notes and Fragments*. Edited by Paul Guyer. Translated by C. Bowman, P. Guyer, and F. Rauscher. Cambridge: Cambridge University Press, 2005.
———. *Anthropology, History, and Education*. Edited by G. Zöller and R. B. Louden. Cambridge: Cambridge University Press, 2007.
———. *Observations on the Feeling of the Beautiful and Sublime and Other Writings*. Edited and translated by P. Frierson and P. Guyer. Cambridge: Cambridge University Press, 2011.
Kass, Leon R. *Toward a More Natural Science*. New York: Free Press, 1985.
———. "The Permanent Limitations of Biology." In Kass, *Life, Liberty, and the Defense of Dignity: The Challenge for Bioethics*. San Francisco, Calif.: Encounter, 2002.
Kennington, Richard. "Review of Jacob Klein, *Lectures and Essays*." *Review of Metaphysics* 41, no. 1 (September 1987): 144–49.
———. *On Modern Origins: Essays in Early Modern Philosophy*. Edited by Pamela Kraus and Frank Hunt. Lanham, Md.: Lexington, 2004.
Kessler, Sanford. *Tocqueville's Civil Religion: American Christianity and the Prospects for Freedom*. Albany: State University of New York Press, 1994.
Klein, Jacob. *Greek Mathematical Thought and the Origin of Algebra*. Translated by Eva Brann. Cambridge, Mass.: MIT Press, 1968.
———. *Lectures and Essays*. Edited by R. B. Williamson and E. Zuckerman. Annapolis, Md.: St. John's College Press, 1985.
Korsgaard, Christine. "Skepticism about Practical Reason." *Journal of Philosophy* 83, no. 1 (1986): 5–25.
Koyré, Alexandre. *Études d'histoire de la pensée scientifique*. Paris: Gallimard, 1966.
Krause, Sharon R. *Civil Passions: Moral Sentiment and Democratic Deliberation*. Princeton, N.J.: Princeton University Press, 2008.
Krause, S., and M. McGrail, eds., *The Arts of Rule: Essays in Honor of Harvey C. Mansfield*. Lanham, Md.: Rowman and Littlefield, 2009.
Kraut, Richard. "Two Conceptions of Happiness." *The Philosophical Review* 88, no. 2 (April 1979): 167–97.
———. *What Is Good and Why? The Ethics of Well-Being*. Cambridge, Mass: Harvard University Press, 2007.
Lachterman, David R. *The Ethics of Geometry: A Genealogy of Modernity*. New York: Routledge, 1989.

Lamberti, Jean-Claude. *Tocqueville and The Two Democracies*. Translated by A. Goldhammer. Cambridge, Mass.: Harvard University Press, 1989.

Landau, L. D., and E. M. Lifshitz. *The Classical Theory of Fields*. Reading, Mass.: Addison-Wesley, 1962.

Laplace, Pierre-Simon. *A Philosophical Essay on Probabilities*. Translated by F. W. Truscott and F. L. Emory. New York: Dover, 1951.

Laporte, Jean. "La finalité chez Descartes." *Revue d'histoire de la philosophie* 2 (1928): 366–96.

Laudan, Laurens. "The Clock Metaphor and Probabilism: The Impact of Descartes on English Methodological Thought, 1650–65." *Annals of Science* 22, no. 2 (June 1966): 73–104.

Lawler, Peter A. *The Restless Mind: Alexis de Tocqueville on the Origin and Perpetuation of Human Liberty*. Lanham, Md.: Rowman and Littlefield, 1993.

Leibniz, G. W. *Nouvelles lettres et opuscules inédits de Leibniz*. Edited by A. Foucher de Careil. Paris: Durand, 1857.

———. *Die Philosophischen Schriften von G. W. Leibniz*. 7 vols. Edited by C. I. Gerhardt. Berlin: Weidmann, 1875–90.

———. *Sämtliche Schriften und Briefe*. Edited by the German Academy of Sciences. Darmstadt: Walter de Gruyter, 1923–.

———. *Philosophical Papers and Letters*. Edited by L. E. Loemker. Second edition. Dordrecht: Reidel, 1969.

———. *Philosophical Writings*. Edited by G. H. R. Parkinson. London: Dent, 1973.

———. *Philosophical Essays*. Edited by R. Ariew and D. Garber. Indianapolis, Ind.: Hackett, 1989.

———. *New Essays on Human Understanding*. Edited by P. Remnant and J. Bennett. Second edition. Cambridge: Cambridge University Press, 1996.

Lindley, David. *Where Does the Weirdness Go?* New York: Basic, 1996.

Locke, John. *The Works of John Locke in Nine Volumes*. London: C. and J. Rivington et al., 1824.

———. *Essays on the Law of Nature*. Edited by W. von Leyden. Oxford: Clarendon Press, 1954.

———. *A Letter concerning Toleration*. Edited by James H. Tully. Indianapolis, Ind.: Hackett, 1983.

———. *Two Treatises of Government*. Edited by Peter Laslett. Third edition. Cambridge: Cambridge University Press, 1988.

Lodge, P., and M. Bobro. "Stepping Back Inside Leibniz's Mill." *Monist* 81 (1998): 553–72.

Machiavelli, Niccolò. *The Literary Works*. Translated by J. R. Hale. London: Oxford University Press, 1961.

———. *The Chief Works and Others*. Translated by Allan Gilbert. 2 vols. Durham, N.C.: Duke University Press, 1965.

———. *Florentine Histories*. Translated by Harvey Mansfield and Laura Banfield. Princeton, N.J.: Princeton University Press, 1988.

———. *Il Principe*. Edited by Giorgio Inglese. Turin: Einaudi, 1995.

———. *Discourses on Livy*. Translated by Harvey C. Mansfield and Nathan Tarcov. Chicago: University of Chicago Press, 1996.
———. *The Prince*. Translated by Harvey C. Mansfield. Second edition. Chicago: University of Chicago Press, 1998.
———. *The Prince with Related Documents*. Translated by William J. Connell. Boston: St. Martin's, 2005.
MacIntyre, Alasdair. "Hume on 'Is' and 'Ought.'" *Philosophical Review* 68 (1959): 451–68.
———. *After Virtue: A Study in Moral Theory*. Second edition. South Bend, Ind.: University of Notre Dame Press, 1984.
Maier, A. *Zwei Grundprobleme der scholastischen Naturphilosophie. Das Problem der intensiven Größe. Die Impetustheorie*. Rome: Storia e letteratura, 1951.
Maimonides, Moses. *The Guide of the Perplexed*. 2 vols. Translated by S. Pines. Chicago: University of Chicago Press, 1974.
Malcolm, Noel. *Aspects of Hobbes*. Oxford: Clarendon Press, 2002.
Manent, Pierre. *Tocqueville and the Nature of Democracy*. Translated by John Waggoner. Lanham, Md.: Rowman and Littlefield, 1996.
———. *Modern Liberty and Its Discontents*. Translated by D. Mahoney and P. Seaton. Lanham, Md.: Rowman and Littlefield, 1998.
———. *Les Métamorphoses de la cite*. Paris: Flammarion, 2010.
Mansfield, Harvey C. *Tocqueville: A Very Short Introduction*. Oxford: Oxford University Press, 2010.
———. "Intimations of Philosophy in Tocqueville's *Democracy in America*." In *Tocqueville's Voyages; The Evolution of His Ideas and Their Journey Beyond His Time*, edited by Christine Dunn Henderson. Indianapolis, Ind.: Liberty Fund, 2014.
Mansfield, Harvey C., and Delba Winthrop. "Tocqueville's Machiavellianism." *Perspectives in Political Science* 43 (2014): 87–92.
Masugi, K., ed. *Interpreting Tocqueville's Democracy in America*. Savage, Md.: Rowman and Littlefield, 1991.
Maudlin, Tim. *Quantum Non-Locality and Relativity*. Malden, Mass.: Blackwell, 2002.
Maxwell, James Clerk. *Theory of Heat*. New York: Dover, 2001.
Merrill, Thomas W. "The Rhetoric of Rebellion in Hume's Constitutional Thought." *Review of Politics* 67, no. 2 (Spring 2005): 257–82.
Mill, John Stuart. *A System of Logic*. London: Longmans, Green and Co. Ltd., 1941.
———. *Utilitarianism, On Liberty, Representative Government*. Edited by A. D. Lindsay. London: Dent (Everyman), 1948.
Morrisson, Iain P. D. *Kant and the Role of Pleasure in Moral Action*. Athens: Ohio University Press, 2008.
Nederman, Cary J. "Amazing Grace: Fortune, God, and Free Will in Machiavelli's Thought." *Journal of the History of Ideas* 60, no. 4 (1999): 617–38.
Neuhouser, Frederick. *Rousseau's Theodicy of Self-Love*. Oxford: Oxford University Press, 2008.

Newman, Lex. "The Fourth Meditation." *Philosophy and Phenomenological Research* 59 (1999): 559–91.

Newton, Isaac. *Opticks*. New York: Dover, 1952.

———. *Mathematical Principles of Natural Philosophy*. Translated by Andrew Motte and Florian Cajori. New York: Greenwood Press, 1962.

———. *Unpublished Scientific Papers of Isaac Newton*. Edited by A. R. and M. B. Hall. Cambridge: Cambridge University Press, 1978.

Nietzsche, Friedrich. *Sämtliche Werke. Kritische Studienausgabe*. 15 vols. Third edition. Edited by G. Colli and M. Montinari. Berlin: Walter de Gruyter, 2009.

Noll, Mark. "Tocqueville's America, Beaumont's Slavery, and the United States in 1831–32." *American Political Thought* 3 (2014): 273–302.

Norton, David Fate. *David Hume: Common-Sense Moralist, Skeptical Metaphysician*. Princeton, N.J.: Princeton University Press, 1982.

Orwin, Clifford. "Machiavelli's Unchristian Charity." *American Political Science Review* 72 (1978): 1217–28.

Owen, J. Judd. *Making Religion Safe for Democracy*. Cambridge: Cambridge University Press, 2015.

Parfit, Derek. *Reasons and Persons*. Oxford: Oxford University Press, 1984.

Pauli, Wolfgang. "Naturwissenschaftliche und Erkenntnistheoretische Aspekte der Ideen vom Unbewussten." *Dialectica* 8 (1954): 283–301.

Penrose, Oliver. "An Asymmetric World." *Nature* 438 (December 15, 2005): 919.

Perrin, Jean. *Les Atomes*. Paris: Librarie Felix Alcan, 1913.

Peterman, Larry. "Dante and the Setting for Machiavellianism." *American Political Science Review* 76, no. 3 (September 1982): 630–44.

Petrarch, Francesco. *Remedies for Fortune Fair and Foul*. 5 vols. Translated by C. H. Rawski. Bloomington: Indiana University Press, 1991.

Pippin, Robert. *Idealism as Modernism: Hegelian Variations*. Cambridge: Cambridge University Press, 1996.

Plantinga, Alvin. *God, Freedom, and Evil*. Grand Rapids, Mich.: Eerdmans, 1977.

Plato. *Collected Dialogues*. Edited by E. Hamilton and H. Cairns. Princeton, N.J.: Princeton University Press, 1961.

———. *The Republic of Plato*. Translated by A. Bloom. Second edition. New York: Basic, 1991.

———. *Complete Works*. Edited by John M. Cooper. Indianapolis, Ind.: Hackett, 1997.

Poincaré, Henri. *Science and Method*. Translated by Francis Maitland. New York: Dover, 1952.

Ponet, John, *A shorte treatise of politike pouuer* .... Strasbourg: Printed by the heirs of W. Köpfel, 1556. Transcription by Text Creation Partnership, 2004-03 (EEBO-TCP Phase 1). Available at http://name.umdl.umich.edu/A09916.0001.001.

Popkin, Richard. *The History of Skepticism from Erasmus to Spinoza*. Berkeley: University of California Press, 1979.

Prezzolini, Giuseppe. *Machiavelli Anticristo*. Rome: Gherardo Casini, 1954.

Prufer, Thomas. *Recapitulations: Essays in Philosophy*. Washington, D.C.: The Catholic University of America Press, 1993.

Reich, Klaus. "Kant and Greek Ethics." Translated by W. H. Walsh. *Mind* (New Series) 48 (1939): 338–54. Reprinted in Klaus Reich, *Gesammelte Schriften*, edited by M. Baum, U. Rameil, K. Reisinger, and G. Scholz. Hamburg: Felix Meiner, 2001.

Reisert, Joseph R. *Jean-Jacques Rousseau: A Friend of Virtue*. Ithaca, N.Y.: Cornell University Press, 2003.

Renan, Ernest. *Œuvres complètes*. Edited by H. Psichari. Paris: Calmann-Levy, 1947–.

Rescher, Nicholas. *The Philosophy of Leibniz*. Englewood Cliffs, N.J.: Prentice Hall, 1967.

Riezler, Kurt. *Physics and Reality: Lectures of Aristotle on Modern Physics at an International Congress of Science*. New Haven, Conn.: Yale University Press, 1940.

Rilke, Rainer M. *Werke, Kommentierte Ausgabe*. 4 vols. Edited by M. Engel and U. Fülleborn. Frankfurt am Main: Insel, 1996.

Rohlf, Michael. "The Ideas of Pure Reason." In *The Cambridge Companion to Kant's* Critique of Pure Reason, edited by Paul Guyer. Cambridge: Cambridge University Press, 2010.

———. "Emotion and Evil in Kant." *Review of Metaphysics* 66 (June 2013): 749–73.

Rousseau, Jean-Jacques. *Œuvres complètes*. Edited by B. Gangebin and M. Raymond. Paris: Bibliothèque de la Pléiade, 1959–69.

———. *Œuvres complètes*. Edited by J. Fabré and M. Launay. Paris: Seuil, 1971.

———. *Emile or On Education*. Translated by Allan Bloom. New York: Basic, 1979.

———. *The Reveries of the Solitary Walker*. Translated by Charles E. Butterworth. Indianapolis, Ind.: Hackett, 1992.

———. *The Discourses and Other Early Political Writings*. Translated by Victor Gourevitch. Cambridge: Cambridge University Press, 1997.

———. *The Social Contract and Other Late Political Writings*. Translated by Victor Gourevitch. Cambridge: Cambridge University Press, 1997.

———. *The Major Political Writings of Jean-Jacques Rousseau*. Translated by John T. Scott. Chicago: University of Chicago Press, 2014.

Ruelle, David. *Chance and Chaos*. Princeton, N.J.: Princeton University Press, 1991.

Russell, Bertrand. *A Critical Exposition of the Philosophy of Leibniz*. Second edition. London: Allen and Unwin, 1937.

Rutherford, Donald. *Leibniz and the Rational Order of Nature*. Cambridge: Cambridge University Press, 1995.

Rutherford, E. "The Scattering of α and β Particles by Matter and the Structure of the Atom." *Philos. Mag.* 21 (April 1911): 669–88.

Salart, D., A. Baas, C. Branciard, N. Gisin, and H. Zbinden. "Testing Spooky Action at a Distance." *Nature* 454 (August 14, 2008): 861–64.

Sartre, Jean-Paul. *L'Existentialisme est un humanisme*. Paris: Nagel, 1946.

———. *Cahiers pour une morale*. Paris: Gallimard, 1983.

Schelling, Friedrich W. J. *Einleitung zu dem Entwurf eines Systems der Naturphilosophie*. In *Ausgewählte Werke: Schriften von 1799–1801*. Darmstadt: Wissenschaftliche Buchgesellschaft, 1980.

Schilpp, Paul Arthur, ed. *Albert Einstein Philosopher-Scientist*. La Salle, Ill.: Open Court, 1969.

Schleiffer, James T. *The Making of Tocqueville's Democracy in America*. Second edition. Indianapolis, Ind.: Liberty Fund, 2000.

———. "Tocqueville, Religion and *Democracy in America*: Some Essential Questions." *American Political Thought* 3 (2014): 254–72.

Schmitt, Carl. *The Concept of the Political*. Translated by George Schwab. Chicago: University of Chicago Press, 2007.

Schneewind, J. B. *The Invention of Autonomy: A History of Modern Moral Philosophy*. Cambridge: Cambridge University Press, 1998.

Schroedinger, Erwin. "Discussion of Probability Relations between Separated Systems." *Proceedings of the Cambridge Philosophical Society* 31, no. 1 (January 1936): 555–63.

Schuster, Heinz Georg. *Deterministic Chaos*. Weinheim: VCH Verlagsgesellschaft, 1989.

Schutt, Hans-Peter. *Die Adoption des "Vaters der modernen Philosophie": Studien zu einem Gemeinplatz des Ideengeschichte*. Frankfurt am Main: Klostermann, 1998.

Seneca. *Moral Essays*. Translated by John W. Basore. Cambridge, Mass.: Harvard University Press, 1938.

Shaftesbury, Anthony Ashley Cooper, Third Earl of. *An Inquiry concerning Virtue or Merit*. In *Characteristics of Men, Manners, Opinions, Times*, edited by Lawrence E. Klein. Cambridge: Cambridge University Press, 1999.

Shattuck, Roger. *The Innocent Eye: On Modern Literature and the Arts*. New York: Washington Square Press, 1986.

Shelley, Mary. *Frankenstein*. London: Penguin, 1994.

Shostak, Stanley. *Becoming Immortal: Combining Cloning and Stem-Cell Therapy*. Albany: State University of New York Press, 2002.

Simmons, Alison. "Changing the Cartesian Mind: Leibniz on Sensation, Representation, and Animal Consciousness." *Philosophical Review* 110 (2001): 31–75.

———. "Sensible Ends: Latent Teleology in Descartes' Account of Sensation." *Journal of the History of Philosophy* 39 (2001): 49–75.

Smith, Steven. *Spinoza, Liberalism, and the Question of Jewish Identity*. New Haven, Conn.: Yale University Press, 1997.

Sorell, Tom, ed. *The Rise of Modern Philosophy: The Tension between the New and Traditional Philosophies from Machiavelli to Leibniz*. Oxford: Clarendon Press, 1993.

Spinoza, Baruch. *Spinoza Opera*. 5 vols. Edited by Carl Gebhardt. Heidelberg: Carl Winters, 1972 [1925].

———. *Theological-Political Treatise*. Second edition. Translated by Samuel Shirley. Indianapolis, Ind.: Hackett, 2001.

———. *Complete Works*. Translated by Samuel Shirley. Edited by Michael Morgan. Indianapolis, Ind.: Hackett, 2002.

Starn, Randolph. "The Republic Regime of the 'Room of Peace' in Siena, 1338–40." *Representations* 18 (Spring 1987): 1–32.

Strauss, Leo. *Natural Rights and History*. Chicago: University of Chicago Press, 1953.

———. *Thoughts on Machiavelli*. Chicago: University of Chicago Press, 1958.

Suárez, Francisco. *Disputationes Metaphysicae*. 2 vols. Hildesheim: G. Olms, 1965.

Sullivan, Vickie B. *Machiavelli's Three Romes*. DeKalb: Northern Illinois University Press, 1996.

Swift, Jonathan. *Gulliver's Travels*. Edited by C. Rawson and I. Higgins. Oxford: Oxford World's Classics, 1948.

Tarcov, Nathan. "Machiavelli in *The Prince*; His Way of Life in Question." In *Political Philosophy Cross-Examined: Perennial Challenges to the Philosophic Life,* edited by Thomas L. Pangle and J. Harvey Lomax. New York: Palgrave Macmillan, 2013.

———. "Machiavelli's Critique of Religion." *Social Research* 81, no. 1 (2014): 193–216.

Tegmark, M., and J. A. Wheeler. "100 Years of Quantum Mysteries." *Scientific American* (February 2001): 54–61.

Tessitore, Aristide. "Tocqueville's American Thesis and the New Science of Politics." *American Political Thought* 4 (2015): 72–99.

Thomas Aquinas. *Summa contra gentiles*. 5 vols. Edited by V. J. Bourke. Translated by A. C. Pegis, J. F. Anderson, V. J. Bourke, and C. J. O'Neil. South Bend, Ind.: University of Notre Dame Press, 1975.

———. *The Division and Methods of the Sciences*. Translated by Armand Maurer. Toronto: Pontifical Institute of Medieval Studies, 1986.

Thomson, W., and P. G. Tait. *Treatise on Natural Philosophy*. Oxford: Clarendon Press, 1857.

Tocqueville, Alexis de. *Oeuvres Complètes*. Edited by A. Jardin. 18 vols. Paris: Gallimard, 1967.

———. *Oeuvres*. Edited by A. Jardin. 3 vols. Paris: Gallimard, 1991.

———. *Democracy in America*. Translated by Harvey C. Mansfield and Delba Winthrop. Chicago: University of Chicago Press, 2000.

———. *Writings on Empire and Slavery*. Translated by Jennifer Pitts. Baltimore, Md.: Johns Hopkins University Press, 2001.

———. *Tocqueville: Lettres Choisies, Souvenirs*. Edited by Françoise Mélonio and Laurence Guellec. Paris: Gallimard, 2003.

———. *The Ancien Régime and the Revolution*. Translated by A. Goldhammer. Cambridge: Cambridge University Press, 2011.

Villiers de l'Isle-Adam, Auguste. *L'Ève Future*. Edited by N. Satiat. Paris: Garnier-Flammarion, 1992.

Wallace, William A. *From a Realist Point of View: Essays on the Philosophy of Science*. Lanham, Md.: University Press of America, 1983.

———. *The Modeling of Nature: The Philosophy of Science and the Philosophy of Nature in Synthesis*. Washington, D.C.: The Catholic University of America Press, 1996.

Welch, Cheryl. *De Tocqueville*. New York: Oxford University Press, 2000.

Wheeler, J. A., and W. H. Zurek, eds. *Quantum Theory and Measurement*. Princeton, N.J.: Princeton University Press, 1993.

Whelan, Frederick. *Order and Artifice in Hume's Political Philosophy*. Princeton, N.J.: Princeton University Press, 1985.

Winthrop, Delba, "Rights: A Point of Honor." In *Interpreting Tocqueville's Democracy in America*, edited by K. Masugi. Savage, Md.: Rowman and Littlefield, 1988.

Wodehouse, P. G. *Jeeves in the Offing*. London: Penguin, 1963.

Wolff, Christian. *Oratio de Sinarum philosophia practica/Rede über die praktische Philosophie der Chinesen*. Edited by Michael Albrecht. Hamburg: Felix Meiner, 1985.

Wolin, Sheldon S. *Tocqueville between Two Worlds: The Making of a Political and Theoretical Life*. Princeton, N.J.: Princeton University Press, 2001.

Wood, Allen W. "The Supreme Principle of Morality." In *The Cambridge Companion to Kant and Modern Philosophy*, edited by Paul Guyer. Cambridge: Cambridge University Press, 2006.

Zuckert, Catherine. "Not By Preaching: Tocqueville on the Role of Religion in American Democracy." *Review of Politics* 43 (1981): 264–86.

Contributors

RÉMI BRAGUE is emeritus professor of Philosophy at the Universities Paris I and Ludwig-Maximilian (Munich). His recent publications include *Le Règne de l'homme* (Paris: Gallimard, 2015); *Où va l'histoire?* (Paris: Salvator, 2016); and *The Legitimacy of the Human* (South Bend, Ind.: Saint Augustine's Press, 2016).

MICHAEL GILLESPIE is professor of Political Science and professor of Philosophy at Duke University. He is the author of *Hegel, Heidegger and the Ground of History*; *Nihilism before Nietzsche*; and *The Theological Origins of Modernity*. He is co-editor of *Nietzsche's New Seas: Explorations in Philosophy, Aesthetics, and Politics*; *Ratifying the Constitution*; and *Homo Politicus Homo Economicus*.

PAUL GUYER is the Jonathan Nelson Professor of Humanities and Philosophy at Brown University and Florence R. C. Murray Professor in the Humanities *emeritus* at the University of Pennsylvania. He is the author, editor, or translator of numerous works on and by Immanuel Kant. His most recent books include *Kant*, second edition (New York: Routledge, 2014); *A History of Modern Aesthetics* in three volumes (Cambridge: Cambridge University Press, 2014); and *Virtues of Freedom: Selected Essays on Kant* (Oxford: Oxford University Press, 2016). He also edited Edmund Burke's *Philosophical Enquiry into the Sublime and Beautiful* for Oxford World's Classics in 2015.

RICHARD F. HASSING is research associate professor in the School of Philosophy at the Catholic University of America, specializing in the history of physics, the philosophy of nature, and early modern philosophy. He edited *Final Causality in Nature and Human Affairs* (1997), and is the author of *Cartesian Psychophysics and the Whole Nature of Man: On Descartes's* Passions of the Soul (2015).

NICHOLAS JOLLEY is emeritus professor and research professor of philosophy at the University of California, Irvine. He is the author of *Leibniz and Locke: A Study of the New Essays on Human Understanding* (Oxford: Clarendon Press, 1984); *The Light of the Soul: Theories of Ideas in Leibniz, Malebranche, and Descartes* (Oxford: Clarendon Press, 1990); *Locke: His Philosophical Thought* (Oxford: Oxford University Press, 1999); *Leibniz* (New York: Routledge, 2005); *Causality and Mind: Essays on Early Modern Philosophy* (Oxford: Oxford University Press, 2013); and *Locke's Touchy Subjects: Materialism and Immortality* (Oxford: Oxford University Press, 2015).

HARVEY C. MANSFIELD is William R. Kenan Jr. Professor of Government at Harvard University and senior fellow at the Hoover Institution, Stanford University. He is the author of books on political parties, executive power, liberalism, indirect government, and manliness. He has translated Tocqueville's *Democracy in America* and three of Machiavelli's works.

THOMAS W. MERRILL is associate professor of government and associate director of the Political Theory Institute in the School of Public Affairs at American University in Washington, D.C. He is the author of *Hume and the Politics of Enlightenment* (Cambridge: Cambridge University Press, 2015) and a co-editor of two edited volumes: *Apples of Gold in Pictures of Silver: Honoring the Work of Leon R. Kass* (Lanham, Md.: Lexington, 2010) and *Human Dignity and Bioethics* (Notre Dame, Ind.: University of Notre Dame Press, 2009). His articles have appeared in *Review of Politics*, *Polity*, and *Perspectives on Political Science*.

STEVEN NADLER is the William H. Hay II Professor of Philosophy and Evjue-Bascom Professor in the Humanities at the University of Wisconsin-Madison. His books include *The Philosopher, the Priest, and the Painter: A Portrait of Descartes* (Princeton, N.J.: Princeton University Press, 2013); *A Book Forged in Hell: Spinoza's Scandalous Treatise and the Birth of the Secular Age* (Princeton, N.J.: Princeton University Press, 2011); and *Spinoza: A Life* (Cambridge: Cambridge University Press, 1999). His book *Rembrandt's Jews* (Chicago: University of Chicago Press, 2003) was named a finalist for the Pulitzer Prize.

MICHAEL PAKALUK is professor of ethics in the Tim and Steph Busch School of Business and Economics at the Catholic University of America. He is the author, with Giles Pearson, of *Moral Psychology and Human Action in Aristotle* (Oxford University Press).

MICHAEL ROHLF is associate professor of philosophy at the Catholic University of America and previously taught at Brown University and Skidmore College. He is the author of many articles on Kant and modern philosophy, including the general entry on Kant in the online *Stanford Encyclopedia of Philosophy* (2010).

TAD M. SCHMALTZ is professor of philosophy and James B. and Grace J. Nelson Fellow at the University of Michigan, Ann Arbor. He has published articles and book chapters on various topics in early modern philosophy, and is the author of *Malebranche's Theory of the Soul: A Cartesian Interpretation* (Oxford: Oxford University Press, 1996); *Radical Cartesianism: The French Reception of Descartes* (Cambridge: Cambridge University Press, 2002); *Descartes on Causation* (Oxford: Oxford University Press, 2008); and *Early Modern Cartesianisms: Dutch and French Constructions* (Oxford: Oxford University Press, 2016).

NATHAN TARCOV is professor in the Committee on Social Thought, the Department of Political Science, the Committee on International Relations, and the College of the University of Chicago. He received his B.A. in history from Cornell and his Ph.D. in political science from Harvard. He was on the faculty at Harvard, served on the Policy Planning Staff of the State Department, was a secretary of the Navy senior research fellow at the Naval War College, and was a fellow at the Siemens Foundation in Munich. He is the author of *Locke's Education for Liberty*, co-translator of *Machiavelli's Discourses on Livy*, co-editor of *The Legacy of Rousseau* and Locke's *Some Thoughts Concerning Education and Of the Conduct of the Understanding*, and author of articles on Machiavelli, Locke, the American founders, Leo Strauss, constitutionalism, democracy, and tyranny.

Index

The Modern Turn was designed and typeset in Minion by Kachergis Book Design of Pittsboro, North Carolina. It was printed on 60-pound House Natural Smooth and bound by Sheridan Books of Chelsea, Michigan.